From Brooklyn NY to Brookline MA

SIDNEY KRIMSKY

ISBN 978-1-950818-68-6 (paperback)

Copyright © 2020 by Sidney Krimsky

All rights reserved. No part of this publication may be reproduced, distributed, or transmitted in any form or by any means, including photocopying, recording, or other electronic or mechanical methods without the prior written permission of the publisher. For permission requests, solicit the publisher via the address below.

Rushmore Press LLC
1 888 733 9607
www.rushmorepress.com

Printed in the United States of America

Contents

Chapter		Page Number
	Title Page	1
	Copyright page	2
	Contents	3
	Glossary of phrases and terms	7
i	Dedication	19
	Old Cover	21
ii	Encouragements	22
iii	Purpose	25
1	Paternal Family	27
1.1	Uncle Munya's Letter to Sheldon Krimsky Dated 10 December 1990 Translated from Russian	37
2	Maternal Family	43
3	Early Childhood	56
4	Move to Baltimore, Maryland	63
5	Return to Brooklyn, New York	75
6	Baseball	90
7	My Zadie	95
8	My Maternal Relatives	102
9	Mark Twain Junior High School	107
10	Hebrew School	112
11	Dr. Jacob Kravitz	116
11.1	Mermaid Avenue	118
12	Kaddish for a Canary	125
13	Bar Mitzvah	127
14	Singing career	129
15	Smoking	131

16	Murray Frost	133
17	Entering the Labor Force	135
18	Lessons Learned from My Father	137
19	Lessons Learned from My Mother	141
19.1	Rose Krimsky, Chaya Raisel bas Yitzhak was my mom.	145
19.2	Eulogy for Rose (Skolnick) Krimsky Chaya Reizel bas Yitzchak by Rabbi Elly Krimsky	149
19.3	Eulogy for Grandma Rose Krimsky by Rabbi Jonathan Krimsky	154
19.4	Eulogy by Dorothy Krimsky	157
19.5	Eulogy by Naomi Hollander at the Gravesite	159
19.6	Comments and Corrections for "My Life as a Motherless Child"	161
20	Walk to Zadie's House	166
21	Bullying	169
22	Working on the Boardwalk	170
23	Nathan's Famous	172
23.1	Living in Coney Island during the 1950s	179
24	Abraham Lincoln High School	183
25	Introduction to the Holocaust	189
26	Brooklyn College and City College of New York (CCNY)	191
26.1	Concept of the Almighty	202
26.2	Pay-as-you-see TV	209
27	J. Robert Oppenheimer Lecture	213
28	Selling Bibles	216
29	Sputnik	219
30	Shlomo Breuer	222
30.1	Shabel Family	226
30.2	Visiting His Parents in Israel	228
30.3	Avraham Hoelzel	229
30.4	The Arab-Israel War of 1967	233
30.5	Verbal GPS Location Accuracy	236
30.6	Torah on the Head of a Pin	238
31	California	241
32	Challenger Disaster	246

33	Move to Boston	248
34	AVCO Corporation	253
35	MIT.	259
36	Beth Shalom in Cambridge	261
37	Meeting the Holcers	265
38	Oratory for an Unveiling	275
39	George Gamow Lecture	277
40	GCA Corporation	279
40.1	Edward Teller Lecture	280
40.2	Program CHESS	281
40.3	Milliforce Rocket	286
40.4	Manned Orbital Laboratory (MOL)	290
41	Blowing Shofar	292
42	Smithsonian Observatory in Cambridge	294
43	Meeting and Marrying Dorothy	296
44	Death of Alex Krimsky	304
45	Birth of Our Children	309
46	Rent Control in Brookline	316
47	Lincoln Labs and the Light Gas Gun to Study Missile Reentry Phenomena	328
47.1	My Interaction with Uncle Munya	337
48	Polaroid	341
49	Rabbi Moses Cohn	354
49.1	Climbing Mount Sinai	369
50	Microscience, Anti-Semitism, and Thievery	373
50.1	Consulting at Ciba Corning Corp.	376
51	Department of Defense and My Third Career Start	378
51.1	Act for America	395
51.2	Trips to Berlin, Germany	397
52	Synagogue President	401
52.1	Kaddish for Kadimah	407
53	Life's Goals: Securing Professional Employment, Getting Married, and Raising a Family	411
54	Assisting Deborah Onie to Recover Her Reputation	416
55	Personal Values and Philosophy	425

56	The Divorce	434
57	Grandchildren	441
58	Northeastern University and the RE-SEED Program	450
59	Epilogue	455
60	Peroration: Bye-Bye, Brookline	458
60.1	Remarks on the bat mitzvah of Simma Meira Hollander on 6 November 2011, 9 Cheshvan 5772	465
60.2	Bas-Mitzvah of Tamar Yaffa Hollander on 6 November 2016, 5 Cheshvan 5777	467

Coolidge Corner is at the heart of Brookline, Massachusetts.

Glossary of words, terms, and expressions used in "From Brooklyn to Brookline" listed by order of appearance in the book.

Chapter no.	Chapter	Explanation or translation
Chap 7	My Zadie	My Grandfather
Chap 12	Kaddish for a Canary	Hebrew Prayer for a Dead Person said for a Dead Canary
Chap 13	Bar Mitzvah	Heb: Son of the Commandment- Ceremony for 13 year old boy
Chap 29	Sputnik	Russian Satellite orbiting Earth- means Fellow Traveler
Chap 30.5	GPS	Global Positioning System
Chap 30.6	Torah	Five Books of Moses-Old Testament written in Hebrew
Chap 34	AVCO	Abbreviation: Aviation Corporation
Chap 35	MIT	Massachusetts Institute of Technology
Chap 36	Beth Shalom	House of Peace in Hebrew –Name of Synagogue in Cambridge.
Chap 40	GCA	Geophysics Corporation of America
Chap 40.2	CHESS	Name assigned by Advanced Project Research Agency
Chap 40.4	MOL	Manned Orbital Laboratory – Precursor to Space Station
Chap 41	Shofar	Hebrew: Ram's Horn- Blown during Jewish High Holiday Services
Chap 47	Light Gas Gun	18 Foot barrel used to fire a small projectile
Chap 52.1	Kadish for Kadimah	End of my relationship with Cong. Kadimah-Toras Moshe

Page no.	Word or Phrase	Explanation or translation
22	Z"TS"L	Hebrew abbrev: Means Righteous Person of Blessed Memory
26	hechsher	Rabbinic certification that the meat and preparation was kosher
26	OU	Union of Orthodox Rabbis: agency certifies that food is kosher
26	kosher food	Heb: content, quality, & preparation conforms to Jewish Law
26	matzoh	Hebrew: Unleavened bread prepared according to Jewish law
26	Passover	Jewish Holiday during which leavened bread is not eaten
29	aortic stenosis	narrowing of the aortic valve
30	furrier	person who makes garments from animal furs
46	momentum	product of mass multiplied by velocity
47	WOP	"Without Papers"-pejorative term applied to new immigrants
47	HIAS	Hebrew Immigrant Aid Society
48	Cantor	Person who sings, chants, and reads the Hebrew Liturgy
49	rickets	Disease of soft bones-corrected with cod liver oil and vitamin D
49	heart murmur	aortic heart valve does not completely close detected by EKG
49	putzutzah	Yiddish: female variant of putz (male reproductive organ)
49	PS	Public School

50	Zadie	Yiddish: Grandfather
53	USN	United States Navy
56	Tante	Yiddish: Aunt
58	p'sicha	Heb: Privilege of opening the curtains and door of the Holy Ark
58	Aron HaKodesh	Hebrew: Holy Ark that houses a Torah Scroll
59	Yichus	Hebrew: Family Geneology or background
59	buma	Yiddish: bum
59	IRA	Individual Retirement Account
60	touchis	Yiddish from Hebrew: ass
60	babushka	Russian: Grandmother
60	riebeisel	Yiddish: washboard, board with metal or glass corrugations
61	barabanchik	Russian: drummer boy
65	Bubbie	Yiddish from Russian Babushka: Grandmother
68	COMSEC	Communications Security
83	YMCA	Young Men's Christian Association
83	fungo	tossing up a baseball and hitting the ball yourself
90	bleacher seats	seats in a baseball park furthest from home plate
90	PAL	Police Athletic League
93	mensch	German/Yiddish: worthwhile person with good characteristics

95	Chanukah	Hebrew: Festival of Lights-Candles are lit each day for 8 days
96	Pesach	Hebrew-Holiday of Passover
96	Yiddish	language spoken by European Jews- mix of German & Hebrew
96	kneidlach	Yiddish: matzoh balls usually served in chicken soup
96	kreplach	Yiddish: meat dumplings with spices served in chicken soup
96	kugel	Yiddish: potato or noodle pudding baked in a vessel
96	sedarim	Hebrew: plural for seders or talk + meals served at Passover
98	Nachum der Roite	Yiddish: Nathan the Red Haired Person
106	plut	Russian: trickster
113	Shaari Zedek	Hebrew: Gates of Righteousness (typical name of synagogue)
113	Haganah	Hebrew: Israel Defensive Military Force before 1948
113	Pushkie	Container with slotted top to insert coins & dollars
113	shul	German: school; Yiddish: synagogue – place of learning
119	bialy	Roll with partial hole named after Town of Bialystock in Russia
120	OPA	Office of Price Administration: Federal Price control during WWII
121	ALHS	Abraham Lincoln High School on Ocean Parkway in Brooklyn

129	Kriat HaTorah	Hebrew: Reading from the Five Books of Moses
129	Chazzan	Cantor who conducts services in the Hebrew Language
129	Chazzanut	Melodies sung by the Cantor
130	Magen David	Hebrew: Six pointed Star of David
131	LSMFT	Lucky Strike Means Fine Tobacco was a ubiquitous ad
138	EPA	Environmental Protection Agency
138	OSHA	Occupational Safety and Health Administration
141	gefilte fish	yellow pike & carp ground with eggs & made into patties & boiled
141	mondel bread	home-made cookies made with almonds
143	kasha	Russian: buckwheat
143	borsch	Russian: beet soup
152	nachas	emotional pleasure from children and grandchildren
154	tzimis	Yiddish: cooked mixture of carrots, sweet potatoes & prunes
154	blintzes	Yiddish: baked or fried dumplings filled with cheese
154	latkes	Yiddish: fried or baked pancakes made of potatoes and onions
154	Pessadik	Hebrew/Yiddish: adjective meaning appropriate for Passover
155	Shep Nachus	Derive pleasure usually from grandchildren

155	shayna ponim	Yiddish: beautiful face
155	challah	Yiddish: Special bread served on Sabbath and Jewish Holidays
156	mazinka	Yiddish: last child to be married
156	bli ain hora	Hebrew: Unseen by the evil eye
156	Tehinish masatz....	Hebrew: May you be bound in the holy life
159	Baruch Hashem	Hebrew: Blessed is God or Thank God
166	Yom Kippur	Hebrew: Day of Atonement, Day of introspection and fasting
167	lekach	Yiddish: Honey cake
167	baalebatim	Hebrew/Yiddish: Members of the Synagogue
185	CCNY	City College of New York
185	SAT	Scholastic Aptitude Test
192	ROTC	Reserve Officers Training Corps
192	M-16	Rifle used during WW II
193	DC-3	Douglas Commercial Aircraft No. 3
195	RADAR	Radio Detection and Ranging
195	ADC Radar	Advanced Design Corporation Radar
195	SAGE Radar	Semi-Automatic Ground Station Radar
195	JFK Airport	Airport named after Pres. John Francis Kennedy
196	CAD-CAM	Computer Aided Design-Computer Aided Manufacture
196	DVD	Digital Video Disk (verbal and video)
196	2D/3D	2 dimensional/3 dimensional

205	RAMBAN	Hebrew: Rabbi Moses ben (son of) Nachman
207	CERN	City in Switzerland-houses the Large Hadron Collider
209	FCC	Federal Communications Commission
241	CATV	Cable Television Committee
224	Hagadah	Hebrew: Narrative in a book describing the exodus from Egypt
227	Mincha	Hebrew: Afternoon prayers
227	Maariv	Hebrew: Evening Prayers
230	FOCK	Fund of Common Knowledge, common to most Americans
231	CD	Compact Disc (verbal only – no video)
234	IDF	Israeli Defense Force
238	MBIT	MEGABITS or Million Binary Digits
239	Talmud	Collection of stories, commentaries and arguments from Torah
239	Mount Menucha	Hebrew: Cemetery in Jerusalem—Mount of Consolation
240	HaRav	Hebrew; The Rabbi
240	Saba Hagadol	Hebrew: Grandfather the Great One
241	RAF	Royal Air Force
242	A/C	Air Conditioning
242	PERT	Program Evaluation and Review Technique
242	IBM	International Business Machines Corp.
242	Hollerith Cards	IBM punch cards named after inventor Herman Hollerith

243	BOAC	British Overseas Airways Corporation
244	AFB	Air Force Base
244	BRAC	Base Realignment and Closure (DoD Order to close bases)
246	UCLA	University of California at Los Angeles
253	NASA	National Aeronautics and Space Administration
255	USN	United States Navy
263	Kohain	Heb: Descendants of Priestly Class who presided in the Temple
263	Levy	Hebrew: Assistants to the Kohain
263	Baal Koreh	Hebrew; Male who reads from the Torah in the synagogue
263	brachot	Hebrew: Blessings said before and after reading from the Torah
263	kiddush	Hebrew: Small collation with wine after synagogue services
263	Gabbai	Hebrew: Congregant who manages the synagogue services
265	Rosh HaShonah	Hebrew: Jewish New Year Holiday or Holyday
269	shammas	Hebrew: Sextant
269	yahrzeit	German/Yiddish: anniversary of the death of a loved one
270	ketubah	Hebrew: Certificate of Marriage
270	lehening Torah	Anglicized German Variant of lesen "Reading from the Torah"
273	sukkah	Hebrew: Book of the Talmud about Holiday of Tabernacles

273	kever	Hebrew: grave
273	HaShem	Hebrew: The Name; appellation of the Almighty
277	quasar	quasi-stellar radio source
283	PM	photo-multiplier tube (measures light intensity)
283	rpm	revolutions per minute
293	baal tokiah	Hebrew: person who blows the shofar
310	brit milah	Hebrew: circumcision
310	bris	Hebrew: contraction for brit milah
310	Yom Tov	Hebrew: Good Day – Any Jewish Holiday
310	sandek	Hebrew: male relative on whose lap baby rests for circumcision
310	seudah mitzvah	Hebrew: communal meal after circumcision
311	mohel	Hebrew: person who performs circumcision
322	BTC	Brookline Tenants Council
328	MA	Massachusetts
329	CG	Center of Gravity
335	ARPA	Advanced Research Projects Agency
339	Chumish	Hebrew: Five Books of Moses (Old Testament)
339	Gemorrah	Hebrew: Commentaries & Laws derived from the Chumish
339	Rambam	Hebrew: Rabbi Moses ben (son of) Maimon
342	SERI	Solar Energy Research Institute

344	EPA	Environmental Protection Agency
354	PTA	Parent Teachers Association
355	Derech Eretz	Hebrew: Way of the World
356	psak	Hebrew: Decision based on Jewish Law
356	BOD	Board of Directors
364	TRIO	The 3 Parents assigned to meet with the school committee
368	FUGU	Japanese: fish
380	EHF/UHF	Extremely High Frequency/Ultra High Frequency
380	MILSTAR	Military Strategic and Tactical Relay Satellite
380	MITRE	MIT Research & Engineering Corporation
383	DIRNSA	Director of the National Security Agency
383	DCGS	Distributed Ground Control Stations (battle space awareness)
383	JTIDS	Joint Tactical Information Distribution System
384	CIA	Central Intelligence Agency
384	FMS	Foreign Military Sales
385	Y2K	Transition from 31 December 1999 to 1 January 2000
388	SECDEF	Secretary of Defense
408	JCC	Jewish Community Center
409	HafTorah	Hebrew: Words of the Biblical Prophets read on the Sabbath

409	Davened Shabbos	Hebrew: Recited the morning prayers on the Sabbath
409	Shachris	Hebrew: morning or morning prayers
409	Parshat Parah	Hebrew: Story of the Golden Calf in the Torah
409	YCT	Hebrew: Yeshivat Chovevai Torah
409	Chovevai rabbi	Hebrew: rabbi trained outlook more liberal than conservative
409	KTM	Hebrew: Congregation Kadimah-Toras Moshe
409	Smiuchat	Hebrew: Rabbinic Ordination
420	CJP	Combined Jewish Philanthropies (Boston, MA)
422	Parshat Mishpatim	Section of Talmud dealing with judges and judgements (torts)
424	Mindick Legal Case	Landlord tenant dispute in Boston settled by Jewish Court
425	tschuvah	Hebrew: repentance
428	DER	Disproportionate Emotional Response to trivial irritation
428	kvetches	Yiddish: people complaining or squeezing out complaints
429	FIRPS	feckless incapable of responding to problems (bureaucrats)
429	feckless	lack of initiative or strength of character
430	WIMPs	weak individuals managing people (managers & supervisors)

431	Shalom Bias	Hebrew: Peace at Home -substitute for being correct sometimes
431	bais din	Hebrew: Jewish Court of law
433	YMCA	Young Men's Christian Association
437	kippah	Hebrew: head covering
449	RE-SEED	Retired Engineers &Scientists Enhancing Education............
458	CATV	Cable TV Committee
459	US PO	United States Post Office
465	Lech Lecha	Hebrew: "You Go" opening words in Chap 12 of the Torah
466	bas Israel	Hebrew: Daughter of Israel (implying virtuousness)
469	Yishayahu	Hebrew: Isaiah was a Prophet in the Old Testament
470	Noach	Hebrew: Noah in the Old Testament (Story of the Flood)

Chapter i

DEDICATION

This book is dedicated to the many people who influenced my life including my wife, our children, their spouses, and our grandchildren without whom life would be empty.

Dorothy Irene (Chaya Devorah Goldstein) Krimsky without who my life would be without meaning. She made it possible for me to engage in all the political activities and employment opportunities described in this book, and her participation added value and corrected my deficiencies.

Alex (Eliyahu ben Shlomo) Krimsky, my father
Rose (Raizel bas Yitzhak) Krimsky, my mother

Rabbi Alec Seth (Eliyahu Shais) Krimsky
Yocheved Krimsky and their children
Yaakov Yedidiah Krimsky
Rachel Krimsky
Yakira Krimsky
Moreh Naomi Ilana (Krimsky) Hollander
Yitzy Hollander and their children
David Baruch (Ephraim Baruch) Hollander
Joseph (Yossi) Kalman Hollander
Simma Meira Hollander
Tamar Yaffa Hollander

Rabbi Jonathan Isaac Krimsky
Cheryl (Chaya) Krimsky and their children
Aryeh Leib Krimsky
Tziporah Krimsky
Yeshaya (Shai) Simcha Krimsky
Malka Krimsky
Akiva Krimsky
Shoshana Raizel Krimsky
Reuven Krimsky

David Baruch (Ephraim Baruch) Hollander
Leah Hollander and their child
Shaina Hollander

FROM BROOKLYN
New York

TO BROOKLINE
Massachusetts

SIDNEY KRIMSKY

Chapter ii

ENCOURAGEMENTS

Dear Rosa,

I have wanted to respond to your thoughtful, beautifully handwritten letter. The banquet for Rabbi Halbfinger and work for the rabbinic search committee have consumed my attention since February 2004. The banquet is over, and the search is completed.

    I can't imagine whatever caused you to write such a poignant letter to me that reflected your inner feelings. I really do not think I did anything so extraordinary that merited such focus. Fortunately, I was there at the time when Paulette and you needed some help and I was also searching for human connections. Prof. Shlomo Breuer. Z"TS"L appealed to my head, your father Rabbi Moses Holcer Z"TS"L appealed to my heart and your mom appealed to my stomach. It was an accident or a series of unlikely events that caused our paths to cross. You know very little about me other than my interaction with your family. I am a product of a different world. Yes, I am a first-generation American with an affinity for Polish and Russian immigrants. My grandfathers, father, mother, and aunts from my paternal grandfather all emigrated from the Ukraine. I thought that I would tell you something about myself that I could also share with my children and grandchildren. I tried to condense this story, but my memories kept urging me to write further. It was Benjamin Franklin who commented that old men like to write their memoirs.

FROM BROOKLYN NY TO BROOKLINE MA

I appreciate your follow-up telephone call and encouragement for me to continue writing. I can't imagine who else would want to read all this. I realize now that I grew up in an age of innocence, when no harm came to kids roaming the streets of large cities, when the government of the Unites States was trustworthy and efficacious, when the US Capitol was open twenty-four hours a day for Americans to visit and explore, when teachers really tried to teach and not babysit students until graduation, when standards meant something, when mothers did not have to work outside the home, when parents took responsibility to discipline their children without the advice from all the psychologists and liberal do-gooders, when miscreants were identified and jailed, and when the words of a teacher, principal, and policeman carried weight.

I sense that what I furnished earlier is not sufficient to douse the fires of your curiosity. I continued to probe my memory and put my observations into words and historical context.

I grew up in an age of exaggerated fears of the Communist hegemony and the response of our government that would ultimately provide employment for millions of Americans and opportunities for people of integrity to work as guarantors of national security.

I appeared out of nowhere in Cambridge in 1960, but now you know more about me after all these years that you never knew or wanted to know. My experiences as a child of immigrants pale into insignificance with what your parents endured, but your family was there at a critical time in my life in which I had to structure a future. Your family and Shlomo Breuer's family were models for me to emulate. The rest you know or thought you knew. I hope this adds to your understanding and appreciation of our interactions. The next version will have illustrations.

Sid Krimsky
June 2005

Mrs. Rosa Drapkin viewing this book for the first time.
Photo taken by her husband, Dr. Mark Drapkin.

Chapter iii

PURPOSE

My purpose in recording this document evolved after I started to write my recollections about the influences of Mr. Holcer and Shlomo Breuer on my life. My intention was to share my experiences of growing up during the 1940s–1950s sometimes called the age of innocence after which the United States had prevailed during World War II and the enormous impact this victory had on the collective American psyche. This victory was followed by an enormous economic expansion of peace and opportunities even during the cold war. It was a time when mothers stayed at home, public education was viewed as essential to achieving satisfaction and economic success, children played in the streets without adult supervision, and most important is that most people believed in the righteousness of the federal government. I hope this window explains this to my children and grandchildren. The world has changed many times since then, and I hope this document opens a larger window to history during eight decades and the small part I played working for the military industrial complex and private industry.

Franklin Roosevelt was a godlike icon, and his death shocked America, but Harry Truman continued his liberal legacy as the leader of the Democratic Party. It was a time when storekeepers did not use metal grates to prevent break-ins. It was a time when teachers and policemen were really respected in the community. It was a time when immigrant parents knew that their children would have a better life in America than anywhere else. The material life prospered, but the spiritual life was set aside and ignored by the vast collection of Jewish immigrants as leading nowhere. All the rabbis and their daily prayers could not stop Hitler and could not stop the destruction of European Jewry. Only the army and navy of the United States could stop Hitler and Tojo. Religious Yeshivas were tolerated as curious inefficacious schools mired in medieval teachings having little connection to economic opportunities, national defense, and rising expectations.

On the radio Sunday morning on WBVD, we heard Yiddish music and Yiddish jokes. On the lower East Side in New York, we were able to buy Moshe's pumpernickel and Gus's pickles and Ratner's knishes. In Coney Island, we all knew that the all-beef frankfurter sold at Nathan's was sort of kosher, but no rabbi gave a *hechsher*. Nathan did not need it. His business prospered without a hechsher. We never heard of OU or any kosher symbol, but on Passover we bought Manishewitz and Sons matzoh, and the "Kosher for Passover" labels were put on Breakstone's dairy products. My uncle Izzy (Aunt Annette's husband), a grocer, was skeptical and saw this as a way of earning money for the rabbis who added no value to the products on which they put labels. Yet the shuls were crowded on the Jewish Holydays. Everyone attended. The feeling was there, but the intellectual underpinnings were largely absent from the masses of Jews living in New York. I performed as a choir boy for a few years in many shuls in New York City during the High Holy Days. People attended out of duty to socialize and to commiserate after the Holocaust, but the real spiritual underpinnings were absent and certainly escaped me.

Our teachers in public school were mostly Jewish men and women educated in the thirties and forties. The men went off to war among the sixteen million persons under arms, returned from the war, and received an education under the GI Bill, one of the most generous acts of the Democratic Congress under Harry Truman. They became parents and schoolteachers and educated me. I am the product of that era.

My children know nothing of my early years and the influences on my life. This book should fill that void.

Chapter 1

PATERNAL FAMILY

The origin of the name Krimsky may come from the Yiddish word *Krum* or *Krim*, which means *crooked* or *squint eyes*. An alternative spelling is *Krimm* or *Krum* (with two dots over the *u*). It also means *shop* or *store*. *Krym* in Russian means *Crimea*. The name ending "sky" means associated with or from.

From the Jewish gen birth records, I learned that my paternal great-great grandfather was named Yekheskel Krimsky. His father's name was Boruch. Yekheskel's wife was named Yuta. Yuta's father was named Avraham.

My paternal great-grandfather Yakov Krimsky, son of Yekheskel, was born in the town of Kishinev in the province of Bessarabia (now Moldova) on 4 July 1839 (the fifth of Av). Uncle Munya confirmed that his father was named Yakov when Munya stayed with us for a week in 1969.

Menachim Manis Feldman had two daughters, Sonya and Pessie. Sonya lived from 1882 to 1945. She died 7 August 1945, one day after WWII ended. Pessie lived from 1872 to 1959. Sonya married Shlomo Yankelevich Krimsky, and Pessie married a Mr. Katz. Pessie was the mother of Max Katz and Fannie Katz. Max was born in 16 February 1904. Max married Sonya and had one daughter, Evelyn. Evelyn married Avraham Sternklar and had one son. Fannie married Philip Fidel. Pessie was seventy-seven years old at my bar mitzvah party in 1949. We called her Bubbie Pessie. I never spoke with her. Bubbie Pessie had a brother, Yosif Feldman, who married

Zelda. Both died in Israel. Yosif and Zelda had a daughter, Chaya Gitel.

Bubbie Pessie had another brother, Avruhom Feldman, who died in Brooklyn. He had a daughter, Jennie, who married Dr. Hirsch. Dr. Hirsch was my first doctor. Avruhum Feldman attended the wedding of my father and mother. Some of the relatives of the grandmother of Max Katz escaped to Buenos Aires, Argentina, and San Paulo, Brazil, during or before WWII.

My paternal grandfather, Shlomo Yankelevich Krimsky, born in 1878 (anglicized to Samuel), immigrated alone to the United States in 1911 six months after the birth of his fifth child, my aunt Annuita (Annette). He and his wife, Sonia Feldman, born in 1882, had five children each about two years apart: Manis, Paulina, El, Rachel, and Annuita. My grandmother was left impoverished in Tulczin, South West Ukraine, after Samuel left for America. She worked in an orphanage where she cooked for everyone, so her five children would have something to eat. Poverty was rampant. The children had no opportunity for Jewish education and little opportunity for secular education. He was unable to contact his family until 1923 because the First World War interrupted postal service. My grandfather lived in Philadelphia at 924 North Franklin Street, worked as a presser of ladies garments, saved, borrowed, and sent money through an agent to bring the two eldest of his five children to America. The plan was for the two eldest to work, save earnings, and help to bring over the remaining four members of the family. Manous (Munya as he was known) at eighteen was the oldest male, and Paulina (Pessie in Yiddish) at seventeen was the oldest female. Their names, specifically requested by my grandfather, were written on the visa.

Munya, eighteen, was a member of the Komsomal (Communist Youth Organization) and had a girlfriend, Frieda. He was an ardent patriot and refused to emigrate. My grandmother begged him. Visa time was running out. She scratched off his name and wrote the name of my father, El or called Elyosha, who was sixteen. El was born March 8, 1908, in Tulczin. A lover of horses with minimal schooling, he worked as a printer before coming to America. He and his older sister Paulina packed their bags and traveled by wagon and boat to

FROM BROOKLYN NY TO BROOKLINE MA

Riga, Bremen, and then to Ellis Island aboard the SS *America*, arriving in 1924. Elyosha was sick on the boat with an intestinal disorder and was detained for two weeks in a room at the Ellis Island infirmary. Paulina stayed with him until he was well enough to travel. I walked into the infirmary rooms at Ellis Island and could imagine the chaos among all the nurses, doctors, and patients who spoke different languages. I suspect that my father and Paulina never saw a doctor in the Ukraine. Munya's letter to Sheldon describes the early years is in chapter 1.1.

My father did not talk much about his short life in Russia. He was chased by Cossacks and shot in his leg, which bore a visible scar. He rolled down a hill and stuffed cigarette paper into the wound to stop the blood flow. He wanted to see his older brother Munya before it was too late. He never did see him after my father left Russia.

I learned much later that the whole family in Ukraine became sick with serious influenza. My grandmother sent out my father to acquire water for their illness or for cooking. He brought back buckets of water and may have contracted rheumatic fever or strep throat, which was not treated with antibiotics. My father was later diagnosed with aortic stenosis. We think it came about from the untreated strep throat. In his later years, he developed a shortness of breath exacerbated by smoking.

Elyosha Krimsky was born 8 March 1908 in the town of Bratslov in the region called Podolia. He arrived in the USA on 5 January 1925 from Bratslov, Podolia. He became a citizen from his father's citizenship paper issued in Philadelphia. He received his own citizenship paper on 28 February 1944 in Baltimore, Maryland, no. A102465. He had to answer basic questions from a judge and pass a basic literacy test. My father told me that he was proud to be an American citizen. He learned to read by himself and learned to write by copying the headlines from local newspapers. There were no ESL classes to learn English, and he and his sister Pauline had to work full-time to repay the loan taken by their father to pay for steamship tickets to come to America and to raise the money to bring his sisters and mother from Russia to America. My father never considered himself a hero; he just did what his moral conscience told him to do.

Elyosha (anglicized to Alex) and Paulina (anglicized to Pauline) were put to work upon arrival. I located their names on the microfilm of the ship's manifest stored at the National Archives in Washington DC. My father loaded fruit wagons, and Pauline worked as a furrier. My grandfather, my father, and my aunt worked to save money to bring over my grandmother and two daughters: Rachel, fourteen, and Annuita, twelve. In 1926 they arrived aboard the SS *Mauritania* at Ellis Island. The two girls were put in school. They knew how to read and write Russian and spoke Yiddish. My grandmother's education was minimal. In the villages, education for women was a low priority. She did speak to me in English. The family moved to New York, and Aunt Rachel (anglicized to Rae) was put to work in a dress shop where she learned how to be a seamstress. Annuita (anglicized to Annette) continued in school. In 1941 Germany invaded Russia. The Red Army withdrew from Tulczin to regroup elsewhere, and the local Ukrainians massacred the Jewish inhabitants of Tulczin. Chaos reigned; there were no mail deliveries between the United States and Ukraine. The immigrant family lost contact with Munya.

My grandparents never again saw Munya. My grandfather left Russia in 1911 when Munya was seven years old and my father was three. Munya married his girlfriend, Frieda, and had one son, Salim. Munya was conscripted into the Russian Army. His wife and son were sent to Siberia for protection against the rapidly moving German armies. He ended his military service as a major in the artillery corps, pushing the Germans west until the Russians reached Konigsberg (Northeast Prussia) when the war ended. Konigsberg was annexed to the Soviet Union in 1945 and renamed Kaliningrad. The Russians viewed this annexation as a small compensation for all the pillage endured by Russia during the war. Munya was demobilized and returned to civilian life and found work as a printer. I met him in 1969 on his only trip to the United States. His wife, Frida, was not permitted to accompany him.

My father was disappointed because he never saw his older brother in America. My father died on Chanukah 1966 from a coronary about four months after Dorothy and I were married. Munya came to the United States for a visit arranged by Pauline and stayed a week with us. We spoke in Yiddish. He knew no English, and my parents never spoke Russian because for them Russia was part of a bad dream and schooling in Russia for them was nonexistent. Munya remained an ardent Communist even when he saw how we lived. He thought the American government, because of his visit, assigned me the apartment at 403 Washington Street. During those years from 1928 until the 1960s, Munya told me that they all starved. Long bread lines were ubiquitous throughout Russia. On Munya's deathbed around 1987, he admitted to his son, Salim, that he made a mistake by not coming to the United States when his name was on the visa in 1924. I can't say with certainty that my father wanted to leave Russia even though he was chased and shot by the Cossacks. The bullet grazed his leg, and he described to me how the hole eventually healed after he stuffed cigarette paper into the wound. A visible deformity remained on the surface of his calf.

My paternal grandfather died of a heart attack at age fifty-two in 1930. My father wanted to return to Russia after the death of his father, who lived and died in the USA but whom he really never got to know. My aunts and my father all married immigrants. Aunt Annette married Isadore Weisleder from Poland. Pauline married Willy Asrilant from Russia. Rachel married Meyer Eisenstadt from Canada. My oldest cousin, Stanley, son of Aunt Annette, was born in 1933 and named after Grandfather Samuel. His sister Elaine was born in 1941. Jerry, son of Pauline, was born in 1935. He died needing a kidney transplant on 23 October 2011. He had been undergoing dialysis. My cousin Elaine told me that he died peacefully in his favorite chair in his sleep. I was born 1936 about six years after my grandfather died, so he never saw me. I do remember my grandmother, Bubbie Sonya, as we called her. My grandmother died in New York at age sixty-three in 1945 of a cerebral hemorrhage.

My parents moved to Baltimore during the war, and there we received a telegram announcing her death. There were few private phones. I recall how my mother went to an outdoor phone booth on Broadway to call a local grocery store in east New York to ask someone to summon my maternal grandfather, telling him that we were coming to New York for the funeral and if he could provide housing for my brother and me. Important phone calls were made that way. My brother was four years old. We took a train to New York City. I remember Bubbie Sonya because she visited us in Baltimore and cared for me as a child. She lived with my aunt Rae (Rachel in Russian) in Brighton Beach after the death of her husband, Samuel. My paternal grandparents are buried in Mount Hebron Cemetery adjacent to Main Street in Queens. I have been there. They sacrificed a great deal to come to America. They lived through the stock market crash and economic hard times. There was no welfare or Social Security. They sacrificed, so their children could have a better life in America than in Russia. Their children continued to sacrifice, but at least in America, their hard work would reap benefits for their grandchildren.

My cousins, my brother, and I all graduated from colleges in New York City, which prepared them for professions in insurance, finance, engineering, law, and philosophy. Two generations suffered. We stand on their shoulders.

My cousin Salim remained in Russia, graduated as a metallurgist at a Moscow technical institute, and went to school at night to study music. Music was his great love. He married a music teacher, Galina. They have two children, Anna and Igor. Anna is a concert pianist, and Igor is a piano teacher. Igor has two children, Daniel and Svetlana. Daniel studies computers. Salim is a member of the Russian Composers Union. His original symphonic compositions of Jewish music were performed in Russia and at Tufts University.

FROM BROOKLYN NY TO BROOKLINE MA

Birth Certificate of Alex Krimsky in Russia Bratzlav
Podolier Gibernia (Podolier Region)

SIDNEY KRIMSKY

TRANSLATION

THE RABBI OF THE TOWN OF BRATZLAV
STATE (GOVERNMENT) OF PODOL

TRANSCRIPT FROM THE BIRTH RECORDS OF THE BUREAU
OF VITAL STATISTICS

This Birth Certificate was issued by the Rabbi of Bratzlav, under his signature and provided with the stamp of the Government, in accordance with the birth records of the Bureau of Vital Statistics of the Jews of the Town of Bratslav of the year 1908, Entry No. 11, Section Male Births, stating the following:

There was born to Shlioma Yankelev Krimsky, father, and Sura, the mother, a male child on March 7, 1908, named "El".

This Birth Certificate was issued for the purpose of use as a document whenever necessary.

Issued in the town of Bratslev on March 28, 1920

    (signed) signature illegible
                    The Government Rabbi of Bratslav

STAMP (reading) The Chief Rabbi of
                    the Town of Bratslav

Translation of Birth Certificate of Alex Krimsky signed by the Government appointed Rabbi of Bratslov. His father's Hebrew name is Shlomo Yankelev (Samuel) and his mother's name is Sura (Sonia).

FROM BROOKLYN NY TO BROOKLINE MA

Bubbie Sonia and Grandpa Samuel Krimsky in Russia

Bubbie Sonia's naturalization paper retained by my father

Taxicab license of Alex Krimsky. He was proud of his license and his safe driving record. His heart condition forced him to surrender his license. Other photo shows Grandma Rose at the Golda meir House in Newton, MA.

Chapter 1.1

UNCLE MUNYA'S LETTER TO SHELDON KRIMSKY DATED 10 DECEMBER 1990 TRANSLATED FROM RUSSIAN

Dear Nephew Sheldon,

Igor related to me the contents of your letters. Thank you for your letter to me. It was very interesting. You ask many questions. It is only natural since you wish to learn more about my life, as well as the lives of other members of our family.

First I want to thank you for the news about your mother. I was glad to learn more about her life. When I visited you, I told Sidney that he should have her stay with him. She had enough working and living alone. He promised, but he has not done it. Send your mother my best regards.

Now to my memories. All the things I remember could make up as a book, but I do not have a skill to be a writer. I was born in 1904, at the beginning of the century. All the twentieth century is a difficult time of revolutions and wars, especially here in Russia. We had much to live through and experienced many sorrows.

My father (your grandfather Samuel Krimsky) left for America in 1911 with the intention of sending for his family within three to four years. He found a job at a textile factory and made a good living. He frequently sent us letters and money, and we dreamed of joining him.

We were Mother, I, Polla (Paulina), Elik, your father (we called him Allosha), and Rahil. Mother was pregnant. Anuita was born in 1912. In 1914 World War I started. Communication with father was severed. We starved. I dropped out of school so that I could find work. I found a job as a janitor at a library. There I mopped floors and dusted bookshelves. There I also read a lot at night by candlelight. I was fourteen years old and had read novels by Tolstoi, Dostoyevsky, and other Russian authors, as well as American writers such as Jack London and Theodore Dreiser. That is how I improved myself.

We lived in the town of Bratzlav then. We starved; and Rahil, five, and Anuita, three, had to beg in the streets.

Later I found a job as a messenger in the print shop. Later I learned typesetting and became a typesetter. I attended a youth club and joined a chorus. There I met Freda, and later we got married. This was in the town of Tulchin where I had moved.

When I worked in the library, I told the director about my family. She advised that we move to Tulchin and promised to help get the children into a children's home (he says it is a boarding school, but the word means orphanage-mh). We moved to Tulchin, the children were admitted to the children's home, and Mother got a job as a cook. Our situation improved. Rahil and Aniuta were good students and did well in music. Allosha did not want to study. He spent his entire days at the stable and helped there with the horse, brought water from the well for the home. Mother was unhappy with Allosha, but he would not listen. He was also very interested in gymnastics. That is how he probably damaged his heart. The doctors diagnosed arrhythmia (?) and heart disorder; he had it for the rest of his life.

In 1924 we received a letter from Father after we had not heard from him for ten years. He sent money and transit papers (ship cards?) for me and Pollia to go to America. I refused (probably because I was a Komsomol member). Mother cried, but I would not listen. She had to go to the office that handled immigration and transferred the papers to Allosha. He and Pollia left in 1924. Next year in 1925, Mother, Rahil, and Aniuta also left for America. Before they left, Frida and I frequently visited the children's home. We played and danced with children, and Aniuta and Rahil played the piano. These were happy times for us.

FROM BROOKLYN NY TO BROOKLINE MA

In 1926 I was drafted into the army. Frida sent me monthly packages with cigarettes and home-made cookies. Then I stayed in the army as a volunteer. I was sent to the city of Baku. In 1929 I returned to Tulchin to get married to Frida so that she could come with me. In 1930 we had a son. We named him Salim (Sholom in Yiddish). At home we called him Sioma.

In 1941 World War II started. I was at the frontlines from the very first day. Frida and Sioma were evacuated to the east. I participated in the battles near Moscow. With my military unit, we moved westward, liberating towns and villages from the Fascists. I participated in the battle for Kenigsberg, the second capital of Germany. After that, we were sent to the Chinese border. According to the treaty with the United States, we were supposed to fight in the war against Japan along with the American forces.

After the war, I got a job at a book factory as a typesetter. Frida worked at a textile factory. Sioma started to attend the Polytechnic Institute, Department of Metallurgy. When he graduated, he was sent to the Urals. There he worked as an engineer at ironworks.

Ever since, Sioma was a student; and later, when he worked at the ironworks, Sioma was very interested in music. He managed to be accepted to the correspondence division of the Urals Conservatory in Sverdlovsk and successfully completed his studies there. There he met Galia, and they became friends. They graduated from the conservatory in the same year and got married. They began working in a music school in the Northern Caucasus region. Igor was born in 1962, and Aniuta was born in 1974.

Igor and Svieta met in the music school, then studied in a conservatory. They got married in 1983. In 1984 their son, Daniil, was born. Now Svieta and Igor work in a music school—teach piano forte. They settled in Seliatino not far away from Moscow.

Their daughter, Aniuta, studies in the central music school sponsored by the Moscow Conservatory. It is a regular school as well as a music school. She is a very good piano player and recently played Beethoven concerto with a symphony orchestra.

Sioma, Galia, and Aniuta live in Moscow. Galia does not work now.

Frida died in 1987. I was left alone and was unhappy. I moved to Seliatito where Igor lived with his family, and now I live with them.

Sioma's family often comes for dinner, and we enjoy music together.

Sometimes Svieta and Igor leave for work at the same time. Then I stay with Daniil. I play with him and take him to the park. He is a good boy. I love him very much. He is precocious. He already can read, and he memorizes songs and tunes he hears on the radio and TV. Maybe he will follow in his parents' footsteps and become a musician. Children should be loved. They carry on our lives.

It has been twenty-two years since I visited you, but I remember everything clearly.

My health is getting worse. Last summer I spent a month in the hospital, but most of the time, I feel all right, although my eyes and hearing are getting worse. The glasses I have are not helpful. I can read only with a magnifying glass (triple magnification). I have not found a large lens with greater magnification.

On my last trip to Kiev, Polia let me know of Rahil's request to buy a balalaika. I bought it and gave it to Polia. If it is properly tuned, one can accompany songs, especially Russian ones.

Igor and Svieta dream of visiting America for one month. To accomplish this, they need an official invitation. Can you help? My best wishes to your wife and children.

Sincerely,
Your uncle Munia

FROM BROOKLYN NY TO BROOKLINE MA

Uncle (DYADYA) Munya and Aunt (TEOTKA) Frida in Russia.

The Tombstone of Samuel Krimsky who died before I was born. He is buried on Mt. Hebron Cemetery in Queens near Main Street.

Chapter 2

MATERNAL FAMILY

The name Skolnick, Schkolnick, or Shkolnik comes from the word *Shkola*, which means *school* in Russian. In Ukrainian or Belarusian, *Shkola* means *a synagogue* or *a school*.

My maternal grandfather, Itzhak (Isadore) Shkolnick, was born November 15, 1888. He departed the village of Biela, near Yampol, Southwest Ukraine, for New York City the day after my mother, Chaya Raizel, was born. We think that my mother was born on June 25, 1914, although she assigned herself a birthday of 1 June 1914. She did not know her real birthday. My grandmother, Chaya Sarah, died when my mother was between four and six years old, probably as a result of the 1917–1918 worldwide influenza pandemic that claimed millions of lives. My mother remembers how her mother was laid out on a flat board with candles burning at the head of the corpse. My mother was raised by her two aunts. I was named Chaim Israel after my maternal grandmother, Chaya Sarah. My mother lived in a one-room village house without running water, indoor plumbing, etc. She recalls how the lambs were brought inside the house when it was really cold outside. My mother had no shoes and could not recall going to school.

Photo of the two aunts who raised my mother:

From the Ellis Island passenger record, my grandfather Itzko Schkolnick, as listed on the ship's manifest, arrived at Ellis Island 10 July 1914 on the ship *Lusitania* that departed from Liverpool. He was sponsored by his brother, Kupel (variants are *kappel, kopel,* etc.). My grandfather was twenty-six years old and reported to the immigration agent that he spoke Russian and Hebrew. The immigration agent recorded that his last place of residence was Dzygowska, Russia. His Hebrew name was Yitzhak (*Itzik* in Yiddish). His name in Russia was Shkolnikoff. He left Ellis Island with the new name Isadore Shkolnikoff. Both names are shown on the ancestry database. Years later, he changed his surname to Skolnick. The agent listed his marital status as "single," which is strange. It was either a mistake or he said *single* to avoid answering further questions.

Kopel (however it is spelled) is a variation of Yakef according to a book of names and variants I read at YIVO. Yakef is another way to spell Yaakov or even Yankel. The English variation is Jacob. Yankel Schkolnik was born in 1868 and arrived in the USA on 18 May 1906 in New York on the ship *Caronia*. He came from Russia. He married Dora Wasserman in 1912 (marriage certificate number 5874). He was forty-six years old in 1914 when he sponsored my grandfather to the USA. Kupel worked for New York City as a garbage collector. He died of cancer as did his sister Yudel.

From the *Wikipedia*, *Lusitania* met a disastrous end as a casualty of the First World War when she was torpedoed by the German submarine *U-20* on May 7, 1915. The great ship sank in just eighteen minutes, eight miles (fifteen kilometers) off the Old Head of Kinsale, Ireland, killing 1,198 of the people aboard. The sinking turned public opinion in many countries against Germany. It is often considered by historians to be the second most famous civilian passenger liner disaster after the sinking of *Titanic*.

According to the passenger list on the *Laconia*, Meyer and Mollie Schkolnik arrived in the USA 17 August 1914, which was after my grandfather arrived in the USA. He sponsored their arrival with his brother, Kupel. Meyer's age was fifty-five at arrival, which means that he was born in 1859. The spelling of both names was anglicized from Meir and Malya to Meyer and Mollie. Their gravestones show that Meyer was born in 1861 and died 11 November 1930 and Mollie was born in 1861 and died on 12 February 1934. Meyer came to the USA with a daughter, Ida. I suspect that she died before my aunt Ida was born. My aunt Ida was named after her aunt Ida.

Grandma Rose arrived in 1928, and she met both grandparents. Aunt Ida was born in 1922, and she remembered both grandparents. Their names and ages are listed on the 1925 census as follows— Meyer, sixty-two; Molly, sixty-five, and Ida (daughter), twenty-two— which do not agree with the dates carved on the gravestones. Their occupations are listed as follows: Meyer, rag sorter; Molly, housewife; and Ida, cloak finisher. The New York State Census of 1925 says Meyer was born about 1863 and was sixty-two years old. The ancestry (Galicia, births marriages, and deaths) states that Molly was born in Jagielnica in 1864 and Meyer was born about 1859 in Jizevka. The ship's manifest says that he came from Jizevka and arrived at the port of New York on 16 August 1914, which was about two months after Grandma Rose was born. Grandma Rose remembered that Meyer worked with rags. Arriving at the truth using gravestones, US census records, New York State census, ship's manifest, and ancestry data is like specifying the location and momentum of subatomic particles at the same time based on measurements—an impossible task. But it was an interesting effort for me to go to YIVO, and with some help, I located the documents of interest.

On 21 November 1919, my grandfather reported in his declaration of intention to become a US citizen that he was married to Sarah residing in Russia. He reported his address as Sixty-Fourth Mckibben Street in Brooklyn. He listed his occupation as a presser. He listed his age as thirty-one years old. He was born in 1888.

He learned that his wife in Russia, Chaya Sarah, died around 1919 probably from the Spanish Influenza epidemic. He married Anna Matz on 6 March 1921 in Kings County (certificate number 3001).

In his petition for naturalization dated 24 April 1922, he reported that he arrived in New York on 14 July 1914 and was married to Anna who was born in Babruysk, Russia. My mother was between four and six years old when Sarah died. He listed his occupation as a presser. He reported his address as Thirty-seven Morgan Avenue in Brooklyn. He reported that he had two children: Rose, born on 25 June 1914 in Russia, and Ida, born on 3 January 1922. Their address was Thirty-seven Morgan Street in Brooklyn. In a petition event on 21 November 1923, in the Southern District of New York, the record shows that he changed his name from Scholnikoff to Schkolnick.

Anna was born on August 28, 1900, in Russia. Her maiden name was Anna Matz. The 1940 census indicated that she completed one year of school probably in Russia and my grandfather completed four years of school also in Russia. He and Anna had three children: Ida, Nathan, and Harry. The census reported his age as fifty-two and her age as forty-eight. He listed his occupation as a self-employed painter. She listed her occupation as a housewife. About ten years later after he had arrived in America, he had saved enough money to bring my mother to America. He engaged an agent to arrange all the papers. The agent stole the money, and my grandfather had to resend money. My mother arrived at Ellis Island as a girl of fourteen on 9 March 1928 on the French Line, according to the port authority records, but she appeared younger. An older couple was supposed to look after her on the ship during the voyage, but they did not. We could not find any record of her arrival to Ellis Island. Her name was not recorded in the ship's manifest that was eventually put on microfilm. My brother and I looked on the microfilm of the ship's manifest and never found her name, the maiden name of her mother (Millman), or the name of any female about her age. My grandfather tried to meet her upon arrival but was told she was in the infirmary. My mother was sick during the ocean voyage. He returned the second day with a cousin, Harry Lieber, to meet her.

She became a citizen upon arrival from her father's citizenship papers. Her father became a citizen in on 1 June 1923 (number 1818679) in Brooklyn, New York.

I visited Ellis Island. At the end of the great hall where the newcomer immigrants waited to be processed into America by answering questions of the immigration officers who stood at their desks (shtenders), there is a down staircase that leads to an exit from the main building to a dock and ferry to the mainland. My mother remembers nothing about how she actually sneaked into the United States. I suspect that she walked behind the agents recording names of arrivals. The agents standing at their desks ignored a small peasant girl without parents, without an adult guardian, who spoke no English. She entered the USA without papers (WOP), without a birth certificate, and without luggage. She remembers bringing luggage on board ship, which she recalls as being her mother's bedding. WOP is a pejorative term that was applied mostly to Italians during the 1950s and 1960s. Similar pejorative terms such as *greenhorns*, *mockies*, *micks*, *chinks*, and *kikes* were used to debase newly arrived immigrants. I heard them all on the streets of Coney Island. Some people resented the new immigrants because they had government assistance to find housing (in short supply) and were given some financial assistance (perhaps from HIAS).

My mother, small for her age and feisty, just walked away from the crowd, in the confusion sneaked around the agents, and walked downstairs where my grandfather and a cousin, named Harry Lieber, probably saw her and called Roseh. They were waiting for her. Harry was married to Bessie. Bessie's brother was Cantor Chaim who married my mother and father, and Ida and Perry. He also officiated at my bar mitzvah. They took a ferry to the mainland and then went to Williamsburg, the home of my grandfather. The Shkolnick family moved shortly after to Hinsdale Street in East New York and then eventually to 456 Alabama Avenue in East New York. The records of the Jewish Historical Society in New York on Sixteenth Street show no evidence that my mother ever arrived in America.

The aunt, sister of her mother, who raised her in Russia asked my mother to send her letters upon her arrival in America. My mother regrets that she never wrote to them. But my mother never learned to write in Russian or even Yiddish. Her aunt never learned if she arrived safely in America unless my grandfather wrote to them. I am not aware if he did write to them. I regret not understanding all this when he was alive so I could ask him questions. Aunt Raizel and Uncle Yossel sent a letter to my grandfather that my mother kept until this day. They asked my mother and grandfather to write them about their life in the USA. Their letter and translation are in the rear of this manuscript. I suspect that my grandfather wanted to forget his former life in Russia and could not send them money.

The German front in WWII extended north of Biela, so I suspect that nothing remained of Biela after the Germans invaded. Yampol still exists on the map.

My mother was enrolled in the third grade in a Brooklyn public school and felt embarrassed; there were no special schooling arrangements. According to the historical records at the Jewish Historical Society, she completed the fifth grade. My mother was enrolled in public school for three years and left at age sixteen to go to work. During those three years, she learned to read and write English and do arithmetic. My grandfather hired a tutor for six months to teach her how to read and write Yiddish. My mother could speak Yiddish but not write; she had no schooling in Russia. My grandfather's second wife, Anna, had three other children from this marriage, one child in diapers, and never bargained for another child from a former marriage. Ida was born first on 3 January 1922. My mother reported that she was mistreated by her stepmother by denying her food. Anna complained to my grandfather that she was not helping around the house. Anna asked or expected my mother to change Heshy's diapers. Anna could not read or write any language. She spoke Yiddish and some English. My mother recalls that my grandfather gave my mother $5 per week for lunch because Anna would not provide her with food. Sometimes she bought candy for lunch. Her teenage diet was poor. She was malnourished, which was probably why I was born with rickets, heart murmur, and arms smaller than my father's. I noticed that years later when I watched him paint ceilings without tiring. My mother wanted to remain in school. She received good reports from her teachers but left after three years at age sixteen and went to work as a salesperson, earning $9 per week. My mother has bad memories about her stepmother. Her stepmother demanded she contribute to the household by giving $5 a week. After a year, my mother stopped payments so she could buy some nice clothing and have a social life. Anna objected to the stop payments, and I can imagine the arguments that ensued. My mother resented whenever I called Anna Bubby. My mother always referred to my grandmother as the *putzutzah*, which I believe is the female equivalent of *putz*. She just made up the name without knowing how she came to it, which reified her feelings about her stepmother.

In order to receive an employment certificate, she needed to have a physical exam. A carbon copy of the form states that she was four feet eight inches and weighed ninety-four pounds. Her pulse rate was eighty. Her teeth, throat, glands, hearing, vision, and lungs were good. Her nutrition was listed as only fair. She was in the fifth or sixth grade at PS 171. She was vaccinated against smallpox. She passed the physical exam and was entitled to leave school and go to work.

In May 1931, my mother was issued an employment certificate by the New York City Board of Education. Her birthday was listed as 1 June 1915. She left school at age sixteen, the minimum age for acquiring working papers in New York. She listed her address at 754 Pitkin Avenue, Brooklyn. The employment certificate stated that "this minor is required to attend continuation school." My mother went to work and did not attend continuation school.

After she met my father at a Russian club, my mother befriended Bubby Sonya. Conditions became unbearable at 456 Alabama Avenue, and my mother left her Alabama home and moved into the apartment of Bubby Sonya for six months before she married my father. Bubby Sonya insisted that my mother and father visit Zadie and explain that she and my father want to be married.

On 22 December 1934, the city clerk of New York issued a marriage license to Alex Krimsky and Rose Skolnick. Both addresses were listed as 1905 Daugton Street. His age was listed as twenty-six, and her age was listed as twenty. His occupation was listed as painter, and her occupation was listed as cutter. Both places of birth were listed as Podolsk, Russia. Podolsk is the region in which Tulchin and Bieleh were located. Sarah Feldman was listed as his mother's name, and Sarah Milman was listed as her mother's name. Both were listed as first-time marriages.

Zadie approved the marriage and hired a cook for $35 to prepare a wedding feast. They were married in the shul across the street from 456 Alabama Avenue, the shul my Zadie refused to attend. Bubby Pessie, the aunt of my father, walked my mother down the aisle. I can imagine the argument that ensued because my mother did not want Anna, her stepmother, to walk her down the aisle. So Zadie refused to walk her alone, and the solution was to have pareve Bubby Pessie walk her down the aisle. Cantor Chaim performed the ceremony, the same chaim who performed my bar mitzvah ceremony. I never knew him or saw him elsewhere except on those occasions. Bubbie Pessie attended my bar mitzvah party. I never spoke with her.

Zadie demanded half of the wedding presents because he had to pay for the cook. They were married on 20 January 1925 at the address listed as 445 Alabama Avenue, which I believe was the shul across the street from Zadie's house, 456 Alabama Avenue. The sum of 4+5+6 = 15, which is a special number as 15 equals the number of words in the priestly blessing. My mother's name on the ketubah

(Jewish marriage certificate) was listed as Chaya Raisel b'Reb Yitzhak although she never mentioned her middle name to us growing up.

Mom and Dad went to the Half Moon Hotel for their honeymoon for one day. The hotel was located on Twenty-Ninth Street and the boardwalk in Coney Island. The Half Moon Hotel was named after the ship used by Henry Hudson to sail up the Hudson River when he explored New York State. During and after WWII, the hotel was used by the navy as a recovery center for wounded sailors. I saw wounded sailors sitting outside in the sun to recover from their war wounds. No one took me to visit them. The hotel was demobilized as a hotel and remained there until the 1980s when it was torn down and replaced by housing for elderly, mostly Russians who immigrated to America.

The 1940 census shows Mom and Dad living at 639 Blake Avenue in Brooklyn. She reported as twenty-six years old and Dad was thirty-two. He listed his occupation as a house painter.

I telephoned my grandfather right after Naomi was born in March 1970 and described her red hair. He told me about Nachum der Roita (Nathan, the red-haired one) who was a distant cousin of my grandfather but who was dead. He became Nachum der Toita (Nathan the dead one). He once told me when I visited him that "Americaner haben moireh far die Toiten." It means that Americans are afraid of the dead. Americans do not want to deal with death. Americans want death sanitized. Death was part of life, and at his age, he saw plenty. He used to visit sick people in the hospital as a mitzvah just as he visited his beautiful granddaughter with blonde hair and blue eyes in the medical institution that cared for her. She was the daughter of Natie and Silvia Skolnick. My aunt Ida called him the mayor of Alabama Avenue because he seemed to know everyone on Alabama Avenue and connected with all of them. He did not like the shul across the street but never told me why.

Zadie worked as a housepainter, as did my father. He never learned to drive. I noticed that his hands were large and calloused. His wrists were larger than mine. His hands were those of a Russian muzhik, laborer or peasant. He told me that he taught my father how to paint. My father dismissed that idea.

Alabama Avenue became dangerous for older Jews, and my aunt Ida and her husband paid the increased rent to have him relocate. My zadie and bubby moved from 456 Alabama Avenue to an apartment on Fountain Avenue, which was still in Brooklyn but closer to the ocean. Brownsville and East New York quickly became free from Jews during the 1960s. The synagogues were abandoned, and the merchants slowly disappeared.

My grandfather selected his own gravesite in the Old Mountefiore Cemetery on the side of a lane so his gravesite could be easily found. He was a house painter as was my father. He painted the entrance gate to the family plot red so his lane could be easily spotted. He claims he taught my father how to paint, but my father always disagreed with that assessment. My father taught himself to mix colors and watched other painters. My zadie died after Pesach, April 30, 1970, at age eighty-two (24 Nisan), shortly after Naomi was born. I continued his custom of red painting the First Zigifker entrance gate to the lane where he is buried whenever I visit the cemetery. Anna moved to a nursing home, Haber House, in Coney Island. My aunt Ida handled the expenses. My mother was furious when she learned that I walked from Neptune Avenue to visit her on a Shabbos. Bubby Anna died April 9, 1976, at seventy-six years of age. I regret that my mother informed me too late to attend her funeral. It was the last chance to see my three stepuncles and aunts all together. I had nothing against them. Of course, my mother did not attend her funeral and did not want me to attend. It was rude of me not to go. How could I explain this to my uncles and aunt? My grandmother treated me well as her grandchild. She was solicitous of me whenever I visited my grandfather and slept over and went to shul on Saturday. He had a mysterious aura by carrying the Jewish culture from Russia to America, which my paternal relatives did not have. They were more pragmatic and brought to these shores a Ukrainian culture of dance, art, and music. Religion played no role in their lives, and Jewish teachings were minimal. The Russian government saw to that.

My grandfather's two children, Ida and Nathan (Natie), graduated high school but did not go to college. I do not think Harry (Heshie) graduated high school. Natie served in WWII as a soldier, and Heshie served in the USN at the end of the war. Ida married a businessman, Natie's friend Perry, and they had two children, Mark and Linda. Mark and Linda each married. Linda attended Brooklyn College and studied art in Paris. Mark studied business. Linda had a bad marriage, lived as flower child of the sixties. Her husband abandoned her. She died of breast cancer about 1995. My aunt Ida told me that she returned from Paris a changed person. I saw Linda only once when she was a few weeks old during a visit to my grandfather's apartment on Alabama Avenue. After she died, Ida refused to put her in the ground where she could be eaten by worms. She is buried in a vault somewhere in New York. Ida lives in Great Neck, Long Island, and cared for her husband, Perry, until he died from Alzheimer's disease in 2011. Perry was born as Peretz Fishbein. His English name was Phillip, and he later changed it to Perry because that is what everyone called him. He is buried in a vault. Linda and her husband had two children, Jessie and Allana. Both lived in Florida. Linda's husband abandoned his family. The children have nothing to do with him. Ida and Perry supported them after their mother died so they could at least continue college education and have a place to live.

Mark has two children, Jason and Evan. Jason married a non-Jewish woman, divorced her, and remarried an Israeli woman from Russia. They married in Israel. Jason has a child from his first marriage. I know nothing about the conversion of the first son. I met Mark only once at the funeral of my grandfather. I never met his children or Linda's children.

Natie married Sylvia in 1945 or 1946. I attended their wedding on Long Island. They moved to Alabama Avenue and lived there for a while. I remember visiting them only once and saw and smelled bacon cooking on the stove. Sylvia had no concept of kashruth or did not care. I felt that this was a betrayal of my grandfather's principles. I recall that she asked me if I wanted something to eat or drink and I politely said no. I could not eat from her trefe home. Natie was part owner and worked in a candy store down the street on Alabama Avenue. He dispensed egg creams and ice cream and rang up the money into the cash register. He was a cool guy, a natural for that kind of work just as my uncle Izzy, husband of Annette. They both had a natural way of interacting with customers. The streets were teeming with Jewish people after the war especially since the young veterans returned to live with their parents until they were able to construct their own independent lives and move away from teeming central Brooklyn into the suburbs.

Natie had three children: a brain-damaged girl, Steven, and Michael. My grandfather visited the blonde blue-eyed girl in a special institution almost every week. He told me about it, but she barely recognized him. I knew it hurt him, but he had a strong constitution coming from Russia. Natie and Sylvia could not bear the pain of seeing her. Natie had serious money disagreements with Steven. Steven borrowed tens of thousands of dollars for a business and refused to repay the loan even when he prospered. Sylvia died in 2007 of Alzheimer's disease. Natie and Michael have a good relationship. Natie kept busy cooking and working at Sears in Albuquerque, New Mexico as of July 2008. He died in 2009. I regret that I never saw him for about fifty years. He seemed like a cool uncle when I knew him, and he worked in a candy store on Alabama Avenue. The neighborhood was teeming with demobilized Jewish veterans of WW II. There was life on the streets day and night, and it was safe to walk. I used to play ball in the school yard of the Thomas Jefferson Public School. In later years, the Jews moved away, and the neighborhood was unsafe.

Heshie married twice and had one child with Marilyn, his first wife. His son was a slow learner. Heshie moved to Los Angeles and died in 1994 from the stress of the earthquake for which the epicenter was Northridge in the San Fernando Valley where he lived. My grandfather's children and other grandchildren had no Torah education (except for my brother and me who did attend Hebrew school), and that is one reason he doted on me.

A short history of the Jewish community of Yampol, Ukraine may be found in Kehila Links. On 18 June 1941 Yampol was occupied by the invading Nazi forces. Many Jews evacuated with the retreating Red Army. Most of the remaining Jews were murdered by the Germans. My mother left Bieleh, near Yampol, before the German invasion.

FROM BROOKLYN NY TO BROOKLINE MA

In July 2011, my last uncle, Perry Fishbein, died. His wife, Ida, Zadie's daughter, was a dutiful wife who took care of him at home as best she was able. I never had a relationship with him or my uncle Natie who died a few years earlier in Albuquerque, New Mexico. My uncle Heshy died in Northbridge, Los Angeles, after an earthquake. I regret never having a relationship with the families and cousins on my mother's side. The divorce between my brother and me is payback for constantly criticizing the half brothers and sister and in-laws on her side because of her hatred for her stepmother. Would you want a relationship with someone who constantly criticized your mother? Around 1950 my father formed a business relationship with a Mr. Yampolsky. He came to our apartment and showed me a business card, "Krimsky and Yampolsky, Painters." His relatives may have come from Yampol.

Bubbie Anna and Zadie Isador Skolnick

Chapter 3

EARLY CHILDHOOD

My mother and father met at a Russian social club. My mother moved out of my grandfather's house into an apartment on Watkins and Pitkin Avenue with Bubbie Sonya before she was married to my father. My mother could not stand living at home. Moving out before marriage was not the custom at the time. Girls lived at home until they were married. My parents were married in the Alabama Street shul in 1935 followed by a reception in my grandfather's apartment, 456 Alabama Avenue, in East New York. My father's aunt Tante Pessie walked my mother down the aisle. My mother did not want her stepmother to walk her down the aisle. This caused arguments in the house between my grandfather and grandmother. Pessie was the mother of Fannie Fidel and the sister of Bubbie Sonya. Pessie attended my bar mitzvah. I saw her only once or twice. I had no relationship with her. She looked ancient, part of a lost world, totally outside of my experiences. Pessie was the mother of Max Katz. Fannie and Max were siblings. Both observed kashruth and Shabbos, the only ones in my paternal family. Fannie and her husband, Phillip, were a mystery to me. I did not relate to them. Max and his wife, Sonya, attended my bar mitzvah and my wedding. Max moved to Arizona because Sonya had tuberculosis and she needed dry air. I spent one Shabbos with him because I could not get home before Shabbos after a conference in Las Vegas. Bubbie Pessie walked my mother down the aisle. Cantor Chaim, family chazzan, a favorite of my grandfather, performed the ceremony. Aunt Pessie accompanied my mother to the *mikveh* (ritual bath) for the first time. Prior to marriage, my mother never heard of a mikveh. I know nothing about Pessie's husband or how they came to America. Pessie was married to Rabbi Katz in Russia. He taught the father of Leonard Bernstein his bar mitzvah lessons in Russia. Rabbi Katz died in Russia before Bubbie immigrated to America.

Max and Sonya had one daughter, Evelyn. She was a beautiful teenager with dark eyes, older than me, and far more mature than me at my adolescent age. She married an Israeli pianist Avraham Sternklar who left Israel to play and teach in America. Evelyn mocked her father's religious practice. Max told me this himself in Arizona. He stopped talking to his daughter. Only Sonya talked to her daughter. I felt sad for him. He read the weekly portions from the Torah in the Young Israel shul in Tucson, Arizona. Abraham had a car accident in America that ended his piano-playing career. He continued to teach. I never heard him play. Evelyn took voice lessons, but I never heard her sing. Max visited us once in a while in Coney Island to enjoy the beach. His face had a perpetual smile. He was unassuming, and I really liked him. In New York City he worked as a milliner and in Arizona learned about electricity and worked as a radio and TV repair technician. Max died in Arizona, and Sonya moved to a nursing home in New York and died.

In 1965, I visited Israel for the first time, traveled to Beer Sheva, and walked on the circular staircase to the top of the minaret near the shuk. The minaret was built during the Turkish occupation before WWI. The minaret had a balcony with a concrete parapet at the top about chest level that permitted me to see out in the distance on all sides. I saw the name "M. Katz" deeply scratched into the horizontal concrete surface surrounding the cylindrical minaret. I returned to America and asked Cousin Max if he was responsible for carving his name, and he admitted doing that a few years before I visited Israel. When I revisited the museum a few years later, I wanted to see if the weather had eroded his name scratched on the concrete parapet. A locked gate at the entrance to the cylindrical staircase blocked me from walking up to the top of the minaret.

The honeymoon of my parents consisted of spending one day and night at the Half Moon Hotel on Twenty-Ninth Street in Coney Island, which was adjacent to the boardwalk. The uncle of my son-in-law, Rabbi Kalman Sodden, recalls going into the Alabama Street shul as a youth. Attendance dwindled, and the beautiful building, squeezed between two apartment buildings, was demolished during the 1960s. This was the fate of all the shuls in Brownsville, East New York, and the shul in Coney Island on West Nineteenth Street in which I became a bar mitzvah.

After I was born, my parents moved to another apartment on Riverdale Avenue near Blake Avenue. Later my grandfather stopped attending the Alabama Street shul, directly across the street from 456 Alabama Avenue. He favored the Pennsylvania Avenue shul about half a mile away. Something happened, was probably insulted, and stopped attending the Alabama Street shul directly across the street from his apartment. He proudly told me that he purchased *p'sicha* (opening the Aron HaKodesh or Holy Ark) for an entire year in the Pennsylvania Street shul. My parents never spoke to me in Russian or Yiddish but strived to learn English. He spoke to me in English with Yiddish words thrown in. When I had measles, he mentioned to my mother that someone also "gemeaselt." He combined the past tense of Yiddish *Ge* with the noun *measles* and created a new past participle *gemeaselt*. He made a verb out of a noun by combining two languages. That was cool. My first real exposure to Yiddish was in Hebrew School in Coney Island where we learned to translate the Chumish into Yiddish. It was torture since Yiddish was rarely spoken in my house, but I absorbed some Yiddish from my grandfather. I visited him many times for Shabbos, and he doted on me more than his own four children. After graduating college, I wrote to him in Yiddish from California and even called him up before Yom Kippur.

FROM BROOKLYN NY TO BROOKLINE MA

Half Moon Hotel on West Twenty-Ninth Street and the boardwalk. Building was used as a naval hospital during WWII. It was eventually demolished during the seventies or eighties and replaced by the Shore Front Jewish Geriatric Center that cost $3 million dollars to build and replaced the Brooklyn Hebrew Home and Hospital for the Aged that was located on Howard and Dumont Avenues in Brooklyn.

My father repeated the following story. During the time he was courting my mother, he called for her at the home of my grandfather, which was the custom at the time. My grandfather knew nothing about my father's family, so he asked about my father's *yichus*. He wanted my mother to marry someone of substance, not give her away to a *buma*, which in Yiddish means a *lowdown person*. My father was not a person of substance, and my mother had no dowry. My father, his mother, and his sisters struggled to survive in America without welfare, without health benefits, without IRAs, without rent control, and without a real education. So my father responded to my grandfather's inquiry about yichus by saying "Yichus Touchis [Family background my ass]," which angered my grandfather so much that he threw my father out of the house by asking him to immediately leave. He left but returned to court my mother. My grandfather never again asked about my father's yichus. Of course, my grandfather was only one level above peasanthood status since he could at least read and write Yiddish. According to the census records, he only completed four years of schooling in Russia. He never boasted about his yichus. His wife, Bubby Anna, could not read anything. She knew how to cook and clean—a real model of a Russian peasant babushka. She completed one year of schooling in Russia.

My parents moved into 217 Watkins Avenue in East New York where families shared bathrooms. My mother was malnourished. I was born on March 17, 1936, in Beth Moses Hospital in New York. The pediatrician determined that I had rickets and a heart murmur. My mother was worried because she thought that I had a heart condition, and that is why she always tried to restrain me from vigorous physical activity. The pediatrician prescribed a daily teaspoon of cod liver oil and daily exposure to sunlight to strengthen my bones, which I later learned caused me to make vitamin D3. His treatment must have worked because I never experienced difficulties in walking or having crooked legs. I still remember taking cod liver oil daily and the oily taste lingered in my mouth. I can still taste it. The taste did not bother me. I just accepted cod liver oil as a necessary treatment. This is still the recommended treatment for rickets. A teaspoon has 400 IU of vitamin D. Vitamin D promotes the absorption of dietary calcium, which is needed for strong bones. The murmur was something else. It was barely discernable, but it was there. I was lucky because it never interfered with physical activities in my youth. But I did notice shortness of breath after running for less than a mile. I could never do a marathon. My mother cleaned diapers in a bathtub using a washboard made with glass corregations(*riebeisel* in Yiddish) that she saved for me and I still have. She saved it so I could know how hard she worked at home. Who can know when riebeisels and slide rules will again prove useful? The Second World War started. My father liked to work outdoors, and he liked to build and repair things. My father tried to join the navy construction battalions (Seabees) but was classified 4-F because of a heart irregularity.

My birth certificate records that we lived at 217 Watkins Avenue in East New York. I was born in Beth Moses Hospital that that merged later to become the Maimonides Medical Center near Fort Hamilton Parkway. My mother was malnourished when she was married and malnourished when I was born. It took me many years to understand that I was born small, with thin arms and wrists, with a heart murmur and rickets. The doctor explained this to my mother, and she believed herself as responsible if I had a bad heart. The doctor explained about murmurs to her, and this was always on her mind when she tried to restrain me from active physical work or sports. Although I was built like my father, his arms, wrists, and muscle structure were more powerful than mine. She objected when I used to jump the eight feet off the boardwalk onto the sandy beach at Coney Island or when I would jump from roof to roof on the small bungalow buildings when they were unoccupied and we were exploring. My mother told me how she dropped me, because she was malnourished, near or on a hot radiator when I was a baby, and she apologized for this several times. I do not recall being dropped.

One night I recall waking up in a crib holding on to the rail wearing pajamas with a buttoned flap that opened in the back. My mother was whispering to my father, and there was a siren noise outside. She told me to go back to sleep. I stood up in the crib and listened and heard. Years later I learned that my father volunteered as an air raid warden during the early year of the war, and I saw that he wore a special white hat. He went outside telling people to close their curtains and window shades so city lights could not assist the Germans to bomb New York or assist enemy ships to slip into New York Harbor. This was an exercise in preparation for an attack. He was proud of his service as an air raid warden.

I must have been three or four years old when my father came home from work with a red toy drummer with a wind-up key. He would wind up the key, and the drummer would beat on the drum with two drumsticks. My father called it a *barabanchik* or *drummer boy* in Russian. I remember my mother scolding my father for spending money on such things. I can't recall exactly what she said, but she was verbally unhappy with his purchase. Money was tight, and my mother managed the family budget. She did not work at the time. Later, he also bought me a small table with a mallet and pegs. I was supposed to knock the pegs into a pegboard that had lots of holes. For hours I sat on that table, knocking pegs into holes. I learned how to remove the pegs and knock them back into the pegboard. The toy occupied me for hours.

In September 1941, I was enrolled in kindergarten in New York PS 175 on the corner of Blake and Hopkinson Avenues.

Pearl Harbor was attacked on December 7, 1941.

Sid Krimsky on a pony circa 1940

Chapter 4

MOVE TO BALTIMORE, MARYLAND

From my birth to October 1936, we lived at 217 Watkins Avenue in Brooklyn. From October 1936 to October 1939, we lived at 496 Williams Avenue in Brooklyn. From October 1939 to September 1940, we lived at 637 Blake Avenue in Brooklyn. From September 1940 to February 1942, we lived at we lived at 169 Dumont Avenue in Brooklyn. Sheldon, my brother, was born 26 June 1941. From February 1942 to November 1945, we lived at 255 Herring Court in Baltimore, Maryland, on the second floor of an attached house. We moved in November 1945 to 2995 West Twenty-Ninth Street in Coney Island, Brooklyn. My parents and brother continued to live there for a few more years after I moved to Sacramento, California, in August 1958.

In February 1942 we moved from Dumont Avenue to 255 Herring Court in Baltimore, Maryland, where my father obtained work as a second-class engineer, building liberty ships at the Bethlehem Naval Shipyard. He worked in a machine shop and learned to use a metal bending machine from which he formed a bracelet for my mother out of monel (molybdenum nickel alloy) metal by pig-tailing two one-eighth-inch rods and compressing the pigtail between two hardened rollers. She refused to wear it. I still have it unworn by anyone. He also made for himself a wedding ring out of a solid rod of monel metal that I wear this day. I remember watching a ship launching on the wharf while sitting on my father's shoulders. He was short but powerfully built. I was enrolled in public school number 2.

We lived in a brick house, a three-story walkup in a housing project especially built for defense workers employed by Bethlehem Naval Shipyard. The houses were attached (as townhouses) and designed to minimize construction costs. The front of the houses faced small playgrounds with a series of vertical poles for affixing clotheslines. The outdoor entrance was a concrete staircase leading to three doors. The left door opened to the left-side apartment on the first floor. The right door opened to the right-side apartment on the third floor. The center door opened to a staircase for the second floor. We lived on the second floor. The entire housing project accommodated several hundred families. We lived there from 1942 to 1945. The buildings were efficiently designed at the lowest cost. They are still in use.

Author and brother are standing outside 255 Herring Court in Baltimore.

My brother Sheldon and I standing at the steps opposite 255 Herring Court in Baltimore, Maryland.

FROM BROOKLYN NY TO BROOKLINE MA

Sidney sitting on the steps outside 255 Herring Court Baltimore, Maryland.

I recall that my father took me to greet Santa Claus on a winter day in a large department store. I waited on line with my father to receive a present from Santa Claus. I did not sit on his lap, but I did receive a small box of tanagrams. These are small acute triangles, rectangles, parallelograms, rhombuses, etc., that may be rearranged to show different shapes. The instruction booklet showed how to make birds, chickens, etc., from assembling the different shapes. This small gift was not terribly exciting and challenging to a seven- or eight-year-old, but Santa was poor and there was an ongoing war. I was too young to understand what was happening around the world, but I do remember the gold stars on the small hanging flags on the windows of the houses all along the streets. Some flags had multiple stars. It was a symbol of pride.

Bubbie Sonya came to pay us a visit perhaps to help take care of us because my mother was in the hospital. I was put in a kindergarten at age five. Bubbie Sonya was supposed to pick me up after the school day. One day after everyone went home, I was alone. There was a big chain-link fence in the outside playground. I grasped the links and cried. No one was there. Everyone left the schoolyard so it seemed. It was getting dark. Finally, she showed up and apologized for being late. I never forgave her for being late. My mother found out and also apologized to me later. I did not trust Bubbie Sonya to come on time. There was no repetition of that incident.

One day I decided to greet my father on his way home from work. I knew what time he arrived at home. The shipyard was located at the wharf on lower Broadway, only a fifteen-minute walk from our apartment. Our apartment was situated between two major parallel streets, Pratt and Lombard Streets. The Jewish butchers, food stores, and shops were on Lombard Street. A major synagogue was situated on Lloyd Street, a block from Lombard and only a few city blocks away from our apartment. The Jewish Museum of Maryland is presently located on the site. The synagogue is a national historic site.

In the evening before supper, I walked left from our apartment toward Gough Street, turned right on Broadway, and waited to meet my father returning from work. He would be carrying his familiar metal lunchbox with a thermos bottle and be surprised to see me. I wanted to surprise him. I waited on the corner. He did not show up, so I walked down Broadway toward the wharf. I kept walking wondering, why I did not see him. Finally, I turned around and started to walk back. I saw both my parents about a city block away from the direction I had walked. I learned that my father walked home on that day on the other side of Broadway and missed me. My mother expected him to be with me and panicked when he came home alone. I never felt threatened walking down Broadway alone as a child of about seven years, which is probably why these same safe feelings persisted after sixty years upon my return to the same streets although the neighborhood appears seedier in 2005 than in 1941–1945. My wife and children would not understand my explanation. I grew up without fear of walking alone anywhere. The housing project of three-storied buildings is still there between Pratt and Gough Streets and between Broadway and Caroline Streets. The clothesline poles are still there between the buildings.

One day I woke up with my neck tilted to the right, and I could not straighten it out. It hurt if I tried. I worried: was this to be permanent? My mother worried about polio and asked neighbors about a neurologist. Polio was a feared disease during the 1940s and 1950s. I did not know anything about polio. She walked me down Broadway toward the wharf to a doctor. I recall walking up a wide set of stairs, with my neck still tilted at an ungainly angle, into an office with a large desk and books, and a doctor sitting behind the desk. He was nicely dressed and looked real professional. He sat in front of a large circular window that looked out into Baltimore Harbor. All the ships and activity in the harbor fascinated me. The doctor asked my mother and me some questions. He then walked to where I was sitting, pulled up a chair, and put his probing fingers around my neck, asking about pain. He put his large hands on my cheeks, pushed my cheeks together as if my head were in a vise, and quickly snapped my head in the other direction. Wow! I felt a millisecond of pain, and miraculously, my neck was straight. I had regained full motion. When I saw the movie, *The Hunchback of Notre Dame*, I always wondered if a neurologist could have helped Quasimodo if he had lived during the twentieth century.

The Apex and the Cluster were two movie theaters on lower Broadway. The Apex is near Pratt Street, and the Cluster was farther down Broadway toward the wharf on the other side. My mother took me to a scary movie in the Cluster. We saw *Tomorrow the World* with Frederick March as head of the family. The Nazi leaders used the phrase "Tomorrow the world" to articulate the aggressive policy of German hegemony and world influence. In German, the complete phrase reads "Heute Deutschland, Morgan die Welt [Today Germany, tomorrow the world]." The movie described an American family to house and care for a German youth, named Emil,(Skip Homeier) whose father was friendly with the head of the household. Emil had been indoctrinated with Nazi ideologies and hatreds. He tries to get his way by bullying. His behavior was nasty to the host family. This movie was clearly antiwar that portrayed the world view and eventual planned implementation of the Nazi ideologies if unstopped. I never again saw the film although I have been looking for it. It was my first exposure to institutional evil. The movie stayed with me for many years.

In 1994 I had an opportunity to travel to Baltimore on business. I would spend a week learning about communications security (COMSEC) at the National Security Agency at Fort George Meade in Maryland, south of Baltimore. I always wanted to revisit the 255 Herring Court site and see if it is still there and retrace my early years. Herring Court, part of a larger housing project, was not on the street maps. I remembered that it was near Lombard Street, Pratt Street, and Broadway. I located these major streets on the detailed street map. I drove my rented car to the approximate area, parked my car, walked up and down the streets, closed my eyes, and tried to recall the project layouts when I lived there from 1941 to 1945. The area had clearly changed. The Jewish shops were gone, replaced by empty lots, an elementary school, and seedy shops. The two movie theaters on Broadway displayed XXX-rated movies. Bethlehem Shipyard was gone. Putting logic on hold, I allowed my intuition to control my brain, always a dangerous precedent for me. An unexplained inner force directed me to walk several blocks toward a group of low-rise brick buildings where I saw the Herring Court sign and walked to house number 255. For a few minutes I was transfixed in a time warp and controlled by another force. It really was weird. The clothesline poles and small playgrounds were still there. I also noticed the black skin color of people walking and standing. I had the eerie feeling I was being watched. I did not fit in that neighborhood, but I did not feel unsafe. I worried about my rented car that was parked on the street. It was getting dark. I walked around the building, meandered for a few minutes, glanced over my shoulders, and departed. I returned a few years later with Dorothy, and she reluctantly exited the car and walked with me to number 255. She absolutely refused to allow me to knock on the door, introduce myself to the occupant, offer cash for the favor of admission, and ask to see the apartment.

I recall when President Roosevelt died. It was a hot day in April, and I was walking with a friend, Bobby Goss, when an older kid walked up and said that President Roosevelt died. I had heard President Roosevelt speak on the radio. He was the nearest thing to God. The older kid said that Truman is president. I remember asking, "What's a Truman?" The mother of Bobby Goss operated a candy store nearby, and we used to hang out together. I never saw his father. He might have been overseas. People on the street were sad and everyone located a radio so they could hear the news. We did not have a telephone and certainly not a TV. We listened to the radio, and my father explained what happened. I was really sad when we moved to New York City, and I never again saw Bobby Goss.

Every morning before class started, we would recite the Pledge of Allegiance followed by the chorus of "Let's Remember Pearl Harbor." I recall the melody and some of the words:

> Let's Remember Pearl Harbor
> as we go to meet the foe.
> Let's remember Pearl Harbor
> as we did the Alamo.
> We will always remember how they died for liberty.
> Let's Remember Pearl Harbor
> and go on to victory.

There were shortages of rubber, metals, and consumer items during the war. I remember collecting rubber bands from school and on the street, winding them in a huge ball and bringing them to a collection center. I also remember collecting pieces of tinfoil from my father's Camel cigarette packages plus whatever pieces of aluminum or metals I could find on the street and making a large tin ball and bringing that to a collection center. I remember the tin ball was the size of a softball and heavy. The government and schools encouraged these collections and also encouraged victory gardens. I tried to make a victory garden in an old Breakstone's cream cheese wooden box. The box was approximately three inches by four inches by twelve inches and would sit on a windowsill to get the sun's rays. We filled it with dirt and planted some seeds and provided water. I was not successful in getting anything to grow.

The photo below shows my mother seated between my brother and me on the steps leading to 255 Herring Court in Baltimore, Maryland.

Mom, Sheldon and me sitting on steps of 255
Herring Court Baltimore, Maryland.

At the Baltimore Naval Shipyard my father worked in a machine shop. He had no prior experience whatsoever with machines or bending metal. He learned on the job. I even inherited some of his adjustable wrenches on which he inscribed his initials. In order to improve himself, he purchased a book published by Audell Company called *Machinist and Tool makers Handy Book*. I once saw him exploring the book at night in bed. The book came in a nice cardboard box, and he treasured it. There were drawings of jigs and fixtures and practical instructions for operating millers, planers, lathes, boring mills, shapers, etc.—basic tools in any machine shop. There were descriptions of trigonometry, geometry, solid geometry, basic algebra mensuration techniques instruments, etc., as described in the back of the book. As I grew older, I understood that it was impossible for anyone to understand the math in the book without a high school education. Only later in life did I empathize with my father's frustration in not having an education that would have allowed him to understand the basics of the book. His knowledge was from doing and not from learning anything from books. After the war ended, he never returned to working in a machine shop. In Russia he was apprenticed to work as a printer. I still have Audel's book and even referred to it when I interacted with machinists at Polaroid to have then make or modify what I designed. In February 1946–March 1946, we moved back to New York City. I was in the fourth grade in Baltimore. I recall being tested in PS 188, and for some reason, I was promoted to the fifth grade. Perhaps the schools in Baltimore were advanced. I graduated from the sixth grade in PS 188 in June 1947, one year ahead of my normal class. In later years, I always viewed the promotion as a mistake because I never learned how to print English letters taught in the fourth grade in New York City and was not nearly as socially mature as my classmates. My mother was proud that I was promoted. I was indifferent to all this.

255 Herring Court in Baltimore, MD.
We entered through the center door. Our apartment was on the second floor. We played outside the building. We always felt safe. The houses were built quickly by the Federal Government to house shipyard workers. The buildings still stand.

Apex Theatre on Broadway, Baltimore, in which I saw "Tomorrow the World" with my mother.

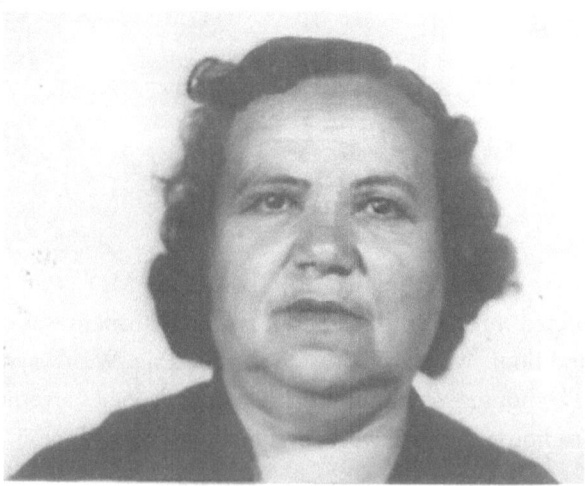

Bubby Sonia Krimsky

Gravestone of Bubbie Sonia Krimsky

Sidney & Bubbie Sonia

Mom, Bubbie Sonia &
brother Sheldon

Mom & Bubbie Sonia

Chapter 5

RETURN TO BROOKLYN, NEW YORK

The war ended, and so did my father's job. Empty apartments were scarce everywhere. A cousin located an apartment in Coney Island, Brooklyn, and we returned to New York City and moved into a two-bedroom apartment with a private bathroom and kitchen. The fire escape of our apartment was near the window in my bedroom. I learned how to use it and jump to the street, and that made my mother nervous. Fortunately, we never had to use it. My parents used the living room as a bedroom, and my brother and I shared a small bedroom. I attended a Hebrew school in Baltimore and transferred to the Sea Gate Sisterhood Talmud Torah in Coney Island on West Twenty-Third Street. I entered Public School (PS) 188. I was promoted one whole year upon transferring to PS 188—a big mistake for which I suffered socially later and always felt insecure in the presence of classmates with superior verbal skills. I skipped the entire fourth grade.

I missed Bobby Goss, my one friend from Baltimore. There were lots of kids older and younger than me living on Twenty-Ninth Street. I did not initially integrate well; I was on my own. My classmates did not live nearby. I was small for my age and was called shrimp, pee-wee, or punk. I would tease those who teased me and run away and was never caught because I was the second fastest runner on the block. Only Billy Bloom, who lived above me on Twenty-Ninth Street, was faster, but we got along. His sister, Beverly, attended

PS 188 in a different class. His mother was a gentile, but she married a Jewish fellow from whom she was divorced. We never spoke about it. Beverly got married to a teacher in California, Leonard Thomas; and I once had dinner at her apartment in Sacramento, California. The last time I saw Billy Bloom was in 1959 on a return trip from California. I was working and had some money. We met in an ice cream parlor on the corner of Mermaid Avenue and Twenty-Ninth Street. It is no longer there.

In public school 188, Maxine Rich sat in front of me. She was particularly obnoxious because she used such big words, such as *modify*, that I did not understand. One day, I wiped my nose mucus on her long hair that swept across the front of my desk. I was careful not to tug her hair. She never knew. At least she never spoke to me about it. She was in my high school graduating class. I never spoke with her. She never spoke with me. Girls just seemed stuck-up.

We used pens and inkwells in those days. The ink covered our fingers and sometimes spilled on our clothing. One day, Muriel Goldberg brought in a ballpoint pen; it was expensive. She claimed it wrote upside down and underwater. We continued to use fountain pens even into high school. One boy was appointed monitor, and the job was to fill the inkwells every day in the morning. Girls were not appointed. Their dresses had to be clean. In a few years, the inkwells disappeared.

During the war, the whole country was mobilized to defeat Italy, Germany, and Japan. All consumer items were in short supply during and even after the war until demobilization was completed. Meat, milk, and gasoline were rationed. Even after the war ended, my mother gave me ration stamps and cash to buy milk at the local grocery store, Wenig's Grocery, on West Twenty-Ninth Street in Coney Island, New York. The government provided the ration stamps freely to each family at post offices, but they were limited. Ration stamps could be exchanged. They were not to be sold, but a large black market arose for buying and selling ration stamps. The Office of Price Administration (OPA) fixed prices of all consumer items. Manufacturers, wholesalers, distributors, resellers, and consumers criticized the OPA. President Harry Truman abolished the hated OPA as one of his first postwar acts.

On one birthday when I was about nine years old, I received an electric train set from my uncle Natie. It came in a box about three feet by three feet by perhaps eight inches high. I loved to set up the train set and watch the trains move on the tracks. I inserted the male plug into the receptacles and watch the trains go round and round on the metal tracks in my bedroom. The train ran under the beds because there was so little room. About a year or two later, my mother asked me to return the train set to Uncle Natie because he wanted it for his son Stevie. What could I do? I could tell how sad my mother was to even ask me to do this. She must have struggled with the issue when she spoke with Natie. I kept all the parts neatly in the box and surrendered the train to her. It disappeared in a few days from my house. I recall the events vividly. Uncle Natie was an "Indian giver," but what could I do? He must have been desperate. He never thanked me for having surrendered the train. My mother appreciated that I put up no resistance. I never had a chance to set it up for my younger brother. However, Natie received his reward many years later after he lent a large sum of money to Steven and Steven did not want to return it. Steven made bad economic decisions and refused to return the borrowed money all told to me by Aunt Ida.

In Wenig's Grocery, on Twenty-Ninth Street close to our house, pickles and green sour tomatoes were sold in wooden barrels for a nickel each. The odor of garlic, dill, mustard seeds, and other spices was overwhelming. A customer would dip his arm into the pickle barrel that was filled with brine and select a pickle and/or a sour tomato. Sometimes we ate them right from the barrel as a refreshing treat, and sometimes we washed them before eating. No one got sick from contaminated pickles or tomatoes. No germs could live in the salty brine. I never saw the brine disposed. It was reused. I suppose eventually it was poured down the sewer and replaced with new brine or a whole new pickle barrel.

Mr. Wenig added a separate barrel of sauerkraut to his selection and required that we had to use tongs for both pickles and sauerkraut. I preferred to use my hands. Pickles, tomatoes, and sauerkraut floated to the top of each barrel. We picked up sauerkraut with special tongs, allowed the sauerkraut to drain into the barrel since the weight included the salty brine, and sauerkraut was sold by the pound. I then transferred the wet sauerkraut onto a stack of heavy waxed paper on the counter. The grocer pulled out the top sheet, placed the sauerkraut, folded the paper several times, and weighed it. He placed it into a bag on which he wrote the price. The bag still leaked on the way home, but once at home, I placed the sauerkraut into a jar. I usually spilled some brine on the floor, and my mother knew I bought sauerkraut. Besides, the refrigerator would smell.

We lived a city block from the Atlantic Ocean. My father taught me how to swim in the shallow water near the sandy beach by holding my hands and encouraging me to kick the water. I spent days on the beach and in the salt water, never tiring of diving into the waves crashing into the shore. I used to swim out to the third barrel. The air filled barrels were tied together to ropes and anchored into the ocean floor. The third barrel must have been two to three feet above my head. The lifeguards watched us, and we could always hold on to the ropes. I used to dive into water, swim underwater, and search around until I surfaced. There were no pools nearby and no formal lessons. Everyone somehow learned how to swim. My mother never learned how to swim. She told me that she was afraid of the water.

During the summer hot months, every evening Jewish refugees from Eastern Europe would gather in the covered pavilions on the boardwalk, talk in strange tongues, and sing ethnic and Yiddish songs. I regret never being able to understand or record those melodies. I was an outsider. I observed but did not know enough to participate. I did not understand their world. They did not understand my world as a first-generation American born of immigrant parents. My parents did not participate in those song fests.

During the winter the streets were empty. It became dark quickly after returning from school. I used to walk on the boardwalk after school or on weekends just to clear my lungs, west toward Sea Gate and sometimes east toward Stillwell Avenue, inhaling the fresh salty ocean air. It was dead quiet. I never felt threatened or afraid during the day or at night within our neighborhood or walking alone on the boardwalk. No one watched us. I never experienced anti-Semitism during those years or any time I lived in Coney Island. Of course,

I did nothing to stimulate anti-Semitic reactions. I looked like any other Jewish kid living in Coney Island.

During the long winter months, after school I listened to my favorite radio programs by sitting down in front of the single radio on a small table in the hallway that separated the kitchen from the living room. I knew the schedule and listened every week to the *Lone Ranger*, *The Shadow*, *Jack Benny*, and *Superman*.

During the summer, the days were long, and we filled them by playing games on the street without any adult supervision or direction. The games were spontaneous depending on who and how many kids were outside and the weather. Punch ball, stickball, 1-2-3 ringolevio, hit the penny, Johnny on a pony, and off-the-wall were favorites. We threw a pink Spalding rubber ball off the wall of a nearby apartment building or off a concrete molding for others to catch. Points were rewarded for catching the ball.

Ringolevio was an advanced version of go hide and seek. It was a favorite of mine. We divided ourselves into two teams: hunters (jailers) and escapees. The hunters had to find one of the escapees, tag them, and pronounce them captured by saying 1,2,3 ringolevio, and bring them back to the jail. The jail consisted of a small area against a house, an alleyway, or a vestibule in an apartment building or near a hydrant. There were plenty of places to hide in the neighborhood, alleys, behind buildings, entranceways, cellars, etc. I knew them all. Uncaptured escapees could free all the captured escapees by tagging them in the jail before they were tagged. The jailers had to recapture the escapees. The faster and more agile boys performed the best. I was one of the best. I was the second or third fastest runner on the street. The game was sometimes played after it got dark, and it became more interesting. Bedtime ended the game, or we all stopped to see the fireworks from the boardwalk every Tuesday night.

Johnny on a pony consisted of one team jumping onto a line of boys, each one bending over and holding on to the waist of the boy in front. The first boy leaned against a building, and the second boy grabbed his waist. With enough weight, the line collapsed. If the line did not collapse, then the bottom team won the game. Hit the penny consisted of two players, each one throwing a pink Spalding rubber ball to hit a penny placed in the crack between two concrete blocks on the sidewalk. The first player to hit the penny thirteen times wins the game. Sometimes we migrated to Kaiser Park to play baseball or have batting practice.

We also played with marbles on the empty lots and on the streets. Marbles were called immies, aggies, and jumbos. There were two basic games. In one game, we drew a large circle on the ground and each player put into the circle one or more marbles. Each player had a chance to shoot a marble using his thumb and index finger and knock a marble out of the circle. He kept the marble if he knocked it out of the circle, and if not, then the marble was left in the circle and another player had a chance to knock it out. The winner had the most marbles when the game was called (ended) usually when it became too dark to play. Another marbles game consisted of a banker and players. The banker had a cigar box or a cream cheese box in which holes were cut to allow marbles to enter. The shooter stayed about three feet away and tried to shoot the marble into the holes in the box. The distance between shooter and box and the size of the holes determined the reward for shooting a marble through the holes. The banker owned the box, and he had to reward the shooter five, ten, or more marbles if the shooter's marble penetrated the box. We positioned the boxes on the gutter adjacent to the curb. There were fewer cars on the streets, so we had plenty of street space. Sometimes the banker left with more marbles, and sometimes the shooter left with more marbles. A bag of marbles cost $0.10. In any case, there was no great loss or great gain.

Somehow we all knew when to put on our metal skates. Half a dozen or more preadolescents put on metal skates and skated on the asphalt gutter. The boys made up games such as races and rope pulling where someone in the center not on skates held on to a rope while someone on the other end was pulled around in a circle. Another game was to skate toward a small wooden ramp, build up speed, skate upward, and jump as far as you could. Some of the boys made wood scooters by separating the front of the skate from the rear and tying each half of the skate to opposite ends of a two-by-four wooden stud. We nailed the wood to a vertical stud and nailed on a handle. The metal skates consisted of a heel and toe and flat portion all held together by sliding metal parts and bolts and nuts. The skates were adjustable to almost any shoe. Two toe clips and straps secured the skate to the shoe. The toe clips were tightened by means of a skate key. The skate key turned a worm gear that really locked the toe clamps. Each skate had four roller wheels. Each wheel had a raceway and ball bearings. The four wheels provided good support to the bottoms of the feet. One could stand on the skates without ankle pain as compared with roller blades or ice skates. Losing the skate key had consequences because without loosening the worm gear and toe clamps, the skates could not easily come off the shoe. We wore the skate key around our necks. The skates were heavy and awkward. I never saw girls wearing these skates. After an hour of this, we put our skates away and played something else.

The girls did not play in any of these games. They played potsy (some call it hopscotch) on the sidewalk and drew their own potsy boxes with chalk. (The phrase *hopscotching around the world* means jumping or flying from one country to another.) They jumped rope. I was uncoordinated at jumping rope. They also played jacks. I found it very difficult to throw the ball and pick up jacks. I could never figure out the girls or why anyone would want to play these games. The girls seemed to have certain motor skills I did not have. The boys devalued their games because the games did not involve speed and strength.

The giant stickball games attracted people from all around the neighborhood usually Saturday and Sunday afternoons. The older people played and also bet on the outcome of the games. One player, Murray Goldstein, lost one arm in the war and was the best stickball hitter in the neighborhood. People came from all around to see him play. A manhole cover was always used as home plate or second base. It was an obvious choice. The stick was a broom handle without the broom. We threw the Spalding pink rubber ball up in the air about four feet. It bounced once or twice, and then we whacked it with the broom handle. Depending on the location of cars in the street, the outside tire of a car would be first and/or third base. Sometimes the ball bounced off parked cars and buildings. We made up our own ground rules. As in baseball, we played nine innings or until it became too dark to play. The team scoring the most runs won the game. Next day we played again with different players.

Punch ball was played with the same rules as stickball but without a stick. We threw the ball in the air in front of us, made a fist, and hit the ball as hard as we could with our fist. Sometimes I missed the ball, so I learned to slap the ball by spreading out my fingers. A punched ball traveled farther than a slapped ball.

Sam the barber had a shop down the street. He charged $0.35 for a haircut. I went by myself (without my parents) even at a young age, and he cut my hair until I graduated college. He raised his price during my college years to $0.50 because of inflation. I was sixteen when he commented that I was losing my hair on the top of my head. Wonderful! I could do nothing with that factoid. It made no difference to my social life since I had none. Some of my friends used grease on their hair (called pomade) to smooth it back. (This is the origin for the title of the movie *Grease* with John Travolta about life during the fifties.) My hair stood up, and I cut it short. I never allowed it to grow too long. Some of my friends thought it's sexier to have long hair and use pomade.

Benny's Pharmacy was located on Surf Avenue and Twenty-Ninth Street. The pharmacy was embedded in the corner of a multiple-story apartment building on the northwest side of West Twenty-Ninth Street and Surf Avenue. Benjamin Siegel did more than dispense drugs. He was the local first aid person and the first person to see bleeding kneecaps and children with dirt or hairs in their eyes. Everyone knew him and trusted him. He removed dirt and hair from eyes and applied first aid. Everyone in the local neighborhood was a loyal customer; and he had a prosperous business that included a soda fountain that dispensed egg creams, ice cream, and seltzer. An egg cream is unique to New York. It consists of chocolate syrup, whole milk, and seltzer. After adding the ingredients, the seltzer is dispensed into the glass. The result is a delicious liquid topped with an inch of foam, a great thirst quencher in the summer. Many years later I went into a spa in Cambridge, Massachusetts, and asked for an egg cream. The salesperson asked how I wanted my egg and with what kind of cream. Although I moved back to the East Coast, I knew I was still far from New York City. Benny Siegel employed my brother to work in the store during the summer months when business boomed because of the increased population of the "bungalow people" who rented bungalows during the hot summer months. The building was demolished and replaced by a YMCA.

On Twenty-Ninth Street between 2995 and Surf Avenue, there were a number of stores: Wenig's Grocery, Sam the barber, Barney the tailor, and a Luncheonette on the corner. Barney had a wife named Minnie, and we called her Minniehaha after the river in the poem "Hiawatha." Sam charged $0.35 cents for a haircut, and he increased the price to $0.50 when I attended high school. Now a haircut costs me $10, which is a 4.9 percent annual increase compounded over seventy years.

When the daytime weather was too hot to play games in the street, I would walk to Kaiser Park and find someone with whom to play handball or have a catch or play fungo. Fungo consists of tossing a baseball about two feet into the air and hitting it with a bat as the ball falls. If the ball is caught in the field on the fly, the player catching it takes the bat.

On languid summer days, I might walk or ride my bicycle to Tom Tesauro's Lumber Yard near Cropsy Avenue and acquire some small pieces of wood that they would throw away. I would make something of the wood by borrowing my father's hand tools. He owned no electric tools except for one electric drill. I would watch him work with his hands and then do something on my own. Sometimes I used a large screwdriver to disassemble disposed wooden crates left on the streets near the fruit stores to obtain wood panels. The Hobby Shop on Coney Island Avenue offered a collection of balsa wood that I would buy for carving. They also sold model airplanes for $0.25 that I would buy to assemble and hang up in my room. We used a smelly airplane glue made by Tester to bond the paper thin sheets to the wooden structure of the wings and fuselage. Later I learned that some kids sniffed the glue to get high. This was my first exposure to abuse of technology. The models were of B-17s, Mustangs, Thunderbolts, P-40s, Black Widows, Hellcats, and B-24s. A collection of army and navy airplanes hung from the ceiling in my room. The air force became a separate service in 1948 and had its own logo.

One of my playmates, Fred Rebeiro, built larger models with an actual engine in front. Wow! He obtained some gasoline and flew the airplane in a park. Flying such an airplane was an expensive hobby. He had no father or siblings. He and his mother lived alone in an apartment in our building. She used to sew sequins on dresses in her apartment to earn a living. Her apartment was filled with many fancy dresses on racks. Freddy wanted to work in the aviation industry when he grew up. He attended the high school of aviation trades in New York, and I went on to Mark Twain Junior High School and Lincoln High School on an academic track.

On some really hot days, we went to the Surf Theater on Surf Avenue and West Thirty-Fifth Street or to the Mermaid Theater on West Twenty-Ninth Street and Mermaid Avenue to enjoy the air-conditioning. Movies cost $0.10 to $0.15 for each admission. The Mermaid Theater was an incredible dump. The bathrooms were foul with graffiti written all over the walls. The Surf Theater was better maintained. I was able to read the marquee from standing on the ocean side of the corner of Twenty-Ninth Street and Surf Avenue. My eyes were that sharp until about age fourteen in high school when I had to squint to read the marquee. I needed glasses in high school. I believe my eyes became nearsighted from all the close reading I did in high school plus solving sets of math problems.

The movies we watched at the Surf Theater were the comedies, Westerns, and WWII action movies. I remember seeing Johnny Weissmuller as Tarzan, the Three Stooges, Groucho Marx, Alan Ladd as Shane, Roy Rodgers, Gene Autry, John Wayne, Randolph Scott, Liz Taylor, Marjorie McBride, Thelma Ritter, Gregory Peck, Boris Karloff, Lon Chaney, Clark Gable, Edward G. Robinson, Kirk Douglass, and so many actors of the forties and fifties. The scariest movies were *Frankenstein* and the *Wolf Man*. There was a strict moral code. The movies were not rated, but Hollywood did not make movies unsuitable for family viewing. Some movies were violent but not gory or lascivious.

FROM BROOKLYN NY TO BROOKLINE MA

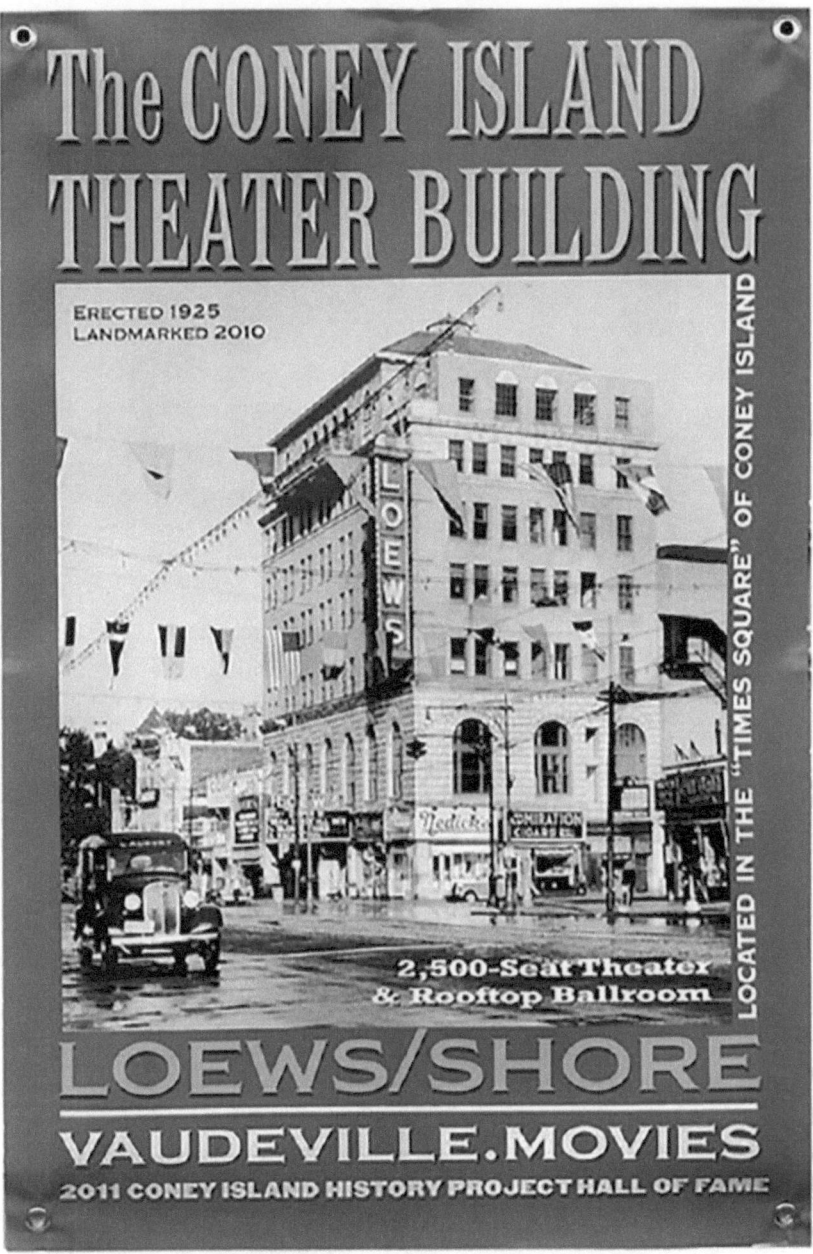

Old Loews Theater opposite Nathan's Famous on Surf Avenue. It is now an office building.

Former Lowe's Theater across the street from
Nathan's Famous-Now an office building

2995 West 29th Street in Coney Island where I lived on the second floor
in the rear from 1945 to 1958. We played stickball and punch ball on
the street unsupervised. We sat on the brickwork in front of the house.

FROM BROOKLYN NY TO BROOKLINE MA

Former site of 2995 West 29th Street building in Coney Island. Now it is the Surf Side Gardens for nearby apartment dwellesr. The Geriatric center is the other large building, formerly the Half Moon Hotel.

YMCA replaced Benjamin Siegel's Pharmacy

Shorefront Jewish Geriatric Center replaced the
Half Moon Hotel near the Boardwalk

Geriatric center as seen from the Boardwalk

Steeplechase Pier dedicated to Pat Auletta owner of a sporting goods store on Stillwell Avenue near Surf Avenue. He supported Little league baseball and all sports. His son Richard was in my High School graduation class. Richard became a noted writer and author.

Chapter 6

BASEBALL

My uncle Harry (Heshy) took me to my first professional baseball game in Ebbets Field when I was nine years old. I arrived from Baltimore a few months earlier and did not know how to travel in New York City. He put nickels into the slots above the turnstile, and in we walked up the stairs to the subway platform. Upon arrival, we walked through a large parking lot, and a crowd gathered around Carl Furillo, right fielder for the Brooklyn Dodgers. He signed his autograph on a brown bag in which I carried my sandwich. Unfortunately, I lost the bag. His throwing arm was the best in the National League.

Baseball was important during my preadolescence. Everyone followed the Brooklyn Dodgers. We attended games in Ebbets Field and sometimes in the polo grounds in Manhattan and, rarely, in Yankee Stadium in the Bronx. Traveling to the Bronx was a long subway trip. Bleachers cost $0.50 at Ebbets Field but I joined the Police Athletic League (PAL) of New York City at the Coney Island Sixtieth Precinct Police Station, received a pass, and paid only $0.35 at the gate. We listened to Red Barber and Vince Scully on the radio and were annually disappointed because the Dodgers always choked at the season's end just as the Red Sox did until 2004. Red Barber was the most colorful sportscaster I ever heard with the exception of Mel Allen who reported games for the Yankees. The radio sportscasters broadcasting had to describe verbally what was happening on the field so the listener could visualize the entire action. It is easier now with TV, so the sportscasters add value to the broadcast by mentioning statistics and other baseball trivia. Red Barber came from the South and spoke with a distinct Southern accent while he sat in his "catbird" seat at Ebbets Field above home plate. He spoke kindly about all the players including Jackie Robinson. Red Barber extolled the performance of Jackie Robinson as he stole bases and made double plays from Reese to Robinson to Hodges. It must have been difficult for him to see the first black man play in the major leagues, but he set aside his prejudice.

We played baseball almost every day during the summer in Kaiser Park that faced the northwest side of Gravesand Bay. The park was named after Leon Kaiser, a noted educator and former principal of Mark Twain Junior High School. On Sundays we watched the bigger boys play baseball. We organized ourselves into teams without adult supervision. Little Leagues were nonexistent. When I was about fourteen and small for my age, I played with the younger boys. Everyone thought I was twelve. We sought a sponsor for our team, any local merchant who would purchase team uniforms with an advertisement stitched on the back of the jackets and shirts. An adult identified the Major Meat Company in Coney Island as a potential sponsor. They sponsored other baseball teams. Major Meats was a butcher store or chain of stores that sold all kinds of meats in the retail market. To prove our ability, an adult arranged for us to play against a Catholic school baseball team, St. Bernadettes. This was to be an important game, and I could not sleep the night before the game. It rained during the evening before the game. Field number two in Kaiser Park was reserved for the game. Baseball fields had to be reserved by calling the New York City Department of Parks. We woke up early and warmed up outside on the street by throwing and catching baseballs to one another. We walked to the park, had fielding and batting practice, and continued to warm up. The other team arrived and started their warm-up and batting practice. They looked organized, and they fielded and batted well. They had played as a team for a while, had coaching, and meant to beat us.

I played second base. I was fast on my feet, but my reaction to ground balls was slow, and I was too small to be a good hitter. I swung and missed most of the times, and when I did connect, I hit ground balls. I tried to get to first base via "base on balls" by taking advantage of my height. Sometimes it worked, but the pitchers caught on and pitched low fastballs to strike me out. We lost the game, and I was a weak link although I did nothing so bad that caused us to lose the game. At the end of the game, an adult coach, who was trying to obtain sponsors for us, told us to meet him under a tree in the park away from the field. He showed us a stack of uniforms and said that we were in a league. He had succeeded in acquiring a sponsor and team uniforms, but some players had to leave to strengthen the team. There were not enough uniforms for everyone. He said that "not everyone can be a good baseball player, and it is no crime not to be on a team." He told me that I was to be replaced by Elliot Yaeger, a boy slightly younger than me who was well built, taller than I, and with quick hands. I saw him practice before the game, and I knew he was a better ball player than me. I was really disappointed. I asked the adult if I could take the uniform home for one evening, wear it at home for one night, and return it the next day. He must have sensed how sad I felt because he knew how much I worked for this and how much it meant to an immature fourteen-year-old. I took the uniform home, put it on and admired myself in it, imagined I was someone else, took it off, rewrapped it, and returned it to the adult coach the next day in the park at a practice session that I would no longer attend. I walked home dejectedly, feeling sorry for myself, went to my room, and opened my stamp and coin collection, an escape into different worlds. It was my first real experience with rejection. I had to learn to live with a major disappointment. It made an impression. Many years later, when I returned to the park, the tree was still there. I sat under it and felt sad. Having a good memory is not always worthwhile.

 I watched the great Brooklyn Dodgers players of that generation such as Gil Hodges (1B), Carl Furillo (RF), Pee Wee Reese (SS), Duke Snider (CF), Roy Campanella (C), Don Newcomb (P), Billy Cox (3B), Jackie Robinson (2B), and Joe Black (Relief Pitcher). There were fewer home runs then as compared with now. There was more emphasis on fielding, base running, and strategy. Jackie Robinson was the best of the best. I watched him dance on the bases, make pitchers nervous, steal second base, run to third base on a hit, and steal home. Watching him was more exciting than watching a home run. In my opinion, he was the most colorful player of his generation, a behavioral model for youth, and a real mensch. The Brooklyn Dodgers fans loved him, and he never let us down. I never heard any racial epithets against the black team members from Dodgers fans.

Since we did not own a TV, I was invited to watch the October 3, 1951, final playoff game for the National League pennant in the apartment of a friend, Sanford Axelband, between the Dodgers and Giants. It was the ninth inning of a three-game playoff for the National League pennant. With one out, Bobby Thompson hit the second pitch off Ralph Branca to smash the ball down the left field line just above the 315-foot sign and landed five rows deep in the stands. Thomson's home run gave the Giants a 5–4 victory over their biggest rival and a trip to the World Series. It was a heartbreaker. I was shocked for days afterward. Both players came from nowhere to become an instant celebrity and an instant goat. Destiny can be glorious and cruel.

I felt betrayed when Walter O'Malley transferred the Dodgers from Brooklyn to Los Angeles in 1956 after the Dodgers won their first World Series against the Yankees. How could he do that? I lost my interest in baseball. I learned that baseball was a business. That whole story should have been titled "Triumph and Tragedy," but Winston Churchill already used those same words in one volume of his massive work of the Second World War. I later learned that Walter O'Malley argued with Robert Moses, premier architect of New York during the first half of the twentieth century, about the importance of a baseball stadium near Atlantic and Pennsylvania Avenue when Moses wanted to build the Interboro Parkway (later renamed the Jackie Robinson Parkway). O'Malley wanted the land for a new stadium, and the mayor Robert Lindsay and Robert Moses opposed the request so the Dodgers left Brooklyn. Moses was the chief planner for the city of New York, a construction czar. He did not believe that taxpayers should provide space for a private enterprise. The departure of the Dodgers was an enormous tragedy at the time. No other team in the National League was more intensely beloved during the

1950s than the Brooklyn Dodgers. The Atlantic Avenue and Jackie Robinson Parkway area remains undeveloped, seedy, and unsafe to walk alone after dark, a miserable eyesore to what could have been a remarkable development.

Rear view of a statue of Pee Wee Reese placing his arm around Jackie Robinson during a game at Crosley Field When Robinson was booed by baseball fans. The booing stopped after this gesture by Pee Wee Reese. Statue is outside the Cyclone Baseball Park in Coney Island. Brooklyn Dodger fans loved Jackie Robinson.

Chapter 7

MY ZADIE

My grandfather used to visit us every few months but especially during Chanukah when he would give my brother and me "Chanukah gelt." (Chanukah money) It was his pleasure. I think about this during Chanukah time, and at the same time, I am reminded about the death of my father on the day of the sixth candle, 30 of the Hebrew month of Kislev. Zadie rode several subways to get here and my father drove him home. On one trip, they decided to visit Silver's Baths near the boardwalk a few blocks away from our apartment. I asked to go. They took me along. To this day, I recall how enjoyable that was. The tiled rooms were filled with big, burly hairy Russians speaking a motley of languages. Some were sitting on wooden benches in a steam room while someone poured water over their heads. Some were swimming in a smelly chlorinated pool, and some were sitting under a stinging needle shower. We were naked; there was water and steam everywhere. Visibility was limited. I ran from station to station, trying different combinations of hot water, steam, cold water, needle showers, and swimming pools. It was exhilarating. There was a dry room before exiting. There was nothing lurid. It's too bad that Silver's Baths closed.

I recall once that my grandfather treated my brother and me to a deli lunch in a small restaurant on Alabama Avenue. I remember ordering a pastrami sandwich with mustard and pickles and a Coca-Cola. Romanian pastrami and corned beef was always a favorite of mine. My mother used to make pastrami and eggs in a fry pan.

Nothing tasted as good and filled me up as fried pastrami and eggs. Perhaps someday someone will make a soy equivalent. My taste in food has changed, so I may not enjoy it the same way as I did on Alabama Avenue.

One summer my grandfather invited me to visit him in the Catskill Mountains where he had rented a summer cottage for a few weeks. This was exciting. My mother gave me some pocket money and prepared a toiletry bag with a toothbrush and a small tube of yellow Ipana toothpaste. Now this was really cute because toothpaste was not widely available, especially small tubes. We used to sprinkle tooth powder on a toothbrush and hold it under the water faucet for a short time to make a paste. My father drove me to a bus station. I entered the bus and exited at the right stop. My grandfather met me. He even found a friend, Louie, who took me around and showed me how to fish. Bubby prepared a bed in a corner of the cottage. We went swimming in the pond and just hung around for a few days. It was my first and only trip to the mountains as a youth. I remember visiting a small store and bought something to eat with my own pocket money. It was a strange feeling to reach in my pocket and pull out some money. I was there for less than a week, but it felt grown-up to travel such a long distance and return home. That was my only experience going to the mountains until I left home for California.

During Pesach, we visited my grandfather who made a seder for us. The seder was a mysterious ritual with special foods and prayers. I looked forward to saying the four questions in Yiddish, and he kvelled. My grandmother prepared the chicken, kneidlach, kreplach, and small kugels made of matzoh meal. The food was bland, and my younger brother commented that everything had the same taste. His seders were my only experience with sedarim until Rabbi Broznan in Sacramento, California, in 1959 invited me to his seder. I knew so little and felt out of place at his seder. My grandfather's children were never present at the seders I attended. I never asked about my uncles and aunt. It was special for me, my brother, and my parents.

My grandfather brought with him from Russia some of the old Jewish traditions and mores to which were a mystery to me and never explained. But he treated me as something special and introduced me to all his friends in shul and made me feel important. He was proud that I stayed in school and intended to attend college. I learned from him that it is important for grandparents to tell their grandchildren how proud they are of their accomplishments.

My grandfather had a friend in Russia, Mr. Braverman, who immigrated to Israel at the time my grandfather immigrated to the USA. They corresponded by mail. When I went to Israel in August 1965, he told me about Mr. Braverman, provided an address on Ibn Gabirol Street, and requested that I visit him. Houses were not well numbered, but somehow I found him and introduced myself as the grandson of Yitzik Skolnick. He and his wife welcomed me with open arms. I could tell that they were poor people. My grandfather must have sent them money on occasion. I visited them at night and had no flash on my camera so I could not photograph them. We spoke in Yiddish. Both were fluent in Hebrew. He told me that his son, Zohar, was killed in the War of Independence. He had one son and one daughter. He said in Yiddish, "Mir haben bazahlt far Eretz Israel," meaning "We have paid for the land of Israel." I felt really sad when he told me that and saw photos of Zohar as a young man. My grandfather never saw Mr. Braverman after they separated in Russia. Telephone communication was almost nonexistent. They communicated by mail. He told me how wonderful were the grapes grown in Israel. He took pleasure in small things and kept asking me how my grandfather was getting along. I'm certain that Mr. Braverman had quite a story to tell after leaving Russia about 1922 and living through the British occupation and the UN vote. I was in no position to record his history. Small tape recorders did not exist. My grandfather and the generation of Europeans who came to America supported the State of Israel by sending food, money, and clothing. The Jewish cemeteries are filled with a hundred thousand such people who lived during the last half of the twentieth century.

If the Jewish dead in the cemeteries could talk and were asked about BDS (boycott, divestment, and sanctions), they would think the question absurd and reverse BDS to be SDB, which means support, develop, and buy bonds. That generation supported the State of Israel without question although there were still "self-hating" Jews such as Arthur Ochs Sulzberger, publisher of the *New York Times*, who pushed stories of the atrocities in Europe to the back pages.

Mr. Sam and Mrs. Clara Dauer were an older couple living in our apartment building. She asked my mother if I would write letters to her son-in-law and daughter, Harry and Bert, who lived in Fargo, North Dakota, since Sam and Clara were unable to write English. She insisted paying $0.50 per letter. She dictated the words. So during my junior high school years, every few weeks, I was asked to write letters. My brother continued the practice after I entered high school. Mr. Dauer was in a wheelchair and spent most of the day watching TV. The word *dauer* means *to last* in German, and it seemed that he lasted a long time.

Isadore Skolnick, my Zadie. I called him after Naomi Krimsky was born. He died 30 April 1970 about one month after the birth of Naomi Krimsky. He explained that her red hair came from his dead cousin Nachum der Roite. Now he was Nachum der Toite, meaning Nathan the dead one.

This Synagogue was located at 455 Alabama Avenue and was opposite my Zadie's apartment building at 456 Alabama Avenue. The Synagogue was founded in 1909 and demolished during the 1970s. t was called Beth Shalom Tomchei Halav. I believe that my mother was married there and the reception was held in his apartment across the street. Whenever I visited, it was the Synagogue that my Zadie refused to attend. I never set foot in the building. He never told me why he refused to attend but I suspect that he was insulted. He walked to the Synagogue on Pennsylvania Avenue about 5 blocks away from his apartment.

Gravestone of Meyer Skolnick, my great grand father.
Buried in the Old Montefiore Cemetery.

Isadore Skolnick—My Zadie. Yitzhak ben Meir.
Buried in the Old Montefiore Cemetery.

FROM BROOKLYN NY TO BROOKLINE MA

Mollie Shkolnick 1860-1934. My Great Grandmother.
Buried in the Old Montefiore Cemetery.

Anna Skolnick 1900-1976. My Grandmother Henya bas
Zvi Hersh. Buried in the Old Montefiore Cemetery.

Chapter 8

MY MATERNAL RELATIVES

My zadie and bubie Annie had three children: Nathan (Natie), Ida, and Harry (Heshy). In my earliest recollections, Natie was a soldier who was sent to France during WWII. I believe he drove military vehicles. Heshy entered the navy toward the end of the war or after the war. I never heard any serious war stories from either of them.

Natie married Sylvia after WWII, and I attended the ceremony and reception held in a private home on Long Island. I suspect it was the home of Sylvia's parents. I recall nothing about the reception except that I was there. Natie always spoke to me jokingly and tried to bring me out of my natural shyness. He and Sylvia moved into an apartment on Alabama Avenue, a few houses down the street from my grandfather. During a trip to my grandfather, I was invited upstairs into Aunt Sylvia's apartment and smelled bacon cooking for the first time. I saw it in her kitchen. The smell never left me. She asked me if I wanted something to eat, and I politely said I was not hungry. I told no one about this, but I knew she was cooking pig. I felt she betrayed my zadie.

Natie worked behind the counter in a small candy store that sold cigarettes, ice creams, frappes, coffee, and sandwiches. He had a likeable personality and interacted with customers. I admired him and thought his job was really "cool." I wanted to work behind a counter. My hands worked fast, and I knew how to make change quickly at nine years old. The street was really crowded at the end of the war since all the soldiers were demobilized, getting married, with insufficient available apartments. Construction started quickly on Long Island, and within a few years, all the young Jews left East New York, leaving behind all the parents and grandparents and old synagogues.

A year or so later, Natie bought me an electric train in a cardboard box. It had a few cars, tracks that needed to be assembled, and a variable transformer that would increase the speed of the cars. Tracks were straight and curved so I could make a big oval and make the trains go. Toys like these were not made during the war. I played with these for a few years, and one day my mother told me Natie wanted the train set returned for use by his son, Steven. It was clear that my mother was sad making that request of me. I read it in her eyes. I still remember her asking me to surrender the train. I did not argue. My brother was not old enough to play with it by himself. Since I retained the cardboard box, I was able to carefully pack the train and the tracks with all the parts into the box and gave it to my mother. I even wrapped a string around the box to keep the end flaps from opening. Later years in school, I learned the words *Indian giver* and reflected how that applied to Uncle Natie. After he moved from Alabama Avenue, I saw him the next time at my bar mitzvah party. I never spoke of the train set. We accepted his bar mitzvah gift, and he never asked that it be returned. He and Sylvia were not invited to my brother's bar mitzvah celebration (there was no party in a hall), and they were not invited to my wedding. My parents made the invitation list and excluded my zadie's three children. My mother did not interact well with her three stepsiblings. That is another story.

Natie and Sylvia had three children. One child, a female, was severely retarded at birth. She was placed into a special home. Natie and Sylvia could not bear visiting their daughter; it was too painful. She was not able to see, but she knew when my zadie visited her. Only he visited her. He described how he touched her face and she responded. She had blonde hair. Zadie suppressed his emotions and visited her with regularity until he was no longer able to make the trips or she expired. He never spoke about his granddaughter in my older teenage years.

Aunt Ida married Perry Fishbein. I was not invited to attend the wedding. Perry was also a soldier during the war. Ida told me that he was sent to the South Pacific. I have a photo of Perry and Natie in Paris. I dreamed of someday going to Paris and seeing what the soldiers saw. Dorothy and I went to France. I saw graves of the soldiers who died at Normandy. It was a moving experience to read the names and ages of the young boys who died so I could live out my life as an American. Ida and Perry had two children, Linda and Mark. I recall visiting Zadie a week or so after Linda was born. Linda was the first unclothed baby I ever saw. I never again saw her. I learned she attended Brooklyn College and went off to Paris and somehow adopted an alternative lifestyle. She lived in a commune, married twice, and may have experimented with drugs. Her last husband left her, or she asked him to leave. She died about 1990 about age fifty from breast cancer and was placed in an above-ground vault. Her mother could not bear placing her in the ground to be eaten by worms. Linda had two children who lived in Florida. The children were financially helped by Ida and Perry, their grandparents. Their father abandoned them. I found my aunt Ida friendly and emotionally low-keyed and regret that we were never able to establish a family relationship because my mother hated Ida's mother who was my mother's stepmother, whom my mother labeled the putzutzah.

I saw Uncle Heshy very infrequently, perhaps four or five times in my whole life. Zadie complained that he spent time in pool halls after WWII. He attended my bar mitzvah reception at the Melrose Chateau in Brooklyn. The next time I saw him was at Zadie's funeral. I had nothing to say to any of Zadie's children. Heshy was pushed into marrying Marilyn who bore one son. I never met the son. Heshy eventually divorced Marilyn, remarried, and moved to Northridge in Los Angeles. He suffered a heart attack after the Los Angeles earthquake and died. I did not attend his wedding or any life-cycle events of my maternal relatives. They were just names associated with photographs.

Zadie's children grew up during the 1920–1930s. Opportunities for Jewish education were limited to Orthodox Yeshivas in which the students had to surrender hope of achieving economic independence by surrendering observance to Shabbos and surrendering the restrictions of the "old fashioned" Jewish laws and traditions. This was decades before "Torah and Maddah." Zadie came to the United States with the Yiddish language and the shtetel traditions. Although he had to work on Shabbos, he never forgot Yiddish, Hebrew, and the associated rituals. However, he was unable to transmit this rich culture to his children. They grew up with a minimum, if any, of Jewish education. What they knew, they learned on the street. The practical needs of an impoverished family to rise above the economic barriers were the first priority. Of course, the Yiddish culture was all around the neighborhood. East New York was filled with synagogues, butcher stores, kosher delicatessens, clothing stores, grocery stores, etc. Almost every adult spoke English with an accent. Only at the public schools did I hear unaccented English spoken.

I was the only grandchild who showed any interest in Jewish culture and traditions. Zadie made Passover seders for me after I asked. His children did not attend. He doted on me and wistfully complained about his own children showing no interest. He was the only relative who came to the United States with an inheritance of Jewish traditions from the old country, and I learned by watching him. When he was too old to work as a house painter, he would visit the sick in hospitals and attend services with more regularity. He spent his last days visiting with friends in local senior clubs. Fortunately, Aunt Ida was in the best position to help him economically, and she did. He told me about her help and he was grateful.

He knew that I was studying engineering at CCNY and he asked me if I was going to change my name. He told me that a relative, who was an engineer, changed his Jewish name so as to be able to find work. I suppose this was customery during the 1920s to avoid appearing too Jewish. I told him I would not change my name. The thought never occurred to me.

The neighborhood deteriorated around 456 Alabama Avenue, and Zadie and Bubbie moved to Fountain Avenue (Canarsie) into new affordable apartments assisted by Aunt Ida. He joined a senior club and paid $1 a month membership dues. Dorothy and I visited him there, and he was satisfied to be away from the deteriorating neighborhood. He died a few years afterward. I was notified and attended his funeral. Before he died, he promised me his gold watch. I told him he should enjoy a long life, but he said that he would not be able to attend Alec's bar mitzvah. I never expected a gold watch. My mother heard of his promise and said that he was a "plut" without ever knowing what it meant. I heard her use the word many times as an insult for my zadie. How could he be a plut whatever that meant? *Plut* in Russian means *trickster*.

Bubbie moved to Haber House in Coney Island where I once visited her. She died a few years later, a lonely old forgotten woman, in a nursing home. My mother informed me after the funeral occurred that Bubbie died. Had I known, I would have attended the funeral and paid a shiva call. My mother did not want me to show Bubbie, the putzutzah, any respect and did not want me to attend her funeral. I sent to Ida a letter of condolence.

Chapter 9

MARK TWAIN JUNIOR HIGH SCHOOL

I entered PS 239 or Mark Twain Junior High School in September 1947 at seventh grade and was assigned to a class destined for an academic high school. More about that later! Mr. Sexter was my homeroom teacher for the first year, and Ms. Irene Kehoe was my homeroom teacher for the ninth grade. Mr. Sexter was a soft-spoken teacher who left me with no impression. Ms. Kehoe made an impression. She never raised her voice, but she really controlled the wise guys in the class. She would put up with no nonsense. She took attendance every day as did Mr. Sexter. I was never absent from class. I even received 100 percent attendance certificate awards. I was the smallest in my class, so I was excited when Ms. Nalalie Novick, teacher and cafeteria manager, asked for volunteers to work in the cafeteria and be "in charge." I was promoted to lieutenant of the cafeteria squad. I learned that no one listened to me; I had no desire to control anyone and dictate to them. I served in the cafeteria squad for two years. In later years, I learned that I preferred to control things rather than people. I never ate the food in the building because it was real, not kosher. It smelled bad, it looked bad, and it cost money. My mother packed a lunch every day in my metal lunch box with a glass thermos bottle. I was satisfied with whatever she cobbled together. A favorite of mine was a bulkie roll (called a kaiser roll) smeared with peanut butter and filled with cottage cheese—yum, yum. There were no snacks, candies, Tootsie Rolls, etc., in my lunch bucket. I usually bought a small container of milk in school for $0.04.

We had recess twice a week. There was a gymnasium inside the building. Sports were organized. We learned gymnastics and played a form of dodge ball. I'm not sure what the girls did. I remember that the gym teachers Mr. Williams and Mr. Warshower lined us up to throw the basketball into the hoop. Then they would organize teams for intramural sports. I was not able to throw the ball anywhere near the hoop. The ball fell considerably short of the hoop even when I was close to the hoop. This was embarrassing. I was the only kid who could not throw the basketball. I was the smallest in my class. When weather permitted, we had recess outside the building where there were handball courts and a softball field. The bigger kids organized themselves into teams while Mr. Warshower provided softballs and bats. Each team had nine players, and they all knew who would play in what position. I was never selected for these teams. I did manage to occasionally play handball with Murray Schecter and Maurice Josephs. These were the brightest kids in the class. I could tell from their demeanor and their vocabulary. They were soft-spoken. I really thought they would become teachers or university professors. I was pleased that they even asked me to play handball with them. I was not in their league. When the handball courts were occupied, I just sat around and watched the big kids play. The gym teachers acted as umpires for the softball games. The idea was to get the kids outside but not to allow them to wander away from the school grounds. Maurice Josephs graduated from Lincoln High School. I don't know what happened to Murray Schecter.

During recess, some kids walked around, asking students for money. I was asked once or twice, said I have no money, and walked away. I viewed these kids as evil. Two kids were especially frightening to me; Dominic Mickelizzi was a little taller than I with rimless glasses who later reminded me of Heinrich Himmler who also wore rimless glasses. The other kid was Nickolas Agastinacchio, a taller kid with blond hair who seemed to be good at sports. They did not ask me for money, but I always stayed away from them. I never saw them at Lincoln High School.

After class in the spring and fall, my friends gathered together to play baseball in Savino's parking lot located near Surf Avenue and West Thirtieth Street near the boardwalk. Summer bungalows surrounded the lot, and sometimes we entered the bungalows through an open window. But we just went exploring, not stealing anything and not doing any damage. People who wanted to leave the hot city rented the bungalows in the summer. The parking lot had the right dimensions for a baseball field. After completing junior high school, the bungalows and Savino's parking lot were all demolished to construct a massive middle-income apartment housing project extending from West Twenty-Ninth Street to about West Thirty-Third Street. I watched the destruction of everything there and the construction of what there is today by walking around the chain-link fence surrounding the property.

At Mark Twain, I discovered that I had a penchant for foreign languages especially French. I would hold my nose when reading the text for my teacher, Mr. Jacobs, and he would enjoy that. I scored high grades but intensely disliked having to memorize dozens of irregular verbs. Even the regular verbs were irregular. I would ask my mother to test me at home by asking me English words that I had to translate into French. We had homework after every class, and I was diligent. I came to class prepared. I admit that I enjoyed learning a foreign language and culture.

At the end of the second year, the class leaders were preparing a "class prom" or big party for all the graduates. It was to consist of music, food, dancing, and dating. The idea was to inculcate the students with manners and proper etiquette especially with female classmates. During recess, dancing lessons were made available in the gymnasium. Teachers were mostly female students. Their job was to tame the wild boys with proper manners and etiquette. One needed a date to go to the prom. Mary del Pozo tried to get me to come into the gym, but I wanted no part of this sissy stuff. I just refused and walked away. I did not understand the music and could not understand how people moved to it. Besides, I had nothing to say to females. I always had difficulty making small talk about clothes, prices, shopping, and the usual trivia. No one could force me to go. I did not attend the prom.

During the winter, when the weather was really inclement, after school ended, the window shades were pulled down in our homeroom; and we viewed Tarzan movies. Jane appeared to be a helpless creature always rescued by Tarzan. They had a son named Boy. Tarzan spoke few words but initiated big actions. He avoided speaking "Lashon Horah (hateful speech)." The jungle animals were his friends especially the orangutans, monkeys, and elephants. To the elephants, he would say "Ungawa" and the elephants moved along with Tarzan on top. In *Discover* magazine January/February 2015, page 70, "elephants recognize humans by voice." So indeed, Tarzan was able to communicate with the elephants. So Hollywood was proven correct after sixty-five years. Tarzan and his family lived in a tree house. There was always plenty of food and fresh water in the jungle. Tarzan was the personification of "good" because he chased out the hunters, and those who would defile the jungle. Tarzan was a pharmacist because he knew all the plants and roots and their medicinal values. With his knowledge, he healed the jungle residents, both man and beast.

Site of the old Surf Theater on Surf Avenue and West Thirty-Third Street. I was able to read the marquee while standing on Surf Avenue and Twenty-Ninth Street without glasses up to age fourteen to fifteen. At age sixteen, I needed reading glasses from all the close-up reading I did and math homework. Later, the theater gave out silverware to movie attendees to compete with free TV shows, mostly *Milton Berle*. It was later demolished for a housing project.

The New York school system had three tiers of high schools: academic, commercial, and vocational. The academic high schools included school for gifted students such as the Bronx High School of Science and the School of Music and Art. The commercial high schools taught business skills to students not destined for academic high schools. The vocational schools taught automotive, aircraft maintenance, and other mechanical and electrical skills needed for a growing technically complex society. By the fifth grade, teachers already had an idea who should go where to maximize the potential of each student and not place them in a frustrating environment. I had no way of knowing this or having any choice in the matter. Most of my playmates with whom I connected when I first moved to Coney Island in February–March 1946 did not attend Mark Twain Junior High School and were not in attendance at Lincoln High School. I was nine years old when we moved to Coney Island. Junior high schools were set up to capture late bloomers or to correct any mistakes in sending children to the wrong high schools. The standards in Mark Twain Junior High School were high as I recall. We had to read stories, write reports, read about current events and present our comments in class, study a foreign language, and learn algebra. Success required some intelligence but also an effort in class, doing homework and proper conduct in class.

Graduation ceremonies from PS 239 occurred on June 27, 1950, at the Tilyou Theater, 1611 Surf Avenue near West Fourteenth Street in Coney Island starting at 9:30 a.m. A few weeks later, I received a postcard informing me to report to Abraham Lincoln High School room number 330 before 8:45 a.m. in September 1950. That would be my homeroom for the next three years. Mrs. Neufield would be my homeroom teacher.

Chapter 10

HEBREW SCHOOL

My mother enrolled me in Class aleph in the Sea Gate Sisterhood and Talmud Torah on West Twenty-Third Street and Mermaid Avenue in Coney Island in February 1946. We moved in February 1946–March 1946 to Brooklyn. Prior to enrollment, I remember being asked to read Hebrew by a rabbi whom I learned later was Rabbi Yehuda Galinsky. I learned how to read Hebrew from classes in Baltimore. I waited outside his office in the basement while he spoke with my mother about selecting an appropriate class level for me and payment for tuition to attend five classes a week after public school. They agreed that she would pay $4 per week for tuition. My teachers were Mr. Beychik and later Mr. Resnick. The class had about ten boys. Mr. Beychik sometimes slapped the boys on their backside for misbehavior. He never struck me, but he did on occasion throw small pieces of chalk. He also threw yardsticks at the students. I found the classes boring and the mandatory lessons of Chumish translations into Yiddish torturous. The teacher did not really explain the meanings behind the Chumish. We learned how to read Hebrew and Yiddish without understanding. I had no enthusiasm for those classes. I felt that I was inadequate because I had no interest and no mind for that kind of rote learning. Many decades later, I learned from the writings or Rabbi Joseph Soloveitchik that the whole movement of post-WWII after-school Jewish education was a failure and I was not at fault that I learned so little. I was eager to end the classes after my bar mitzvah.

The Talmud Torah raised operating funds by appealing to Jewish neighbors on all the residential streets in Coney Island. A flat truck would appear every few weeks in daylight hours during the summer. Men with pushkies would fan out in the crowd, and a spokesman would make an impassioned plea for funds through a microphone and loudspeaker, "How much will you give to Yeshivah Shaari Zedek and the Seagate Sisterhood and Talmud Torah?" These visits on our street interrupted our stickball game, and we just waited until the flat truck left. I listened to the language employed in the appeal. It stuck with me. It was unlike anything I heard from my teachers in public school. The speakers were immigrants as were almost all the adults I knew growing up in Brooklyn.

We learned about displaced persons from our teachers and the heroic efforts of the Haganah transferring Jews to Palestine shown in the newsreels. We were asked to help by collecting canned goods from neighbors and bringing the goods to the Hebrew school basement from which they would be transferred to a truck and then to a ship bound for Israel. Boys were paired, and we knocked on hundreds of doors in multistory buildings largely occupied by Jewish people. Tenants answered the doors and donated canned goods that we placed in my partner's red wagon. The most popular items donated were Del Monte canned vegetables and small cans of sardines. We trundled the filled wagon down the elevators and through the streets to our Hebrew school without incident. People knew what we were doing. The "food for Israel" program was described in the newspapers. The shul basement was stuffed with boxes and crates to be packed and shipped. I continued to learn until my bar mitzvah. I was glad to complete my Jewish education. Years after college did I realize that my Jewish education was too short and wholly inadequate.

Gravestone of Rabbi Judah Galinsky.

Yeshivah Shaari Zedek on Mermaid Avenue and West Twenty-Third Street in Coney Island. Hebrew school entrance was on the side facing West Twenty-Third Street. The building was abandoned, used as a crack house, set on fire, and eventually demolished.

Former site of the Sea Gate Sisterhood Talmud Torah. Now it is a Police Station for the New York City Housing Authority. My car with ski racks is in front of the building on the corner of 23rd Street and Mermaid Avenue in Coney Island.

Chapter 11

DR. JACOB KRAVITZ

I was rarely ill. A few times I contracted bad colds (upper respiratory infections). My mother used a rectal thermometer to take my temperature, kept me indoors, and called Dr. Jacob Kravitz. His office was in a walkup house on the corner of Mermaid Avenue and West Twenty-Ninth Street, two blocks from our house, in which he lived with his family and aging mother. He made house calls. He drove a big black car, always wore a nice suit with a starched white shirt, and carried a medical black bag. He parked on the street near our apartment house. Neighbors knew immediately something was wrong when his car arrived. The children stopped playing punch ball or stickball on the street to avoid hitting his car. He walked in to our apartment and spoke with my mother briefly, who proudly provided temperature data. I felt better immediately. He opened his bag and removed a stethoscope with which he checked my heart. Then he wrapped a mirror around his head and used tongue depressors to peer into my throat. He looked into my ears with a tapered metal tube. He looked into my eyes. He spent ten minutes examining me and asking me a few questions. I eagerly awaited his conclusion to the questions, "Will I be OK and when can I return to the playground?" He gave my mother the usual instructions. Drink fluids especially orange juice, grapefruit juice, soup, and tea with lemon. I was to gargle every few hours with salt water. I had to remain indoors until my temperature was normal. I prepared the gargle compound myself consisting of one tablespoon of Diamond Crystal kosher salt mixed into boiling water that was allowed to cool. I loved to drink a fifty-fifty mixture prepared from one quart of pure grapefruit juice with one quart of pure apricot juice—a combination recommended by the next-door housewife, Mrs. Frost, mother of Murray Frost. My ordeal usually ended within twenty-four hours, and I was back on the street.

Once I acquired severe sunburn from languishing on the beach and the skin on my back formed blisters with a white fluid. My back hurt, and I had a fever. My mother called Dr. Kravitz in a panic. He examined me the usual way but without knocking on my back with his fingers while listening to his stethoscope. I had a serious burn. He punctured some of the larger boils, gently dressed the wounds, and told me to avoid the sun for several weeks and then to wear a shirt and use tanning lotion if I wanted to go to the beach. He warned me that a second exposure might produce worse effects and I was to avoid direct sunlight. He recommended Noxzema cream that we always kept in the house for gentle burns. My mother thanked him for coming, paid the $3 for a house call, and I already felt better. He charged $2 for an office visit. Dorothy and I made sure our children always wore shirts and sunscreen when they were playing on the beach. I lived at 2995 West Twenty-Ninth Street (near Surf Avenue) in Coney Island from November 1945 until August 1958.

Chapter 11.1

MERMAID AVENUE

My father was employed as a metal worker at the Bethlehem Steel Naval Shipyard in Baltimore Harbor during WWII. After WWII ended, the shipyard workers were demobilized, and we had to leave US government housing that was built for the shipyard workers. Apartments were in short supply immediately after WWII, but my father found an apartment in Coney Island, helped by a distant relative. We moved to Coney Island in November 1945. I entered PS 188 in February 1946, skipped a grade, and eventually graduated PS 188 in June 1947. I entered Mark Twain Junior High School in September 1947 and graduated in June 1950. I entered Abraham Lincoln High School in September 1950 and graduated in June 1953 at age seventeen and three months. Intellectually I was ahead; socially I was behind.

Trolley car tracks on Railroad Avenue lay between Surf and Mermaid Avenues. I rode the trolley from Stillwell Avenue to Twenty-Ninth Street. I recall the final destination, Tomkins Point, that ended somewhere in Seagate, the gated community on the very west end of Coney Island. The trolley fare was $0.05. One could walk along Railroad Avenue toward Stillwell Avenue but had to leave where the tracks ascended above Gargiullo's Restaurant to the elevated station above Stillwell Avenue. Around 1950 the buses along Surf Avenue replaced the charming trolleys. The railroad ties and tracks remained into the 1970s until they were eventually removed.

Dr. Jacob Kravitz lived in a private house on the corner of Mermaid Avenue and West Twenty-Ninth Street with his mother.

FROM BROOKLYN NY TO BROOKLINE MA

His office was in his home. Dr. Kravitz practiced general medicine. He drove a shiny black car appropriate for a doctor at that time. He made house calls and parked his car on the street. There were no meters. There were few cars then, and we played punch ball and stickball on the street, deliberately avoiding touching or hitting his car. He was a man we respected and were in awe of him whenever he visited a patient. The neighborhood people knew his car and who was sick. He charged $3 for house calls and $2 for office visits in the late 1940s. He treated me a few times for influenza and once for second-degree burns from exposure to the bright sun when I played unprotected on the beach. When he walked into our apartment, he was always dressed with a dark suit and starched white shirt, carrying a black bag. His very presence made me feel better. I had confidence in him. He had tongue depressors and instruments in his black bag. He looked in my ears, nose, throat, eyes, and listened to my heart and breathing. He integrated the information, made a diagnosis, and usually wrote a prescription. My mother paid him in cash. He engaged in no small talk, but when he left, I definitely felt better.

The Mermaid Theater was on Mermaid Avenue near Twenty-Ninth Street. The inside was dirty, and graffiti was written all over the bathroom walls. I went there only half a dozen times, preferring the cleaner Surf Avenue Theater.

I remember Rosenberg's Deli on Mermaid Avenue between Twenty-Ninth and Thirtieth Streets with the corned beef, Romanian pastrami, and salami hanging from the ceiling on strings. On those days when my mother was too busy or too tired to prepare supper, I was sent to buy "deli" with potato salad and coleslaw from Rosenberg's. Sometimes I bought "specials," which were fat frankfurters that she broiled in the oven.

I remember a grocery store between Thirtieth and Thirty-Second Streets selling herring and lox for $0.20 per pound. On Sunday mornings, my mother would send me to buy herring (called solatka in Russian) or lox. I would stop at the Bialy bakery on the way home for bialys and some cookies. We would feast on herring, boiled potatoes, bialys, cream cheese, and milk. Now the combination of salt, saturated fat, and dairy cholesterol makes this something to avoid.

Wenig's Grocery Store was on Twenty-Ninth Street near Surf Avenue. I remember going into the store with ration stamps. Food was still rationed for months after the war ended until President Truman terminated the OPA(Office of Price Administration). Milk was sold in bottles that were only pasteurized. Homogenized milk was introduced a few years after WWII ended. The machinery had to be designed, built, and distributed to the milk processing plants. It was a real treat not having to shake up the bottle or remove the cream that collected at the top. Mr. Wenig would allow us to dip our hands into the brine barrel and select a pickle for $0.05. When sauerkraut appeared in barrels, we had to use tongs and bring our own jar. We used the tongs to pick up the sauerkraut and allowed the brine to drip back into the barrel before placing the produce onto special waxed paper to be weighed. The waxed paper was folded and placed into a bag that always dripped. All the grocers added up the prices on the bag into which they placed the goods. I was amazed at how fast they added. They all spoke with accents but did arithmetic in their heads.

Cream cheese was sold in boxes about four inches by four inches by ten inches. We used to ask the grocer or take them from the trash heap, carve out one-or two inch rectangular holes in the sides, and play marbles. The idea was to roll a marble into the hole from a distance of about two feet with several tries. The banker kept the marbles that did not enter the hole. The shooter earned perhaps ten marbles if his shot entered the hole.

Day or night during preadolescence or adolescence, I never feared for my safety walking along Mermaid Avenue. I used to window-shop especially in front of hardware stores. I was fascinated by the variety and ingenuity of all the tools and hardware I saw in the windows.

There was a Woolworth's on Mermaid Avenue near Twenty-Fourth Street that sold school supplies and some art supplies. There were little pads, crayons, notebooks, construction paper, and fountain pens. Ballpoint pens were introduced around 1947, and we still used liquid ink and fountain pens until ballpoint pens were available to everyone. The ink invariably spilled on the desk, clothing, floor, homework, and books. Only boys were assigned to be ink monitors and keep the small jars filled with ink. Girls might spill ink on their pretty dresses. This was to be avoided.

The public library on Mermaid Avenue near Nineteenth Street opened around 1947. I walked there from Twenty-Ninth Street and was transfixed by the collection of reference material. How could I possibly learn everything in these books or read everything? We had very few books at home and anyway no place to put them.

Almost all the food and clothing stores in Coney Island were on Mermaid Avenue. Even Seagate had no commercial property. It was strictly residential. Unheated bungalows for the summer people who came in June and remained until September were on Surf Avenue. They filled the beaches and boardwalk. Surf Avenue had large undeveloped lots of land while Mermaid Avenue was covered with stores.

One of the exceptions was Harry Kronberg's Store on Surf Avenue around Nineteenth Street. He sold stationery and art supplies mostly wholesale but some retail. I bought my first stapler from this store and was fascinated by the design. I kept taking it apart and filling it with staples, using it, until it jammed, and then I removed the jammed staples with a pair of pliers and started to use it again. The store was stuffed with school and office supplies from floor to ceiling. I think he sold to the schools.

Pat Auletta's Sporting Goods store was located on Stillwell Avenue between Mermaid and Surf Avenues. Pat was a sports enthusiast, active in the community, and an avuncular salesman for sporting goods. His store had lots of sporting pictures on the store windows and walls. I bought my first and second baseball gloves and a set of spiked shoes from this store. I could not afford to buy bats and baseballs. He sold the ubiquitous pink Spalding rubber balls that had so many uses. He had a large selection of sporting goods for an eleven-year-old. His son, Richard, graduated Abraham Lincoln High School (ALHS) in June 1953. Dick Auletta became a writer, researched the federal government's case against Microsoft, and wrote a book about Microsoft's alleged violation of the Clayton Act (restraint of trade). The Steeplechase pier off the Coney Island boardwalk is named after Pat Auletta. *Steeplechase* is a word borrowed from the British fox hunts in which lines between church steeples were the boundaries of the hunt.

The Sea Gate Sisterhood and Talmud Torah and Yeshiva Shaarai Zedek (Gates of Righteousness) buildings were on the corner of Mermaid Avenue and West Twenty-Third Street. The building entrance faced on Mermaid Avenue, and the top had an onion-shaped dome reminiscent of the design features used in Eastern European synagogues before WWII. The building on the corner housed a synagogue, and the adjacent building on West Twenty-Third Street housed an afternoon Hebrew school. I attended daily classes after dismissal from public school and attended parties in the building social hall celebrating various Jewish holidays.

After WWII ended, the Hebrew school students were asked to collect canned food for distribution overseas to help the displaced persons in Europe. A classmate and I would pull a red wagon down Mermaid Avenue and walk down the side streets, knock on doors, and ask the residents for canned food. We trundled our wagon filled with canned goods up and down the elevators in the large apartment buildings, knocked on doors, received canned goods, and filled our wagon. Residents trusted us. They knew why we asked for canned goods. Theft never entered our minds or the minds of the residents.

We returned via Mermaid Avenue to the synagogue building. I saw how we contributed to the mountains of cans that were placed into boxes and stacked on pallets for shipment overseas. I was told that refugees were suffering, and it felt good to be able to help. I did not know the full extent of what happened. My parents never spoke to me about events in Europe.

During the summer months, a flat truck with loudspeaker would drive up and down Mermaid Avenue and the side streets, park at a densely settled or busy commercial area, and the speaker would ask for donations for the Sea Gate Sisterhood and Talmud Torah. After an emotional appeal by the speaker with a European accent, the listeners and neighbors contributed enough money so the truck moved elsewhere. "How much will you give for Yeshiva Shaari Zedek?" blared the speaker. The contributors never asked for receipts, and none were issued. There was an inherent trust between the contributors and the recipients. I never heard of scandal. My parents would have found out and told me. The flatbed truck interrupted our stickball game by parking on the street covering first base, but we stopped the game to watch the appeal and resumed our game after the appeal ended in about thirty minutes.

The synagogue and school building fell into disuse from the 1960s and was sealed. The nonmaintained building fell into disrepair, was used as a crack house for drug addicts, and was finally demolished by the city. A low-rise municipal building now resides on the site.

Irving Herzenberg's optometry clinic was on Mermaid Avenue identified by a large pair of eyeglasses mounted on the front of the store and visible for several blocks. If you could not see the large pair of glasses from one block distant, you needed his services. I think he provided glasses for everyone in Coney Island. He was a big man with a smile to match his belly. He was involved in community improvements for Coney Island and worked for revitalization including a Jewish Community Center to be built around West Thirtieth Street. I heard that there was such a facility off Mermaid Avenue but was unable to find it.

Al Sinrod had a classy tuxedo sales and rental place on Mermaid Avenue. Only Fred Astair wore a tuxedo. It was all too formal for my peasant tastes. I never wore a real formal tuxedo with a cummerbund; that was for the movies.

My mother remembers shopping at Bortnick's grocery store on Mermaid Avenue but cannot recall the location.

Major Meats was located on Mermaid Avenue near Twentieth Street. Various kinds of preserved meats hung in the window, and unpreserved meats were available under the refrigerated counters. Major Meats supported the amateur baseball leagues playing in Kaiser Park. They provided the jackets and the uniforms for one of the teams that played baseball during the summer weekends. It was a real privilege to be on one of the teams and play well enough to have a uniform and a jacket. I never qualified.

The Good Humor man would drive his ice cream truck with regularity on Mermaid Avenue up and down the side streets during the summer. There were no one-way streets. Ice popsicles or ice cream popsicles, called pops, cost $0.10. A peculiar ring preceded the arrival of his truck. He lingered for ten or fifteen minutes, enough time for the children to run upstairs and ask their parents for some small change.

There was a candy store on Twenty-Ninth Street near our house. The store was the neighborhood-gathering place to exchange news; buy ice cream, packaged foods, newspapers, and skin lotion to prevent sunburn; and receive telephone calls. Private phones were not available until a few years after WWII ended. A neighbor would answer the public phone in the candy store. The same or another person would walk to the residence to notify the person for whom the phone call was intended. Everyone in the local neighborhood knew one another. Among the dairy items sold in the candy stores were ice cream, frappes, malteds, banana splits, milkshakes, and egg creams. On rare occasions during the hot summer months, a thick malted milk with two large pretzels replaced lunch. The store sold bubble-gum with baseball cards. A handful of pistachio nuts emerging from a glass bowl cost $0.10, a glass of seltzer cost $0.02 cents, and the *Daily Mirror* and the *Daily News* cost a nickel.

Chapter 12

KADDISH FOR A CANARY

My younger brother asked my parents to purchase a small canary as a household pet. During the dark winter days, we would provide birdseed and daily change the dirty water. We would insert our index finger into the birdcage, and the canary would rest on our finger. We would watch the bird sharpen its beak on a special bone and on occasion hear it chirp and jump from horizontal bar to bar. I named the bird Carey, a nondescript name, for a bird of unknown gender, Carey the canary. We all had responsibility for cleaning out the birdcage weekly by removing the bottom removable slide covered with paper and bird poo. Within a year, Carey died. My brother was saddened by this unexpected death. My mother appealed to me to do something; we simply could not dispose of Carey in the trash.

I would bury Carey with dignity. I made a small box of cardboard, lay the bird inside, stroked the bird's feathers for the last time, sealed the box with Scotch tape, brought a pair of yarmulkes and a siddur, found a small metal shovel in a beach pail, and went downstairs. My brother and I walked to the abandoned lot on Twenty-Eighth Street opposite our apartment house. It was overgrown with weeds and brush and a few old toilet hoppers. We found a clearing. I dug a hole big enough for the bird coffin. I placed the box into the ground, replaced the dirt into the hole, and added some additional twigs and brush. At least the roaming dogs and cats would not disturb Carey. I recited Kaddish over Carey the Canary. I also dumped the contents of the birdcage elsewhere in the lot.

Within a short time, my brother saw the empty birdcage and asked that we buy a parakeet. I named this new acquisition Fogel (or *bird* in German). My father, brother, and I all played with Fogel. He lived alone in his cage and died within a year. I repeated the ceremony. This time the birdcage remained empty. Perhaps Fogel would have lived longer if he had a mate.

Chapter 13

BAR MITZVAH

Mr. Resnick taught me parshat parah for my bar mitzvah and wrote my Yiddish speech that I delivered flawlessly in shul attended by my aunts, uncles, and grandparents. Mr. Resnick lived alone, a man in his fifties. He taught me in his apartment in a residential building near the boardwalk. He always wore a gray sweater with front buttons, and he seemed perpetually sad. My parents were proud of me and took me to a recording studio in Manhattan where I made a record of my HafTorah and Yiddish speech. In later years, I realized that the speech had no Torah content. It was pure emotion. What did I know?

In addition to performing in shul, my parents made a party at the Melrose Chateau in Brooklyn. I walked down an aisle between my cousins and uncle to chazzan Chaim who was a distant relative of my grandfather. I sang a song I learned from my choir days and was blessed by the *chazzan*. My relatives sat around round tables while a photographer took pictures for an album. My parents could barely afford this extravaganza. I never asked for it. The whole thing was bereft of Torah and any meaning for me. For them, it was a matter of pride. They did nothing like that for my younger brother. I received some books, money, and the traditional Waterman's fountain pen for my bar mitzvah. My mother commented that some relatives were "cheap."

During and after my bar mitzvah lessons, I attended shul on Shabbos mornings, but shortly after bar mitzvah, my interest dwindled and my attendance ceased. There was no attraction to continue attendance. No one took an interest in me or even befriended me. I had no friends there. The old men lived in a different world. I knew of no option to extend my Jewish learning beyond bar mitzvah. Hebrew day schools were called parochial schools with the perception that the curriculum was traditional but narrow, unrelated to the modern world, and the students perceived to be nonathletic, unwholesome nebbishes learning from rabbis who smoked in and out of class.

The synagogue on West Twenty-Third Street and Mermaid Avenue housing the Sea Gate Sisterhood and Talmud Torah was abandoned in the 1960s and used as a crack house. The building was demolished in the 1980s and replaced by a building for New York City Housing Police.

One of my mother's favorite photos of my Bar
Mitzvah at the Melrose Chateau in Brooklyn.
My mother was proud when we were all dressed up.
Considering her background, this was a big deal.

Chapter 14

SINGING CAREER

When I was eleven years old, Mr. Elchik Conviser, musical conductor, asked around the neighborhood if any young Jewish boys were interested in joining his choir to perform for the high holidays in various synagogues in New York. He lived in the apartment house across the street. It was an opportunity to earn some money and spend the holidays in strange places. His apartment was filled with musical books, portraits, and a piano. I saw on the wall a certificate of graduation of Lionel Conviser, his son, from the Julliard School of Music. Julliard was a prestigious school, so I had to assume that Lionel had some talent although I never met him. I auditioned, learned that I could sing on key, and was accepted with three other boys and two adults into a choir. We practiced on Thursday nights one month before Rosh Hashanah. I was an alto. One boy was a tenor who later became a well-known chazzan, Steven Stein, and the adults were baritones. We were paid $25–$35 for three days' work plus singing for Slichos late at night before Rosh HaShonah. That was a lot of money.

Members of the shul provided us with housing and food. It was considered a privilege to house choirboys. The chazzanut was much different than today. The pace was slower, with more wailing. The shul was packed on Kol Nidre night. I recall vividly the silence and crying during Yizkor on Yom Kippur, the moaning wails of the Chazzan, and the Kiddush clubs during Kriat HaTorah on Rosh Hashonah in which old people disappeared into a small alcove downstairs, drank whiskey, and ate honey cake. I too ate honey cake but without the whiskey. The rabbis spoke in Yiddish, and I barely understood what they said, but the audience did. I absorbed these events emotionally but not intellectually. In a few years, my voice changed. My brief attempt at stardom ended when I became an ex-choir boy.

One year we performed in Knesses Israel, a shul in Sea Gate. Sea Gate is a gated community at the western tip of Coney Island. In May 2005, I entered Sea Gate and recognized the synagogue after fifty-seven years. I remembered the large circle on the front brick wall made with colored glass and a Magen David. It was closed but is still used. I hope to return and see the inside where I sang duets with Bobby Schwartz.

Chapter 15

SMOKING

My father learned to smoke in Russia as a boy to quench the constant hunger pangs. He and my aunt Raizel (Ray) were addicted. Both exhibited smoker's coughs in their fifties. My mother disdained the odor and sent my father outside to smoke. We never were exposed to secondhand smoke. My father's clothing reeked with the odor of cigarette smoke. Some of my street friends started to smoke at ages thirteen. Smoking was for the in-people who wanted to be more popular especially with the opposite gender. It was OK to smoke. The newspapers, subway signs, TV, and the radio all told us that doctors (or people who looked like doctors) and athletes smoked. Humphrey Bogart smoked in the movies and in real life. The subway, TV, and radio advertised Lucky Strike Means Fine Tobacco (LSMFT), the advantage of a Marlboro cigarette (filter flavor and flip-top box), and Camels with its desert scene and a camel in the desert. The camels never smoked. More doctors smoked Camels than any other cigarette. I viewed all these ads as bogus. Yet my classmates and childhood playmates smoked outside of school. It made them feel cool, part of the in-crowd. I felt left out because I regarded smoking as irrational and expensive. No one accepted my views. There were no medical reasons not to smoke. I was just being a nerd, and a stubborn one at that. Doctors, surgeons, teachers, and rabbis smoked. If the rabbis who communicated with the Almighty smoked, then it was OK for their students to smoke. I saw this with my own eyes. After all, the gemorrah did not forbid smoking. The rugged Marlboro Man died of cancer.

I once tried chewing beech nut chewing tobacco since so many athletes chewed tobacco. Some of the big boys who played baseball every week in Kaiser Park chewed tobacco and then spit out a huge saliva wad. I got a headache, went to bed early, and explained nothing to my parents. My mother wondered what was wrong with me because I went to bed so early. It was stupid to chew tobacco. It was legal to buy and chew tobacco. I never did it again.

Presently cigarettes, cigars, marijuana, vaping, (except perhaps for flavored leaves, and opioids (when prescribed by doctors) are all legal. "Vaping is the act of inhaling and exhaling the aerosol, often referred to as vapor, which is produced by an e-cigarette or similar device. The term is used because e-cigarettes do not produce tobacco smoke, but rather an aerosol, often mistaken for water vapor, that actually consists of fine particles. Many of these particles contain varying amounts of toxic chemicals, which have been linked to cancer, as well as respiratory and heart disease." Statement was Published 2018. by "Center on Addiction."

I believe that it is unhealthy to put any foreign substance in your lungs. I always believed that smoking is unhealthy, expensive, addictive and therefore irrational. .However there is a sinister reason why these substances are not declared illegal. The manufacture and sales of these substances provide revenue to state and the Federal Government from taxes paid by customers, manufacturers, and employees. Manufacturers contribute to political campaigns. The state and Federal Government would prefer that people who engage in these unhealthy acts prematurely expire before their life expectancy to avoid receiving entitlements such as social security, Medicare, or pensions from the state or the Federal Government.

Chapter 16

MURRAY FROST

Murray Frost was my next-door neighbor, and on winter rainy days, we played monopoly on the steps leading to our apartments next to our doorways. In summer we played chess and a card game called pisha paysha on the beach. Pisha paysha is a card game for two players, one of whom is usually a child; the deck is placed facedown with one card face upward; players draw from the deck alternately, hoping to build up or down from the open card. The player with the fewest cards when the deck is exhausted is the winner.

 I learned the art of stamp collecting from him, and I would spend pennies buying canceled stamps from a dealer on Mermaid Avenue who sold stamps from all countries of the world. Murray Frost became one of the world's great scholars on historical philately. He eventually earned a PhD in political science, and I visited him in Goleta, California, during a business trip around 1961. He was the longtime editor of the *Judaica Philatelic Journal*, and for nearly ten years beginning in 1991, he authored the popular "Judaica Philately" column in the *Global Stamp News*. Dr. Frost died of pancreatic cancer in September 2000. He wished that his writing and research continue to be made available to others who share his interest in stamp collecting and Jewish lore. He prided himself on reading the *New York Times* at a precocious age and taught us how to fold the *New York* Times while sitting on the subway. He was a member of my high school graduating class, but we rarely interacted in high school. He was the youngest of three siblings. The siblings lived next to us in small quarters. His older bookish brother Charlie graduated college and became a librarian. His older sister Elsie married and moved to California. I once visited her and her husband who managed a pizza parlor near San Francisco. The siblings all left Coney Island from their crowded quarters and could not wait to leave and explore the world.

Chapter 17

ENTERING THE LABOR FORCE

I was about ten years old when I learned about stamp collecting from my next-door neighbor Murray Frost. I collected stamps both canceled and unused. Returning GIs from WWII handed me foreign stamps and foreign money. A few years later, I purchased the Master Global Stamp album, into which I mounted all my stamps from the US and foreign countries. I learned to read the strange alphabets, learned about remote places shown on the stamps, first-day covers, and the history behind the American stamps. My brother continued the hobby when I moved to California. I sold the stamp album, first-day covers, and stamps to a dealer for $100 in 1967 or 1968 and split the revenue with my brother. I retained the coin collection.

At age thirteen, I decided to seek work to support this inexpensive hobby that was disapproved by my parents, so I rode the streets on my bicycle during the summer looking for work. Mr. Weissberg, a butcher on Neptune Avenue, needed help with deliveries. He owned a live chicken market. On Wednesdays and Thursdays, women selected their live chickens, and the shochaits in the rear accommodated the women. The feathers were burned off the dead chicken by several non-English speaking babushkas sitting around a gas stove. They pulled out the *pankes* (quills) after the feathers were burned on the dead chicken. The dead chickens were soaked and salted in the store. The chicken was again cleaned, wrapped in heavy paper, and packaged for me to deliver. I delivered packages on my bike to the housewives in apartment buildings and received a customary $0.50

tip in addition to a small salary for doing menial work around the butcher shop. The housewives including my mother recleaned the chickens, resoaked the chickens with coarse salt for a few hours, and rinsed them to extract all the blood. Everyone used Diamond Crystal kosher salt. It was packaged in a box with a metal spout, just as today. Salt from the chickens was washed down the drain. These old apartment buildings no longer exist in Coney Island. I suspect that the constant exposure of the black iron drain pipes to weekly coarse kosher salt from thousands of households contributed to the deterioration of the waste plumbing in these old buildings. The coarse salt should have had a warning sign: "Use of this product may cause your waste plumbing pipes to deteriorate. Flush with plenty of water after use." Every Jewish housewife knew how to kasher a chicken without ever attending a shiur.

When I was fourteen, after failing at baseball, I applied for work at Dunkel's Grocery on Surf Avenue between Twenty-Eighth and Twenty-Ninth Streets. My job was to stock shelves, sweep the floor, deliver packages, and help customers locate products. After two weeks, he short-changed my salary by a few days. I complained, and he fired me. My mother was furious that such a man, a corrupt capitalist, would take advantage of a kid. My father advised me to go to the New York State office of labor affairs at the corner of Surf and Stillwell Avenues. I did not have working papers. One needed to be sixteen to acquire working papers. I went anyway and explained every detail to a sympathetic lady behind a large desk. She promised me she would take care of this matter within a week or two. I believed her, and I knew she believed me. I received a penny postcard from her office directing me to return to Mr. Dunkel and he would pay me what I was owed. I walked into his grocery and showed him the postcard. He grumbled, opened the cash register, and withdrew what he owed me. I never again frequented his store. That is how justice was done. Lawyers were not involved. One phone call fixed the problem. I learned a lesson from that experience that I carry with me this day: silence in the face of wrongdoing only causes resentment and anger to the victim.

Chapter 18

LESSONS LEARNED FROM MY FATHER

My father came to the United States with minimal education. He was employed as a printer before he came to America. This involved placing moveable type made of lead into a type holder prior to inking and printing. The work was dirty. The lead got on your fingers. Lead was used because it had a low melting point and could be molded into letters just like melting lead into molds for making bullets. He learned to speak English by listening and learned to write by copying English letters from the newspapers. He obtained work for Smilen Brothers, a fruit importer and retailer with fruit stands in East Coast cities. During the war we moved to Baltimore because jobs were made available and he was hired as a second-class engineer metal worker in Bethlehem Naval Shipyard. After the war, he learned how to paint houses both inside and outside and joined the painters' union. Most large-scale jobs were only granted to union members. He learned how to work the scaffolding outside tall buildings where he painted woodwork and other exposed surfaces. Outside work made my mother nervous, and she often asked him to find work indoors. Working the scaffolding ropes required strength and coordination with the other painter.

My father taught me how to mix colors, wipe rubbing stain, use varnish, and clean brushes. All paint had lead. Industrial water-based paint such as latex did not exist. Benzene was used to clean brushes. Brushes had to be cleaned after every job or they would harden and become useless. The brushes were expensive. He washed his fingernails and hands with benzene after using paint. Benzene was also used to remove paint spots from clothing. He did not smoke when he painted. He understood the fire hazard. After a while, the outside work became too hard, and he only accepted indoor work. I learned twenty years later that benzene is a carcinogen. Benzene is outlawed for consumer use. It is used in some industrial processes under strict EPA and OSHA guidelines.

As an adolescent in the summer, I accompanied him on a few jobs in Long Island. He assigned the closets for me to paint because no one looked inside the closets. He mixed the paints and prepared the brushes. I saw how he painted walls and ceilings. Painting ceilings is tiresome. He was neat, carefully dipping the brush into the paint bucket and withdrawing the brush without spilling a drop. He would paint the ceilings without leaving any brush traces. Paint rollers had not been invented. I tried but could never achieve his rhythm or his neatness. He told me that he took me along so I would work hard in school to never become a house painter. He taught me not to complain but to overcome adversity by hard work and independence. He never complained even when he was sick. He taught me responsibility and not to be a victim.

I watched while he made household repairs for my mother and his sisters. He rewired lamps, and I was ten years old when I imitated him. All lamps and wall receptacles were not polarized at that time, and the neutrals and hot wires were interchangeable. No wonder it seemed so easy. I bought lamp cord and rewired many lamps. Later at CCNY I studied electrical engineering and learned about hot wires, neutrals, and grounding. I did receive 110-volt electric shocks. The electrical code changed in the sixties to where the use of polarized plugs, polarized receptacles, grounds, and neutrals became standardized.

My father was a kind and generous man. The earliest recollection I have is when we lived in Baltimore in a new two-family walkup built for shipyard workers. A man knocked on the door downstairs and asked to speak with my father. He explained that he missed his ride home and asked if he could have something to eat. He knew my father from the shipyard. My father asked my mother to make a sandwich and offer him some milk. He ate downstairs at the foot of the staircase. I watched all this from the railing on the second floor. He ate and drank, thanked my parents, and left. I never saw him again. It was an act of kindness.

My mother managed the money in our house. She had a head for figures. My father just gave her all the money, and she gave him what he needed. She did all the food shopping, and I helped when she sent me to the grocery store. Shopping was an opportunity for her to display her negotiating skills. She was conscious of every penny and walked city blocks to save pennies. She verified the grocer's addition since the numbers were penciled on the grocery bag. My father trusted her completely to handle money. There were no separate accounts. It was a model of trust that remained with me. Dorothy controlled our checkbook for thirty years until we started to use credit cards. She no longer has to carry the checkbook in her purse. I balance the checkbook.

My brother and I never received an allowance, but my father always had pocket money for ice cream cones for us during the warm summer evenings when he was downstairs smoking in the local candy store. An ice cream cone cost $0.10. My father painted houses in Nassau County, and I wonder if he painted the house we purchased in November 2013. Painting all day long using oil-based paint and cleaning brushes with turpentine and benzene makes one want to breathe fresh air. Try painting all day long, and you will see what I mean although present latex paint is water based. That is why he wanted to leave the house at night during the summer and be outside.

During the winter months, he was not able to find work indoors. He visited the union halls and sometimes found odd paint jobs. Sometimes a week passed in which he found no work. My mother did not work outside the home. Very few mothers worked outside the home during those years. There were no household washing machines. Mothers stayed home, did the wash in bathtubs, later used a public Laundromat, shopped daily for groceries, cooked, baked, sewed, and watched their children grow up and attend public school.

In his spare time, my father made a doll house for Stanley's daughter, Mindy. He loved to do things like that. Stanley was his sister's son.

As he grew older, my father was no longer able to paint houses. He loved to drive his car and applied for a taxi license to work for a cab company. He did not need a taxi medallion. Only the owners of taxis or a fleet of taxis needed medallions (special licenses), which cost tens of thousands of dollars. He drove taxis all over New York City until he once blacked out and had to surrender his license. In 1964 he had his first heart attack after sailing and helping me to lift a tech dinghy from the Charles River onto the dock of the MIT boathouse. He sat on the bench outside the boathouse on Memorial Drive and just keeled over. He was taken by ambulance to Massachusetts General Hospital. He recovered, but the doctors could do nothing for him except prescribe nitro-glycerin pills. Bypass operations and valve replacements were being researched and were not in operational use. He stopped working, continued to smoke, did odd jobs for my mother around the house, and collapsed in the downstairs hallway on Neptune Avenue. The neighbors called a doctor who had an office in the building. He died on the way to Coney Island Hospital on the day of the sixth candle lighting, Chanukah 1966, a few months after Dorothy and I were married. He did not attend my brother's wedding. He never saw his grandchildren. He would have adored them. He would have been proud of his sons. He is buried in Montefiore Cemetery in Long Island on Springfield Boulevard. I still think about him and what he never saw. Alec is named after my father, Eliyahu ben Shlomo, Alex son of Samuel.

Chapter 19

LESSONS LEARNED FROM MY MOTHER

I used to practice reading to my mother. She would test my spelling and words in English and French that I had to memorize. She only had three years of school in America and no years in Russia. My mother was always around. After school, there was always something good to eat in the refrigerator that was made at home. She worked from raw materials. We did not eat processed food. She made the best gefilte fish that I ever tasted. Her honey cakes and cookies were light and fluffy, and only my wife and daughter can compete. My mother made mondel bread that compared with Mrs. Holcer's. My grandfather and my mother told me to avoid eating fat from red meat, so she trimmed the fat from the lamb chops and rib steaks we ate each week. She removed the fat from the chicken soup we had every Friday night. My mother worried about everything. She anticipated the worst. "Come home early because you will hurt yourself playing in the dark." I came home late. "Don't jump between the roofs of the small bungalows." I jumped between the roofs. "Don't jump from the boardwalk onto the beach. It's too high." I jumped from the boardwalk to the beach. "Don't go to Ebbets Field by yourself. You'll get lost." I took my younger brother, and we did not get lost. After a while, I ignored her because she constantly underestimated me.

She came to school during open school week at Mark Twain Junior High School, but I felt sad that I was not called upon to recite. She was always there preparing cookies and cakes for consumption that I ate after school with a whole quart of milk. She insisted that we drink fresh orange juice every day. She cut each orange in half and rotated each half orange over a glass juicer that squeezed out the liquid and pulp from the rind and then poured everything through a strainer to collect the liquid. Orange juice in wax-covered boxes or bottles had not yet been developed. She did most of the shopping, but sometimes she asked me to purchase food. I felt she trusted me; but she would have selected a better-quality lettuce, beets, etc., and better negotiated with the grocer. I could not compete with her careful selections and her negotiating skills. No one could buy fish the way she did. She just knew what was fresh and what was old. No one bought the yellow pike, carp, and white fish (ingredients in gefilte fish) except her. She trusted no one to buy these precious ingredients except her. I could buy bagels, lox, carrots, potatoes, beets, milk, and eggs but not fish and meat. Oh no, not fish, chicken, or meat. I could buy delicatessen, coleslaw, potato salad, and specials (really fat hot dogs) from Rosenberg's Delicatessen. The corned beef and pastrami were fully processed ready for eating.

    She cleaned the house, cleaned the dirty laundry, and hung up the wet clothes on a clothesline using wooden clothespins. My father was responsible for repairing the clothesline whenever it collapsed. Large lag screws into a telephone pole were required to support the weight of the pulleys and the weight of all the wet clothing and bedding; otherwise, the line broke, and everything fell to the ground. Later I learned to install and repair clotheslines. Clothing that is dried on outdoor clotheslines is fresher and seems cleaner than clothing dried in a gas drier. In the winter, the clothing developed rigor mortis when dried outside. She sorted, folded, and stuffed the stiff clothing into drawers that quickly filled with expanded stiff clothes. I recall putting on freezing dried clothing that quickly warmed from my body heat. It was a strange feeling.

    During the winter, our apartment frequently had no heat. The owner, Mr. Koten, was a plumber and told us that the building was old. My mother complained, but his apartment was never cold. He became the object of my mother's wrath. It was cold when we woke up to attend school, and my mother had awakened early to turn on the gas oven in the kitchen and prepare hot cereal, usually Wheatena. Wheatena is like kasha. I still enjoy a bowl of kasha. It filled my belly and kept me going until lunchtime. I carried $0.14 with me every day to high school. The bus cost $0.05 each way, and a half-pint container of milk cost $0.04. My mother packed a lunch. One of my favorite lunches was cottage cheese with peanut butter spread onto a bulkie roll. Yum, yum! I never ate the hot lunches prepared in the school cafeteria. The lunches cost $0.50 but were still considered more expensive than Velveeta or cottage cheese in a bulky roll.

Before Passover each year, she insisted we visit Mirsky's or a similar clothing store on Pitkin Avenue in East New York near my grandfather's house. It was a ritual I detested. Why do I need a new suit? Who cares? Daddy does not need a new suit. "You have to look nice for Yom Tov," said my mother. Why and for whom do I have to look nice? We are all Russian peasants anyway. It was incomprehensible to me how she bargained with the tailor who took my measurements and who would cut the material to make a boy's suit. The unclothed female mannequins pushed to one wall in the store were a source of curiosity and awakening. I wore a suit to my junior high school and high school graduations. My mother was proud that I wore a suit. I still felt like a peasant.

My mother sent me to buy bialys, cream cheese, lox, and herring Sunday mornings. I went to the bialy bakery that opened very early Sunday morning. Lox cost about $0.20 a pound. The herring was very salty with small bones, and we ate it with boiled potatoes. Now I wash off the salt from the boneless herring served at Kiddush in shul, and it does not taste the same.

I watched my mother cooking and actually learned how to prepare food. I regret that I never learned how to bake or make gefilte fish. From her, I learned how to prepare borsch, fish, and schav from raw materials. I learned about kashruth, koshering a chicken, and separation of dishes. We never ate milk and meat together but never knew why.

My mother had a weak stomach and rarely complained when we were young. She watched her diet and watched our diet. We never had soda in the house. We drank New York water from the taps. I was hardly ever sick and rarely saw a doctor when we lived in Coney Island.

After my father was sick, my mother who had not worked since marriage had to find a job. She knew how to sew and found work in Manhattan as a seamstress and later as a quality checker for women's clothing. Working kept her going after my father died. Riding the subways, shopping, and preparing her own meals exhausted her. My brother accompanied her to a Social Security office with a doctor's note and applied for Social Security at age sixty-two. She lived in a high-rise building on 435 Neptune Avenue until my brother submitted her name in a lottery for elderly apartments in the Golda Meir House in Auburndale, Massachusetts. Her name was selected, and she moved into the Golda Meir House.

She attended all my graduations and accompanied my father in his car when he drove me to the airport to leave Brooklyn for my employment in California. It was exciting for me. It was an emotional low for her. I called her few days later. Phone service was not readily available as now.

My mother passed away on 26 December 2012 after bouts with pneumonia and a broken hip bone. The memorial service was held at Levine's Chapel in Brookline on 28 December 2012. She exhausted her CDs that she was saving for my brother and me to pay for her hospice care. She left the world of the living penniless just as she arrived on Ellis Island. The following eulogies were delivered at Levine's Chapel.

Chapter 19.1

ROSE KRIMSKY, CHAYA RAISEL BAS YITZHAK WAS MY MOM.

*I*f there were one word to describe my mother's life, it would be "struggle." Her response to life's struggles was verbal suffering. She struggled and relished talking about her struggles. After a while I grew tired of hearing about her struggles and all the offenses committed against her by our relatives. So I buried myself in homework and reading Time Magazine at the supper time while she would remind me of her struggles. I said, "Mom, I already heard this several times." She would say, "It is good for me to get this off my chest." But I already heard this and what good is it to constantly talk about what happened 25 years ago. She responded, "You don't understand and you should never know from this." I would try to reason and she would terminate the conversation, by saying "Don't aggravate me." That ended all attempts at logic.

My mom's struggles started when she was born in a Ukrainian village Bieleh north of Odessa. Her father left the day she was born; there was no brit milah and no reason for him to delay his trip to America. Mom's mother died when she was 3 or 4 and she was raised by two aunts. She did not go to school and on cold days the lamb was brought into the one room house. My grandfather remarried and twice sent money to bring mom to America. The first time, the money was stolen by the agent. She left the village, with tickets, and a box with her bedding, and travelled to the ship that would bring her to Ellis Island in 1928. Someone on the ship was supposed to watch her but no one did. She wandered around the ship, became seasick, and after two weeks landed at Ellis Island. The first day she was confined to the infirmary with sea sickness.

Ellis Island as a point of departure for immigrants was a mass of confusion. Multiple languages, multiple ages, multiple statuses but everyone had to be questioned by the US Immigration Agents standing in front of their desks before anyone could descend downstairs to the dock where the ferry would take people ashore to the streets of New York and freedom. Immigration agents were like the TSA today but without technology. They questioned every immigrant, "How much money do you have, where will you live, what is your name, the name of your children, who is your sponsor, are you a communist, and do you plan to overturn the US Government by force?" I recovered the arrival record of my father and his siblings at the National Archives in DC. I found no record of my mother. I searched for many hours during multiple trips. The genealogy room closes at 8:45PM. My mother heard someone calling her name, probably snuck behind the agent and ran downstairs to see who called her. It was her father.

My mother was anxious about riding on a boat and on a subway, with a strange man she had never known. They spoke in Yiddish. She was placed in elementary school and struggled to learn English. She moved up rapidly and completed three years of public school and had to leave at age 16 to go and work. Her teachers begged her father to allow her to remain in school but they needed the money during the 1930's. She struggled to get along with her stepmother who could neither read nor write any language. She moved out of her home to live with her future mother-in law, whom she adored. She met my father at a Russian Club and they married. My grandfather insisted that my mother give half of the monetary wedding gifts to him to pay for wedding costs.

They moved to a flat where bathrooms were shared with other families and rodents. Keeping the apartment clean was a struggle. My mother was malnourished and I was born sickly with rickets. Drink milk and be exposed to sunlight was the remedy. My mother apologized several times, even last year, for having dropped me onto a hot radiator because she was weak. WW II started and my father found work as a metal worker in the Baltimore Naval Shipyard so we moved. Apartments were scarce after the war ended, so my father was lucky to find an apartment in

Coney Island, near the Ocean. The building was poorly heated and my mother struggled to keep us warm. Complaining to the owner was useless. My father also struggled to find steady work as a house painter and my mother struggled to cook the meals without prepared food, shop for food and clothing, clean our three room apartment, and do the laundry without household washing machines and dryers. She was a real mom and always did the best she could for her family. Her family was her life. She handled all the money and paid the bills. She checked the addition on the grocery bags until she trusted me to add the figures. She helped me with my homework and went to Open School Week. She struggled with her relationship with her father whom she claimed let her down by favoring his wife, the step mother. She never ceased to verbalize her dislike for her step mother who treated me well, she was my bubby.

My father became too sick to work and died in 1966, five months after Dorothy and I married. Once again, my mother struggled to find work in the garment district. She was always feisty and insisted on being independent. She struggled with low energy reserves, preparing breakfast, lunch, climbing the steps to take the subway to Manhattan every day, shopping on the way home and repeating the process until she was eligible to collect social security. All during those years she struggled with doctors whose advice she frequently ignored. "They are practicing on my body" I frequently heard. I would argue rationally and she would respond, "Don't aggravate me."

She moved to Golda Meir House about 20 years ago and struggled with congestive heart failure and other medical problems. Tufts University assigned medical students to talk with residents at Golda Meir House to make them more sensitive to patient needs. Her long history with doctors was recorded by medical students from Tufts University and she relished telling them about her struggles. She disliked medical advice and medicines but she went anyway to doctors and complained about the waiting time. She felt important in being interviewed. Someone was listening to her struggles.

She asked me when she was in the hospital receiving intravenous fluids and being cared for by the wonderful doctors and nurses, "Why am I being tortured?" and I answered "So you will have something to talk about when you recover."

'In June she contracted pneumonia and that started her rapid medical decline. She struggled to speak and to walk. On 26 December 2012 someone from LaSalle Rehab Center called me to say that her condition was worsening. I asked the caller if she was being seen regularly. The caller said that the doctor will see her in the evening. I drove to LaSalle Rehab Center and stayed at her bedside for about 20 minutes. It was Xmas evening and there were few nurses visible on the floor. The nurse on duty said she was seen every hour. She was on her back asleep. Her breathing was labored. Her chest was moving up and down. I went home. My brother was probably in New York otherwise I am certain he would have come to LaSalle.

In the morning I received a phone call that she expired. I drove to LaSalle and assembled her belongings. She had been moved to Levine Funeral Home before I arrived. I spoke to an aide and asked what happened. The aide said that the doctor never came but gave instructions to the nurse to administer morphine to ease her breathing. I asked for the daily inspection sheet that is initialed by the aides and nurses who are supposed to check on patients every hour. I saw that the boxes for the previous day were unsigned. I asked the nurse and she said that the aides just were too busy to sign the sheets because there were fewer aides on duty the previous day. She was supposed to be checked hourly.

The effect of a morphine injection is to slow down the heart. I believe the doctor administered too large a dose. My mother could not take the recommended doses of any medicine. She usually only took half because she understood her own body's response to medicines better than the physicians.

Her struggles finally ended on the morning of 26 December 2012. She proved the doctors were wrong, they could not save her. Her struggles ended. I will miss her verbal suffering.

Sid Krimsky
28 December 2012

Chapter 19.2

EULOGY FOR ROSE (SKOLNICK) KRIMSKY CHAYA REIZEL BAS YITZCHAK BY RABBI ELLY KRIMSKY

Before I begin words of tribute to my beloved Grandma a'h, I want to offer gratitude to so many people who made her last few years as absolutely comfortable as possible. All the professionals at the Golda Meir House; everyone at the Laselle Rehab Center where she finally succumbed; the staff of unbelievable doctors and nurses at Newton Wellesley, with a special mention of our life-long friends Rosa and Dr. Mark Drapkin. I want to thank Mr. Howard Block who cared for my grandmother as if she were a relative. I want to thank the wonderful caregivers who gave my grandmother 24-7 coverage and security in her last months. Most of all, however, I want to thank my Uncle Sheldon, who really assumed the role as primary caregiver and decision maker for Grandma and for our family. You kept all of us abreast of everything we wanted to know in a concise, honest and caring way. Grandma truly knew all that you were doing for her. She expressed it to me on almost every occasion we spoke the last few years. You never failed her and she trusted you and for good reasons. And you know better than I that she didn't trust just anyone.

The title of this week's Torah portion is *Vayechi Yaakov*, which means "and Jacob lived"; yet it describes the passing of Jacob, and the subsequent passing away of Joseph, the viceroy of Egypt. Our sages taught us a profound lesson. Life is a cycle. It does not begin with birth and does not end with mortal death. The soul is an eternal being that makes a stop on its odyssey here on earth. We were privileged to have had my beloved Grandma—Rose Krimsky—on this earth for quite a while. Jewish tradition teaches that the soul is present at the time of the eulogies. I know, Grandma that I cannot possibly do you justice, and I beg your forgiveness. But I must try!

Grandma, when I will think of you, I will always think of a fairy tale. Your life may not always have resembled a fairy tale and I can almost hear you laughing at me right now. But if you'll give me a few minutes to explain, I think you'll agree with me.

Grandma, I think of you as Cinderella. We all know the story—the rags to riches fantasy about the unlikely princess, who wins the hand of the prince. She was the adopted daughter who was sentenced to cook and clean for her siblings the rest of her life. The night of a grand ball at the palace which her step-sisters attended, while scrubbing and cleaning a fairy appeared, fitted her with a beautiful dress, a coach and dispatched her to the ball. The prince fell in love with her. As the clock began to ring twelve, Cinderella ran off, knowing she would turn back into rags at the stroke of midnight. She inadvertently left a shoe during her flight. The prince, wanting to see her again, sent his entourage to find the woman whose foot fit the shoe. So many young women tried to manipulate the shoe into fitting, but it wasn't meant to be. Indeed it fit Cinderella perfectly, the fairy transformed her back into the princess and they lived happily ever after.

Grandma, your early years were difficult, hardly a fairy tale. And you never missed an opportunity to remind us. And we needed those reminders, to show us just how great you were for overcoming unspeakable obstacles, ones to which we can barely relate! Your father left Russia when you were born and your mother died when you were just a baby. He re-married in New York and started another family. You lived with cousins and eventually came to America. Your father paid some folks to take you across the ocean in steerage, so your name doesn't even appear at Ellis Island. You joined your father and his new family as Cinderella. It was the depression and things were tough. It was hard for your father's new family to accept another mouth to feed, but it was harder for you being the odd one out and the lowest rung on the family totem pole. I know you would want me to state here in this tribute to you, how badly you were treated by your father's wife, traumatic wounds that never healed. Never! Despite being highly intelligent, you were never granted a proper formal education. Your father and his wife sent you off to work in the garment industry at a very young age, an age that would be illegal today, where you worked for decades. I remember once being in your home at Warbasse in Brighton Beach. When I went to school in New York, I relished my visits to your apartment, taking the long subway ride from Washington Heights. I remember once I was writing something and asked you for a piece of paper. In your typical Jewish Grandmother fashion, you started running around your apartment looking to help. You delivered to me about half a ream of paper and expressed your willingness to run to the store to buy more if I needed. I laughed, only needing one piece and said to you, 'Grandma, you didn't need to chop down a tree!' You looked at me as if I was speaking a foreign language. I realized that you may not have known that paper comes from trees, something we learn in grade school which you were denied.

But boy were you smart! Nothing got past you—even into your very old age. You and I would talk about the mayoral races in New York City, you were up on the muggings taking place in your Brooklyn neighborhood, presidential politics, everything. During my last visit to you a few weeks ago, I remember seeing all the magazines you were reading. No one could pull the wool over your eyes! You had street smarts that were second-to-none! Only a few years ago, you noticed some irregularities in one of your bills. You pursued it and were correct. Just months ago, when you said you weren't feeling well and something was wrong, you, in the end, were right; you showed the doctors that something was not right, not just old age.

Grandma, as your oldest grandson, the being whose birth made you a Grandma—(you became a Nanni years later with Alyssa's birth)—I knew you the longest from our generation. What can I say? You were the typical Jewish Grandma, but so much more! I remember driving you back to your apartment in Brooklyn after Yossi, Noami's second child's bris. I was driving back to Maryland; getting off the Ocean Parkway exit on the Belt was literally 500 feet out of my way—maybe 1,000 feet round-trip. I asked if I could walk you in to your apartment. You told me not to be crazy, that you were fine and I would never find a parking place. You then gave me a $20 bill for gas—gas from Queens to Brooklyn. Even today, it wouldn't be that much: even with an SUV. I refused the money and you got insulted. So you won; I took the money. I knew you wanted to give it to me, why should I deny you that *nachas*?

With my other grandparents moving to Florida when I was very young and my father inheriting your thriftiness (and stubbornness), we never went down to Florida and as a result, you were the Grandmother we knew best. We were so excited when you would join us for the holidays. We would pick you up at the train station and you would give these warm hugs. We so looked forward to your visits. We would smell the sponge cake, which almost miraculously seemed like it just came out of the oven. And you were so proud of all of your grandchildren, all five of us. And when we married and had families, you took such great pride in all of our families. We could always count on receiving the check for our kids at their birthdays, and if we didn't call to acknowledge receipt you would worry that the check did not arrive.

I always spoke with you before the holidays, usually within an hour of candle-lighting. On those occasions when Yizkor—the memorial prayer—is recited, you would remind me that you purchased the 24 hour lights and were going to light 4 of them: for your mother, for your father, for Grandpa Alex your one and only soulmate, my name-sake, and for Bobbi Sonia, your mother-in-law, who took you in and treated you like a daughter. Only recently—in the past ten years or so, you shared with me the story of how you and Grandpa Alex met; you were at a club and he expressed interest in you. You didn't take him too seriously because he didn't look Jewish to you. Only after sharing that he was indeed Jewish would you agree to date him. Only a few weeks ago, my parents and I met Cousin Stanley at a Manhattan Café, and he told my father that he saw a lot of Grandpa Alex in me. I was blown away. That was a great compliment. I wish I could have shared that with you.

Grandma, there's one last thing I want to say today. There's a part of the classic Cinderella story that particularly holds true for you. No one but no one could fit that shoe except Cinderella. Grandma, no one could have survived the way you did. You told me relatively recently on the phone that because both your mother and husband died prematurely, you felt a desire to live a long life: you told me that you wanted to do it for them. You succeeded! But you gave all of us a gift. We got you for so long! And every moment we had you, was a blessed moment. And there's no other person I could ever dream or desire of having as my beloved Grandma.

When the patriarch Jacob dies in the end of this week's Torah reading, the Torah says that he breathed his last breath and was gathered to his nation. The term "he died" does not appear as it does regarding Abraham and Isaac. The sages of the Talmud declare that Jacob never died. This statement is challenged. But Joseph ordered that his father be embalmed. Would they do that to a living and breathing man? Of course not! The meaning of the statement is metaphorical. One's legacy can be their family; can be their accomplishments, can be their contributions to the advancement of society. The rabbis conclude: Jacob lived on because his children lived on. Grandma—you live on!

Chapter 19.3

EULOGY FOR GRANDMA ROSE KRIMSKY BY RABBI JONATHAN KRIMSKY

In this week's Torah portion, Vayechi, we read about the final chapter of the life of our forefather Yaakov. Throughout his life, Yaakov had constant struggles and challenges that he had to overcome. Despite his initial hardships, during the last chapter of his life he lived peacefully surrounded by his family. Grandma Rose too had struggles and challenges throughout her life. Like Yaakov, she too was blessed with the love and care of her family over the last stage of her life. The love and affection that her children, grandchildren, and great grandchildren expressed to her was a result of the deep love and affection that she had for all of us. I will always remember Grandma coming to visit and preparing her fresh delicious tzimis, blintzes, fish cakes, latkes, Pessadik sponge cake and all the other traditional Jewish delicacies. She showed that same affection to my children, her great grandchildren. Grandma's cards to her great grandchildren, always the first to arrive and often accompanied by an apology that she couldn't give as much as she would have liked, alerted us to upcoming birthdays. Our children couldn't wait to visit "grandma Rose's house" where they were always treated to a container of Hood's ice cream and whatever other treats Grandma thought they may like. It wasn't merely the ice cream but Grandma's warmth and love that endeared her to our children. Just last week, before our trip to Boston, my oldest son Aryeh said that his favorite thing to do in Boston was visiting Grandma Rose. All of our children were disappointed when they weren't allowed to join my wife and me when we visited Grandma Rose this past Sunday.

Grandma sheped nachas from the accomplishments of all her family. Until recently, when traveling became difficult, Grandma Rose made sure to be a part of every milestone in our lives. I can still feel her pinch on my cheek when I was a child as she referred to me as a shayna ponim. She was proud of both her son's academic and professional accomplishments; as well as all the accomplishments of her grandchildren. A little over ten years ago my father was honored by his synagogue—Kadimah Toras Moshe—for his service as president. My siblings and I came in for the event and Grandma joined us as well. My father was in the middle of thanking Grandma when the emcee asked my father to pause and requested that "Mrs. Krimsky" i.e. Grandma stand up. Grandma obliged and the audience erupted in an impromptu round of applause. The image that has never left me from this event was the radiance that emanated from the face of Grandma Rose when she stood up. She was very proud not only to be the mother of the honoree, but to be the mother of someone who had dedicated so much time and effort to his synagogue. When I got engaged she understandably was happy and proud. In addition to a very generous gift she gave us for our wedding, she insisted on taking us to the Israel Book Shop on Harvard Street so we could pick something for her to get us. After browsing for a while we picked out a blue challah cover. We have used that Challah cover almost every week for the past 7 plus years, and Please GOD will have the opportunity to use it for many more years to come.

I feel fortunate and blessed that Chaya and I had the opportunity to spend some time with Grandma this past Sunday. While it was hard to understand all that she said, we were able to have a relatively normal conversation. We talked about all the events of our children, nephews and extended family. She mentioned that her oldest great grandson called her from the Old City of Jerusalem, and as usual we had to ensure her that it really is not an expensive call these days. She asked how Chaya's brother's wedding was last month and even made reference to the fact that this was a mazinka, as it was their last child to get married. On Monday evening after we packed up our car to head home, we decided to stop by Lasell to see Grandma again before we head west on the Pike. I got to room 315 as a nurse was checking her vitals. I was not able to speak to her however, for by the time I got to the room she had fallen asleep. I tried to talk in a low key to see if she was just dozing, but she did not get up, and I obviously did not want to disrupt her. I left the room and was ready to take the elevator a few feet from her room down to the first floor. Not knowing GOD's plan and realizing life is tenuous, I decided to go back to the room one more time to say goodbye. I looked at her sleeping uncomfortably on the bed and said bye, I love you Grandma.

Despite all of his struggles, or more appropriately because all his struggles, Yaakov was able to look back at his life feeling a sense of accomplishment. Grandma, you came into this world with challenges: both in the Ukraine where you were raised by your aunt and uncle and when you first arrived as a young teenager in New York City. Yet, look what you accomplished. You leave behind 2 children, 5 grandchildren, and 12 bli ain hara great grandchildren (as of now). All of your offspring, who were old enough, forged an everlasting bond with you. We admired you for your honesty, your altruism, your faith and your tenacity. Well, Grandma, on behalf of the whole family I say bye, we love you Grandma. Tehinish masatz rurabitr zrurash achayim.

Chapter 19.4

EULOGY BY DOROTHY KRIMSKY

Those of you who knew my mother-in-law Rose Krimsky knew that she was a small woman. Don't be fooled by her size, she was a fighter.

My father-in-law Alex Krimsky died in December of 1966. After the shiva we invited Mom to come back to Boston and spend some time with us. She stayed for a short time and then decided that she has to go back home and fight the loneliness and adjust to her new way of life.

Mom decided in one visit to Boston that she will teach me how to make gefilte fish. Although it was not my favorite food and my mother also made gefilte fish, I decided to get my lesson. We bought a round wooden bowl and a chopper. We made the fish and she told me to soak the bowl. I told her that the instructions said not to soak the bowl and she told me she knows better. The bowl cracked and she said she will take care of it. She brought it back to the store and indeed got her money back or we got another bowl, I don't remember which.

All of her life she was fighting doctors. All doctors wanted to do was give her medicine and she wanted to take as little medicine as possible. She was ahead of her time with cooking. She cooked healthy food from scratch. She did not buy processed food. One day she called us up and was very upset because a doctor charged her for a visit she did not make. I asked her what she was going to do. She told me a few days later. She called the fraud division of Medicare or Blue

Cross Blue Shield and complained. Not only did the doctor take away the charge, but she also received an apology from the doctor.

One day Jonathan's wife's parents, Chatz and Libby Lazarus came to Boston to spend a few days with us. Mom was not able to travel to NY for either Jonathan's or Elly's weddings so they never met her. After a day touring Lexington and Concord, we drove to Golda Meir house to pick up Mom and we all went drove to China Fair. I sat in the back of the car with Chatz and Libby and Sid and Mom were in the front. Sid asked her about her day. She told us that some doctors in training came to Golda Meir House to speak to the residents about how they could become good doctors. She told them about all of the mistakes doctors made with her so that they would not repeat the same mistakes. She was so fired up it was like watching a comedy show.

Mom was coughing for three weeks in June and the doctor gave her medicine without seeing her. She said she was too weak to go to the doctor. She fell and in the hospital she was diagnosed with pneumonia. They gave her heavy doses of medication and she could not take it. She thought that she would never return to her apartment at Golda Meir House. She got better and then went to Lasell Rehab center. Sid and I were to leave for Berlin and were deciding whether or not we should go on the trip. Before we left I told her that she was a fighter and if she wants to go back to Golda Meir she has to get out of bed and walk to the bathroom with her walker and walk back. We did go on the trip and Alyssa and Jonathan sent us such encouraging e-mails about her progress that we were able to relax and enjoy the trip. Upon our return, she was able to return home with full time help.

There was one doctor that Mom liked, Mark Drapkin. When she went to Newton Wellesley Hospital over the years Mark would visit her and her face would light up when he walked into the room. She felt that she was not important and yet this important doctor came to visit her. It made her feel important. Thank you Mark for caring! Rosa also made many visits to Mom, fed her and bought her first Teddy Bear. She told me that no one ever bought her a Teddy Bear before.

Over the past few months, Mom had pneumonia twice and fell and broke her hip. It was too much to bear and she was too weak to fight. Mom, we will miss you, and may you rest in peace.

Chapter 19.5

EULOGY BY NAOMI HOLLANDER AT THE GRAVESITE

I wasn't going to speak. I didn't speak on friday, but last night…or I should say this morning…as I had a very hard time sleeping, so many things went through my head. I felt so blessed that as a child I had the opportunity to really get to know you. You lived in New York at the time, and I lived in Boston, but you came and visited.

Around the birth of my second son, Yossi, you moved to Boston, but still knew my children, your great grandchildren. You shared in each of their milestones with pride. I am so grateful that my children really knew their special great grandchildren.

My family and I had an opportunity Friday night and Shabbos afternoon to tell special stories about you, grandma. Many of these stories my siblings and parents told kept going through my head last night. But then I kept thinking about a conversation we had not too long before you passed away and I felt I had to share it.

I was on the phone with you, grandma, and you asked me… So how is Ephraim doing in Israel? I had been asked this so many times over the past few months and I answered you that, Baruch Hashem Ephraim is doing so well. He is happy and he is growing on so many levels. You then said to me,…Nomi, How are YOU doing? I paused for a moment because that is not a question I am frequently asked. I replied I am doing ok, grandma. It is hard letting go of your oldest child. I know he is well but it's still difficult.

You then said to me, Nomi, I remember like it was yesterday, when your dad left and moved out to California. It was so hard for me, but I knew It was good for him. Grandma then said, At least when your dad left, I still had Sheldon, so it made it a little bit easier. But, when Sheldon left me, grandma said, that was really hard, but you have a while for that. It's hard, she said, but you have to let them go.

Grandma, despite your small frame, you were a large personality.

You were so right, and as I say my last goodbye to you today, I know it's hard…it's so hard, but I have to let you go. Your memories will be with me and my siblings, Elly and Jonathan and with Elliot and Alyssa, your sons, your grandchildren and great grandchildren…Ephraim, Yossi, Simma, Tamar, Aryeh, Tziporah, Shai, Malka, Yedidya, Racheli, Andrew and Benjamin.

It is very hard to let you go, but we have to believe it is for the best We will continue the traditions and strong values you taught us all. We all love you and we will all miss you.

Tehiye zichro Baruch

Chapter 19.6

COMMENTS AND CORRECTIONS FOR "MY LIFE AS A MOTHERLESS CHILD"

My Life as a Motherless Child was a self-published book by Rose and Sheldon Krimsky. The purpose of the book was to explain her history of coming to America, her struggles, and the mistreatment she experienced at the hands of her stepmother.

I had no knowledge about this book until after it was written. I was not consulted. I did not comment on the accuracy when Mom was alive because my comments would be interpreted as criticism. However, there are some inaccuracies, incomplete information, and some paragraphs require further explanation.

Page 1: In a letter written in Yiddish, the spelling is Bet Yud, Lamed Heh for which the best English spelling is Bieleh.

Page 2: Isadore Shkolnick was born in 1888, not 1889.

Page 14: Life was hard. There were no social entitlements or welfare. I would surmise that few fathers provided "fatherly support and guidance." Those are not my mother's words. This is a statement using twenty-first-century language of comfort to criticize 1928 behavior. My father and my mother also could not provide "fatherly support and guidance" because my world in America was totally different from their world in Europe.

Page 17: My mother entered third grade and ended up in the seventh grade. She was skipped once. She attended school for three years. If she arrived at thirteen, she left school at sixteen, which was the minimum age for acquiring working papers. Junior high school ended at the seventh grade, so my mother did not make graduation. I'm certain she regretted that, but she could not do anything. She was always very thankful that my brother and I completed high school and college. Unfortunately, teaching immigrants dirty words is universally practiced.

Page 18: Following blindly ancient rituals is a theme that permeates my brother's writing. No one explained these rituals to my mother. She lit candles every Friday night without knowing why. She bought kosher meat and did not mix milk and meat without knowing why. She kept separate dishes without knowing why. Even my father did not know why, but he never challenged the origin of these rituals. *Blindly following rituals* are my brother's words. Questioning the origin of these rituals is what I would expect of an educated person.

Page 19: The stepmother was uneducated. She signed her name with an *X*. She could neither read nor write any language. My mother was feisty, quick to criticize, and without diplomatic skills. I definitely take after her. I spoke back and argued with her in the same way she argued with her stepmother. I learned from her to stand up for what is right and don't worry about someone else's feelings. Just do what is right.

Page 20: Seventy years later in her nineties, my mother still blamed her stepmother for making her anemic and malnourished all her life. Seventy years passed, but she was convinced that her condition at age ninety-eight was a result of her teenage years.

Page 20: Her grandfather Meir Shkolnick was born in 1845 and died in 1930.

FROM BROOKLYN NY TO BROOKLINE MA

Page 22: *Chaleria* comes from the word cholera (bad, bad, bad).

Page 33: The comment about benzene is not from my mother. This is my brother's bias against man-made chemicals. Benzene is classified as a carcinogen and is outlawed for consumer use. We used benzene to clean paint brushes or to remove oil paint from clothing. My father soaked paintbrushes in benzene pails in his locker in the basement of our house in Coney Island. I went there often to borrow tools and some paint for projects. I always asked him before using his tools. He insisted that I put everything back where I found it because he depended upon his brushes for his livelihood. My father died of a heart attack unrelated to benzene. I remember putting my hands in benzene because I was sloppy when I painted and got paint on my hands. No one wore gloves.

Page 39: My mother mentioned several times that she dropped me and apologized each time she reminded me. Each time I told her to forget it. I got over it. It bothered her. She was malnourished, and I was born with rickets as a result. I was born with a heart murmur and an irregular pulse.

Page 41: Alex tried to join the Navy Seabees Construction Battalions, but he was rejected. He may have been too old or had two children or failed the physical exam. He was looking for adventure and a steady income. Then he applied for shipyard work in Baltimore.

Page 42: It was Sidney, not Sheldon, who walked down Broadway to meet Daddy coming home from work. I remember clearly what happened. I walked on South Broadway on the west side of the street opposite the Apex Theater toward the wharf. That is how he always walked home. He carried his black lunch pail with a thermos bottle. I walked to the wharf and did not meet him, so I turned around and walked back. My father did not see me, and both went out on the street looking for me. It turned out on that day my father walked home on the east side of the street. South Broadway is a broad street with grass growing down the middle. I was about six or seven years old; and Sheldon was much too young to know where to meet him, cross streets, and walk alone on a big street.

Page 43: *Putsutsa* is a variation of *putz*. Relations with my mother's half sister and two half brothers were estranged. They dutifully attended my bar mitzvah, but contact was broken. They heard the constant invective against their mother. I regretted not having any real contact with my aunts, uncles, and cousins from my grandfather's side. I never met Uncle Natie's or Uncle Heshy's children. I met Cousin Linda once (Aunt Ida's daughter) right after she was born and Mark (Ida's son) at the funeral of my grandfather. I never met Ida's grandchildren.

Page 49: My parents purchased *The New Standard Encyclopedia* from a salesman. They wanted us to have a good education. It was an expensive investment for them at the time. There were lots of pictures and lots of words. I spent hours exploring the encyclopedia. Some students in my class owned the *Encyclopedia Britannica*, the king of encyclopedias but also the costliest. I wrote many book reports based on the words in the encyclopedia. This was a sacrifice for them. We had hardly any books in the apartment other than textbooks. There was no bookshelf, no room for a bookshelf, and buying books was a novel idea for my parents who grew up without such luxuries. There was a public library on West Sixteenth Street and Mermaid Avenue where I went on occasion to write a book report. My father drove me because it was too dark to walk home alone at night.

Page 49: My job was to clean the meat grinder. I dissembled all the pieces, washed them thoroughly, and reassembled all the parts. I enjoyed doing that, and my mother trusted me not to lose parts and to clean them thoroughly to prevent bacteria from growing on the surface.

Plate 9: Alex and Pauline came together to America. Rae did not come with them. Rae, Annette, and their mother, Sonya, came together two years later.

Plates 15–17: The days in Baltimore were the happiest days of my mother's life. She was needed, she lived in a clean apartment, the streets were safe, Alex had a steady job and could walk to work, we had no car expenses, Bubbie Sonya came to visit and help my mother, and her two children were young enough to listen, and she bought fresh unprocessed food from grocers on Lombard Street and had enough energy to cook and clean. The kosher butchers were all on Lombard Street. My mother told me that she was able to save money from my father's steady salary. It all went to pay for his car when we moved to Brooklyn. He needed a car to work in Nassau County painting houses.

Chapter 20

WALK TO ZADIE'S HOUSE

I was thirteen years old, and it was Yom Kippur, Monday, 3 October 1949. I wore a suit and walked into the Young Israel shul on the corner of Surf Avenue and West Twenty-Eighth Street, just two city blocks away from our apartment on West Twenty-Ninth Street, and prepared to relate to the almighty. The shul was a single-story small brick building with stained glass windows and a corner stone named after Lt. Maxwell Quartner. Lieutenant Quartner (called Mackie)—a member of the 515th Squadron, 376th Heavy Bomb Group—was declared MIA after his airplane ditched over the Adriatic Sea near Mezzocorona, Italy, because of bad weather on 11 November 1944. He was another brave lad called to service for the defense of freedom whose short life enabled me to live my life in freedom. I stayed awhile in the shul, pretended to follow the services, but the language was incomprehensible. No one approached me, the prayer books had no English, so I lost interest and left. I felt sad that after so many years in Hebrew school, I could not relate to the prayers. What to do? It was about 10:00 a.m. I was fasting. I fancied that a young boy belongs with his grandfather on Yom Kippur. I decided to walk to Zadie's house in East New York. Eating and riding were not options for me on Yom Kippur. I asked my brother to accompany me. He was eight or nine. My mother objected, saying I would get lost, but she always overestimated the difficulties and underestimated my abilities. My brother could walk the distance after he ate lunch. I knew Brooklyn

Streets; I studied the map and told her how I would proceed. She had no concept of directions. I do not recall asking my father.

We left in the warm afternoon walking east on Surf Avenue, north on Ocean Parkway, northeast on King's Highway, east on Linden Boulevard, and north on Pennsylvania Avenue. The shul was on Pennsylvania Avenue near Blake Avenue. My brother complained about the heat and was tired, but I encouraged him to continue. We walked along Ocean Parkway and saw people riding on horses on the horse trail in the middle of the wide parkway. Horses were rented in Prospect Park, one terminus of Ocean Parkway. From central Brooklyn, Ocean Parkway led to the ocean. We passed many shuls along the way with people lingering and loitering outside. On King's Highway, we passed closed shops with Jewish sounding names. We walked for about four hours, about ten miles, and we arrived at Zadie's shul around neelah time. I walked into the shul, searched briefly, and found my zadie. His eyes opened wide when he saw us and embraced us as Yaakov embraced Joseph. How did we get here? Who brought us? At first he did not believe us when I told him that we walked. He said that he would never forget this for the rest of his life. My brother looked exhausted, so we went downstairs where Zadie proffered honey cake (lekach) and water. Zadie proudly introduced us to the *baalebatim* (members) of the shul, telling them how we walked from Coney Island to East New York. I was his oldest *einekel* (grandchild), and he doted on me. I was not exhausted. My brother was ready to fall asleep.

I recall that I visited my grandfather on a few occasions Friday night by taking the D train from CCNY and changing at Chambers Street for the New Lots Avenue subway and leaving at Pennsylvania Avenue and Livonia Avenue. Then I would walk the few blocks to Alabama Avenue passing the eponymous Fortunoff's Department store on Livonia Avenue. Fortunoff started as a small store and expanded to a chain of stores. I saw beautiful lamps and furniture that were unafordable.

After neelah, we walked to Zadie's apartment, and he quickly explained everything to Bubbie Anna. There was not much to explain. We just showed up. We called home, Coney Island, 6-1950. My mother was relieved. Zadie kept talking to my mother about what we did. He could not get over it. We broke the fast, and my brother fell asleep. My father arrived and brought us home, driving south on Pennsylvania Avenue. At Linden Boulevard, the roadway became a two-lane unlighted bumpy road to the Belt Parkway. He drove west on the Belt Parkway past the Canarsie malodorous edaphic landfill operation, past Coney Island Avenue and Ocean Parkway, and exiting at Cropsy Avenue. The car made so many trips to Zadie's house that it could drive itself. The trip normally took forty minutes. We were home, and I enjoyed inherent satisfaction doing to what my mother had objected and whose difficulty she overestimated.

During WWII, the phone companies worked for the military. After the war, phones and telephone lines were in demand, and two families had to share phone lines. These were called party lines. In 1950, Bell Telephone Company technicians installed a telephone in our apartment. The number assigned was CO 6-1950—easy to remember. Prior to the installation, phone calls would ring in the public booth at the local candy store. A patron would answer, announce who was being called, and a neighbor in the store would ring our doorbell to inform us that someone was waiting on the phone. Everyone in our teeming neighborhood knew everyone else, and people thought nothing of calling someone to the phone. Phone calls were infrequent. Communications were mostly by letter and telegrams for really important communications. Local telephone calls from a booth cost ten cents for unlimited time. The airwaves had plenty unused bandwidth space. Later, the phone company charged for longer time usage.

Alabama Avenue as it appeared during the 1950s looking North toward Dumont Avenue.
The Synagogue appears on the right side and my Zadie's three-room apartment (456 Alabama Avenue) was opposite the Synagogue. The tall building on the left is the Thomas Jefferson High School.

Chapter 21

BULLYING

My younger brother attended Mark Twain Junior High School when I was already in Abraham Lincoln High School. My mother complained to me that an older and bigger kid, asking for money, etc., was bullying him. She asked me to do something. I said I would handle it. She was worried I might do something rash and wanted to know what I would do. She worried that it might backfire on my brother. If I told her what I planned, she would complain to my father and regret that she told me because she feared I would make things worse. I could never quiet her anxieties. I learned who the bully was and where he lived. In the evening, when I knew he would be home, I visited the bully and his mother. I wore clean clothes and explained softly and with extreme confidence that unless he stayed away completely from my younger brother; his mother would be called to pick him up at Coney Island Hospital. I told my mother what I did and she was nervous there would be retaliation. I told her not to worry because his mother read the determination in my eyes and she knew I was not lying. Leslie never again bothered my brother. I learned valuable lessons from this experience. Evil people have to be confronted.

Chapter 22

WORKING ON THE BOARDWALK

At age sixteen, I walked the boardwalk to seek summer work. My friends told me about a small concession on West Twelfth Street on the boardwalk. I needed to find summer work to support my habit of collecting stamps and have some pocket money. My father struggled to earn a living, and I felt guilty asking him for pocket money. I never asked except to buy ice cream cones that cost $0.10. I walked the boardwalk and saw a Help Wanted sign at a small hot dog concession on the Coney Island boardwalk on West Twelfth Street and applied for work. The owner, Philip Handwerker, was the brother of Nathan Handwerker, founder of Nathan's Famous Hot Dogs on Surf and Stillwell Avenues in Coney Island. My job was to make pizza; cook hot dogs, hamburgers, and french fries; and sell food and drinks. Phil and his wife, Nellie, were in the concession every day during the summer. They spent winters in Florida. Nellie kept the place clean. I learned how to make pizza. The dough came preformed. I poured the tomato sauce onto the dough, sprinkled on the graded cheese, and put the pizza into the oven using a big wooden ladle. The cheese smelled bad, but I never ate the pizza. One day, upon removal of the cooked pizza from the oven, the pizza pie slipped off the wooden ladle and fell onto the wooden floorboards with the tomato paste side down. The greasy dirty floorboards were for walking. I panicked. I asked Phil what to do. "Never mind," he said, "turn it over, pour on some more tomato sauce, sprinkle on some more cheese, put it back into the oven for ten seconds, remove it, and sell the slices. Give 'em and let 'em eat." Nellie rinsed the wooden floorboards with a hose. I sold the slices. My mother was appalled when I told her what happened. My tale reinforced her belief that these capitalistic exploiters could not be trusted. I was never to eat that food. I didn't. Each day, I showed up on time, and he paid me on time. I served the customers. I knew my job, and he was willing to hire me for the following summer. My task was "to give 'em and let 'em eat."

The concession must have changed hands in the Handwerker family. It is been rebuilt and modernized at the same site on West Twelfth Street on the boardwalk.

Boardwalk and 12th Street in Coney Island where I worked summer 1952 selling cold drinks, french fries, pizza, and hot dogs. Phil Handwerker, brother of Nathan Handwerker was the proprieter.

Chapter 23

NATHAN'S FAMOUS

Next year at seventeen, I applied to work at Nathan's Famous Hot Dog stand in Coney Island. This was the big leagues of hot dog concessions. Nathan Handwerker, who emigrated from Poland, opened the store in 1916. Murray, son of Nathan, interviewed me. He tested my mechanical dexterity by having me assemble pegs in holes and mental ability by computing change. His uncle, Phil, was my reference. I was hired and put to work immediately, first working in the large kitchen cleaning big pots and then as a counterman selling hot dogs, french fries, drinks, hamburgers, root beer, but not regular beer. I learned later that Murray was a real marketer, and his younger brother Sol was a Socialist. Sol wanted to turn over management and profits to the workers. Nathan transferred management responsibility to Murray. Everyone who worked there was an immigrant except for one law student whom I befriended. Nathan's Famous has expanded and even penetrated the Atlanta and Orlando airports. Hot dogs cost $0.15 when I started to work, and now they cost $3 as of July 2008, an annual compounded increase of about 5.5 percent.

Selling franks or hot dogs, as they were called, required a certain finesse and rapid hand-to-eye coordination. A manager would oversee the operation, replace people as needed, send us to lunch and break, adjust the natural gas under the griddles, replace the mustard and paper plates, and bring out the boxes of raw hot dogs from the inside refrigerators. We did these activities when business was slow.

We arranged the franks on the griddle in rows and kept them moving from right to left, with our tongs, until they were cooked at which time the skin slightly ruptured. We used tongs to turn the franks and the buns that were being toasted on the griddle. During the summer, day and night, demand was furious. We handled the food without plastic gloves, but we washed our hands after lunch and after using the lavatory. The selling process was fast. A customer would request to buy franks and hold a dollar above the counter after we told them to have their money ready. Quickly, we used our metal tongs to snatch the dollar from the customer's fingers and thrust the dollar bill into a wooden box under the counter. All singles were inserted into the moveable wooden box under the counter. The managers provided five singles for $5 bills. Managers would remove and replace the boxes several times a day. The box had a slot just wide enough to accommodate the tongs. With our left hand, we took the necessary change from the pockets of our apron and put the change on the counter top. Using my left hand and a pair of tongs, we presented the patron with his order of franks in buns on a paper plate. The process was fast—real fast. The customers had no time to complain their dollar was snatched so quickly. We surrendered our aprons to the manager when we left the workstations.

    Occasionally a customer would complain that dollar bills were not sanitary and I should use my hands to collect money, not use the tongs. Sometimes I nodded, and other times, I said to a testy customer that if I did not use tongs to snatch his money, my hands would touch dollar bills and buns so there was no difference. Now the food handlers use gloves, and another worker collects the money or handles the credit cards. I never heard of anyone getting sick from the way we collected the money and served the customers. I never heard of frankfurters having salmonella. We moved them fast from the refrigerator to the grill to the customer in minutes during busy times and ten to fifteen minutes during slow times.

    Jake Stein started selling franks about the time Nathan Handwerker opened the concession in 1916. He was a small man with a prune face who worked the corner. Customers approached him from two sides. He had to be fast, and he was. He was a master hot dog cook and salesman with a rhythm I tried to imitate. He said few words. His sad eyes spoke for him. Nathan made it big, and Jake did not. Nathan did not have to work and Jake did. Nathan promised Jake he would always have a job selling hot dogs. When Jake came to work, out of respect, we swapped positions to let him work the corner. I saw him less frequently during the last few years I worked selling hot dogs. I asked about him, and people shrugged.

I worked six days a week from 3:00 p.m. until midnight and sometimes until 3:00 a.m. during busy weekends. Nathan's never closed. I started at $0.75 per hour ($6 per day before 3 percent FICA and taxes) the minimum wage. I had no other benefits except entitlement to one daily free meal and a freshly cleaned apron and clean trousers. My mother packed a lunch, but I ate the fries and root beer. The white trousers and aprons had pockets for change. I surrendered the change apron to the managers when I left for lunch or home. I placed all personal change and dollar bills from my trouser pockets in my locker during work. I could never be accused of transferring change from my apron pockets to my trouser pockets. I walked to and from work to save the $0.10 bus fare no matter how hot or late at night. I smelled bad when I came home, showered, slept late, monitored my stamp and coin collection, listened to the radio, and returned to work the next day. I worked there for five summers. I could have remained there and perhaps worked up as a manager. I was asked to edit the monthly *Frankly Speaking* newsletter. I asked employees questions about their lives that might be of interest such as new births, etc. I found a home but not a future. The managers liked me. I showed up on time worked fast and never gave anyone reasons to distrust me. I enjoyed working there. I did not have to travel into New York City sitting on the subway and perhaps wearing formal office clothes.

One hot summer day, as I was opening a Coca-Cola bottle with a mounted bottle cap opener, the neck of the glass bottle snapped, my hand slipped down, and the glass cut my wrist. I bled all over my apron, trousers, and shirt. The manager, Nick DeLuca, opened a first aid kit, bandaged my wound, and hustled me with a fellow worker into a police car. I was still bleeding. With the sirens blasting, we arrived at Coney Island Hospital into the emergency room. No one asked if I had medical coverage. I had none. The nurse hustled us into a medical office, and a doctor appeared in a minute. I needed about two inches of stitches across my wrist and a tetanus shot. My wound did not sever an artery or vein. I never heard of tetanus. The doctor explained "lock jaw." I was released from the emergency room in a few hours, with my wrist stitched, bandaged, and numb from the local anesthetic. The fellow worker and I taxied back to Nathan's where I expected to resume work. Nick sent me home and said I would be paid for the day. I replaced my white trousers, but my mother saw my bloody shirt. I explained that everything was fine and I was well treated. The following day was my day-off, so I returned the day after and resumed work with my wrist bandaged. I was surprised that everyone including Murray Handwerker asked me about my wrist. Consulting a lawyer was inconceivable. I had an industrial accident. Under present law, an OSHA investigator would be assigned to the case, Nathan's would pay a fine, and Coca-Cola Company would be investigated for making unsafe bottles.

The police were eager to help with the car ride to the hospital. I used to prepare hot dogs, french fries, hamburgers, and quarts of coffee each night for the police stationed at the Sixtieth Precinct as a daily courtesy from Nathan's. Upon return to work, I continued to sell Cokes. I have a two-inch scar across my right wrist as a legacy of the broken Coca-Cola bottle. I was treated well by the doctors at the hospital and by my employer. That is how it was done.

Nathan's famous during busy season.

Nathan's Famous after Hurricane Sandy. Front was demolished from waters from Gravesand Bay

I always wondered what happened to Nathan's Famous. I just happened to see an advertisement in a Jewish newspaper that the grandson of Nathan Handwerker, William Handwerker, would be present at Ben's Restaurant at 140 Wheatly Plaza in Greenvale New York in November to sell his book, "Nathan's Famous, the First 100 Years." I showed up, exchanged our recollections, and traded my book for his book. William is the son of Murray Handwerker, the man who hired me in 1953. Murray died a few years ago. Nathan's went public in 1971 to fund a Times Square location. A private equity firm launched another IPO in 1993 and the company engaged in an expansion with franchises around the world. William Handwerker worked at Nathan's in various executive positions and finally left the company about 15 years ago. He became a financial consultant and now owns his own company. The most dramatic change I saw was that the cooks do not sell directly to the public. A customer places an order and a complement of hamburgers, frankfurters, French fries may be presented to the customer in paper on a tray instead of the customer having to move from station to station. The entire order converges to the customer which is easier for the customer. I presume the food is kept warm by infrared lamps until passed to a counter-person who presents to the customer and collects payment. All the workers wear latex gloves. Business practice such as outsourcing, selling, and sanitation regulations have all changed from when I was employed.

FROM BROOKLYN NY TO BROOKLINE MA

The corner was my sometimes work station dispensing hot dogs right off the grill into a toasted bun. The original signs are still there.

William Handwerker, grandson of Nathan Handwerker displaying his book Nathan's Famous at Ben's Restaurant, Wheatly Plaza, Greenvale New York.

Chapter 23.1

LIVING IN CONEY ISLAND DURING THE 1950S

- The subway, bus, and the trolley cost only a thin dime; and if you are older, you will remember that it cost a nickel to ride.
- New York City schools were the showcase for the whole country.
- Tuesday night during the summer was fireworks night sponsored by Schaefer Brewing.
- There was very little pornography.
- There were the bath houses: Silver's, Steeplechase, and Brighton Beach Bath Houses.
- There was a respect for teachers and older people in general. There was almost no violence. A great day was going to the beach at Coney Island or Brighton.
- Nathan's had the best hot dogs, and there were no better french fries than the Nathan's thick ripple cut.
- There were very few divorces and few single parent families. There were no drugs or drug problems in the lives of most people.
- The rides and shows of Coney Island were fantastic. Steeplechase Park: the horses, the big slide, the barrels, the zoo (maze), the human pool table, the Cyclone Roller Coaster, the Tornado Roller Coaster, the Thunderbolt Roller Coaster, the Bobsled, the Virginia Reel, the Wonder Wheel, the bumper cars, the Tunnel of Love, Bat Away, the loop, the

Bubble Bounce, miniature golf, the whip, the many merry-go-rounds, the penny arcades, Luna Park, the Thompson Roller Coaster, the Parachute Jump, Faber's Sports land and Fascination, toffee and cotton candy stores, custard stands, Pokerama, Skeeball, prize games, the House of Wax, various restaurants, rifle ranges, and push cart rides. Only after I started working was I able to try out some of these rides.

- The street was visited by the fruit man selling from the back of his truck, the tool sharpener or tool grinder, the junk man and the man who sold watermelons from a wagon pulled by a horse. The street was sometimes filled with horse droppings washed away by the rain into the street drains.
- There were three theaters—Surf, RKO Tilyou, and the Mermaid—that cost $0.25 viewing cartoons and two feature films.
- Potato and kasha knishes were sold at Stahl's in Brighton or Shatzkins on the boardwalk. Sometimes a man would peddle knishes from a shopping bag walking on the beach.
- Pickles were sold out of the barrel—for a nickel.
- The Brooklyn Dodgers were known by everyone: Duke Snider, Pee Wee Reese, Jackie Robinson, Preacher Roe, Roy Campanella, Junior Gilliam, Clem Labine, Big Don Newcombe, and Carl Furillo, and Gil Hodges. Ebbets Field was a shrine. Happy Felton's Knothole Club was an institution for each ballgame. The home of the Coney Island baseball team called the Cyclones resides on Surf Avenue and Twenty-Third Street. Outside the stadium on Surf Avenue is a statue of Pee Wee Reese placing his arm around Jackie Robinson during a baseball game at Crosley Field in Chicago in which Robinson was booed by the fans in 1947. The single act by Pee Reese quieted the attendees. Robinson was booed because he was black. Reese's singular act sent shockwaves through the baseball community. Reese came from Louisville Kentucky. If he could accept Robinson as a player, then the fans in the South and elsewhere had no choice but to also accept Robinson.

- We played games in the street depending on your gender. Boys played ringaleaveo, Johnny on a pony, hide-and-seek, three feet off to Germany, red light-green light, kick the can, hit the penny, dodgeball, stoop ball, punch ball, handball in the park, stickball, relay races, and softball in the park. People played card games such as canasta, casino, hearts, pinochle, war, and 52-card pickup.
- In Brooklyn, a fire hydrant was called a Johnny pump.
- Everyone had metal roller skates for use on the sidewalks and gutters. They made noise on the sidewalks.
- Rides on a truck came to the neighborhood during the summer. Rides cost a dime.
- Everyone lived near a candy store and grocery store. Jahn's Ice Cream Parlor near Brooklyn College gave you a free sundae if you brought your birth certificate.
- We waited for the Good Humor Man pushing his cart. Trucks came later. A small cup cost a dime, and larger cups cost $0.15. Movie stars pictures were on the bottom of the Dixie Cup lids.
- As a kid growing up during the 1950s, other kids would spend money on bubblegum baseball cards (complete with a stick of bubble gum) and candy. Full-size candy bars were $0.05 each or six for a quarter. My mother never bought candy or soda in the house. We did buy seltzer.
- There were interesting coins in circulation. Dimes and quarters had some silver in them. Mercury head dimes were still available and were replaced by Roosevelt dimes. Sometimes buffalo head nickels, Indian head pennies, and rarely the 1943 steel penny were given as change. Most pennies were wheat backs; they did not get the familiar Lincoln Memorial on the reverse side of a penny until 1959.
- Pat Auletta's sporting goods store was on Stillwell Avenue opposite the subway station. His son Richard was in my high graduating class and became an author. Pat was a generous man with his time supporting many sports teams in Coney Island. The Steeplechase Pier off the boardwalk is

named after him. I purchased my first baseball glove from Pat Auletta.
- There were railroad tracks from Stillwell Avenue going East and West to Seagate. The tracks went over Gargiulo's Restaurant, which is a Coney Island icon and is still there. During inclement weather, I used the railroad when I attended Hebrew school going from Twenty-Third Street to Twenty-Ninth Street. The tracks were removed after 1950, and the land must have been sold because there are houses where the tracks used to run.

Coney Island revisited:

Many of the small stores along Mermaid and Surf Avenues disappeared. The single-family homes have been replaced by huge apartment buildings that provide affordable housing.

Our old house on 2995 West Twenty-Ninth Street was demolished, and vegetable gardens cared by nearby residents are on the land on which the house used to stand.

Former site of Covered Pavilion. Sand was pushed under the boardwalk to fill all the space previously occupied by kiosks. One walked from the beach under the boardwalk to the street. Sand was filled in to eliminate isolated hidden spaces used by drug addicts and potential criminals.

Coney Island pavilion before 1970. The pavilions were torn down during the 1970s because of storms and non-maintenance. There were kiosks under the boardwalk from which beach supplies and cold drinks were sold. Kiosk merchants also accepted used soda bottles and gave 5 cents to anyone who returned bottles.. During the warm summer evenings people gathered in the pavilions talked and sang songs in many languages from the countries from which they emigrated. The area under the pavilions were eventually filled in with sand because they became sites for drug dealers so I was told. Credit for the image is the Coney Island History Project.

Chapter 24

ABRAHAM LINCOLN HIGH SCHOOL

I was transferred to Mark Twain Junior High School at the completion of the sixth grade at PS 188 to an SP class. Only later did I learn that SP meant "special" for potential college-bound students. At the end of the ninth grade at Mark Twain Junior High School. I was transferred to Abraham Lincoln High School on Ocean Parkway. I had to take a bus to school. My eyes opened up after the first day in school when we were assigned to a homeroom and various academic classes. Most of my friends in earlier years with whom I played in the streets and on the sand lots disappeared from sight. They either dropped out of school or were assigned elsewhere. I had free periods on my schedule during which time I could go to the library, lunch room, and outside the building as a senior. Free periods were not really free.

    My geometry math teacher, Ralph Ellis, called me Krimsky Korsakoff after Rimsky Korsakoff, composer of Scheherazade. He used colored chalk to draw all the figures on the blackboard to prove triangles congruent. He was so logical and systematic to build a case out of almost nothing except pure logic. Every day in his class was a new exploration into the unknown to discover new relationships between triangles, lines, and planes. His teaching struck a responsive chord in my brain and an interest I never knew I had. I regret that I never thanked him. He died a few years ago.

In my plane geometry course, Mr. Ralph Ellis stated that it was impossible to trisect an arbitrary angle just using a compass and a straight edge. I quietly accepted the challenge.

I tried for weeks at home to trisect an angle staying up late at night. My mother would ask why I am up so late, and I would explain that I am trying to trisect an angle because the teacher said it was not possible. She was befuddled. Only a nontrusting skeptic would attempt something the teacher said was not possible. How could she understand? I never told anyone that I tried and failed. Mr. Ellis also taught us that Fermat's last theorem, which was unproved at that time, stated that the equation $X^n + Y^n = Z^n$ is not satisfied with X, Y, and Z being real numbers and n>2. So I tried for months making substitutions to find three real numbers that satisfied the equation. Of course, I failed. A few years ago Fermat's last theorem was finally proven. I looked forward to the math classes every day. It was like being taken on an expedition. Mr. Ellis would reveal the amazing properties of geometric figures, circles, triangles, polygons, squares, and rhombuses. My language expanded as I learned strange theories, axioms, and corollaries of rigorous geometric proofs of congruent and similar triangles. I absorbed the material like a sponge and scored high grades. It was a strange world where everything was perfect, lines, planes, points, angles, polygons, dodecahedrons, tetrahedrons, and icosahedrons. I learned how to think in two and three dimensions, an essential requirement for mechanical drawing.

The most memorable moment was the Friday Mr. Ellis asked us to solve the simple quadratic: $x^2 + 1 = 0$. I raised my hand and said it can't be factored because of the negative square root. He told me to wait and return Monday to class. I tried all weekend to factor that equation. I would show him and become a mathlete hero. I tried everything from substitutions to squaring both sides. Nothing worked, of course. I eagerly returned to class on Monday, and he explained imaginary numbers and complex variables. I was dumbstruck. It was as if I entered a new world, a new dimension, a new reality. Complex numbers are used extensively in electrical engineering especially for signal processing. Complex numbers are also used to solve the fluid flow Navier-Stokes differential equations that describe laminar flow over a cylinder. I learned complex numbers from him and CCNY amplified my understanding.

Mrs. Harriet Weissberg taught world history and political science. We spent hours and days studying Latin American history. We had to memorize the terms of the Act of Chapultepec signed in March 1945 by the US and the South American countries. This act was an updated extension of the Monroe Doctrine. It was a real big deal at the time. It is the only subject I remember from her classes.

I was enrolled in an experimental math course for college-bound students called "fusion math" taught by Mr. Benjamin Braverman, Chairman of the math department. The coursework integrated algebra and trigonometry. I learned the logic, beauty, elegance and symmetry of geometry, algebra, and trigonometry in a way that excited students to go home and do the problem sets. (I was distressed to see how math was being taught later at the Maimonides School.) I scored high in math, taking every math course that was offered. I found something I could do and worked hard at it. I even tutored algebra to students one year behind me for $0.50 an hour. My math and mechanical drawing teachers encouraged me to study engineering. There were no SATs but instead rigorous qualifying exams for students who wished to study engineering at the New York City–supported colleges. I was prepared for the exams and was accepted at CCNY to study engineering. I regret never having contacted Mr. Ellis and Mr. Braverman to thank them for preparing me for an engineering career. I did manage to see Mr. Grubman, in the school cafeteria, who taught me mechanical drawing, during one return trip to Lincoln High School one year after I graduated. I never really thanked him.

Mr. Braverman taught me the method of "casting out nines" as a check of addition, subtraction, and multiplication—useful for large numbers. Here is a simple example. Suppose we have to add the following three numbers: 206, 7,898, and 4,581.

0206	8	add:	$0 + 2 + 0 + 6 = 8$	
7898	5	add:	$7 + 8 + 9 + 8 = 32$;	add: $3 + 2 = 5$
<u>4581</u>	9	add:	<u>$4 + 5 + 8 + 1 = 18$</u>;	<u>add: $1 + 8 = 9$</u>
Correct answer is: 12,685	22	add:	$8 + 5 + 9 = 22$;	add: $2 + 2 = 4$

Add single digits of the correct answer: $1 + 2 + 6 + 8 + 5 = 22$; add $2 + 2 = 4$

The number 4 in both cases must always be the same for horizontal and vertical addition. This method is the basis of "parity checks" and is used by digital computers to check the sums of zeros and ones. This method of "casting out nines" also works when the numbers in each column are added vertically. Using the example above:

$6 + 8 + 1 = 15; 5 + 1 = 6$
$0 + 9 + 8 = 17; 1 + 7 = 8$
$2 + 8 + 5 = 15; 1 + 5 = 6$
$0 + 7 + 4 = 11; 1 + 1 = 2$
$\qquad\qquad\qquad$ 22 Add $2 + 2 = 4$ as before

So why is this not taught in many high schools? This method of checking addition may produce *false positives* if the difference between the calculated answer and correct answer differ by multiples of nine. For example, if an incorrect answer to the above addition equals 12,674, then the sum of the digits $1 + 2 + 6 + 7 + 4 = 31$. Note that $3 + 1 = 4$. I would incorrectly conclude that my addition was correct, a false positive.

Amazing! Is it not? It also works for multiplication.

68 x 27 = 1,836	68 add $6 + 8 = 14$ add $1 + 4 = 5$
	X 27 add $2 + 7 = 9$ $9 \times 5 = 45 ; 4 + 5 = 9$
	1,836
	Add $1 + 8 + 3 + 6 = 18$; add $1 + 8 = 9$

So 9 is the same in both cases.

What is more is that the final answer minus the sum of digits, after casting out 9s, is always divisible by 9. The final answer minus the sum of digits is also divisible by 3.

Example: 12,685. The sum of the digits is. 1+2+6+8+5 = 22; 2+ 2 = 4

12,685 - 4 = 12,681; 12,681/9 = 1,409 which is a whole number.

Same thing in subtraction:

Example: 1,836 - 67 = 1769

1836: Sum of digits = 1+8+3+6 = 18, 1+8 =9
67: Sum of digits = 6+7 = 13, 1+ 3 = 4
9-4 = 5
1769-5 = 1,764; 1,764/9 = 196. 196 is a whole number.

The principle is that any number, N - sum of digits = 9 times another number

In math we always seek symmetry. Can we add a number to, let us say, 1,836 and have it divisible by 9 (or by 3)? The answer is yes by adding the digits and subtracting the digits from nine. Use 1,769 as an example: Sum of digits = 1+7+6+9 = 23, 2+3 = 5; 9 - 5 = 4

Now add 4 to 1,769 = 1,773; 1,773/9 = 197. Therefore, (9) (197) - 4 = 1,769.

So why is this not taught in many high schools? This method of checking addition may produce false positives if the difference between the calculated answer and correct answer differ by multiples of nine. For example, if an incorrect answer to the above addition equals 12,674, then the sum of the digits 1 + 2 + 6 + 7 + 4 = 31. Note that 3 + 1 = 4. I would incorrectly conclude that my addition was correct, a false positive.

This method does not produce false negatives, i.e., if the horizontal and vertical additions do not agree, the answer must be wrong. This still remains a powerful method for checking arithmetic operations.

I joined the slide-rule club after school hours. I felt comfortable in the company of nerds. It was essential to know how to operate a slide rule before entering CCNY engineering. There were about ten students in the class. The teacher had six-feet-by-eighteen-inch slide rule with hooks attached to the wall at blackboard height. The horizontal moving slide was dovetailed between upper and lower parts of the stationary rule. We all used small slide rules to follow the instructor as he would slide the rule back and forth to multiply numbers, divide, and exponentiate (raise to high powers) rule. It was a powerful tool, and I used it extensively for the first fifteen years of my professional life.

All during the twelve years of schooling from kindergarten to twelfth grade, the ethnicity of my teachers reflected the ethnicity of where we lived.

In Baltimore the last names of my teachers were Ms. Parrish, Ms. Cascio, Ms. Gallahue, and Ms. Haughy.

In New York the last names of my teachers were Ms. Weiner, Ms. Rifkin, Ms. Novick, Mr. Neveloff, Mr. Blutinger, Mr. Shapiro, Mr. Kaplan (principal), Mr. Ellis, Mr. Braverman, Mr. Lorber, Mr. Grubman, Mr. Sexter, Mr. Warshower, Mr. Williams. Mr. Levine (principal), Mr. Ball, Mrs. Neufield, Mr. Offner, Mr. Silverman, and Mr. Kaiser (principal), Dr. Orgel (dean), Mr. McNally, Ms. Sorrento, Ms. Devin, and Ms. Kehoe. Only four have non-Jewish-sounding names.

Chapter 25

INTRODUCTION TO THE HOLOCAUST

My first exposure to the Holocaust evil was a film of the camps after liberation shown in 1945 at a private neighborhood club on Twenty-Ninth Street near Surf Avenue into which I sneaked. On a hot summer day, I learned of a movie being shown outdoors at the Cresco Club after dark. The club was mostly for seniors with time to play cards and share experiences. A small fee was required, but I had no money. I scaled the high chain-link fence and unobtrusively disappeared into the crowd. No one paid attention to me; a small quiet kid, I was too young to understand what I saw. I previously saw movies of *Frankenstein* and the *Wolf Man* but this seemed more real and more macabre. I stood in the back and recall vividly that the audience was moaning. Years later, I read the Nuremberg trial transcripts in English while at the CCNY library and in the basement archives of MIT and Northeastern University to gain an understanding of what happened.

In Abraham Lincoln High School, I volunteered to assist Ms. Muriel Newton, an English teacher, as the book club monitor during one free period several times per week. I unboxed, organized and sold books, and then repackaged them for the next day's sale. I was able to examine the pocketbooks on display and purchase books of interest. I bought all the books written by George Gamow about cosmology such as *1, 2, 3 Infinity* and the *Birth and Death of the Sun*. I developed an intense interest in astronomy and cosmology from his books that popularized science. A few years ago, I published an article in a Jewish magazine about the "anthropic principle," a subset of my religio-cosmological beliefs.

I displayed and purchased *Scourge of the Swastika* by Lord Russell, an observer at the Nuremberg Trials. It was an account of the horrors during the Holocaust based on testimony of the survivors. It was my second exposure to evil. We heard nothing of the Holocaust during the war, and little was discussed after the war by my parents or by refugees in the neighborhood. We called refugees "greenhorns," and we did not speak of events during 1939–1945. Tomatoes, bananas, and other fruits are green before becoming ripe. That is the origin of "greenhorn." I could not read the book in one sitting. It was too upsetting and gave me nightmares. I promised myself to do what I could to prevent me from ever being trapped in that situation. I fantasized myself rescuing Jews and killing Nazis in my reveries. After fifty years from high school, I acknowledge there is evil in the world, for which no excuses are acceptable, and use of force is necessary. I was fortunate to be in a position to strengthen the forces of the United States that may be used to discourage or even defeat those evil doers during the time I was employed by the Department of Defense.

Until Elie Wiesel was awarded a professorship at BU and lectured about those dreadful years, the Holocaust was all but forgotten. During our trip to Prague, Dorothy and I visited Theresenstadt and Auschwitz. She smelled or imagined she smelled the smoke. I did present a slide showing to our shul members. One of our members, a survivor of Auschwitz, thought he recognized his barrack after fifty-seven years.

I graduated high school in June 1953. I returned for my fiftieth reunion in 2003. It was a moving experience for me to sit in the same classrooms as I did during the 1950s. I remember the large murals in the auditorium and the librarian's desk in the school library where I spent hours browsing through picture books. I met a few people I knew during my stay in high school. I saw the name of my math teacher, Mr. Benjamin Braverman, listed on the honor roll opposite the entrance to the auditorium with other illustrious teachers who are no longer teaching.

Chapter 26

BROOKLYN COLLEGE AND CITY COLLEGE OF NEW YORK (CCNY)

In high school Mr. Benjamin Braverman, chairman of the math department and my teacher par excellence, asked me what I wanted to do after graduation. I enjoyed Mr. Grubman's classes in mechanical drawing, so I answered that I wanted to become a draftsman. I was able to visualize in three dimensions and convert two-dimensional drawings into multiple views. Mr. Braverman suggested that I work toward becoming an engineer. I had no idea what engineers did. I only knew that somehow I wanted to become a professional person. I watched my father struggle to earn a living without an education. My father used to tell me that I could be whatever I wanted, but he would break my bones if I became a house painter. He spoke figuratively, of course. I continued to major in mathematics taking the most advanced courses in solid geometry and calculus at Lincoln High School. I observed that the students were serious students and all directed toward science, math, and engineering.

During the senior year at high school, I applied to Brooklyn College for admission into the pre-engineering program with plans to complete the program at CCNY. Brooklyn College was much closer, and I was advised that that the quality of instruction at Brooklyn College would prepare me for CCNY. Acceptance into Brooklyn College was competitive, and acceptance into the engineering program was even more competitive. I learned later that one-third of my entering class dropped out of the engineering program. Brooklyn

College was part of the college system of New York, and tuition was free. Acceptance was based on grades, a qualifying exam, and character references. I never heard of Cooper Union, and there was no way I could afford to go anywhere else. Late spring of 1953, I received a letter of acceptance. It was a miracle because my grades in social studies and history were average. My grades in French were B+, and my grades in math were A. I was not a verbal person.

AFROTC and Pershing Rifles

During the first week on campus, I explored Boylan and Ingersoll Halls. In the basement of Boylan Hall was a table with brochures describing the Air Force Reserve Officers Training Corps (ROTC). This was an opportunity to join the military, acquire a free uniform, and possibly enter the advanced corps and earn an eventual commission as an air force lieutenant. I would have a job upon graduation. This was particularly attractive, and I would have to take one or two classes a week to learn about the air force and military history and customs. I would have to participate in close order drill sessions during the week fully in uniform. I learned how to carry a rifle and give orders to our company and flight as we marched on the quadrangle. There were no antimilitary views at that time, but there were still people who believed that the military should have no presence at a liberal arts college. Eventually ROTC was disbanded in the 1960s or 1970s by order of the City University of New York. I served as an AFROTC honor guard at the graduation in June 1954 at Brooklyn College.

A military subgroup called the Pershing Rifles named after General John Pershing of WWI fame attracted me. They were more enthusiastic than the regular ROTC students, so I joined. Drill sessions were on Saturday mornings followed by ice cream at Jahn's, a local establishment. I drilled with regularity and eventually learned how to do a Queen Anne salute with an M-16 by throwing it over my shoulder. I was not good at it and worried about dropping the rifle. These fellows became my social friends and during the year, and I was invited to the annual military ball. The experience was daunting. I did not know how to dance, and I did not smoke or drink beer.

So I invited a young lady with whom I was friendly because we rode the same yellow bus to Brooklyn College. She lived much closer to the school. She refused my offer for a date, and this was the first of many refusals. The second year I was set up, and I went to the military ball, but the whole affair lacked content, and I was unenthused. I did not feel that I belonged.

I pledged for Pershing Rifles and was accepted as a pledge. I experienced no physical hazing. However, I could be stopped by any cadet upperclassman in Pershing Rifles and made to stand at attention and answer questions testing basic knowledge about the government, the military, and the cow. The question about the cow went like this:

Upperclassman: How is the cow?

Pershing Rifle Pledge at attention: Sir, she walks, she talks, and she's full of chalk. The lacteal fluid extracted from the female of the bovine species is highly prolific to the nth degree, sir.

I learned all the marching movements for close-order drill and participated in the giant parade down Fifth Avenue on Memorial Day carrying my rifle. I did well on the exams and continued the program next year. My instructor, First Lieutenant Biedencap, invited his students to fly in a DC3 leaving Floyd Bennett field in New York City. I went along and actually handled the airplane controls for five minutes banking the aircraft left and right and going up and down. I felt the power. But flying did not interest me, and wearing glasses would disqualify me from any flight training as a pilot or navigator. The standards were strict. Glasses might fall off in flight or break or become foggy.

In one assignment, I was tasked to create a bombing dossier for a target in New York City. We had to answer such questions as how large is the target, how well is it protected, what is the expected outcome on military capability, how many bombs and airplanes are needed to destroy the target, etc. I chose the storage railroad yards at Coney Island as my target. I measured the geometry from maps. I counted the number of stationary trains at night that would be hit. I estimated the damage and the disruption to the city. I walked all around the storage yards from Stillwell Avenue to Cropsy Avenue and Brighton Beach to get a real feel of the target. I felt like a spy. It was stupid but exciting. I put a lot of work into it. I earned a high grade. I served as a military honor guard at graduation services in June 1954. Academic Dean Dr. Mario Cosenza was awarded with a degree Doctor of Humane Letters. I never learned the content of those letters, the recipients, and their purpose. What was humane about the letters?

As a member of the AFROTC I was asked to participate in Operation Skywatch. Once a week, on the way home from Brooklyn College, I would leave the Brighton subway line walk to a nearby tall building, take the elevator to the top floor and walk to the roof. On the roof was a small enclosed hut with glass all around, a desk with a telephone and a pair of binoculars. My task was to call in airplanes flying toward or from the shore to a call-in center. I had to identify the airplanes as cargo, commercial, or military. I was proud to have participated in National Defense. From Wickipedia below:

The **Ground Observer Corps**, sometimes erroneously referred to as the Ground *Observation Corps*, was the name of two American civil defense organizations.

The first **Ground Observer Corps** was a World War II Civil Defense program of the United States Army Air Forces to protect against air attack. The 1.5 million civilian observers at 14,000 coastal observation posts used naked eye and binocular searches to search for German and Japanese aircraft until the program ended in 1944.[1]

Observations were telephoned to filter centers, which forwarded authenticated reports to the Aircraft Warning Service which also received reports from the Army Radar Stations.

This is my pin that I wore on my ROTC uniform.
I still have the pin.

The second Ground Observer Corps[2] was reformed during the Cold War as an arm of the United States Air Force Civil Defense network which provided aircraft tracking with over 200,000 civilian volunteers. The corps was established in early 1950 to supplement the Lashup Radar Network and a permanent radar network[3] started with "ADC radar site" P-1 (McChord AFB) on June 1, 1950. "Filter centers" (e.g., in New Haven, Connecticut[4] and Baltimore, Maryland[2]) received telephoned voice information from 8,000 posts, and the information was relayed to Air Defense Command ground control interception centers.[5]

By 1952 the program was expanded in Operation Skywatch with over 750,000 volunteers at over 16 thousand posts (98 per post in shifts) and 75 centers. The program ended in 1958] with the advent of the automated 1959 USAF radar network (SAGE) and the automated Army networks (Missile Master). The first officially commissioned rural skywatch tower was the Cairo Skywatch Tower. It was listed on the National Register of Historic Places in 2002.

The Skywatch sessions lasted an hour. I relieved a person before me and was replaced by someone after me. I had to keep a log of my observations. I suspect that all the logs of useless information about flying, arriving and departing aircraft to and from Idlewild Airport (renamed later to JFK Airport) and Floyd Bennett Field were eventually disgarded.

Descriptive Geometry

People asked me about the most difficult college course that I ever took. Without a doubt, the most intellectually difficult course was at Brooklyn College called Descriptive Geometry or known as Design 32.1 followed by Design 32.2. These were mandatory courses for entry into CCNY engineering. Descriptive geometry is probably not taught anymore. The coursework involved converting three-dimensional objects into two-dimensional drawings that could be made in a machine shop or forged from a solid boule in a factory. The second semester involved the design of three-dimensional objects by providing two views plus auxiliary views so that a machinist could make the part. For example, how do you show the intersection of two different diameter pipes at an acute angle? How do you show the intersection of a triangular prism and a tetrahedron? The exercises were mind-bending, and many students dropped out of class. I included two illustrations from a workbook. I also included a photo of Dr. Sowers, the professor who taught the course. The blackboard is filled with intersecting planes, points, circles, and lines. Mr. Grubman taught me mechanical drawing at Abraham Lincoln High School, but that was real easy but Descriptive Geometry was a real mind-bending bear or, in New England language, "a wicked pissah." Currently, CAD-CAM (computer-aided design–computer-aided manufacture) programs do all that and create a DVD that is input to a computer that instructs a milling machine to machine the part. Currently, 3D printing avoids the need for any visualization of the part being made. An entry clerk just selects the part from a catalog, clicks on a mouse, answers a few questions about size and geometry, and the computer directs the printer to make the part. The need for a mechanical engineer to imagine the part, design the part, create the necessary correct drawings for a machinist is no longer necessary except for brand new parts or parts with a unique design for which no algorithm exists. Computer software can provide a visual display of any part from any angle, enlarge it, and show an assembly of multiparts. All this happened within sixty years of my lifetime. I witnessed a revolution in machine design. Design 32.1 and 32.2 sharpened my ability to visualize objects in 3D from 2D drawings and project objects in 3D to 2D drawings, which was the purpose of the course.

CCNY

In January 1956 I switched over to city college. Not gifted enough to major in pure physics or mathematics and not interested in the details of practical engineering, I fashioned a program in engineering-physics and prepared myself for the most difficult courses by studying math for every semester. I worked hard to stay in school riding and studying on the subway and bus two hours each way to and

FROM BROOKLYN NY TO BROOKLINE MA

from Coney Island. I read texts on the subway and scanned the ads and the faces of the monthly Ms. Subways and dreamed of faraway places, forests, mountains, and clean rivers and wondered if I could ever leave Brooklyn to see them. Eventually, I did.

I immediately purchased a slide rule for $24, a lot of money at that time, and burned my name into the inside leather case. I purchased all my textbooks with the money I earned during the summer selling hot dogs. I used the slide rule for the first fifteen years of my working life until the introduction of electronic calculators made slide rules a museum piece. After one-third of my career, I felt that I too belonged in a museum next to the slide rule and Napier log tables.

I found most of the liberal arts courses uninteresting and the engineering courses stimulating and difficult. Memorizing was useless. The daily problem sets in physics, engineering, and math stretched my mind. The most difficult course I ever encountered, a killer, was Design 32.1 and 32.2 taught by Dr. Sowers. We had to prepare front, side, top, and auxiliary views of machine components and then reconstruct the part in three dimensions such as two unequal diameter cylinders intersecting at an odd angle. In 1989 CAD/CAM programs made all that mind-bending work on the drawing board obsolete. No one does that anymore.

I attended summer school to complete language requirements and often attended the outdoor evening concerts at Lewisohn Stadium on the city college campus. I heard Roberta Peters, operatic diva, sing the arias from *Carmen*, and I had goose bumps. I heard the great classical works that summer and later while living in Cambridge, Massachusetts, visited the music library at MIT and purchased open reel tapes so I could enjoy hearing them over and over. I built my own high-fidelity system from Heathkit with all the power electron tubes and circuits that are now unavailable and obsolete. CCNY opened my soul to the beauty of classical music.

50 year reunion at CCNY on 5/30/2008. Food served to us was kosher.

Dr. Sowers teaching Design 32.1 and 32.2—Mind bending training to twist geometric figures to be drawn from multiple views. Course was responsible for for large dropout for engineering students

FROM BROOKLYN NY TO BROOKLINE MA

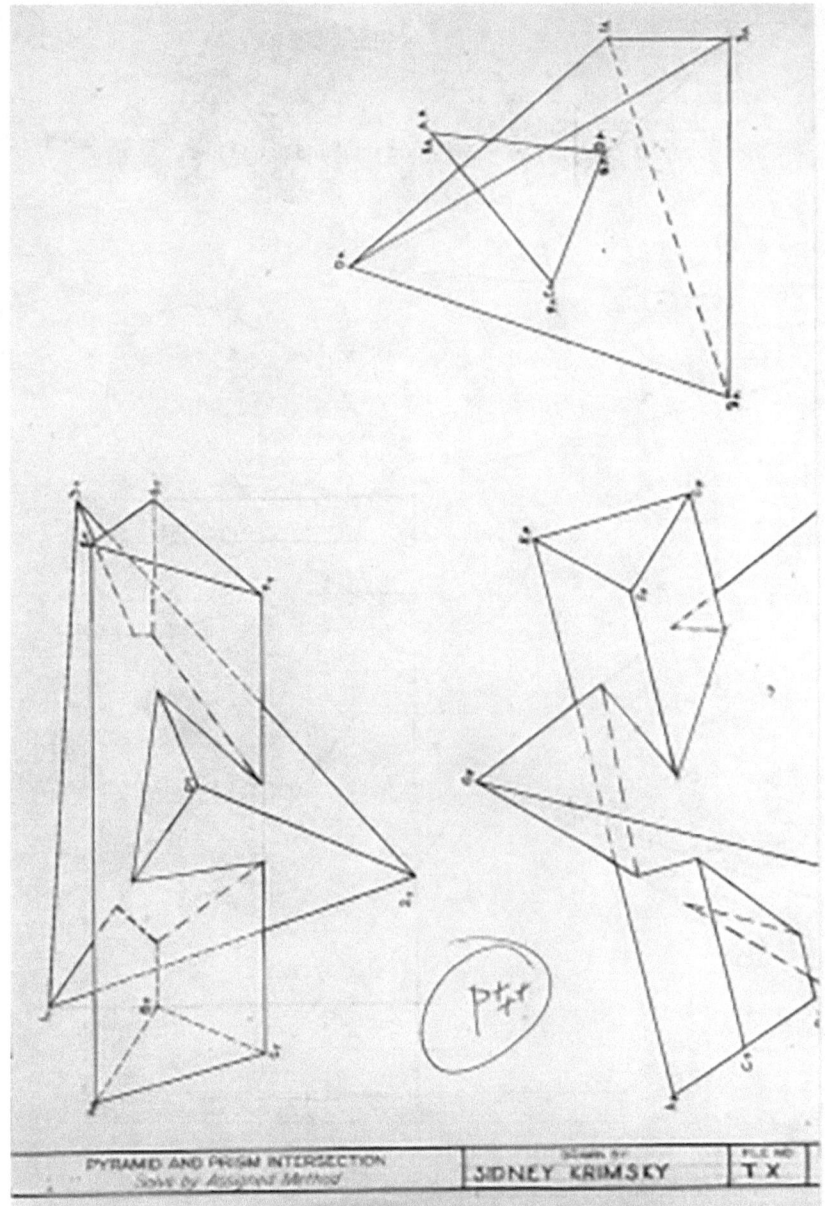

Example from Course Design 32.1
Intersection of a prism and a pyramid.
Draw the intersection in two views showing solid and dotted lines.

Example from Course Design 32.1
Two cylinders intersecting.
Draw the intersection in two views using solid and dotted lines.

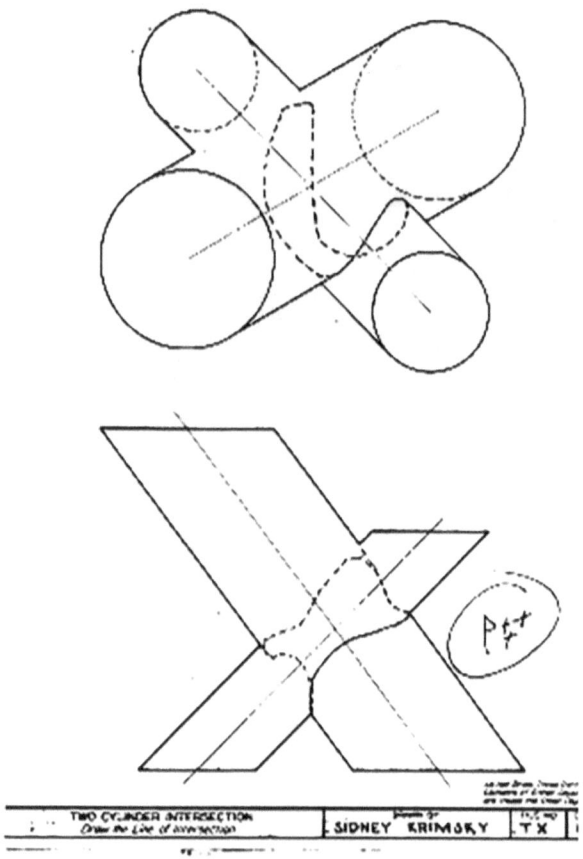

Example from Course design 32.1
Intersection of two cylinders
Draw the intersection in two views showing solid and dotted lines

Sid Krimsky as a member of the Pershing Rifles,
ROTC at CCNY during 1956.

Chapter 26.1

CONCEPT OF THE ALMIGHTY

My concept of the Almighty (God) evolved at CCNY. The elegance of mathematics to describe the physical world was a thing of beauty. Solving the Navier-Stokes equations to describe fluid flow, Maxwell equations to describe electricity and magnetic fields, Fourier equations and Bessel functions for heat flow, and Newton's equations for mechanics and kinematics, and the mathematics to describe thermodynamics, filled me with awe. These equations described the relationships between force, motion, energy, temperature, and material properties that yielded predictive results. I learned in high school about imaginary numbers and learned at CCNY how imaginary numbers were used to solve real problems in electrical engineering that produced measurable results. I learned in high school the equation $e^{ipi} + 1 = 0$ where pi = the Greek letter pi = 3.141592. If that equation is untrue, the whole structure of electrical engineering might collapse.

    I learned that Isaac Newton believed in a cosmological god, a clockmaker who wound up the heavenly bodies and afterward showed little interest. But the equations showed a mathematical construct from atoms to the solar system and how they all behaved. There was a structure to all this phenomena that, in my opinion, had to be designed by a supreme intelligence.

    If the major physical constants such as the universal gravitational constant, Planck's constant, solar constant (energy reaching Earth), invariant velocity of light, Avogadro's number, distance of the earth from the sun, universal gravitational constant, the charge on the electron, the strong force binding protons in the nucleus of cells, etc., differed from their present values, the solar system and universe could not exist as we know it. These are finely tuned constants that could not have been randomly arrived by natural selection or random mutations.

In biology I studied evolution and the belief that humans emerged from an amoeba by a series of genetic mutations over millions of years. All creatures followed a similar pattern. If giraffes slowly grew longer necks to eat plants high up on trees, then we should be able to find giraffe bones with different neck sizes as fossils. The bones of millions of expected transitional species have not been found after looking for over one hundred years. Yes, finches grew larger beaks when the nuts they were eating grew in size. The genetic structure was coded to permit small changes in beaks when the size of the food supply changed. The great paleontologist Jay Stephen Gould recognized this and emerged with a novel idea he called "punctuated equilibrium" in which different species were created in a compressed time, but how did all the varieties of species emerge in a short time? I found it hard to accept that gross changes in species between phyla allowed an amoeba to become a bird through a series of random mutations in a reasonable amount of time. We learned in class that most mutations were not transferred to progeny but were discarded. Punctuated equilibrium pointed to an intelligent process. Some scientists suggested that the earth was seeded by an outside intelligence that landed on earth but offered no evidence. Darwin did not know about DNA, and neither did my biology professors. Changing from an amoeba to a human via DNA changes by mutations seemed even less likely given the time required. I saw no connection between natural selection postulated by Darwin and changes at the molecular level.

Nachmanides (1124–1270) wrote in the thirteenth century that the world started from something the size of a mustard seed. How could he have known that? From the *Wikipedia*:

> *The Ramban explains the creation of the world in a very unique way. It seems to be very innovative*

and intriguing. In his sefer Toras Hashem Temima in perek 7 siman 37, He says,

"When the Torah says (Genesis 1:1) 'In the beginning, G-D created the heavens and the earth.' The word 'in the beginning' means 'at first' like Onkelos explains 'at the beginning' and not a word that means close to the beginning, but rather actually the first thing done. The verse is telling us that in the beginning, G-D, who is the creator of all forces, created the heavens and earth. This means that He created these things from absolute nothingness. The thing that was created was a small object that was as small as a seed of mustard; this was the heavens and everything in it. There was also another small dot that was created and this contained the earth and all that is contained in it. This is the primordial matter for the heavens and the primordial matter for the earth."

The Ramban's first point here is very deep. He is telling us that there is no physicality before this act of G-D. G-D existed before space, time and any type of matter. However, the first thing that happened was the creation of the heavens and earth. G-D created the Earth as well as the heavens (outer space). This seems to be going according to Aristotelian physics that says the Earth is made up of different matter than space. It also tells us that just like G-D is not bound within our Earthly world, he is not contained within outer space either. This is probably why we are able to comprehend what is in space, because we share basic rules with it, but we are still unable to understand G-D's existence.

The Ramban also tells us that G-D is the creator of all forces. I think that this reveals that, according to the Ramban, G-D created all the forces that govern the universe, spiritual and physical, at this time. The physics of the material world, be it space or Earth, have existed ever since the beginning of any existence outside of G-D.

The fact that the Ramban says that G-D created a primordial matter for the heavens and another primordial matter for the earth is remarkable. Also, the fact that he says that these primordial matters were the size of mustard seeds and that they contained everything that was to be in the heavens and the earth shows how scientific the Ramban was. His position is that G-D used these tiny spheres of material, heavenly material and earthly material, to then create everything that was to exist in the heavenly world (outer space) and the earthly world. What does that remind you of? Sounds like a similar scientific approach similar to the big bang and evolution to me. If not directly, it at least leaves the possibility of an evolution of material that uses science and physics to explain the creation of the two worlds.

During the twentieth century, there was an argument among cosmologists as to whether the universe was being continuously created and existed forever or started from a point in space followed by a gigantic explosion. LeMaitre, who was a priest, first came up with the big bang. George Gamow supported the big bang theory, and Fred Hoyle supported continuous creation. Hoyle's ideas were supported by atheists who believe that the universe was forever there and not subject to God-like forces and changes. Gamow's ideas supported the existence of a supreme being and were consistent with the writings of Nachmanides (RAMBAN). Subsequent data on the red shift and expansion of the universe convinced scientists that the universe expanded from a small entity. Finally, this was put to bed by the discovery of Penzias and Wilson of the background radiation that was pervasive in all directions throughout the universe. Their discovery is analogous to the presence of nonvisible heat (infrared) from a large fire after the visible flames have disappeared. From the time-temperature history of the heat, engineers can tell at what time the fire started. Prof. Brian Greene at MIT called the expansion inflation and wrote many books about this subject. But we have to remind ourselves that Nachmanides wrote this down in the thirteenth century:

> *In 1959, a survey was done of leading American scientists. Among the many questions asked was: "What do you believe is the age of the universe?" That year, astronomy was popular but cosmology—the deeper understanding of the universe's physics—was just developing. The responses to the survey was recently published in the Scientific American, the world's most widely read scientific magazine. Two-thirds of the scientists gave the same answer. The answer of the overwhelming majority of scientists was: "Beginning? There was no beginning. 2400 years ago Aristotle and Plato taught that the universe is infinite. Yes, we know the Bible says 'In the beginning', but this is a great story that helps kids fall asleep at night. We sophisticates know better: There is no beginning."*

That was in 1959. Then in 1965, Penzias and Wilson found the echo of the big bang in the darkness of the sky at night, and the world's view changed from believing in an infinite universe to a universe that had a beginning. Science had made an enormous change in its perception of the world.

The world had a beginning. The Torah was right, and only a supreme being of super intelligence could have provided a Torah and provided Nachmonides with such insight.

But is it possible that a small mass could have done this? I learned from Gamow's books that hydrogen, when forced under high pressure and temperature, can be transmuted into helium. This is called fusion and is the source of heat and light emanating from the sun. It is a several step process, but the final mass balance shows that the mass of all of the protons of hydrogen that went into the conversion is greater than the mass of the equal number of protons of helium. The difference is called the mass decrement. The lost mass is converted into energy in accordance with Albert's Einstein's equation $e=mc^2$. Scientists pride themselves in discovering symmetry in physics so is the reverse true? Can energy become mass? The answer is yes. Data from the CERN Large Hadron collider has shown that energy passing through the Higgs field that permeates all of space can become mass. Physicists are still grappling with the cause of all the mass in the universe.

Fast-forward to the *Wall Street Journal*, Friday, December 26, 2014, page A11: "Science Increasingly Makes the Case for God." "Today there are more than 200 known parameters necessary for a planet to support life-every single one of which must be perfectly met or the whole thing falls apart." The author is Eric Metaxas. This is called the anthropic principle, an anathema for atheists.

People evolving from amoebas seem to me to contradict the second law of thermodynamics because the simple organism is growing from less order to a more complex being. The same thing happens when two human cells combine and grow into a baby far more complex than the two cells from which they originated. Even more amazing is that the two cells have no conscience. We know that birds can grow longer beaks over time to reach food that diminishes because of insects or draught or that certain insects can change their color to minimize attacks by parasites. Evolutions call this natural selection. But I believe that the expression of these features is already coded in the DNA of the creatures. But we can't know this until the creature is threatened, and then the defensive feature is expressed.

Even trees when threatened by insect attacks are able to produce a chemical substance that makes their leaves less appetizing to attacking insects.

I left CCNY believing in a supreme intelligence but one that allowed suffering to exist especially among the Jewish people for thousands of years. I spent the next fifty years asking why and never found an answer that satisfied me until I learned from Rabbi Gedaliah Fleer about the role of free will.

Chapter 26.2

PAY-AS-YOU-SEE TV

After WWII and during the 1950s, TV viewing was free. The TV and radio broadcasts were transmitted over the air. Frequencies were regulated by the FCC to avoid signal interference. The airwaves were in the public domain and citizens did not have to pay for their use. About 1950 the FCC started to listen to earnest solicitations from pay-TV proponents, and in March 1958 the FCC agreed to authorize trial runs of various pay-TV systems over the air waves for three years. Pay-TV was debated thoroughly during the 1950s. Should the nation's forty million TV set owners pay only $2 per week to receive programs of their choice? Pay-TV stations would issue a decoder to subscribers. The financial stakes were high. The total expenses would amount to $4 billion per year, a huge amount of revenue at that time that could be taxed. Various schemes were designed to collect the fee from coin boxes to acquire the channel or pay via monthly billing. The proponents of pay TV proposed using telephone wires with large frequency separations between phone calls and TV signals.

The opponents said that audiences will be divided along economic lines and the programming would not be any better than currently viewed. The opponents feared that pay-TV would eventually use the same frequencies as free TV, wiping out free TV.

The arguments favoring pay TV at that time were to improve the quality of transmissions by using telephone wires instead of transmitting signals over the air that could be distorted by atmospheric effects, reflections, interference, etc. Pay TV would stimulate better programming and engineering inventiveness. Pay TV would encourage competition for better programming and better hardware. With better programming, movies would suffer and they did. On Tuesday nights for years, *Milton Berle* followed by the *Texaco Star Theater* captivated audiences all over the country, and the movie theaters were empty. Movie theaters started to offer gifts to Tuesday night patrons to reattract them. However, *Milton Berle*, the *Texaco Star Theater*, *The Honeymooners* and the *Ed Sullivan Show* were huge draws for large audiences and advertisers. Many smaller movie houses closed; they could not compete.

In 1961 the commissioner of the FCC Newton Minow, appointed by President John Kennedy, spoke before the National Association of Broadcasters and said, "When television is good, nothing—not the theater, not the magazines or newspapers—nothing is better.

"But when television is bad, nothing is worse. I invite you to sit down in front of your television set when your station goes on the air and stay there without a book, magazine, newspaper, profit and-loss sheet or rating book to distract you—and keep your eyes glued to that set until the station signs off. I can assure you that you will observe a vast wasteland. You will see a procession of game shows, violence, audience-participation shows, formula comedies about totally unbelievable families, blood and thunder, mayhem, violence, sadism, murder, western bad men, western good men, private eyes, gangsters, more violence and cartoons. And, endlessly, commercials—many screaming, cajoling and offending. And most of all, boredom! True, you will see a few things you will enjoy. But they will be very, very few. And if you think I exaggerate, try it."

"Is there one person in this room who claims that broadcasting can't do better? Well, a glance at next season's proposed programming can give us little heart. Of 73 1/2 hours of prime evening time, the networks have tentatively scheduled 59 hours to categories of 'action-adventure, situation comedy, variety, quiz shows and movies?'

"Is there one network president in this room who claims he can't do better? Well, is there at least one network president who believes that the other networks can't do better? Gentlemen, your trust accounting with your beneficiaries is overdue. Never have so few owed so much to so many."

"Why is so much of television so bad? I have heard many answers: demands of your advertisers; competition for ever-higher ratings; the need always to attract a mass audience; the high cost of television programs; the insatiable appetite for programming material—these are some of them. Unquestionably these are tough problems not susceptible to easy answers."

"But I am not convinced that you have tried hard enough to solve them...and I am not convinced that the people's taste is as low as some of you assume."

Newton Minow's comments hit the airwaves and newspapers like an explosion. TV programming improved, but the plebian interests dominated the airwaves and phone wires with sporting events, mayhem, and weather. Walter Cronkite became the national news anchor and people hung on to his words as they would a college professor. He followed in the footsteps of Edward R. Murrow. In December 1957, in a college class, I participated in a speech debate about the introduction of pay-as-you-see TV. I was assigned the negative side.

Fast-forward to September 1972. In the summer of 1972, the board of selectmen of the town of Brookline issued a call for volunteers to serve on the first Community Antenna Television Committee (CATV). I volunteered to serve on the CATV committee and served for two years. Eighteen people volunteered. The chairman was an electrical engineer familiar with signals transmission.

We conducted our own analysis for the cost to viewers and benefits to the public. Costs for the vendor involved tearing up streets for laying cable; constructing and maintaining broadcasting studios, antenna, and headband construction; and placing cables on telephone poles. Customers would absorb the maintenance costs for the cable system and depreciation costs for the construction of studios. We met with members of the school, health, and building departments to assess their needs and figure out how a CATV system could help them.

After the first year, we concluded that the programming and transmissions were not sufficiently developed to benefit to the town and consumers as compared with free TV.

We met once a week in town hall to evaluate proposals submitted by potential CATV vendors, visited vendor sites and studios where broadcasting was in preparation, and prepared policy recommendations after speaking with community members. A major driver was the potential for improved reception than was available over the airwaves.

After the first year, we concluded that the programming and transmissions were not sufficiently developed to benefit to the town and consumers as compared with free TV. However, we became aware of the tremendous potential to provide two-way communications from the home of the subscriber to the broadcast station. We assessed that the following services were possible: educational networks between schools, police and fire department community services, home alarm systems, remote meter readings, shopping services, library access, and health care services. Eventually, these services all came into existence via cable through the internet.

Meanwhile, The Great and General Court of the Commonwealth of Massachusetts established the Massachusetts Cable Commission. Each city and town was authorized to investigate for itself a general assessment of cable TV and the potential introduction of cable TV into the community. We reviewed the regulations proposed by the Massachusetts Cable Commission.

At the end of the second year, we reversed our decision and recommended that the selectmen issue a franchise to a specific cable company that was committed to broadcasting selectmen's hearings, football games at the high school, and other public events on Cable TV. CATV came to Brookline and with it all the public benefits and costs to the consumer. Free TV was still available; but with tall buildings, multiple reflections, and storms, most people chose cable because of superior reception. I was proud to serve on that committee and share ideas and learn from the senior members. Our committee brought Cable TV to Brookline. I would never have been able to participate in New York City.

Chapter 27

J. ROBERT OPPENHEIMER LECTURE

In my junior year, a notice on the bulletin board of the physics department at CCNY announced a lecture by J. Robert Oppenheimer at Columbia University in the evening, in Pupin Hall, discussing "some outstanding problems in theoretical physics." Wow! I ascended the stairs to the subway at 125th Street and Broadway and emerged at 116th Street, Columbia University. I walked past the Low Library with its large granite dome and magnificent plaza to seek the auditorium in Pupin Hall, the physics building. The lights were dim. Dr. Oppenheimer—technical lead for the development of the atomic bomb at Los Alamos, New Mexico (Manhattan Project)—sat on a barstool-type chair in front of a blackboard on the stage. He was tall and thin, slightly bent, well tailored with a closely cropped haircut. His demeanor and presentation mesmerized me. I was totally unprepared to follow the depth of his thesis and arguments. He spoke about test results from high-energy particle collision experiments from which the collisions produced new particles called mesons and left a track in Wilson cloud chambers that could be photographed. Mesons are too small to be seen. The size of mesons are between a proton and an electron. The word meson comes from the Greek meaning intermediate size. Mesons are composed of a quark and an anti-quark. Quarks were discovered after Oppenheimer. Quarks are believed to overcome the repulsive forces among protons by binding them together in the nucleus. Gluons were discovered later as the source of binding forces.

The components of atoms, namely, protons, electrons, neutrons, and neutrinos, were discovered during an earlier era.

Using high-energy bombardment of matter, recent collision experiments now yielded a plethora of new particles emerging from the collisions. The concept was to bombard the atomic nucleus with higher and higher energy particles and study the breakup of the nucleus. Did the protons and neutrons consist of yet smaller particles? What was the secret of the strong force that binds all the positively charged protons in the nucleus and keeps them from flying apart? The presiding belief was that atomic particles such as protons, electrons, and neutrons cannot be created or destroyed. However, a new class of subatomic particles expressed for very short times were observed from energetic collisions from millions to billions of electron volts in cyclotrons and then bevatrons (billions of electron volts). The challenge to physicists was to explain all this and emerge with a complete model. An analogy in medicine would be to observe that living organisms express antibodies only in response to a disease; otherwise, we would never know that organisms have the potential to express these antibodies. Years later, we learned that at subatomic levels, energy, and matter are interchangeable. In the following years, nineteen different subatomic particles would be identified named quarks in addition to even smaller particles with shorter lifetimes. King Solomon wrote, "He who increases knowledge increases sorrow." The sorrow increased for the high-energy physicists who wanted to probe deeper and deeper into the origin of all matter and were frustrated by finding more complexity and never enough money to build facilities for testing their ideas. Finally, Congress rebelled and refused to fund the billions of dollars needed to build the super collider in Texas. The Europeans built a giant super collider in Cern, Switzerland, for the study of matter in which many graduate students conduct experiments. The super collider will enable protons to collide by traveling in opposite directions at speeds 99.999 percent. The speed of light and detectors will sense the particles and photons produced from that collision that may last a few nanoseconds. This is supposed to simulate conditions that existed at the time of creation of the universe.

The Stanford linear accelerator is two miles long and accelerates particles to 99.99 percent the speed of light. The particles think they are in a three-foot tube because time and distance shrink at such high speeds according to the Lorentz-Fitzgerald contraction I learned about all this by reading George Gamow's books in high school. This is all consistent with relativistic mechanics established by Albert Einstein. George Gamow popularized Einstein's works. I regret that I was unable to ever meet Albert Einstein. He was very modest and approachable. I would have asked him the physical meaning of fourth-dimensional space-time as calculated by the Pythagorean theorem.

General Leslie Groves was the military lead of the Manhattan Project. He was the commanding officer of the Army Corps of Engineers of the District of Manhattan, New York City, and selected by President Roosevelt to lead the effort to develop an atomic bomb and manage the scientists. Oppenheimer reported to Groves. The problems outlined by Oppenheimer have yielded to half century of research only to emerge with new unanswered questions and new particles, too small to measure and having short lifetimes but not too small to contemplate and include in the wave equations that define subatomic matter. The search for small particles continues.

Chapter 28

SELLING BIBLES

As one semester ended, I looked for other ways to earn some income during the summer besides working at Nathan's Famous in Coney Island. I wanted to try something different. I responded to a newspapers ad to make an appointment to learn about a new opportunity to earn full time or part time income with little necessary training. On a warm day in June, I wore a pressed suit and took the subway to midtown Manhattan to learn about this new opportunity. I located the nondescript building, walked into a small open elevator, closed the pantograph-linked doors, and rode the elevator to the middle of the tall building, pulled the lever to open the doors, and found the room number. I knocked and walked in. I saw a small office the size of several closets, with lots of boxes filled with books stacked against the walls, a man sitting behind a desk, not much older than me with a desk stacked with boxes and books. From his language and mannerisms, I concluded he was Jewish and he was operating a business. He explained that he was a regional distributor of Christian Bibles for a national publishing house, and he was constructing a task force to sell Bibles. These Bibles were not available in stores. He wanted me to sell Bibles.

What were these Bibles? These newly printed Bibles were prepared primarily for Catholics and had the papal imprimatur. The Bibles were a work of art. It contained the Old and New Testaments. The edges of the pages were gold; there were lots of color illustrations of the patriarchs, of Moses in Egypt, and of the suffering of Jesus. My potential supervisor explained that these new Bibles will be easy to sell because of the large print, beautiful illustrations, papal imprimatur, red tasseled bookmark, and a new easy-to-read font in English or Spanish. I asked him, "How do I sell these?" He told me to start by visiting the small shops employing women in the garment industry who were mostly Italian and Latinos. He suggested some buildings to visit and I should approach the supervisor and ask permission to present this new beautiful Bible during the employee breaks. I carried a script, order blanks, and only a few demonstration Bibles since these were heavy. Payments could be stretched out upon receipt of the order. Credit cards did not exist, so everything was transacted on forms separated with carbon paper.

I took a few Bibles and visited some small shops in the garment district. The supervisors were gruff and suspicious but allowed me to address the ladies during their break time. I paraphrased a script on the importance of the Bible and the effort to produce an easily read edition with beautiful colored illustrations separated and protected from the printed pages by special tissue paper to preserve the quality of the illustrations and high-contrast font in English or Spanish. There were blank pages to record personal histories and family members. Everyone should own such a new Bible. I made my pitch. No one was interested in making a purchase. Were the books too heavy or too costly, or did I not relate to them? I visited two such shops with the same disappointing results. I sold nothing, felt stupid, and the whole adventure did not feel right. I was better off selling hot dogs in the heat than wearing a suit in midtown Manhattan in the summer.

I called my supervisor; and he advised me to take my samples home, leave the subway, and make cold calls in the Bay Ridge section of Brooklyn occupied by many Italians in attractive brick walkups. I left the subway, selected a street, walked up the steps of several houses, but first checked the names to make sure the occupants were not Jewish. I rang the bells, knocked on the doors, and housewives who were home answered the door. I made my pitch on the doorway. Women were unafraid to talk with me on the doorway; they were used to salesmen knocking on their doors. Besides, this was an Italian section of Brooklyn, and any inappropriate business would be dealt with in Italian fashion. I had no luck making any sales.

Next day, I returned the Bibles, order blanks, and sales material to the regional sales director. I felt relieved because sales are something I did not enjoy doing. A product should sell itself and not need a persuader. I learned that I could not relate to people on their level. It was better for me to sell hot dogs for which there was a high demand and required no selling. I returned to Nathan's Famous to sell hot dogs. Customers did not need convincing.

Chapter 29

SPUTNIK

The first communications satellite Sputnik was launched by the Soviet Union in October 1957 followed by media-frenzied exaggerated fears of weapons raining down on America from space. Prof. Mark Zemansky, chairman of the physics department, conducted a series of seminars for liberal arts students explaining why objects in orbit do not fall to earth. I was amused by the need for a lecture series; any student of physics understood gravity and centrifugal acceleration as explained by Isaac Newton three hundred years ago. Albert Einstein modified Newtonian mechanics with a more sophisticated view of gravity in his general theory of relativity, but he confessed that he did not understand the source of gravity. We still do not understand the source of universal gravitation that pervades the universe, but we still use Newton's equations to describe all ballistic and satellite trajectories in addition to flight paths to the planets.

Sputnik means *companion* and/or *fellow traveler* in Russian and was extended to mean *satellite* since Sputnik was a communications companion.

According to Daniel Boorstin, "Never before had so small and so harmless an object created such consternation" (Daniel J. Boorstin, *The Americans: The Democratic Experience*):

> *"Listen now," said the NBC radio network announcer on the night of October 4, 1957, "for the sound that forevermore separates the old from the*

new." Next came the chirping in the key of A-flat from outer space that the Associated Press called the "deep beep-beep." Emanating from a simple transmitter aboard the Soviet Sputnik satellite, the chirp lasted three-tenths of a second, followed by a three-tenths-of-a-second pause. This was repeated over and over again until it passed out of hearing range of the United States.

The satellite was silver in color, about the size of a beach ball, and weighed a mere 184 pounds. Yet for all its simplicity, small size, and inability to do more than orbit the Earth and transmit meaningless radio blips, the impact of Sputnik on the United States and the world was enormous and unprecedented. The vast majority of people living today, at the beginning of the twenty-first century, were born after Sputnik was launched and may be unaware of the degree to which it helped shape life as we know it. Now is an especially good time to take a fresh and focused look at the event whose impact looms even larger with the passing of time. In the last decade an incredible amount of once-secret material has been declassified and made public. Scholars and writers both inside and outside government have coaxed key Cold War documents out of hiding. Collectively, this material has given new dimensions and twists to almost every aspect of the events leading up to and following the launch of Sputnik.

Time magazine had a picture on the front page of Nikita Khrushchev dressed as a king wearing Sputnik as his crown.

I learned later that the Haystack radio telescope and radar antenna in Westford, Massachusetts, tracked Sputnik. Employees from Lincoln Laboratories operated the electronics equipment to transmit radar, receive the echo, and process the signals. A life-size model of Sputnik with its four-dipole transmitting antennas hangs from the ceiling—a vivid reminder of the consternation it caused half a century ago. The big moveable antenna sits under a geodesic dome and is scheduled for major upgrades within a few years. Thousands of acres separate the large antenna farm from nearby homes.

In response to Sputnik, Congress immediately passed the National Defense Education Act because there was a national perception that the USSR was technologically ahead of the United States. A whole generation of scientists, engineers, mathematicians, and Russian linguists was funded to counter the perceived Soviet superiority. This generation of technologists built space vehicles and designed and tested the weapons that helped win the cold war. I benefited by having various high-tech companies completely finance my graduate school education at MIT and Northeastern University.

CCNY professors taught me to think independently as an engineer, the need for lifelong learning; to dig in to a problem; to accept technical advice; to defend my decisions; and to be unafraid to make decisions in the absence of complete information. I also developed a personal concept of God and philosophy of religious cosmology. The education I received was a gift from the city of New York. I graduated in 1958 with my parents and grandfather in attendance at Lewisohn Stadium. The four children of my grandfather did not attend college. I am not certain if his children graduated high school because of WWII. I was the first of his grandchildren to graduate college.

Chapter 30

SHLOMO BREUER

I met Shlomo Breuer at CCNY in 1956 when we were both enrolled in a required speech class and an elected Yiddish class. I was permitted to enroll in Yiddish in order to fulfill my two-year language requirement. Since I scored high grades in German, I received permission from Prof Liedke to substitute Yiddish for my last semester of German language. Our teacher was Prof. Max Weinreich (1894–1969). He was a real scholar and yiddishist, an escapee from Lithuania. He wrote for his PhD thesis "History of the Distribution of the Yiddish Language." He started YIVO in 1925 (Yidische Wissenschaftlecher Institute [YIVO Institute for Jewish Research]) as a disciplined academic field of study. The whole field of advanced Jewish studies in Yiddish language, literature, and culture is named after him and his son. Lectures are presented at the Jewish Historical Society building Fifteen West Sixteenth Street, Manhattan. He started YIVO in his apartment in Latvia, and it has grown to its current size and attraction to students of Yiddish language and culture.

His scholarly son, Uriel, authored our textbook *College Yiddish*. Uriel Weinreich (1926–1967) prematurely died from cancer. Prof. Max Weinreich was amusing in class, so we did not appreciate the extent of his intellect. Only later did I read about his many intellectual accomplishments. He wrote *History of the Yiddish Language* in two volumes, published in 1973 in Yiddish and republished in 1980 in English. On 3 May 2015, YIVO celebrated its ninetieth anniversary.

Shlomo was charismatic, an object of my intense curiosity. How could anyone so rational, a student of mathematics, also live as an Orthodox Jew? In my view, orthodoxy and rationality were incompatible. Either he was mad, or I was totally uninformed. The truth was in between.

In speech class, each of us on the first day had to introduce ourselves. Without any hesitation, Shlomo said that he came from Israel to study in America and has a wife and daughter. He told the class that in the morning he is a student (attending classes at CCNY), in the afternoon he was a teacher (teaching Hebrew school), in the evening he was a father (attending to Naomi Breuer), and in the evening he was a husband. This extemporaneous outburst caught the teacher off guard; and immediately Shlomo became the focus of attention, hilarity, and popularity.

He invited me to play tennis on a Sunday. I took the train up to 185th Street, and I found the tennis courts. I met Sophie and Naomi for the first time. He invited me to her parents' home on Washington Heights. So I entered and met Sophie's mother, Lilly. I met her brother nicknamed Bookie, who drank water with a straw from a glass. The picture became clear. Bookie was a captive of an extreme religious sect. I read about such people. I had nothing to say to him. My world of math and science at CCNY was alien to Bookie as I was alien to Shlomo's world. Our worlds intersected only at school. I felt sorry for his non-worldliness. Bookie eventually married and had about fifteen children, none of whom attended college. Bookie's real name was Shlomo. Sophie told me that as a young child she could not pronounce *bruder* meaning *brother* in German, so she invented the name Bookie, and it stuck. Bookie died in 2009 in Brooklyn, New York. He was a *sofer* (scribe).

Shlomo needed a few additional credits to graduate so he enrolled in the Yiddish class. Of course, he excelled in Yiddish language because he spoke German fluently. Shlomo graduated CCNY and entered Brown University in Providence, Rhode Island, studying applied mathematics (visco-elasticity) for a PhD. We corresponded during my two years in California. After I returned to Boston in 1960, I visited him in Providence, Rhode Island, many times where I learned about Shabbos and how to live as a Jew. I would tell him that "I am sitting at the feet of the great sage Shlomo Breuer." He would respond with "Don't breathe too deeply."

SIDNEY KRIMSKY

Prof. of Yiddish, Max Weinreich,
Originator of YIVO
1894-1969

He completed his PhD studies in 1962 and sought employment around Boston. I provided a contact at AVCO Corporation that resulted in employment for him for several years until he made Aliyah. Shlomo, his wife, Sophie, and two daughters, Naomi and Michal, moved into Fifty-Eighth Babcock Street in Brookline on the first floor. He and Sophie were very hospitable to me. We laughed and joked and carried on like two imbeciles sometimes keeping his children up at night because they also enjoyed the laughter. He debated returning to Israel. It was a difficult decision for him because he enjoyed the material existence in the USA but also missed his parents and siblings rooted in Israel. Above all, he craved security that he knew was uncertain in Israel. Shlomo joined Young Israel of Brookline primarily to mock the members whom he regarded as stuffy and critical of Israel. He hated pretensions and superciliousness. I attended a Passover seder he gave in Boston. It was most instructive listening to him reading and analyzing the Hagadah to his children, especially Naomi who was the oldest child. I did not have the depth of knowledge to appreciate the subtlety and brilliance of his analogies and connections between various parts of the Torah.

Shlomo hated arrogance, pretentiousness, and superciliousness, which is one reason we got along so well. I told him I was a peasant, the son of peasants, and grandson of peasants. I was direct with him, and we never got into psychobabble. Shlomo hated falsehood "shikur" and loved to hear the truth. He came closest to absolute truth by studying mathematics. His epitaph reads that he hated shikur and loved the Torah. The Torah for him was absolute truth although the entire contents may not be revealed. The study of mathematics presented to Shlomo a glimpse into the mind of God.

Entrance to home of Prof. Shlomo and Sophie Breuer at 35 Zamenhoff Street in Tel Aviv Prof. Breuer standing outside.

Dorothy Krimsky sits on stone entrance to the former home of Prof. and Sophie Breuer.

Chapter 30.1

SHABEL FAMILY

Shlomo befriended John Shabel, a Jew who immigrated to the United States from Latvia. He was imprisoned in several concentration camps during WWII including Buchenwald. His first wife was murdered by the Nazis. He and his American wife, Tobey, lived upstairs from Shlomo on Fifty-Eighth Babcock Street. He was older than Shlomo and had three children: Scott, Anita, and Neal. John came to the USA penniless without much formal education, an intellectual casualty of WWII. He learned how to design kitchens and eventually moved to a house in Milton, Massachusetts. He lived in the same building on Dwight Street.

In 1965 Shlomo invited Dorothy and me to his seder. We walked together from Cambridge to Dwight Street in Brookline and then walked back. Shlomo kept only one day so he asked John Shabel to invite me for the second seder, and he did. I used to play softball with Neal and his older brother in the ball field near the Devotion School when I visited Shlomo.

Unfortunately in 1968, Neal, twelve years old, was hit by a car as he was crossing Philbrick Road outside of Maimonides School. He was brain dead at the hospital, and the Rav Joseph B. Soloveitchik was consulted about harvesting some of his organs. The family gave permission, and the Rav agreed because this was a way to prolong the life of the youth. Neal's kidney was taken for a donation for another boy who, unfortunately, died six months later.

Tobey never recovered from this tragedy. Dorothy and I paid a shiva call. It was one of the saddest shiva calls I ever made. It still bothers me that a twelve-year-old boy full of life and energy had his life snuffed out so quickly. When Dorothy was PTA copresident, she pressed the town of Brookline to place a police officer at the intersection of Philbrick Road and Sumner Street. For many years afterward, the Brookline police provided a school guard at the request of the Maimonides PTA.

John was a hard worker and unpretentious. John discussed and used floor finishing treatments. Once, Shlomo asked John the difference between shellac and varnish. John responded, "Shellac is shellac, and varnish is varnish." Shlomo kept repeating the story. It is a classic answer by a Jew and applies to any question. What is the difference between Mincha and Maariv? Mincha is Mincha and Maariv is Maariv. The questioner expects more, and the answerer has no details to offer. Actually, there is a difference. shellac is alcohol based, and varnish is turpentine based, but John was just a user, not a chemist.

I once met Anita Shabel on the subway in Boston. She attended Boston University. Scott moved to California. Anita became an accountant, and Scott became an attorney. During Passover 1965, on the second day not celebrated by Shlomo, I was invited to the Shabel seder and had a good time with the kids. Naomi Breuer referred to them as the shabelybuttons. Tobey was a heavy smoker. She died, and John remarried and moved to Florida where he later died.

Chapter 30.2

VISITING HIS PARENTS IN ISRAEL

Shlomo could discuss national, state, and shul politics and world history in addition to Torah; and nothing big that happened would escape his keen intellect. John Kennedy was elected in 1960, and the United States was filled with optimism until his assassination in November 1963. Israel was divided. Israel was growing. There was no intifada. In summer of 1965, I toured Israel and visited his parents in Jerusalem. I recall knocking on the door and answering in Yiddish that I was as friend of Shlomo Breuer. It took a while with persistent knocking for them to open the door. Shlomo later explained that they thought I was a mushallech asking for charity. I spoke to them in Yiddish about Shlomo and his family. I felt they were tired. Perhaps I woke them up. I knocked during the day. I only stayed for a few minutes and left giving regards without asking for charity.

Chapter 30.3

AVRAHAM HOELZEL

Shlomo's mind was quick to react even in a raunchy way. Once Avraham Hoelzel had to drive to Chelsea, Massachusetts. Shlomo and I went along. On the way, we encountered a very slow driver in front of us whom we could not pass. I remarked in a clipped British accent, "He's got a car. Why doesn't he drive it?" Shlomo grasped the application by blurting, "He's got a p——. Why doesn't he use it?" I had no way of knowing who used what. He may have referred to Abba Eban, Israel's representative to the UN, whom Shlomo called a "well-groomed eunuch."

Before he and his family made aliyah, they packed their belongings into boxes living at Fifty-Eighth Dwight Street in Brookline on the ground floor. I visited during those packing weeks to say good-bye. Once at the door, just before leaving, I asked him if he knew how a chicken sounded. He did not, so I sounded out "Pock, pock, pock, fock, fock, pock, etc.," until he laughed without end. He opened the door and yelled several times, "Sheba, Sheba." I had no idea who Sheba was, but apparently, Shlomo did not like Sheba. I would continue my chicken sounds, and he would blurt out "Sheba" loudly in the hallway while Sophie begged him to stop. After forty-five minutes, I had to leave because my belly was bursting with laughter.

Since Shlomo was not born in the USA, there were many aspects of our history and culture that he could not know. I would categorize the knowledge that most Americans possessed as all part of the

Acronym FOCK, which means the Fund of Common Knowledge. He would ask me how I knew some obscure fact, and I would reply that it is part of FOCK. Obscure or less-known facts were part of the Fund of Uncommon Knowledge. I leave the task of assessing the acronym to the reader.

Shlomo would attend mathematics conferences in Boston and always stay with us. Dorothy gave him the key to our house, and he came and went as he pleased. He loved to come to Boston and sought relief from "Gibberland," a term he invented to describe the land of the Gebrews or "Giblim" from the Tanach. On one of his last trips, he asked Dorothy and me why we did not tell him about Avraham Hoelzel. We had no idea what he meant until he told us about Hoelzel's adultery. We were not informed about this and felt shocked and betrayed. Shlomo regarded Hoelzel as a true friend. He was a pillar of the Young Israel Community of Brookline, reading from the Torah and attending services. He was also a member of the Maimonides School Committee, making decisions about curricula and hiring teachers. Hoelzel granted his wife a quick *get* (writ of divorce), moved from Brookline, and married his paramour. His children changed their last names. He moved to Quincy, Massachusetts; contracted cancer; and died within a few years. His wife, Yehudit, remarried. Shlomo never again contacted him. Shlomo felt totally deceived that such a person could do this. Hoelzel was a professor of German culture and language at the University of Massachusetts in Boston, an illuminati. I was only a Russian peasant, but even a peasant has values that do not permit such behavior.

He delayed aliyah for a week to attend my wedding and sign the ketubah. He was the scion of a famous family of Jewish scholars, and I was unpretentious, the son of Russian peasants. Only in America could such a nexus exist. In 1966, he accepted a job at Tel Aviv University as professor of mathematics and moved into an apartment on Zamenhof Street, not far from Diezengoff Circle. In later years, he put bars on the windows because of burglaries. He lived there for twenty-seven years. He wrote several math papers and books about numerical analysis and viscoelastic theory and applications. He sent me some of his papers and a book on numerical analysis using computers. He and his wife, Sophie, hosted me, Dorothy, and my children during their stay in Israel in his small apartment that he called a cave. He raised three children in his cave, and one slept in an alcove he called a subcave. At different times, Dorothy, I, and Elly all slept in the subcave. He was a man of routine. He sang the same zemirot Friday nights, criticized the same people, and always commented on the ineptness of the government. He said he studied Shaas (six books of the Talmud) six times, and in the Talmud, he found the truth and stability he craved.

Shlomo attended a math conference in Boston in the summer after the six-day war. He stayed with us. Shlomo did not fight in the war but felt pride in the amazing accomplishments of the Israeli Defense Forces. All the Jews everywhere spoke about the defeat of the three Arab armies from Egypt, Syria, and Jordan and the destruction of their air forces in a few days.

Shlomo and Gideon Zwas consulted to write a book *Computational Mathematics* published in 1975. The book offers students of even basic college math easy-to-understand methods to compute some basic constants such as pi, e, square root of 2, and perform numerical integration. The authors wrote a profound statement, "We think that no student in the seventies should graduate from college without having computed for himself, say, the number pi to a reasonable accuracy. The use of logarithms or statistical tables as 'black boxes,' without the faintest understanding of their construction, should definitely be ended." I studied numerical analysis in graduate school at MIT and found the necessary rigor somewhat tedious. The growth of personal computers (PCs) with choices of CDs and DVDs with algorithms for any conceivable mathematical problem exacerbated the lack of understanding by engineering students of the basis of the disciplines used in numerical analysis. Computational mathematics via the algorithms programmed in CDs and DVDs, in addition to all the engineering simulations based on algorithms, designed, programmed, and tested by students of mathematics, brought engineering and science students even further from a basic understanding of the rigor underlying approximation techniques because of the proliferation of DVDs that outline the solution of almost any conceivable mathematical or simulation exercise. Shlomo's book accomplished the very opposite of what he hoped he would accomplish.

Chapter 30.4

THE ARAB-ISRAEL WAR OF 1967

Boston is known for its radio talk show hosts, and for weeks afterward as information emerged about the complete victory, people called in to give their impressions. Jim Westover was the host, and Shlomo was intensely interested in what Americans thought, not just the Jews. The vitriol from the Arab side continued to hammer the airwaves. Even at the UN the representatives of the Arab nations condemned Israel for waging a war of aggression against the peace-loving Arab people. Day after day, we heard the representatives from the Arab countries saying to the president of the UN General Assembly, "Mr. President, you know who is the real aggressor?" "Mr. President. It is the Israeli who is the real aggressor." We heard that over and over. The Arab representatives not once blamed Gamal Abdul Nasser for closing the Straits of Tiran to Israeli shipping as the cause of war. Their complaints droned on day after day.

I decided to call up the radio station and pretend to be an Arab who was attacked by the Israelis. Shlomo and Dorothy would be listening. My name would be Fowzi Zub, and I would be a citizen of Jordan. Zub is an Arab word meaning *schmuck* or *putz*. I was Mr. Zub. Mr. Westover did not speak Arabic. I spoke in a manufactured Arab accent that I perfected by listening to the UN speeches by the representatives of the Arab countries. I told Mr. Westover that the Israelis entered our homes near the village of Irbil on the West Bank and stole our furniture and our carpets. The soldiers left our women alone but used our water to feed their tanks. I explained that they entered our villages dirty and unshaved and improperly addressed our people. Their machines rumbled on our roads and frightened our goats. "We believed Nasser during the war when he said on Arab radio that the Israeli Air Force was destroyed and the Arab armies were victorious. We are the victims of our leaders," said Mr. Zub. Mr. Zub made up ridiculous claims against the IDF. "I tink dey poison our wells so we can't have children. They even give our children sweets, but we do not trust the Israeli aggressor soldiers." From that conversation on, I was known as Mr. Zub. No one later called up the station and complained that Mr. Zub was a fake. Shlomo would call from New York or Boston about his plans and ask about Mr. Zub. Ibnel Zub means the son of Mr. Zub in Arabic, of course. Abu Chara means the father of *dreck*. Shlomo also mentioned Ibnel Bola, but I am not too sure what that meant in English. Eventually, the UN condemnations ceased. Abba Eban, made the case for Israel at the UN. Shlomo called Abba Eban "a well-groomed eunuch." Shlomo believed that Abba Eban lacked testosterone and the male organ to use it.

Before the common use of emails we exchanged letters every few months and commented on the state of the USA and the non-peace in Israel. Shlomo declared the OSLO agreement as having no value just like "chametz before pesach." Shlomo commented on the idealistic Dr. Gillers who helped Palestinians and worked with Palestinian doctors. Dr. Gillers was killed by Palestinian terrorists. We knew them when he and his wife lived in Boston. They are now forgotten.

In a letter to me in August 1991, Shlomo admitted that he stopped reading from the Torah because of his eyes. I was stunned. He was only sixty years old. I told him that age sixty was too young to stop reading from the Torah. He had probably memorized much of it, but I never understood why he stopped unless the letters from the distance were blurred or too small for him to comfortably read.

In January 1992 I wrote to Shlomo that he was welcome to stay with us during Purim. We told him that he had kitchen privileges, his own keys, but no smoking in the house. He went outside to smoke. He was addicted but would not admit it. Once he tried to stop but gained weight and became sick, so he resumed smoking. He developed a cough even when he was not smoking. I could sense that his lungs were getting worse, but to me he never listened. It was too late; he was addicted. He wrote in 1991 that people were getting murdered in Israel by the terrorists and the government did not seem to care. I told him that he did not have a government but a tenuous coalition of political parties whose only interest is reelections and self-preservation. Shlomo loved to go shopping at Target and Bradley's. Ann and Hope (Chana and Tikva) was a favorite store of his. I would drive him on motzei Shabbat to shop for his grandchildren, all of whom he adored. Shlomo loved to drive a car. He renewed his driver's license at the Watertown Registry of Motor Vehicles even though he claimed that he could not afford a car while he lived in Israel. He would take the bus to Tel Aviv University to teach math and do research.

Chapter 30.5

VERBAL GPS LOCATION ACCURACY

During one trip to Boston, we knew Shlomo would arrive in terminal E used for international flights. Terminal E was huge, and there were crowds of international travelers going through customs and finding their luggage at many of the luggage carousels. We parked at a meter, hoping to find Shlomo in short time before receiving a parking ticket. We had an arrangement for finding each other before the invention of GPS and cell phones. I would climb the stairs to the second floor in the terminal, overlooking the luggage areas, and call out the scream of the schmuck bird, "schmuaaaaaaaack" quickly followed by "Wherethefugareyou?" Shlomo would follow with a response "Schmuaaaaaack" from his location so we could easily find him and escort him to my parked car. The schmuck bird, as I taught him in Brookline, lived in a jungle and tracked lost persons who were walking in a circle. If the schmuck bird failed to locate the lost person, the bird would fly in never-ending decreasing concentric circles until he either located the lost person or flew up his own ass and disappeared, screeching all along the way, "Wherethefugareyou?" That is how we located Shlomo upon his arrival to Boston. Dorothy was with us and was shocked at the crudity of our communication system, but it worked, and we promptly left the airport before I received a parking ticket.

Shlomo loved to drive an automobile during his stay in the USA, which he claimed that he could not afford to do in Israel. He asked me to accompany him to a used car dealer on Massachusetts Avenue near Vassar Street in Cambridge. Someone provided him with a recommendation for a reliable used car dealer. He purchased a car from the salesman whose name was Mr. Pergola. Somehow I remembered the name. He asked me if the man was Jewish, and I said his surname was Italian. Perhaps he was Jewish. Fast-forward to October 3, 2008! The name of Prof. Sergio Della Pergola of the Jewish People Policy Planning Institute of Hebrew University of Jerusalem appears on page 4 of the *Jewish Advocate*. I wonder if the two Pergolas are related.

Chapter 30.6

TORAH ON THE HEAD OF A PIN

I recall vividly a conversation with Shlomo during the 1980s on one of his many trips to Boston, in which he said that it is written in the Talmud that one day the entire Torah of 304,805 Hebrew letters may be written on the head of a pin. During those years, magnetic tape, floppy disks, and diskettes were used to store letters.

I told him at the time that it was not possible because the existing storage capacity of magnetic media was too small to store the entire Torah on the head of a pin. Magnetic tape capacity was fifty kilobits/inch squared. If each letter can be described by eight bits, excluding spaces between words, we have a 2.44 MBIT requirement on a pin head (8 times 304,805).

A common pin head has a diameter of one-sixteenth inch and therefore has a surface area of 0.00307 inch squared. The required BIT density is 2.44 MBITS/0.00307 inches squared = 795 MBITS/inch squared.

The current capacity of a one square inch stick memory, about the size of a thumb, is about two gigabits or two thousand megabits. Therefore, the data that can be stored on a pin head is 0.00307 square inch times two gigabits/square inch or six megabits, which exceeds the 2.44 megabit requirement of the Torah. Two Torahs can be written on the head of a pin.

We would need a minimum density of 3,200,000 bits/0.003 square inch or approximately one gigabit per square inch. Such storage density seemed impossible at the time. Therefore, a stick memory can accommodate more than one Torah because new flash drives can hold more than two megabits.

Fast-forward to 1 May 2015 on page 2 of the *Jewish Advocate* in which it is reported that the world's smallest Bible is on display at the Israel Museum in Jerusalem. The Bible prepared using nanotechnology was created by researchers of the Russel Berrie NanotechnologyInstitute of the Technion-Israel Institute of Technology. The Bible is on a gold-plated silicon chip the size of a pin head. The entire text consists of over 1.2 million letters written on 0.25 millimeter-squared chip. How did the Talmud know that the Torah someday would fit on the size of a pin? How did the rabbis know this, and why was it even included in the Talmud? Shlomo never revealed to me the exact source, and I would like to find it. Present bit density on magnetic media nanotechnology has made an old Talmudic dictum come true.

After retirement at the University of Tel Aviv, he wanted to move to Jerusalem into an apartment with a nice view. I told him he was too knowledgeable to sit around and look through a window. He said that he wanted to be surrounded with students, interact with them, and study Talmud. In 1995, Dorothy sat me down and gently told me that he suddenly collapsed after discussing a section of Talmud with Yair, his oldest grandson, on the telephone. Sophie ran for help and locked the door behind her to where the first responders could not enter the apartment and render first aid. The bars on the window, installed to prevent break-ins, also prevented first responders from providing immediate aid. I'm not sure it would have mattered. I cried when he died. He is buried on Mount Menucha with all the other scholars of Israel overlooking Jerusalem with a better view than he had during all the years he lived on Zamenhoff Street in Tel Aviv. I regret that he was unable to see my sons achieve Smicha and was unable to see the results of his influence on me and how he ensured that my grandchildren will carry Torah into the twenty-first century.

Tombstone of HaRav HaGadol Saba HaGadol Shlomo Breuer Z'TS'L in Har Menuchah in Jerusalem
Translation: "I have hated falsehood and abhored it; your Torah I love." from Psalms 119:163

Chapter 31

CALIFORNIA

Tired of living at the edge of poverty and with a BS in engineering physics, I sought professional work. I scanned the *New York Times* and telephoned for an interview in a hotel in Manhattan for the Aerojet General Corporation. Dr. Werner Kirschner—program manager of the Polaris missile development program, Aerojet General Corporation in Sacramento, California—interviewed me. He asked me technical questions and evaluated my responses although I knew nothing about rockets. He needed bodies and hired me on the spot. I later learned that he was a Polish fighter pilot during WWII and fought with the RAF against the Nazis. The interview resulted in my first offer of employment as an engineer. I was assigned to the advanced design group for development of solid propellant booster rockets. I was thrilled. I borrowed money from my parents for the United Airlines flights and arrived in August at the Sacramento Airport Sunday night. I stayed in the Senator Hotel with air-conditioning, reported to the downtown office in the morning, and was whisked to the solid rocket plant where I completed security forms and reported to work. I was assigned to work in the advanced design group. I did not know then that half my working life would be spent working for national defense.

I looked for an apartment, and in a few days just walking around downtown Sacramento and looking in the newspapers, I found an apartment at 1321 K Street, midtown Sacramento, across the Capitol Building. I could afford the rent. There was no A/C, but there was a fan. I had a small kitchen, living room, and bedroom. Rent was about $65 a month. My salary was $480 a month. I opened a bank account across the street with the Bank of America. I just needed a car to get to work and start my life as a professional employee.

I was assigned to work in the advanced design group of the Polaris missile program under the Navy Special Project Office. My duties consisted of performing data analysis taken from the firing of small rockets using candidate solid propellants. The chemists would change the mix or the manufacturing process, and we would measure the pressure of the gaseous propellant emerging from the nozzle or the thrust via horizontal load cells to achieve the highest specific impulse. The aggregate specific impulse = force x time divided by propellant weight. The SI for the propellant averaged about 240 seconds.

I was enthralled by the enormity of the Polaris missile program. The underwater platform (submarine was built by another contractor) had to accept the configuration of the Polaris missile. This missile was supposed to be a deterrent against Soviet aggression. I learned about PERT (program evaluation and review technique) when I wandered into a large room where the walls were covered with a wall-to-wall schedule and milestone chart for keeping track of the progress of the Polaris design. This was all explained to me by a female industrial engineer, only a few years my senior, who talked as if she had been doing this for a decade. It turns out that PERT was developed in 1957 by the USN as a management tool for scheduling and controlling the Polaris missile program, which involved 250 prime contractors and more than 9,000 subcontractors. PERT kept track of hundreds of thousands of tasks, tests, and milestones using IBM computers and Hollerith cards to represent the schedule of tasks, tests, and milestones.

I bought my first car, and the owner taught me how to drive. I learned to ski at Soda Springs in the mountains north of Sacramento. I entered Sacramento State College graduate school at night studying abstract algebra and fluid dynamics, observed the downhill skiing winter Olympics at Squaw Valley by climbing up the downhill slope and watching from the sides, slept overnight at Yosemite National

FROM BROOKLYN NY TO BROOKLINE MA

Park, and even went out socially. In California, I saw amazing sights of the snow-capped Sierra Nevada, drove through Donner Pass, skied at Heavenly Valley near Lake Tahoe, used the gambling machines in Nevada, saw Alcatraz Island off San Francisco Bay, and experienced the old West in Virginia City.

During my second year in California, Sheldon was in graduate school at Perdue University in West Lafayette Indiana. He required an operation on his kneecap (patella). My parents went to see him, and I thought of going but had little funds and no time off. I was saving for travel expenses to return to the East Coast. I felt bad but was also trapped. I did not have a phone in my apartment and did not know the telephone number. I set it aside. I called my parents from a pay phone and learned the operation went well.

I saved enough money to travel to London and Paris summer of 1959 to attend the convention of the American Rocket Society. I missed most of the sessions to explore London. I saw unrepaired buildings from the bomb damage of WWII and listened to the awful speeches in Hyde Park. I disembarked from the BOAC aircraft at Heathrow, and a British greeter arranged for a small room in the Rose Court Hotel near Hyde Park. I went to Paris for one day by taking a boat train across the English Channel. I was sick during the channel crossing as the boat heaved, and so did I. I took the train to Paris and wondered around Place de la Concord and the Champs d'Elysee for ten hours while recalling my high school French and reading all the store signs, brasserie, boulangerie, and patisserie, and, of course, Kodak. "Avez vous Kodak?" I asked the clerk. "Vous acceptez argent Amercain?" I asked. "Mais Oui, monsieur," answered the clerk. There were no egg creams in Paris, just "caffee au lait et croissant." I never tasted better croissants than in Paris.

I saw test rocket firings at night that lit up the whole sky. I saw government-sensitive movies of a quiet ocean, out of which emerged a giant cylinder pushed by air pressure that seemed to hover above the ocean and suddenly came to life when the solid rocket boosters ignited. The big missile slowly and then quickly accelerated out of view to become a distant dot above the far horizon. These missiles could carry nuclear warheads to attack the Soviet Union. I never believed the United States would ever find a reason to use these behemoth weapons. I never believed the Soviets would give us reason to use them. Stalin and Khrushchev were diabolical but not stupid. These weapons are still in submarines with potential for use.

But something was missing. The spiritual component was missing, but I did not know it at the time. I connected with a synagogue in Sacramento near K Street where I lived, but I was on the margin. I came out of nowhere and felt that I did not belong anywhere. I could not relate to the older members of the synagogue. There were no young people. A few years after I left California, the synagogue was abandoned and burned down. The site was hard-topped over as a parking lot. I always returned to the shul site when I visited McClellan AFB north of Sacramento. McClellan AFB closed after the last Congressional Base Realignment and Closure (BRAC) Act in 1995. I have not been back.

After the first year in California, I yearned to leave and move closer to the East Coast. I found California too hot for comfort, hedonistic, with a large divorce rate, and bereft of any family connections. I searched the newspapers and sent out my résumé to several aerospace high-tech firms. Chicago would have been fine. I received a response from AVCO in Wilmington, Massachusetts, for an interview. I arrived at Logan airport in August 1960 and was met with a serious hurricane. My interview was cut short. My return to California was delayed. Another employer contacted me from another location outside of New York City. An offer of employment from AVCO came through first, and I accepted. If the offer were delayed, I might have settled in a suburb outside of New York.

After I received an offer of employment from AVCO, I accessed the warehouse where all the missile parts were machined and stored. I found a Polaris nozzle. These were shaped as a truncated giant hourglass with a three-inch diameter throat and an eighteen-inch exhaust diameter. Made of tantalum alloys, these were machined from solid tantalum boules with a thickness in places exceeding one inch. I planted a large dieffenbachia with huge green leaves inside one such nozzle. Word spread the next day, and my boss asked if I had done that and asked me to remove the large flowering plant. I could be fired. The design engineers were unhappy. It showed disrespect for their work. I removed the dieffenbachia, replanted it in Henry Siegel's (colleague) garden, and terminated my employment. When I visited Aerojet Corporation, a few years later, people were still talking about the dieffenbachia in the Polaris missile nozzle. I was the first flower child of the 1960s.

Chapter 32

CHALLENGER DISASTER

The chief Engineer of the solid rocket plant at Aerojet was Mr. R. F. Cotrell. He was a dour, no-nonsense mechanical engineer with ability to organize and integrate people and machines into producing the components and assemblies needed for solid rocket boosters. Now fast-forward to 28 January 1986, and the *Challenger* disaster in which teacher Christa McAuliff and the astronauts were killed when their solid rocket booster exploded during an attempt to orbit the earth. There was an investigation by the Congress. Prof. Richard Feynman of UCLA showed in a simple demonstration how Viton O rings lose elasticity at temperatures below freezing. After the *Challenger* disaster, there was a small article in the *New York Times* about Mr. Cotrell, warning NASA about the use of O rings on booster rockets before the *Challenger* was built. I met and knew Mr. Cottrell.

NASA submitted a request for proposal to both Aerojet and the Thiokol Company, a competitor to Aerojet, for the rocket booster business. Aerojet proposed a single long cylinder with solid rocket propellant cast into the cylinder without O rings because Aerojet viewed the use of O rings between cylinder halves as inherently unsafe. However, such a long cylinder would require special handling and transportation apparatus to move it from Aerojet in Sacramento, California, to Cape Canaveral in Florida. Thiokol suggested use of two cylinders separated by O rings. The Thiokol proposal was less expensive to implement than the Aerojet proposal. NASA selected the Thiokol proposal for the Challenger spacecraft. The O rings failed, and the rest is history.

FROM BROOKLYN NY TO BROOKLINE MA

This is taken from the Internet

"NASA's space shuttle Challenger accident was a devastating tragedy that killed seven astronauts and shocked the world on Jan. 28, 1986. Killed in the accident were Challenger commander Dick Scobee, pilot Michael Smith, mission specialists Judy Resnik, Ronald McNair and Ellison Onizuka, payload specialist Gregory Jarvis and Christa McAuliffe, who was set to become the first teacher in space."

"Here's a look at how the Challenger accident occurred:"

"An inspection of the launch pad revealed large quantities of ice collecting due to unusually cold overnight Florida temperatures. NASA had no experience launching the shuttle in temperatures as cold as on the morning of Jan. 28, 1986. The coldest temperature of a previous launch was 20 degrees warmer."

"Morton Thiokol, the builder of the solid-rocket boosters, advised NASA that they believed the O-ring seals in the solid-rocket boosters would perform adequately in the cold."

"To make each solid-rocket booster, the Morton Thiokol factory built four hull segments filled with powdered aluminum (fuel) and ammonium perchlorate (oxidizer)."

"At the launch site, the fuel segments were assembled vertically. Field joints containing rubber O-ring seals were between each fuel segment.

The O-rings were never tested in extreme cold. On the morning of the launch, the cold rubber became stiff, failing to fully seal the joint between the segments."

This incident reminded me of a brief paragraph published in Time Magazine sometime during the 1960s entitled "Death of a Missile." "Then as the failed housing section moved outward, the edge of the fracture rubbed against the outboard clamp, pivoting it on the two molybdenum bolts that held the housing and outboard clamp together. The tensile bending moments caused the molybdenum bolts to shear and the outboard clamp to fail through the trunnion hole."

Chapter 33

MOVE TO BOSTON

I sold my car, packed my belongings into two suitcases and one box with books, flew on United Airlines to Boston, and moved to Cambridge because Cambridge was centrally located and I was fascinated by the ancient shops surrounding Harvard Square. I was able to arrange for transportation to AVCO in Wilmington, Massachusetts, for several weeks until I purchased a new Ford Falcon in Brooklyn accompanied by my father. He wanted to make sure I was not ripped off. I accepted the first apartment I saw at 1200 Massachusetts Avenue only because the rent was affordable at $75 per month, and I had no patience to look elsewhere. Cambridge was fascinating. I loved to walk around the narrow streets, browse in the stores, visit the libraries, and jog along the Charles River. I bought a used bicycle, but within a few weeks, it was stolen. I walked all over Harvard Square, which was not at all a square but more like a triangle.

Route 93 did not exist then, only Route 38 going north and south. I remember getting lost on the way home from work; making all those rotary turns; winding up in strange places, Medford, Somerville, Melrose, Watertown, etc.; and not knowing how to get back to Harvard Square. Maps were useless because of one-way streets and confusing signs. California streets were grid-like unlike streets around Boston that bore no semblance to sanity. Eventually, I grew to enjoy driving around rotaries. I had to learn a new language because Bostonians do not speak standard English or use common idioms I learned in New York. Here are some examples:

FROM BROOKLYN NY TO BROOKLINE MA

Standard English	Boston English
Aunt	Awnt
Basement	Cellah
Black-and-white pastry	Half moon
Boston	Hub
Boston University	BU
Car	Cah
Car keys	Cahkies
Coop (pronounced *cuuup*)	HarvardCooperative Society (Coop)
Cod or Haddock	Scrod
Chelmsford (town north of Boston)	Chemsfd
Female undergraduate at Radcliffe College	Cliffie
Cuba	Cuber
Dark	Dahk
Garbage	Gabbidge
Grocery cart	Carriage
Harbor	Hahbah
Harvard	Hahvud
Haverhill	Havrill
Haymarket Square	Haymahket Square
Havana (Cuba)	Havaner
Here	Heah
Heart	Haht
Horse	Hoss
India	Indiar
Living room	Pahluh
Main public park in Boston	Boston Common
Massachusetts Avenue	Mass Av
Medford, MA	Mehfuh or Medfid
Molasses cookie	Hermit
MIT undergraduate	Techie
Motor Car	Motah Cah

Nonacademic permanent resident of Cambridge or Charlestown	Townie
On account of	Onna Conna
Near	Neah
Park	Pahk
Park in Boston for ice skating	Frog pond
Party platter	Potty plattah
Police car	Cruzah
Celebration for child when toilet trained	Potty pahty
Public gardens	Public gahdens
Really cool occurrence	Wicked pissah
Rear	Reah
Rubber band	Elastic
Small convenience store	Spa
Small cup of Hoods ice cream	Hoodsie
Soda	Tonic
Soup made from fish usually clams	Chowda
Third-year student at Northeastern Univ.	Middler
Traffic circle	Rotary
TV remote	Clickah
Water fountain	Bubblah
Wellesley	Wellslie
Woburn (town in MA)	Wubn
Worcester (City in Central MA)	Woostah
Yard	Yahd

I frequently got lost driving from work in Wilmington, Massachusetts, for the first few weeks to Harvard Square where I lived at 1200 Massachusetts Avenue. Route 93 did not exist, so I had to drive on Route 38. It was dark at night, and the signs were not lit and frequently absent. Once, I crossed over the Longfellow Bridge and somehow made my way driving west on Beacon Street. I did not know where I was, and there were no signs on the main street. I stopped and asked a burly Boston traffic cop where I was so I could locate my position on a map. GPS had not been invented.

His response was "If you don't where you are, you shouldn't be here." Wow! Welcome to Boston. I had to stop the car and walk to find street signs. I made it back to Harvard Square.

I found myself living in the center of American History in Cambridge Massachusetts. I lived at 1200 Massachusetts Avenue, across the Street from Harvard Yard and about a mile from M.I.T. I explored all the historical sights and eventually escorted Dorothy on dates to revisit these sites: I visitedUSS Constitution, Breeds Hill on which the Battle of Bunker Hill was fought. The Americans retreated but the British suffered unacceptable casualties. We visited the Concord Bridge, Faneuil Hall, State House, Lexington Green where the first shots in the Revolutionary War were fired, Dorchester Heights where the colonists brought cannons from Fort Ticonderoga overlooking Lake George., site of the Boston Massacre, the Old North Church where the two lanterns were hung to inform colonists that the British were coming across the Mystic River to Charleston to march North to Lexington, the Towns that provided Minute Men to dislodge the British Army, Castle Island where the civil war prisoners were held, and the State House on Beacon Hill, and walking along the trail taken by Paul Revere passing through Lexington before he was captured.

In later years after Dorothy and I were married and had children, we would go sledding down the hill in Dean Park and Lars Anderson Park in Brookline. We would go for walks around the Brookline Reservoir especially when the dogwood and cherry blossoms were in bloom. We would walk around the longer Cleveland Circle Reservoir inside the fence after Gov Dukakis had the fence removed because the water was no longer used as a reservoir. Boston is a great walking city and the spirit of revolution still is taught in the schools.

Hiking up Mt. Washington (6288 feet) in New Hampshire with my tripod, Rolleicord camera, and knapsack. We passed the plaque in memory of Aaron Levy, Northeastern University student, who died climbing the mountain. Warning sign is just above the tree line.

Chapter 34

AVCO CORPORATION

Dr. Peter Neurath, Dr. Charles Rosen, and Dr. Stan Ruby interviewed me. Neurath was a Viennese physicist. He was a cultured man who spoke softly and was comfortable in the world of art, wine, music, and science. Rosen was a chemist from New York, and Ruby was a physicist from New York. I was hired to work on engineering problems in their group.

AVCO stands for Aviation Corporation. Dr. Arthur Kantrowitz—an aerodynamicist, chemist, and plasma physicist—founded it. An apocryphal story about the company's founding had Kantrowitz talking with some air force officials (before NASA was created) at a party about reentry burn-up problems of ballistic missiles. Between drinks, Kantrowitz suggested that plasma, consisting of high-temperature gases and disassociated molecules, could be used to simulate reentry conditions for testing new materials for use on nose cones. The government agreed, and money was used to start the AVCO Everett Research Labs. The AVCO lab in Wilmington was tasked to find applications for the new science being developed at the Everett labs.

My first assignment was to develop a solar simulator to expose potential materials to be used for ballistic missile reentry heat shields. These potential materials were designed to protect the electronics and explosives from burning up during reentry. We knew from tests and theory that the material surrounding the protective nose cone would experience thousands of degrees of temperature from the friction of flying through the atmosphere during reentry. Would exposure to sunlight above the atmosphere degrade the nose cone's protective layer of material even before reentry? I used a mercury xenon lamp as a light source because its spectrum simulated the spectrum of the sun. The tungsten filament heated and excited the mercury xenon molecules to emit heat and light through a quartz window into a vacuum chamber holding the candidate materials. The materials were exposed to the heat and chemically analyzed for degradation. In that way, AVCO developed candidate materials for heat shields. I wrote reports that were "AVCO Proprietary" that contributed to the final report sent to the sponsoring government agency.

My second assignment consisted of assembling hardware needed to safely and remotely disarm unexploded bombs using transferred arc plasma technology. We had a contract with the Office of Naval Research to demonstrate feasibility. The scientific concept was simple: the engineering was a challenge but requires a small explanation. We would affix battery cables to a bomb casing, making it part of an electrical circuit consisting of sixteen auto batteries, an RF generator needed to strike an arc, one carbon electrode, a container of an inert gas such as nitrogen, and a gun to house the carbon electrode. Switching on the RF generator would cause an electric arc between the carbon electrode and the gun housing. Applying a voltage to the bomb casing would cause the arc to transfer to the bomb casing. An inert gas was injected to pass between the electrode and metallic housing. The high-temperature arc would strike the bomb casing, heat the metal, and the metal would melt and blow away. Simple in theory!

To do this work required an understanding of arc cathodes. I provided calculations of temperature of the tip of an arc cathode. I was pleased that my calculations appeared in a paper entitled "Arc Cathode Emission Mechanisms at High Currents and Pressures" in the February 1963 issue of the *Journal of Applied Physics*.

The USN engineers told us that the explosive material could be washed out with a high-pressure water hose after making a hole in the unexploded bomb casing. The arc technology science was easy but hard to execute into a useful military product. Victor Kajko, an AVCO mechanical designer, provided a drawing for an arc gun consisting of a carbon electrode electrically insulated from a metallic outer shell. AVCO machinists built it for me. These machinists had no formal education, but I remembered my father and respected their abilities. I knew how to talk to them. The gun allowed me to adjust the distance between the electrode and the gun housing. A DC voltage, needed to sustain the arc, was applied to the electrode with the bomb casing at ground potential. In a few minutes, we burned a hole through the one-fourth-inch steel plate. We changed voltages, spacing between the electrode and shell, and gas flow rates to explore trade-off conditions for burn-through.

We prepared for a test at the Naval Explosive Ordinance Disposal Technical Center at Indian Head, Maryland. It was south of Mount Vernon, Virginia, but on the Maryland side of the Potomac River. We drove with our equipment but without the sixteen auto batteries. The USN provided a huge generator delivered by a forklift. The USN provided steel plates of one-fourth-inch to one-half-inch thicknesses. Our device made holes as advertised. We were successful and expected an ongoing contract for further development.

We were surprised when the USN told us that the device had to be portable and be carried on the back of one or two seamen or marines. How could we make portable an energy storage source equivalent to sixteen car batteries or a huge generator? The USN discontinued funding and found other ways to remotely disarm bombs.

Dr. Neurath obtained a government contract to study the effect of exposing fireflies to strong magnetic fields. He discovered that the emitted frequency of light changes in the presence of a strong magnetic field. However, this effect was well-known in classical physics as the Peter Zeeman effect. Fireflies produce light by exuding luciferase and lucifirin from a sac in their abdomen called a lantern that reacts when exposed to oxygen. These light signals are used in courting. This was his first exposure to bioelectrical engineering. I never understood why the government funded such research. Government contracts faded like dying fireflies, and I left AVCO after two years.

Pat Milello and I standing in front of a test station at AVCO Corp. for disarming conventional bombs by means of arc transfer to puncture holes in steel plates to allow water to flush out explosive material. We demonstrated feasibility. Work was performed under a US Navy contract.

Outside AVCO Corp parking lot. The red sideing panels have become dull. AVCO was sold to Textron Corp.

Solar Simulator material testing apparatus for testing materials for use in the harsh vacuum of space. We tested heat shield materials for ballistic missiles. Apparatus consisted of vacuum pumps, stainless steel chamber, quartz viewpost & mercury xenon lamp to stimulate the solar spectrum.

Mercury Xenon lamp for solar simulator to test materials used in vacuum of space exposed to solar radiation.

Chapter 35

MIT.

I was able to enroll at MIT as a special graduate student during work hours, transfer graduate credits from the University of California, and have tuition paid by AVCO as long as I was employed. My teacher of aeronautical engineering was Dr. Sheila Widnall, who became secretary of the air force and a person whom I admire. Some of the engineering professors wrote the textbooks I used at CCNY.

I settled in, learned about MIT Hillel, where I met Willy Kantrowitz, computer science major in the graduate school. We spoke Yiddish during services. He invited me to watch auto accidents at the intersection of Massachusetts Avenue and on Memorial Drive from his window in the dorm. I declined his gracious offer. I attended Hillel services but felt misplaced with the undergraduates. My interest in Hillel diminished. Hal Waller told me about a real shul on Columbia Street in Cambridge. Dorothy and I attended Hal Waller's wedding. Hal moved to Canada, obtained a position as a professor of political science, and secured his outlook as a bona fide liberal. I met him at the wedding of Paul Mermelstein's son, Mark, in Montreal. I met Paul at MIT where we went on many ski and hiking trips together. He learned a love of the outdoors from his native Hungary. Paul's father was deported to Auschwitz in an early alleged roundup for resettlement to work in the country. The war ended before Paul, his mother, and brother was all to be assembled at the railroad station for deportation and resettlement. I attended Paul's wedding and the wedding of his son, Mark, and visited him many times in Montreal. He and Marcia moved to Florida. Paul did original work on speech synthesis at MIT. Now we just take it for granted but voice messaging operators, warnings of danger, etc., use some form of speech synthesis or artificial speech.

In the winter of 1961, I was driving my new Ford Falcon to Mount Snow with Paul Mermelstein sitting in the passenger seat. The car hit a patch of ice and moved into the left lane where I hit another car in a head-on collision. My jaw broke after hitting the steering wheel. There were no seatbelts in cars at that time. An ambulance came and transported us to Massachusetts General Hospital. Paul hit the windshield and broke his nose. I was operated that day by Dr. Peter Kimball who wired up my jaw. I spent two days in the hospital after which I saw Dr. Frederick Poulin who built an appliance to replace my two front teeth that were broken. The appliance lasted over fifty years and finally deteriorated. Dr. Poulin unfortunately died of leukemia a few years after building my dental appliance. My mother came to Boston and prepared liquid meals because my jaw was wired. I was visited in the hospital by my boss, Dr. John Ehrenfeld, and David Lull, an avid skier. But in three days I was back at work, drinking liquid meals with raw eggs prepared by my mom who stayed with me for a few days after my jaw was sewn up. I was paid for the absent days. I had no medical insurance. I have no idea who paid for the operation. I paid for the follow-up dental work.

Chapter 36

BETH SHALOM IN CAMBRIDGE

Having arrived from California in the fall of 1960, I needed to quickly find an apartment and buy a car. I found a small affordable apartment at 1200 Massachusetts Avenue located a few blocks east of Harvard Square, which was not a square at all but an intersection of streets, buses, underground trains, old brick walls, stores, prerevolutionary buildings, boutiques, overhead electric lines, bookstores, apartments, and dormitories. The Broadway underpass near the JFK Law School had not yet been built; and the area was teeming with bicycles, pedestrians, and cars. I wandered past the law school attended by John F. Kennedy who was a candidate for president of the United States at that time. I was plunk in the middle of the intellectual capital of the United States, totally different from the hot, hedonistic, effete, and uninteresting environment of Sacramento, California, from where I had moved a few days ago.

I transferred my undergraduate credits from CCNY and graduate credits from the University of California in Sacramento to MIT and sought admission as a special graduate student in aeronautical engineering. AVCO Corporation, my employer, paid for tuition and I paid for the books. I joined the Harvard Coop and explored the libraries at MIT. I spent hours in the music library after work. I joined the sailing club and qualified to sail tech dinghies on the Charles River. I learned about the Harvard Hillel and MIT Hillel groups and started occasionally to attend services. It was at MIT in the strange silo designed by Eero Saarinen and surrounded by a moat that I met Willy Kantrowitz, Howie Pilet, Lou Schulman, and Hal Waller. The silo served as a multidenominational building for religious services. After a few months, I grew tired of the undergraduate conversations, and it was Hall Waller who told me about a real shul in Cambridge on Columbia Street.

One Saturday autumn morning, I walked for thirty minutes on brick-lined Harvard Street toward Columbia Street and Beth Shalom, stopping to look through the quaint antique store windows and at the fronts of old buildings. I explored Trowbridge, Ellery, and Dana Streets and Broadway walking past Skendarian Pharmacy.

I read the outside bulletin board of Beth Shalom and learned that Joseph Shultz was rabbi and Mr. Moses Holcer was shammas. Once inside I saw a balcony, stained glass windows, oak benches, a traditional bima, and a Torah ark made in the traditional European style. The bima was in the front eastern end of the shul where Rabbi Shultz and the president sat. I never did like this arrangement. In Sephardic shuls, the bima is in the middle of the shul so everyone can equally hear the baal koreh read from the Torah. The older Askenazic buildings resemble churches in that respect. Near the ark, I saw one man sitting and a short man at the bima with a loud voice chanting in clear Hebrew. The building seemed cavernous with barely a minyan in attendance. His voice bounced off the memorial plaque-covered walls. There was a clarity, vibrancy, authenticity, and sincerity to the prayers of the baal tefilah that I found missing at the MIT Hillel despite the best efforts of Rabbi Herman Pollack, Hillel director at MIT. The prayers came into sharp focus as I gradually remembered the aleph beth that I learned in Hebrew school. But this was still an ancient ritual with no relevance to me.

There was something noble and humble about the man at the bima. I sat in the back row, under the balcony, not to be noticed. I did not want my ignorance exposed. The prayerbooks were in English and Hebrew so I could follow along and absorb the meaning. Rabbi Shultz announced the pages and spoke about the contents of the Torah reading. I saw a few students but mostly older people who reminded me of my grandfather. Hesitating to commit myself, I quickly left after services ended.

FROM BROOKLYN NY TO BROOKLINE MA

Something tugged at me, an unknown force perhaps, to return next week Saturday morning. This time, feeling more confident, I sat about two-thirds away from the bima, still under the balcony. I was visible from the front of the shul. I preferred anonymity, but someone tapped me on the shoulder and asked me if I was a Kohain or Levy. I responded no and was asked to come to the bima for an aliyah. I had aliyot in California, so I knew the brachot but not much more. Up I walked and met the Baal Koreh. I recited the blessing over the Torah, shook hands with everyone, and was about to return to my seat when the baal koreh said, "Why do you sit so far away? Move closer." Sheepishly, I said OK. How could I argue with this holy man? I returned to the benches but moved closer to the bima.

Services ended with Adon Olam and Rabbi Shultz announced a Kiddush downstairs to which everyone was invited. There were some teenagers, seniors, a few graduate students, but no nonstudents close to my generation. The rabbi made Kiddush; and the shammas, Mr. Holcer, brought out the schnapps, herring, and crackers. Having been brought up to respect privacy, in a home where "reaching out" was only limited to family and friends, I was pleasantly surprised that people asked me who I was. I felt comfortable talking with a lively, loquacious, delightful little girl with dark doe eyes who did most of the talking while I listened about her adventures in school with her friends and teachers and the situations in which she found herself. I asked her a few innocent questions, and she sensed I was interested, so she continued to talk about her life and her family and what she knew about the people who came to shul. I found a seven-year-old friend who could relate to me. I only had to listen. I learned her name was Jacqueline. I figured she was from France.

I returned next Shabbos to Beth Shalom. The unchanging routine of the prayer service was becoming familiar. Only this time the seven-year-old recognized me and sat down to continue her monologue. Her two older sisters watched her from upstairs in the balcony. She had few verbal inhibitions. I was asked by the gabbai to lift the Torah, something I had never done. I saw it done in California, MIT Hillel, and Beth Shalom but never saw myself doing it. It could not be too heavy. I could lift ninety pounds of barbells over my head.

This had to be lighter. Mr. Holcer explained that the stitching of the Torah parchment should be in the middle of the scroll rather than near the handles, that my hands had to spread the Torah apart before lifting, and three columns were enough. Could I do it? Yes, I believed I could do it. I lifted the Torah but was a bit shaky as I did not properly stretch the parchment. Next time I got it right. But why should the stitching be in the middle? It took years before I realized that for a parchment stretched under constant tension, the stress on the cross-sectional (width times thickness) area of the parchment is greater where the radius of the scroll is smaller. Therefore, the stitching, being the most vulnerable part of the parchment, should not be stretched around a small radius when the parchment is under tension. Later, while working at Polaroid Corporation, I learned from stress equations that when wrapping movie film or magnetic tape around a reel, the tension is always greater when the film is wrapped around a small radius.

Rabbi Moses Holcer and Frida Holcer with Naomi Krimsky circa 1973.

Chapter 37

MEETING THE HOLCERS

I stayed for Kiddush; and Jacqueline introduced me to her two sisters, mother, and father. I learned about their school and home life. It was an uncommon experience for me to see how each member of this family respected one another and was solicitous of one another. The smallest gesture did not go unnoticed. All three sisters were charming beyond description, verbally clever, and worriers. Their mother, Mrs. Holcer, was the biggest worrier; and their father, Mr. Holcer, put his whole trust in the Almighty so he outwardly showed no sign of worry. Emerging from the turmoil of postwar Europe as a Jewish immigrant family, without family roots, without continuity, without security, and not belonging anywhere, I could understand the source of their anxiety.

I concluded these people are refugees, but from where? How did they get here? How are they supported? Why don't they complain? It would take a few years to learn about their story. I did not want to pry into such personal matters, but eventually, their story would emerge.

It didn't take long. The high holidays were coming. I had to plan ahead to observe the holidays. I did not want to drive to Brooklyn. My parents did not really observe the holidays. My grandfather moved into smaller quarters. On occasion, I managed to eat at the Harvard Hillel where Mrs. Robert Morton was the primary chef, but I found little interest in the students' conversations that I found devoid of any real world considerations. Mrs. Holcer invited me to dinner on Rosh

HaShonah. It was the best offer I had. I learned that such hospitality and generosity of spirit was normal for them. Students from local colleges especially MIT were often invited to share Shabbos meals. Mark Drapkin, an MIT undergraduate in the premed program, was a frequent guest. A few years later, I was fortunate to be invited and attend his marriage to Rosa Holcer. It was at these table discussions that I learned about the struggles in school, the politics in shul, and the challenge to meet each day with optimism. I was frequently invited to their home and absorbed through their interactions with me and with one another how they functioned to assist one another, to inspire one another, to share with one another, and to protect each other so the three girls would achieve the best that America could provide. It took hard academic work within a single generation for them to achieve the "American dream" and to recompense American society as teachers and caregivers for the gifts of freedom they received as immigrants.

Every shul has its set of characters, and I learned about President Flaksman, Dr. J. Newton Newman and his young wife, Rabbi Joseph Shultz who enjoyed sleeping late (who doesn't?), and Mr. Koocher who thought he managed the shul. He must have attended Congregation Kadimah-Toras Moshe because I found his personal siddur with his signature on the inside cover among many lost articles scheduled for shamos at Congregation Kadimah-Torads Moshe. I saw the concern for Dr. David and his sibling, Sally David, who seemed to be perpetually ill. I learned about the merger of Temple Ashkenaz on Tremont Street and Beth Shalom on Columbia Street. The merged shul could not afford two shamosim. Either Mr. Hecht or Mr. Holcer had to leave. Mr. Hecht had more experience and was older. Mr. Holcer was younger but more desperate for employment. Charlie Abzug and some of the other graduate students wrote letters and called the new officers from the merged shul. The merged board wanted a shammas who would stay. They selected Mr. Holcer over Mr. Hecht. He repaid their confidence by staying and serving the community for almost half a century.

"You can observe a lot by watching," said the sage Yogi Berra, former catcher for the New York Yankees and now an oft-quoted literary don. I watched the Holcers adjust to American life and the three girls grow as their minds and interests expanded. I lived in a different reality, with different experiences, and the product of a different education; but something continued to draw me to shul and even return on Saturday evenings for mincha and Seudat shlisheet. I realized years later that my interaction with them was a palliative for existential angst that first surfaced in Sacramento, California. I did not understand it in California and did not understand it in Cambridge.

After a few years, the merger was complete, Beth Shalom was sold, and activities centered at Temple Ashkenaz on Tremont Street in Cambridge. Rabbi Shultz departed Cambridge. But how could the immigrant family survive let alone thrive in the twentieth century? The family was in a time warp and would have felt more at ease in the middle of the nineteenth century where science was a mere curiosity and spiritual values permeated village life, where the direction of life was more certain, where choices were fewer, where girls did not worry about examinations in academic subjects, and where marriage arrangements were made by parents and relatives.

Paulette, Rosa, Jacqueline, and their parents learned that success for indigent immigrants in America would depend on some luck, hard work, and education. The girls worked hard in school and achieved academic success. Their father would help them in Hebrew and religious subjects. However, Paulette and Rosa were challenged by the rigor of high school mathematics, the only academic discipline in which I excelled. They needed help just to clarify some concepts and processes in quantitative thinking. I offered to help them weekly with math homework and prepare them for exams. Their background was weak, their intelligence was high, their enthusiasm was unbounded, and failure in high school was not an option. They were willing to work with me to understand and help with their math homework assignments. I could not take their exams, but I could hone their minds and give them the tools to learn the material. I did not expect them to be as serious with math as with their other subjects, but with dogged determination, they persisted, and we reviewed the material to where I believed it began to make sense to them.

I tried to explain the elegance, logic, and simplicity of high school math. I even pointed out that their address, 314 Columbia Street, had special mathematical significance. Since pi equals 3.14, their address was 100 pi Columbia Street. Their parents could not help them as my parents could not help me with the secular subjects. Our math lessons wandered sometimes as I interacted with them and tried to explain the workings of the real world. A hardworking student and responsive teacher is a mutual naches society. Both teacher and student embark on an adventure like planting a seed. The seed eventually flowers, the difficulties are forgotten, but the achievements remain as a nonerasable-stored hologram in the pleasure centers of the mind.

For about four and a half years, Paulette, Rosa, and I worked together. Mrs. Holcer prepared the tea and mondel bread while we analyzed the math problems and occasionally diverted to the other homework and other aspects of their busy social life. They were far more mature than I was at their age, and I realized what I was unable to achieve in high school. The closeness of the family and the relationship to the teachers of Maimonides School made an indelible impression that served as a model for a family that I would be fortunate to be able to emulate in future years. I was fortunate in meeting Dorothy five years later who also saw the benefit in this kind of family structure that was also absent in her youth.

I can recall that Paulette brought home a science kit, a circuitry for a speech synthesizer that had to be wired up and soldered. It resembled a U-DO IT electronics kit. She never held a soldering iron. So we worked together and constructed the kit to where it sounded out several vowels, such as *aaa, eee, ooo*, etc. We were both exposed to the very beginning of synthesizing speech. Now, we take synthesized speech for granted forgetting its humble beginnings. GPS receiver/transmitters and telephone voice messages use synthesized speech.

Between their close family life, structured school life, and spiritual life on Shabbos and holidays, something tugged within me to show the girls the lighter side of life. For me, it was enjoyable to see how they reacted to common pleasures that I took for granted. So we went for rides in my Peugeot with a roof that opened, walked to the Hatch Shell to hear concerts on the esplanade, took a trip to Miles Standish State Park, and drove around Cambridge and Boston where I occasionally would get lost. I was still learning my way around. Their teenage giddy side emerged during the laughing as I tried to redirect their minds from the intensive studies. I felt like an American uncle or an adopted member of the family. I tried to show that America was more than shul, school, and Cambridge.

I recall that on one long summer Shabbos, we all walked to Harvard Square and entered the Busch-Reisinger Museum of Germanic Art on Broadway. I don't think that the rows of medieval armor or any of the other medieval artifacts made any impression on them. Anything from Germany was not a subject to be pursued. The craftsmanship of the armor made an impression on me.

Mr. Holcer rarely came with us on pleasurable auto trips. His wife, Frieda, often came with us as a palliative for winter cabin fever. She enjoyed leaving the confines of her apartment. Once I convinced Mr. Holcer to accompany me to Haymarket Square after the Sabbath because food prices dropped at the end of the day. We purchased a wooden crate of oranges for $1 as well as other foodstuffs whose price had dropped. A *metziah* (bargain) such as this would never again be seen in Boston.

He found a way to earn additional income through preparing and mailing the yahrzeit cards. Coming to the United States without knowing any English, he mastered the postal system and typewriter to mail yahrzeit notices to hundreds of Jewish people who wanted to be annually reminded about the date of the death of a loved one. The cards were sent as a reminder to give charity to the synagogue. The recipients sometimes included a personal check in the return envelope. Many synagogues now use e-mail as a reminder. It is even possible to request that the "kaddish prayer for the deceased" be said by clicking a box on the website of the "Webber Rebbi," thereby depersonalizing the entire process and having the computer absorb the ongoing emotions of mourning. The computer and Internet have become part of the mourning process. Between mailing yahrzeit cards, teaching bar mitzvah lessons, and receiving tips from trips to the cemetery to help people remember their loved ones, and receiving a small salary as shammas, he eked out a living. Mrs. Holcer worked for a few years in a nearby fruit store. Despite the financial hard times, no one really complained; there was ample optimism to spare and to share. At least I did not hear any complaints except about the landlady, Mrs. Koustopoulos, who too often had to raise the rent.

When he was not completing the yahrzeit cards, Mr. Holcer reread the Torah portion of the week so that he would not make any mistakes on Shabbos. His eyes brightened when he read from the Torah, relishing each word as if he heard it directly from Moses. He was a Levi, and as the Levites of ancient times who zealously cared for the Temple, he exuded a zealous energy to coddle each word of the Torah before releasing the words of the Torah to the worshippers. I think he was the only one in the synagogue who really understood the words and the implications of the words of the Torah reading.

Out of respect, I could not call Mr. Holcer anything but Mr. Holcer except after his first grandchild, Shlomo, was born when I renamed him "Saba HaGadol" or "grandfather the great." After Shlomo had a child, I renamed him "Saba HaGadol HaGadol." He reminded me in some ways of my father who had no guile and no ego and was generous to share what he had. Mr. Holcer had no ego and was without guile. He tended to his family needs more than his own. He served his family and his G-d. He would not compromise his personal religious beliefs, yet he tolerated the religious beliefs of the unknowledgeable. He was patient with people who were Judaicly challenged such as me. I was so pleased that he and his family attended my wedding and Mr. Holcer signed the ketubah. We were also privileged to have him sign the ketubah of my daughter, Naomi, twenty-seven years after he signed Dorothy's ketubah. I think that his signature carries weight with the Almighty.

Over a half century, Mr. Holcer catered to generations of college students who came to Beth Shalom, graduated, who were influenced by him, and occasionally returned to Beth Shalom. They all remembered him for his Torah Lehening, shofar blowing, prayers before the Almighty, Kiddush, egg salad, and the lemon-peel-laced vodka. I learned to add lemon peel to the vodka in our shul. It enhances the flavor.

I wanted to ask him how he adapted to the evolving less rigorous religious practices at Beth Shalom, and among Jews in America in general, compared with what must have been a serious religious milieu in prewar Poland. I did not know how to formulate the question without making him feel sad because I believe that he lost so much in Europe, besides his family, that the answer might have precipitated buried painful emotions. So I avoided the subject altogether. Besides, he was comfortable that his daughters were attending Maimonides School and receiving a rigorous Jewish and secular education. If he had moved to Brooklyn instead of Cambridge, their education and my exposure to Yiddishkeit would have been different. I would have missed some wonderful interactions and learning experiences. There was a certain friendship that exceeded more the weekly mathematics lessons that glued our relationship.

He was honored by Beth Shalom on his ninetieth birthday with a huge celebration, and Moshe Holcer Day was proclaimed in the city of Cambridge, a fitting honor to a man of faith who literally changed history by influencing thousands of people with his persona. I wrote the following for insertion into the memory book:

> *The life of Moshe Holcer mirrors the span of Jewish History. Starting from his early beginnings when exposure to the Tanach illuminated his soul and then the years of abject slavery spent in Russian concentration camps followed by years of statelessness and uncertainty and finally freedom in America. Just as Avraham and Moshe left the land of their birth to build anew, Moshe and Frieda left the land of their birth to rebuild in America. During these tumultuous upheavals in his life, the constancy of belief in Torah sustained him during the darkest hours when others despaired. Indomitable, he brought his Torah with him to America despite the physical, emotional, and psychological poundings. Perhaps not communicated directly to the Holcers, coming to America was a special assignment of the Almighty.*
>
> *The Talmud relates that the world exists because of 36 righteous people (zadikim). The selection criteria are unknown. In the Hebrew language, each letter is*

assigned a number. The assigned numbers to the letters Lamed (30) plus Vov (6) equals 36. The Hebrew word lamed vov means "heart" in English. Moshe Holcer whose very heart revitalized a moribund synagogue was born 12/12/12 for which the sum is 36, lamed vov. He and Frieda were married on Chanukah during which 36 candles, plus the 8 shammosim candles, are lit. There is a tradition is that the world rests on the existence of 36 righteous people (tsaddikim) and each tsaddik is called a Lamed Vovnik, one of thirty-six. * Their identities are unknown.

Ninety is a special age since chai (18) plus twice lamed vov equals 90. So we pray the Almighty give a proper accounting for gvurah to Moshe and Frieda for the oncoming years.

The following is taken from the OU web site:

*And it is to this principle that the second-century Palestinian rabbi Shimon ben Yohai, considered by Jewish tradition to be the author of the seminal kabbalistic text of the Zohar, appeals when he is quoted by the talmudic tractate of Sukkah as declaring: "I [alone] could exonerate the world of [God's] judgment from the day I was born to the present—and if my son Eliezer were with me, from the day the world was created to the present—and if Yotam the son of Uziahu [a king of Judah who, according to the Bible, "did what is pleasing to the Lord"] were with us, from the day the world was created to the day it ends." Shimon ben Yohai certainly did not have the modesty attributed by later Jewish legend to a Lamed-Vavnik, but his boast caused the Talmudic sage Abbaye, who lived slightly more than 100 years after him, to add to it. (Abbaye's remark is found in the same passage in Sukkah):

"There are never less than 36 just men in the world who greet the Shekhinah [God's worldly presence] every day, for it is written [in the book of Isaiah 30:18], "Blessed are all who wait for Him" [*ashrei kol h.okhei lo*], and [the word] *lo* ["for Him," spelled Lamed-Vav] is numerically equal to 36."

Mr. Holcer is introduced in chapter 36 of this book, which is a coincidence.

His earthly assignment ended, and Mr. Holcer passed from this life 9 August 2004 to blow shofar for the Almighty and the host of heavenly beings. His shofar blowing repudiated Nazism and Communism, through which he had suffered, and elevated the human spirit to learn the force and use it to serve the Almighty. A memorial stone was unveiled in July 2005 in the Groove Street Cemetery, West Roxbury, Massachusetts.

Elly and Yocheved Krimsky were married on 27 June 2007. I visited the kever of Mr. Holzer several times during the fall 2008 and ask that he intercede with the Almighty for Yocheved to become pregnant with a healthy baby. On 9 August 2009, Yaakov Yedidiah Krimsky was born on the day of the fifth anniversary of the death of Rev. Moshe Holzer. That was weird.

I wrote the following eulogy for his passing to the editor of the *Jewish Advocate*:

> *No obituary for Rabbi Moshe Holcer (August 13–19, 2004 Jewish Advocate) can ever be lengthy enough to connote his life of dedication and service to HaShem from Poland, through Siberia, to Cambridge as a teacher, counselor, parent, and role model. His struggles mirrored Jewish history from his early beginnings at a yeshiva in Poland, through devastation and deprivation,*

and finding a new life in a new land; a land that offered opportunity and sustenance to nurture a family who grew Jewishly to embody the yeshiva values he exuded as charismatic rabbi of Beth Shalom in Cambridge.

In the entire Torah only Moshe Rabbeinu is called a "servant of HaShem" [Deut 34:5] and only in the eighth sentence from the last sentence in the Torah. According to one tradition, Joshua wrote the last eight sentences. I believe that Moshe Rabbeinu was too modest to write that about himself when he wrote the first Torah. In the later writings, Moshe Rabbeinu, Joshua, Nechemia, and Daniel are described as "servants of HaShem." There is no doubt in my mind that when Moshe Holcer is brought to the Holy Court, he will be introduced as a "servant of HaShem." Cambridge will lose a Lamed Vovnick. His whole being resonated with a mystical connection to the Almighty. He viewed his life as a continuum of small and large miracles from his survival in the Russian death pits of the gulag, through the displaced person camps in Europe, to settling in the safety of Cambridge Massachusetts where the Maimonides School embraced his three daughters.

All during the years of his trials he maintained a continual dialogue with the Almighty. I once asked him if the Almighty ever responded to his prayers, and he said, "Yes, in the miracles I see every day." His approach to life was unique. The oldest among us can recall no one to whom he may be compared and the youngest among us, no matter how long they may live, will never see his likes again.

Sid Krimsky
Brookline, MA

Chapter 38

ORATORY FOR AN UNVEILING

Mr. Holcer was trained in Torah knowledge and learned self-control, modesty, humility, courage, and discipline. He prepared himself in the first third of his life for an unknown destiny. His intense mental training was followed by physical challenges in the gulag that would strengthen him for his ultimate but unknown destiny in Cambridge, Massachusetts. During the deprivations in the gulag, the evil supporters of the Communist regime who wanted to break his unbending self-sacrifice of service to the Almighty continually tested him in survival and self-control. I'm sure he heard the evil forces tempting him to forgo the faith of his teachers and succumb to the dark side. In the gulag, he never surrendered his humanity or dignity or lost his self- control or discipline. He gave hope to the weary and courage to the excoriated. From his earlier training, he emerged with the courage and energies to continue to survive in the gulag to eventually overcome the calumnies of his accusers and eventually emerge triumphant. Nazism and Communism ideologies bent on destroying the peace of the world would be defeated, and he would outlive many of their supporters. His story of education, deprivation, humiliation, hope, and emergence would inspire all who knew him. With Torah words and mannerisms he absorbed in his youth, he disarmed the opposition.

For the second two-thirds of his life, he was existentially alone, ripped from the yeshiva as the source of his strength. Evicted from the cesspools of Europe, he was sent halfway around the world as an isolated scholar to a remote Jewish outpost in Cambridge in need of his services to strengthen the Torah forces of belief, faith, and humanity. As a Torah oracle, he was sought for advice and dispensed it in accordance with his rigorous training but spoke with a certain tolerance and flexibility learned from the suffering in the gulag swamp. He will be remembered as one who strengthened the Torah by influencing others to respect and submit to the Torah power and to reject the dark side. Finally, his physicality was returned to the earth and his soul to the heavens.

Tombstone of Rabbi Moshe Holcer, Lamed Vovnick born 12/12/12 and died 8 Aug 2004, birthday of Yaakov Yididiah Krimsky.
12 + 12 + 12 = 36 = lamed vov

Chapter 39

GEORGE GAMOW LECTURE

In 1961, I attended a cosmology lecture at Sanders Theater at Harvard delivered by Prof. George Gamow, a high school hero. How exciting it was to hear the great guru of cosmology after the books I had read in high school. He was a big Russian who spoke with a cigarette between his thumb and index finger of his left hand while his right hand moved a pointer and wrote equations on a blackboard. He spoke about the cosmological discoveries newly exposed with more powerful optical telescopes. He never lived to see the stunning photographs taken by the Hubble telescope in orbit above the clouds, dust, and background lights that distorted distant signals. He never saw the stunning photographs from *Voyager* that is just now exiting our solar system. Galileo would have marveled at the photographs of colliding galaxies, supernovae, red giants, quasars, binary stars, and the surfaces of planets in our solar system. A memorial stone to Prof. George Gamow stands outside the physics building at George Washington University.

Gamow was known as the author of pocketbooks that popularized science. He piqued my curiosity when he wrote about dying stars, age of the universe, relativity and time travel, and the "twin paradox" in which a twin returning from a distant space voyage returned younger than his twin brother who remained on earth. Gamow popularized the ideas of Einstein that make our universe amazing such as the flow of time having gravity dependence. He popularized the big bang theory in the 1950s and opposed the ideas of Fred Hoyle, another outstanding cosmologist, who taught that the universe existed forever and matter is continually being created. I doubt that Gamow ever read Nachmanides who wrote a thousand years ago that the universe started from a small volume, the size of a mustard seed. If Gamow was aware of this, he could not have written it because it would have challenged his credibility as a scientist. Most cosmologists now accept the description of Nachmanides about the origin of the universe as starting from something the size of a mustard seed but are unaware that he first described it.

Chapter 40

GCA CORPORATION

I left AVCO Corporation in 1962 and accepted an offer from the Geophysics Corporation of America, a small company located on Route 62 east of Route 3. One surprising day, staff members were called into a large conference room to meet, to greet, and to attend a seminar presented by Dr. Edward Teller. Wow! He was given an accolade by the division manager, Dr. Norman Wiederhorn, as the chief scientist for the development of the hydrogen fusion bomb or commonly called the "H" bomb. Since GCA employed astronomers who assisted in the development of atmospheric and space-borne instrumentation for exploring the properties of the upper atmosphere, space, and the planets, a lecture from him about space was appropriate.

Chapter 40.1

EDWARD TELLER LECTURE

He sat down at the head of a long table. He appeared physically strong, well tailored, sure of his words, and spoke with conviction. He had a clear Hungarian accent and did have big bushy eyebrows. He appeared just as the media had described him. He excitedly spoke about quasars (quasi-stellar radio sources) that he pronounced as *KVAISARS*. quasars were newly discovered during the 1960s, and astronomers were debating the source of this very distant powerful light. Some thought that quasars were dying stars. Some thought quasars were binary stars rotating about a common axis. Some thought that quasars were distant stars whose light was captured and focused by an intelligent civilization using galaxies as gravitational lenses. I did not want to appear dumb, so I asked no questions. Quasars are believed to contain a billion suns deriving its energy from the center of a rotating black hole located at distances at the edge of the universe. Their spectra have been significantly red shifted because of their high recessional velocity from the earth.

Chapter 40.2

PROGRAM CHESS

GCA had a contract with the Advanced Research Projects Agency (ARPA) to develop an experimental system to detect oncoming ballistic missiles flying over Canada toward the United States, a non-trivial task. (ARPA was later changed to DARPA [Defense Research Projects Agency].) ARPA was given seed money by Congress to encourage private and public organizations to develop new technologies that are applicable to national defense. Program CHESS consisted of dispersing an aerosol in the upper atmosphere, along the distant early warning (DEW) line running thousands of miles from east coast to west coast in Northern Canada below the Arctic Circle. The aerosol host would consist of a gaseous medium (perhaps nitrogen) with very fine particles in suspension. The particles would produce microsecond speckles of light when impacted by fast-moving ballistic missiles above the earth's atmosphere. The speckles of light would be detected by ground-based telescopes fitted with large diameter-short focal-length lenses collecting light for highly sensitive photomultiplier tubes. Signal processing algorithms would convert the raw pulses into meaningful data and distinguish the missiles from an oncoming meteor shower. The particles in suspension would be highly reactive alkali metals such as lithium, potassium, or cesium, and/or the alkali earth metals such as strontium, beryllium, magnesium, or radium. We also considered other metals such as lead and aluminum. It would be a challenge to make this work. We overlooked environmental effects; our mission was national defense.

Successful implementation of Project CHESS would provide New York residents with thirty to forty-five minutes of warning time of a missile attack, sufficient notice to seek shelters underground. Washington DC residents would have an hour to seek shelters. Submarines would launch a military response, assuming POTUS himself authorized the launch of nuclear Polaris missiles. POTUS is a government acronym for President of the United States and was first introduced during the Clinton administration. At that time, we had no means to intercept oncoming missiles.

A GCA team of engineers prepared the aerosols and developed aerosol generators. We constructed a round concrete silo with large diameter vacuum lines, airtight ports with removable sealed heavy quartz windows, sealed doors, and roof ventilators, and tested it for leakage. We purchased and assembled large vacuum and exhaust pumps. We purchased and stored barrels of toxic materials. We conducted daily tests using commercially available aerosol generators and new generators designed by GCA engineers. We calculated particle settling time under different atmospheric pressures and gases by injecting laser light through the quartz windows and measuring scattering coefficients. Aerosols were old technology. Our application was new. The building is still there off Route 62 opposite MITRE. Very few people alive actually know what was done there, the hazardous materials employed, and knowledge of the fifty-five-gallon storage drums that leaked. Ironically, decades later, GCA Corporation sold the office building, land, and silo to Clean Harbors, an environmental clean-up corporation. The abandoned silo is still there near a creek that runs toward Middlesex Turnpike in Bedford, Massachusetts.

The task of our group was to provide sensors to detect the light from the collision of the missiles with the particles in the aerosol. My assignment was to provide a means of testing photomultiplier (PM) tubes for response to microsecond light pulses. If the PM tubes did not respond to the expected short light pulse, the concept would not work and continued funding would be terminated. This was 1963. We bought PM tubes from EMI Corporation in England. They were the best. I had to provide microsecond light pulses to test the PM tubes. A formidable challenge! Rapid solid-state switches did not exist.

From Edmund Scientific, I purchased an optical bench, lenses, prisms, apertures, optical filters and diffusers, and slow- and high-speed motors. From the National Bureau of Standards, I purchased a standard incandescent light source. I designed an optical collimator and focused a narrow beam of light on the surface of a hexagonal prism that was mounted on the shaft of a high-speed synchronous motor that could spin at 3,600 rpm. Five sides of the prism were blackened. As the motor turned, the optical beam whipped around the room too fast to observe. A small-diameter aperture in front of the PM allowed light to enter the PM tube. Filters cut out room background light. The width of the light pulse was inversely related to the distance between the motor and the PM tube. Longer distances meant shorter pulses. I connected the PM tubes to a 555 Tektronix oscilloscope to amplify the pulse and watch the pulses as the motor rapidly rotated the prism. It worked, but the light pulse was tens of microseconds. I needed smaller pulse widths. I increased the distance from motor to PM tube to about forty feet, the longest distance in the lab. The pulses grew shorter to microseconds. But the traces on the oscilloscope were unsteady, I believed as a result of vibration. I believed the building and the trucks on Route 62 contributed to all this vibration. I obtained the keys for the building on Sundays and reran the tests. Bingo! I obtained cleaner results for ten- to twenty-microsecond pulses. I learned to my chagrin that the EMI PMs did not respond to microsecond pulses. Yet they were the most advanced PM tubes at that time. The PM tubes were inadequate to respond to the speckled light produced in the upper atmosphere from a ballistic missile attack. The defense of the United States was at stake. We needed better PM tubes.

We could not talk about this. My data including Polaroid photos taken from the face of the oscilloscope were placed in a locked container. I never saw them again. My apparatus was replaced with a newly available and expensive Kerr cell that could be turned on and off in microseconds in response to an electric signal and produce a single light pulse. The Kerr cell produced the same results as my series of tests, i.e., the response time of the photocells was too slow. After a year, someone woke up in Washington, and ARPA terminated the contract. The silo is used as a storage building. The barrels of hazardous materials are gone. Who knows what hazardous materials were absorbed into the ground and retained by the inner concrete walls? The silo is silent—abandoned but there.

Since the aerosol may have consisted of fine particles of alkali metals, we had to better understand the performance of these metals under high pressure and temperature that would occur behind a shockwave when struck by a supersonic surface on a missile above the atmosphere. I, my colleague Joe Selvitella, and my boss Dr. John Ehrenfeld, developed the equation of state for alkali metals; and the paper was accepted and published in the *Journal of Applied Physics* in May 1966 (QC 1.J3230). The alkali metals (lithium, sodium, potassium, rubidium, and cadmium) are highly reactive; and any parameters that define the equation of state are difficult to measure.

The US Army recycled the name of Program CHESS. It stands for Computer Hardware Enterprise Software and Solutions program. It is the prime source for buying commercial information technology (IT) for commodity buying. CHESS uses a no-fee, flexible procurement strategy for all COTS (commercial off-the-shelf) hardware. CHESS collects requirements and seeks to purchase large volumes that drive down prices.

Test silo for testing aerosol generators for Program Chess. Note quartz windows for firing lasers through the toxic gas into the silo. Sensors on either side were used to measure settling rate and optical properties of the aerosol. Note the large elbow and ducts to exhaust contaminated air outside the silo.

Chapter 40.3

MILLIFORCE ROCKET

One of the most interesting assignments I ever had was during the planning and design of a ten-foot diameter passive communication satellite for reflection of radio waves. The satellite would be made of thin metalized Mylar, placed into orbit, and allowed to expand into a sphere. The thickness of the Mylar was about 0.001 inch, which is about one-half to one-third the thickness of plastic trash bags. The thin metallic coating would reflect radio waves from the earth and reflect the rays of light from the sun to keep the surface cool. One difficulty was that, above the earth's atmosphere, the rays of the sun impinging on the satellite exert solar radiation pressure to cause the satellite to drift out of orbit. Remember, light is both a particle and a wave. The satellite had to remain in a circular orbit to be useful.

We estimated the force on the satellite from radiation pressure as a first step to compensate for the solar pressure. From the literature, we learned that the solar radiation pressure, p, impinging on a surface above the atmosphere is $p = s/c$ where s = solar constant = 0.137 watts/cm^2 and c = the velocity of light (3×10^{10} cm/sec). (The solar constant is the solar radiation that falls on an area above the atmosphere on a line pointed to the sun.)

Therefore, $p = 4.57 \times 10^{-12}$ watt-seconds/cm^3.

Since, 1 watt-sec = 10^7 dyne-cm and 1.45×10^{-5} lbs/in^2 = 1 dyne/cm^2, therefore, $p = 6.62 \times 10^{-10}$ lb/in².

The cross-sectional area of a ten-foot diameter sphere

$A = (3.14)(10)^2(1/4)(144) = 11.3 \times 10^3$ inches²

The force $= (2)(11.3 \times 10^3)(6.62 \times 10^{-10}) = 0.15 \times 10^{-4}$ lbs $= 0.015$ millipound

(The multiplier 2 is needed because the light from the sun is reflected and not absorbed, i.e., the momentum transfer of the photon is mv - (-mv) = 2 mv.)

A small solar counterforce of millipounds had to be applied continuously to the satellite during a polar orbit and partially during an equatorial orbit; otherwise, the circular orbit would degrade into an eccentric ellipse and the satellite would move closer to the earth, encounter upper atmospheric gasses, slow down, deorbit, and burn up. My task was to counter the solar radiation pressure. Since I could not produce another sun on the other side of the satellite to apply pressure in the opposite direction, I decided to design a small rocket that could last for a year and produce a millipound of thrust with a 1.5 percent duty cycle (meaning that it would be turned on 1.5 percent of the time in orbit around the earth).

We estimated that the thrust would equal the force of a mouse fart (MF), so we officially called it our milliforce rocket and unofficially our mouse-fart rocket. Our chemist Dr. Charles Rosen (same person at AVCO) suggested we use a salt such as ammonium chloride that was stable in a vacuum and had a small but finite vapor pressure that could be increased with temperature. The outside vacuum of space would draw out the vapor from the small rocket nozzle. I pressed the salt into a Kodak metal film can, made a small hole in the dome for the vapor to escape, and attached two electrical wires into the salt and completed the circuit with a switch, resistor, and battery. I put the MF rocket into a vacuum bell jar on a very sensitive gravimetric scale that measured to millipounds. I closed the switch, and a small electric current flowed into the salt. The salt became warmer, and the sensitive scale started to move. I was ecstatic. It worked! My understanding of the physical world enabled me to dream this up. My boss Dr. John Ehrenfield consulted with company attorneys, and we applied for and were issued a US patent 3,358,452. However, the satellite program was cancelled, US government funding ceased, and the project was terminated. We were running out of government contracts. I saw the future or the absence of a future and quit the company. I was looking for something with more stability.

Use of solar radiation pressure to power sails in space is being developed by NASA. From the NASA website, "Solar sail propulsion technology bounces a stream of solar energy particles, called photons off giant, reflective sails made of lightweight material 40 to 100 times thinner than a piece of writing paper. The continuous pressure provides sufficient thrust to perform maneuvers, such as hovering at a point in space and rotating the space vehicle's plane of orbit, which would require too much propellant for conventional rocket systems. Because the Sun provides the necessary propulsive energy, solar sails also require no onboard propellant, thus reducing payload mass." The available solar pressure diminishes as the spaceship travels away from the sun and the spaceship cannot travel directly toward the sun but must set the sail at an angle to the sun's rays as does a sailboat sailing into the wind.

NASA announced that a 124-foot wide solar sail has been built and is undergoing testing at the Plum Brook Facility in Ohio scheduled for launch in 2017. The solar sail weighs seventy pounds and will carry instruments to measure space weather. We at the GCA Corporation wrote some of the original papers and proposals for ARPA, and fifty-three years later, NASA is preparing to launch a solar sail.

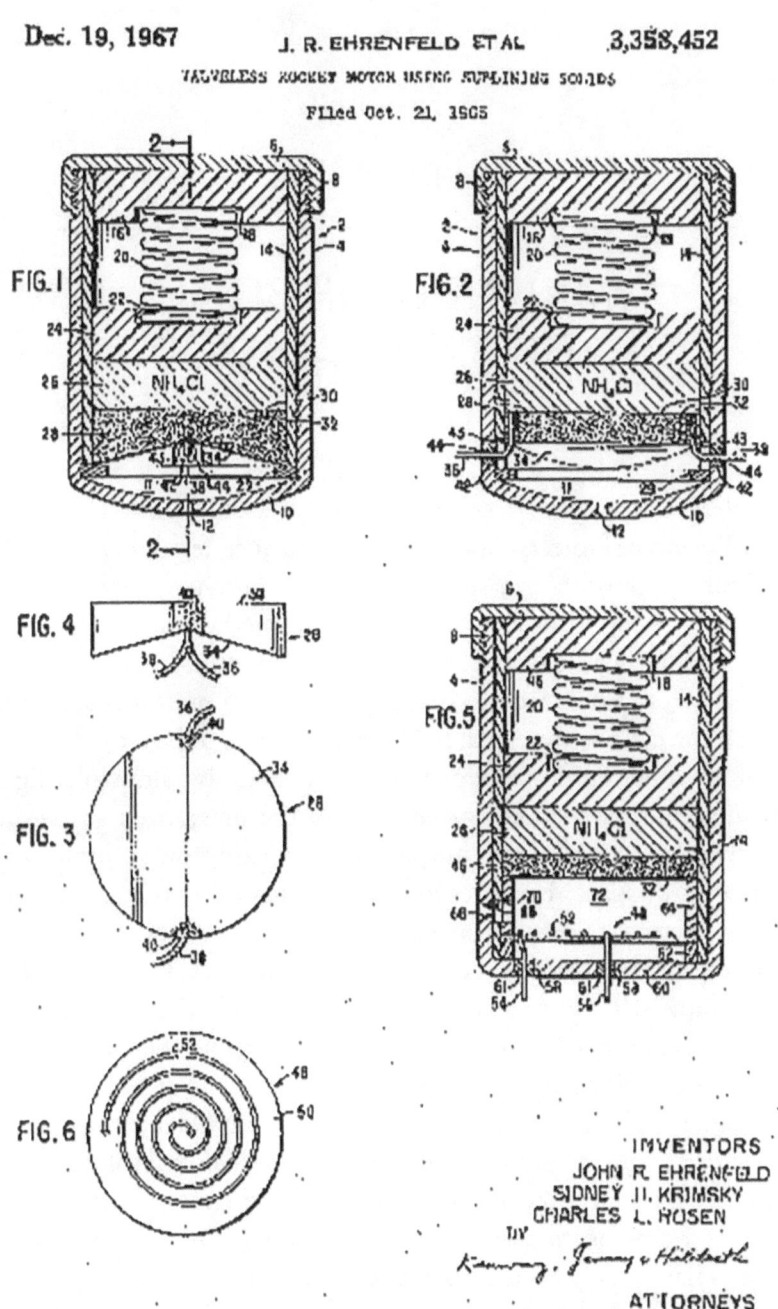

Subliming Propellant Rocket Motor AKA "Mouse Fart Rocket"

Chapter 40.4

MANNED ORBITAL LABORATORY (MOL)

GCA Corporation received a contract from ARPA (Advanced Research Projects Agency) to perform a feasibility study to assess the deployment in space of several prototype pressurized cylinders, differing in design, materials, and method of construction. The cylinders would be packaged in a canister on earth, hoisted aloft by rockets, and deployed in space by releasing a pressurized gas that caused the cylinder to expand. The material was to be a rigid honeycomb or other fabric composite cured in space by ultraviolet light. An impermeable bladder would restrain the pressurized gas within the cylinder. The ultimate purpose was to learn how to build large structures in space. I was responsible for analyzing the gas requirements, thermal transfer properties when deployed, and temperature exposure of the structure because of the sun's rays. Could we build and deploy such a large suitable structure for an MOL? Would it survive the harsh space environment? This was before the construction of the International Space Station.

One application of such materials was to build a hemispherical collector of light, a parabolic cylinder, or a parabaloidal solar concentrator. Solar concentrators would provide the energy to make heat and electricity for the astronauts living in the MOL. Such prototype engines had already been designed to work in space. I was responsible for analyzing the thermal parameters involved in designing, building, deploying, and operating a solar concentrator in space. The astronaut would examine the structure and collect data on performance, thermal risk, and degradation because of meteorites. He might even have to bring back samples of the deployed structure for analysis on Earth.

Another application for a deployed rigid structure above the atmosphere of the earth would be a paraboloidal antenna to capture images of distant stars focused on a photographic plate mounted at the focal plane of the antenna. This was imagined well before the Hubble telescope. No one was contracted to build and deploy such a rigid honeycomb structure to be deployed and epoxy-cured in space. It was a mathematical exercise, and I was paid to have fun playing with the numbers and physical thermal constants.

During the 1960s, the USAF desperately needed a BLOS (beyond line of sight) worldwide communication system. Satellites had not yet been developed. We proposed to build a large Mylar sphere, inflatable in space, that would reflect radio transmissions during orbit from ground-to-ground BLOS. We would need a worldwide array of ground-based antennas. This idea was later scrapped for Project Westford. The USAF commissioned MIT and Lincoln Labs scientists to design an orbital reflecting antenna. The scientists proposed to place 350 million thin copper needles in orbit, each needle acting as a dipole antenna to receive and reradiate transmissions from airplanes and ground based antennas. This effort was declared obsolete after the USAF launched its first communication satellite in 1965. Efforts were made to remove the needles. Some of the needles are still in orbit. Project Westford was named after the town of Westford, Massachusetts, which is home for the large Haystack radio antenna on Millstone Hill in Westford, Massachusetts, north of Boston. Haystack houses models of the first Sputnik satellite launched by the Soviet Union. I have been there several times as a visitor.

Chapter 41

BLOWING SHOFAR

In August 1966, I married Dorothy Goldstein, and she moved from Roseland Street and I moved from Massachusetts Avenue in Cambridge to 329 Summit Avenue in Brighton, Massachusetts. Before we were married, we visited different areas to look at synagogues. Based on what I learned from Shlomo Breuer and the Holcer family, we embarked on an informal path of baal tschuvim. Neither of us had formal training. In September 1969, after the high holidays ended, the shul gabbai, Henry Mazer, asked me to learn how to blow shofar. I was going to replace Mr. Kaplan, who was seventy-two years old and no longer had the strength to blow shofar. Henry's son-in-law, Chaim Feifel, purchased several shofros and asked me to try them and select one. Feifel was a noted chazzan and baal tokiah in Cincinatti, Ohio, where he performed for many years. But I had no musical talent except singing on key some of the time. Mazer insisted that I learn. He was convinced I could do it. The shofros all seemed difficult to make acceptable sounds. I could not do it. Feifel selected the easiest one for me, presented it to me as a gift, and insisted that I could learn by practice. I showed Mr. Holcer the shofar. He approved the shofar and blew it for me, but I was not teachable. He told me to practice and how to clean the shofar: Use a mix of 50 percent clean water and 50 percent pure kosher vinegar. Pour the mixture into the shofar and shake left and right. Use a bottlebrush with small bristles near the mouthpiece. Spill out the mixture and let it dry. Let the shofar remain exposed to air. Don't put into a box.

I blew shofar the first time in 1970 and after a few tekiot, I fainted on the bima. The seriousness of what I was doing and hyperventilation caught me unprepared. I was carried upstairs and revived by congregants, two of whom were licensed nurses, Hawley Levenson and Esther Mazer. My vital signs were normal. The services stopped. In a few minutes, I recovered my composure, walked downstairs, and continued as baal tokiah. I learned a valuable lesson. Later after this event, I could only imagine how Dorothy, my new wife, must have felt.

October 2010 was my thirtieth year as baal tokiah for Congregation Kadimah-Toras Moshe. Blowing shofar meant that I could not visit my children who were living in Connecticut, Long Island, or New Jersey for Rosh HaShonah. I told Rabbi Azriel Blumberg in December 2010 that I would end my career as baal tokiah. He would have to find someone else.

Chapter 42

SMITHSONIAN OBSERVATORY IN CAMBRIDGE

The Smithsonian Observatory in Cambridge advertised for a lead mechanical engineer to address various technical problems. I applied and was hired. My interest in physical astronomy (cosmology) made this opportunity particularly satisfying. I attended the free lectures on Thursday nights at the Smithsonian Observatory on Garden Street. The Smithsonian was only partially funded by the government and primarily funded by private sources, so I thought this would offer more stable employment. The Smithsonian was an old respected organization and not about to fade out of existence.

My first assignment was to investigate and improve the process for capturing meteor images on a Baker-Nunn camera stationed at Wallops Island, Virginia. The camera was developed by Dr. Baker and Dr. Nunn at Harvard University, Department of Physics. The camera had a large diameter and short focal length lens and was used to track meteors. The major problem with this camera was that the focal plane was curved, not flat. The images of meteors off axis were blurred if flat film was used. The astronomers used accurate dividers to measure the distances between the images. Measurements between blurred images resulted in uncertain conclusions about the source, location, and number of meteors entering the atmosphere. Flat film could not be used. Curved film that conformed to the curved focal plane was needed.

The engineering technicians at Wallops Island developed a means of forming flat film into a hemisphere by positioning twelve-by-twelve-inch film between a male and female vacuum hemispherical mold; heating the mold, which softened the film; and then cooling the mold. The final shape resembled a cardinal's hat. The edges were trimmed, and if we were lucky, the hemispherical film retained its shape. This operation was all done in the dark to avoid fogging the film. The film was then placed onto the curved focal plane of the Baker-Nunn camera for exposure. The problem was that the film did not retain its shape after leaving the vacuum mold. Much film was rejected. Process reliability was poor. I was asked to fix this problem.

I recommended strict process controls already in place by the technicians. Excess heat fogged the film. Insufficient heat resulted in shrinkage of the curved film. I requested and received authorization to visit Kodak Park in Rochester, New York, to discuss this problem with Kodak engineers. Perhaps different film with different mechanical or exposure properties might work better than the film we were using. I met with the Kodak engineers, and they could not help me. We were not a large-enough customer for Kodak to invest resources to address our problems. I could not improve what the technicians had been doing. I could only validate their process. I could not fix the problem. Solutions would have to wait until the development of electronic photography and pixilated curved focal planes (like the eye of a fly).

Chapter 43

MEETING AND MARRYING DOROTHY

I met Dorothy at a party in the summer of 1965 at the apartment occupied by Al Goldstein and Marvin Koren that they called Middlesex House named after Middlesex County in Cambridge, Massachusetts. The word Middlesex has nothing to do with sexual orientation. Middlesex sounded like a new gender between male and female. Albert was a PhD student at MIT, and Marvin Koren worked at GCA Corporation and was also a PhD student at MIT. Marvin became an expert in bomb blast theory. Marvin and I worked at the GCA Corporation in Bedford, Massachusetts. Marvin, Albert, Bill Beres (another PhD physics student at MIT) befriended one another. Beres turned to religion a few years later. He died in 2009. I perceived her as an overdressed, overly made-up, amusing, overly communicative, intelligent, and exaggerated young pretty female studying at Harvard Summer School and planning to return to her active social life in Queens, New York City. She was teaching at a public school in Winthrop, Massachusetts. I met her by accident outside the Harvard Coop and suggested we go out, but she had a playdate with her young girlfriends she befriended in Cambridge. I suggested that we all go for a trip to Cape Cod in my Peugeot with its roof that opened. The four of us went on a trip to Cape Cod, and I thoroughly enjoyed myself escorting these young giddy girls. I saw her in a different light. Dorothy and a female roommate moved into an apartment on Roseland Street in Cambridge and found a job teach-

FROM BROOKLYN NY TO BROOKLINE MA

ing at Winthrop High School. We paired off, and the rest is history. We hiked into the mountains of New Hampshire and went skiing. She was a good sport about it coming from the sidewalks of Queens where there were no mountains and no ski sites. We even hiked to the top of Mount Washington with Marvin Koren and Isabel whom he later married. We visited all the tourist sites in and around Boston. We announced our engagement in March 1966 and were married on 18 August 1966.

I did not meet her parents until after we became engaged. Based on what Dorothy told me, I knew they would not approve of a short balding man with orthodox leanings with peasant parents. Dorothy's parents were both born in America. I had to rely on Albert, her brother, to tell them about me and prepare them for what they would see. Albert knew I was no flake. I had a good job, an apartment, an automobile, and a good education. That is the impression I wanted them to have. We became engaged, and it was too late to make any changes. Her parents had to accept me. My parents took an immediate liking of her.

I had to notify my parents. From my apartment at 1200 Massachusetts Avenue in Cambridge, I called my parents with Dorothy present and told them I was engaged. My mother asked if I was drunk, which appeared to be a strange question because I never got drunk. I put Dorothy on the phone, and she introduced herself, and we scheduled a trip to New York to meet both sets of parents. I was confident Dorothy would not back down.

At the time we met, I was formulating a model of the kind of life I wanted to lead. The model was based on the families I observed of Shlomo Breuer and Moses Holcer. Our children would attend the Maimonides School, we would live an orthodox lifestyle, and I would join a synagogue as a paying member. From my experiences in Brooklyn, California, and Cambridge, I concluded that this structured lifestyle was the best environment in which to raise children. However, there remained serious questions. Could I abandon all my gentile and Jewish non-orthodox friends? Could Dorothy adapt to a new lifestyle that she was taught was old-fashioned and obsolete and be subjected to the opprobrium of her parents, aunts, uncles, and friends? Was I asking too much of her? Could I sacrifice attending seminars and traveling on the Sabbath? It was almost as if I changed genders. It was most difficult explaining to my associates and friends that our life was tied to the Jewish calendar. Vacations were limited because of taking days off to observe Jewish religious holidays. We had to absorb new constraints and new rules. These were difficult decisions and challenges. On the other hand, I saw the products of Maimonides School and the public schools. I had an opportunity to extend Jewish education to the end of the twentieth century, and Dorothy and I made the necessary adjustments.

I investigated several synagogues before we were married and found Kadimah-Toras Moshe in Brighton, Massachusetts, to be the friendliest and most accepting of my ignorance. I got to know Henry Ferber, Marvin Levenson, Henry Mazer, and Jack Sugarman. Dorothy befriended their wives. Rabbi and Sylvia Halbfinger were always there to provide insight into Jewish thought and practical advice after I started to attend Kadimah on a regular basis. So we started our journey into orthodoxy with a faith that it would all work out.

Dorothy Krimsky standing next to Royal Canadian Mounted Policeman. In Montreal on our honeymoon.

On Cadillac Mountain, Acadia National Park, Maine

Dorothy Goldstein and Sid Krimsky abord the USS Constitution in 1965 in Charleston Naval Shipyard

Dorothy Goldstein resting on platform on the top of Mt Chocorua in NH.

Ski-School—Blue Hill Mountain in Milton, MA.
Penny Pitou was an olympic skiier.

Dorothy Goldstein as a glamarous young lady

Dorothy Krimsky on a boat ride around Boston Harbor

Dorothy Goldstein hiking up Mt. Monadnock in New Hampshire

FROM BROOKLYN NY TO BROOKLINE MA

Dorothy Krimsky on a boat on the Rideau Canal in Montreal

Dorothy Krimsky operating anti-aircraft gun
on USS Massachusetts in Fall River.

Chapter 44

DEATH OF ALEX KRIMSKY

This chapter is filled with unpleasant suppressed memories and is the most difficult to write. Alex suffered his first major heart attack while sitting on a bench outside the MIT boathouse. After taking him sailing, he insisted on helping me lift the boat off the water and placing it onto the boat racks. He looked pale and slumped over. I called an ambulance that drove us to Massachusetts General Hospital across the Charles River. He was admitted into the emergency room where the doctors stabilized his condition. My mother and I met the next day with an assigned doctor, Dr. Wheeler, who prescribed nitroglycerin pills. He spoke to us about his prognosis. I asked him to tell my father to stop smoking, but the doctor refused. My aunt Annette came to Boston to visit him and stayed at my apartment. She loved listening to my music especially Brahms's concertos. She was the trained musician in my family.

Alex returned to New York, continued to drive a taxi, but had a few blackouts. He stopped driving. He wondered around the housing project aimlessly. His whole purpose in life to support my mother was suddenly taken away from him. He continued to smoke. My mother started to look for work. She had not worked in thirty years. She could cook. She could sew. She found work in the garment district as a seamstress.

On the seventh day of Chanukah, 30 Kislev 1966, five months after our wedding, he collapsed in the downstairs common hallway of my parents' apartment building. People stopped and called the doctor whose office was in the apartment building on the first floor. The doctor called the ambulance. My mother was home, and she and he rode together to Coney Island Hospital. My mother called my aunts, and it was Annette who broke the sad news to me in a phone call. She called my brother who was living in Cambridge, and we plus Dorothy drove to New York City that night to attend a funeral the next day.

The saddest day of my life was being at home at 413 Neptune Avenue and not seeing my father in the apartment and knowing that I will never again see him. He was always there offering a helping hand and useful advice.

Next day we drove to the Midwood Memorial Chapel on Coney Island Avenue to conduct a brief service and say good-bye. A few of Dad's friends showed up as well as his sisters and brothers-in law and my grandfather. I viewed the open casket for a few minutes. The whole experience was surreal. I expected him to come in wearing one of his hats with a twinkle in his eye. After all, this was a family gathering. My mother, brother, and I sat in the hearse and were driven to Montefiore Cemetery on Springfield Boulevard, Long Island. It seemed like a long trip into an out-of-the-way place. The gravediggers placed the casket that my mother selected into the ground. The casket was not a simple pine box but was colored cherry red with fancy metal handles. They placed him near a chain-link fence. I have been back many times to cut the shrubs and to talk and recall our good times together watching TV or when he drove me back to my apartment on Riverside Drive Sunday nights, where I lived for a year during my stay at CCNY, or when he dug into his pockets for a dime almost every summer night so I could buy an ice cream, or when we went out for an early morning breakfast when he drove me to meet my driver to take me to New Jersey where I worked as a shipping clerk and he spoke to the waiter in Russian. That spooked me because he never spoke to us in Russian except to say "Edi-spot," which means "Go to sleep." He never demanded anything for himself except to own, repair, and drive his car. He was a low-maintenance father. I never heard him complain, and I never saw him sick. He loved to drive, and he loved to maintain the engine and the car.

He once painted parts of the engine gold because it lasted him a long time and provided good service. During the severe blizzard of 1948, I remember that I helped him to dig his car out from the snow when he parked it on the street. He never asked me, but I volunteered to help. It was a father and son working together. He could not give us money, but he gave us what he had.

He frequently left for work very early in the morning when I was still sleeping and would sometimes return before I left for work at Nathan's Famous in the summertime. I used to joke with him that we could save money by sharing shoes. His foot was bigger than mine at my age.

We believed that he contracted strep throat as a teenager that developed into rheumatic fever that damaged his mitral heart valve.

EULOGY FOR ALEX KRIMSKY (by Sidney Krimsky delivered at the funeral)

Alex Krimsky came to this country in 1924 as an immigrant boy of 16 years. Penniless and without skills and education he sought work as an unskilled laborer.

He married amidst the depression and started married life with very little.

The war years provided work and Alex tried to enlist in the Seabees for overseas work but was rejected for medical reasons. He was offered and accepted work as a second class engineer at the Baltimore Naval Shipyard to help build victory ships with which to win the war.

The war years ended and the post war housing boom began. Alex moved to New York and worked as a house painter which became his chosen vocation.

Although unschooled himself, he realized the importance of learning. He sent both sons to Hebrew School and provided for the kind of home environment which fostered un-interrupted study so that both graduated high school and went on to college. Those years were rough for Alex because he toiled daily asking so little for himself and giving his all to his family.

Although not wealthy financially he boasted "I'm richer than the richest millionaire because I have a good wife and two sons."

He did not have a multitude of friends but those of us who knew him cannot forget the twinkle in his eye, the cheerful disposition and his willingness to help a friend in need without being asked.

Even in the face of medical disability and inconvenience, his feelings pride, self-sufficiency and independence never wavered.

His cheerful disposition carried his family through his own medical crises. Alex died as he had lived, unafraid, fearless and independent.

EULOGY FOR ALEX KRIMSKY (by Sheldon Krimsky delivered at the funeral)

Alex Krimsky did not actively participate in religious ceremony nor in the communal prayers of Judaism yet he practiced a <u>personal religion</u> that surpassed in value any organized religious practice.

- A personal religion which teaches ultimate duty and self-sacrifice to one's family
- A Religion which surpasses even the Golden rule – since he often did unto others and never anticipated any return
- A Religion without many words but with strong emotional feeling suppressed within the portals of a golden heart
- A religion which taught the values of self-pride and independence

Whatever were the forces and sufferings that confronted him, he often remained silent, hopeful that his silence would screen his own problems from others. That one man alone can conquer the world, which he expressed in his own words as "with these two hands I can do anything", is the fantasy by which he often lived.

He was a man whose avocation and vocation were one; namely the unyielding desire to put in a hard day's work, and receive his due reward.

Amidst the affluence of society his demands were few and simple. Without formal education and with limited skills, he sought the opportunity to improve upon himself; and improve himself he did through the achievement of his sons, in whom a part of him remains.

And what remains as a legacy is a spirit, a spirit of giving. He tried foremost to give peace of mind to those close to him, and so he minimized his ills, and that, took all he had.

Mom, Dad, & Sheldon standing on the Sinclair Weeks Bridge over the Charles River connecting both sides of Harvard University at the time of receiving my MSME at Northeastern University.

Chapter 45

BIRTH OF OUR CHILDREN

Dorothy completed her MA at Northeastern University before the birth of Alec Seth Krimsky. The birth of a first child is an extraordinary experience for anyone but especially for me because of the death of Alex Krimsky in December 1966, only five months after we were married. My father never lived to see his grandchildren or his younger son get married. I choose the name Alec in English because I could not bring myself to call him Alex; it was too close and too painful. I chose Seth as a middle name because Seth was a substitute for Abel who was killed by Cain in the Torah. His Hebrew name would be the same as my father, Eliyahu. For the first two years until Naomi's birth, I doted on Alec. Dorothy stayed home and upon my return from work would say, "Take him. He's yours" to give her a few hours respite, and I would take him. When he started to crawl and walk, I would wrestle with him on the room rug and take him outside to Griggs Park off Washington Street for him to run around and climb the fire engine, which was eventually removed from the park around the year 2010. It appeared to be safe for children to climb. Alec would make up stories and pretend to be someone else to our amusement. He started to talk at an early age, and I learned later that he was verbally precocious. He received his mother's genes because I was never that way.

Alec was born in 1968, one year after Yom Yerushalim, an auspicious day. I tried to attend the delivery, but the hospital rules forbade me from attending. After the birth, I contacted Rabbi Abraham

Halbfinger about what to do for a bris milah. He spoke with Henry Mazer who took care of everything. He bought the food and set it up in our apartment. The bris was on a Shabbos or Yom Tov; there was no eruv, so we could not go to shul. The brit milah was held in our apartment on 403 Washington Street in Brookline. My mom and my zadie, who was sandek, came from New York City. For my zadie, it was a big honor to be sandek for his great-grandson especially at a proper bris and seudah mitzvah. I do not know if his other children had such affairs for their sons. I was not invited, and my mother would have told me if there were such an event.

One month later, my cousin Max Katz served as cohain to redeem Alec during the pidyon Haben, also occurring in our home. I gave him five silver dollars that I collected in 1958–1959 in Harrah's Club near Lake Tahoe in the California–Nevada State Line. At that time, silver dollars were used as gambling chips on the roulette and card tables. One could easily buy them. This practice of selling silver dollars was eventually stopped because the silver made the coin more expensive. Presently, the silver in the silver dollar may be too small an amount for pidyon haben. Rabbi and Silvia Halbfinger, Uncle Al and Aunt Anita Goldstein, Grandma Rose, Grandma Belle, and Grandpa Goldstein were at the pidyon haben. Alec was so small I had to lift his neck to have him look up. His neck muscles were not developed. Once again, Henry, Esther, and Myra Mazer purchased and set up all the food for the seudah mitzvah for the pidyon haben. I learned from the brit milah, but all this overwhelmed me. I was also working full-time.

About two years later, Naomi Ilana was born. Dorothy and I liked the name Naomi named after Nathan, Aunt Lena's husband. I also liked the name Naomi, reminding me of Naomi Berta Breuer, Shlomo's oldest daughter, who made aliyah in 1966 just before we were married. Once again, I tried to be present at the birth at the Boston Lying-In Hospital, but hospital rules forbade my presence. So I waited in the husband's room, and Dorothy emerged tired and serene, holding her little girl. She had red hair. I took some movies of her and Naomi entering the taxi that brought us home. We had a Shalom Nikaivah Friday night and named her Saturday morning in shul. Alec took to his little sister, but I spent most of my time with him walking with him outside to the park sometimes with Naomi in the carriage. We enrolled him in Mrs. Ciment's preschool in Lubavitch when he was four years old where we met the zany Dolly Bloom. Mrs. Ciment advised us that Alec had musical ability that she saw right away. She recommended that we offer him piano lessons. So we did, and from age six until he graduated Maimonides and left to study in Israel, the piano was always in use. He studied piano for ten years. We made the same offer to Naomi, but she tried for a while and lost interest. We offered piano lessons to Jonathan, and Jonathan studied piano for ten years.

Alec was seven years old when Jonathan was born. Esther Mazer slept at our house to stay with the two children when I went to the hospital. This time the hospital allowed me to be present in the delivery room so I saw Jonathan's birth. It was a sight I can't forget. From the spaghetti that covered the head of the emerging baby, I saw a baby emerge. Quickly the nurses cleaned the baby, cut the umbilical cord and removed the afterbirth, and handed the baby to the mother. Dorothy was tired but exhilarated. He was larger than his siblings. I called him a giant baby. I stayed with Dorothy all night and walked home as the sun was rising. This was Succoth. I promised to tell Naomi first, so I woke her up and told her that she had a little brother. She asked me if his hair was red. I said no, and she fell back to sleep. I then woke up Elly, and he smiled after I told him and went back to sleep. Esther Mazer walked the children to shul, and Naomi could not wait to tell everyone that she had a little brother. By the time I arrived, everyone knew.

Rabbi Arnold Wieder was mohel for Alec and Jonathan. The bris for Jonathan was on shemeni atzeret. I visited Rabbi Wieder in his *succah*, and he wanted to know if our shul conducted such events inside the succah. He asked me technical questions, and I referred him to Rabbi Halbfinger. Henry, Esther, and Myra Mazer prepared all the food and set up the tables for the seudat mitzvah after the bris. I selected the oldest man in the shul, Mr. Berlin, to be the sandek. His daughter, Eva Berlin, died in 1990. We named the baby Jonathan Isaac, after my grandfather, Isaac." "We liked the name Jonathan.

Alec and Naomi acted as Jonathan's parents. They spoke for him, translated his wants to us, and engaged him in play. Whenever we asked Jonathan a question, Alec would answer, and Jonathan would say "Ga," so we called him "Ga man."

I tried to teach Alec from early on to be able to argue with me and win on occasion. He approached us when he was four years old and spoke for Naomi, asking me to get her a big bed instead of the crib in which she was sleeping. Eventually, we would have to do this. I argued with him, saying that she could fall out of a big bed. Safety was important. Naomi was two and could not argue for herself. After two sessions, Alec convinced us to provide a railing or a floor mattress so she would not hurt herself in a big bed. So we went out to a furniture store to buy her a big canopy bed with four posters. She liked the canopy bed and the French-style furniture.

FROM BROOKLYN NY TO BROOKLINE MA

IT WOULD HAVE BEEN SUFFICIENT

If he had only becalmed and encouraged us it would have been sufficient.
If he only told us what to buy, it would have been sufficient.
If he had only told us how to set up, it would have been sufficient.
If he had only told us where to buy the food, it would have been sufficient.
If he had only lent us the bridge table, coffee urn and serving platters it would have been sufficient.
If he had only offered to obtain the whitefish, challah and herring, it would have been sufficient.
If he had only obtained the largest challah in Boston, it would have been sufficient.
If he had only baked the delicious kugel and cake, it would have been sufficient.
If he had only prepared the nahit (chickpeas), it would have been sufficient.
If he had only come as a guest with Esther and Myra and enjoyed himself, it would have been sufficient.
If he had only instructed Jim Sullivan to deliver what was needed, it would have been sufficient.
If he had only walked in the rain to share our simcha, it would have been sufficient.
If he had only offered to cater by himself, it would have been sufficient.
If he had only brought Esther and Myra to help him cater, it would have been sufficient.

But he did becalm and advise us, told us what to purchase, told us how to set up, lent us the bridge table, urn and platters, obtained the largest challah in Boston, bought the whitefish, herring and challah, baked the kugel and cake, prepared the nahit, instructed Jim Sullivan to deliver what was needed from the Synagogue, walked in the rain to share our simcha, catered the entire affair, brought Esther and Myra to help him and was modest in all his undertakings.

And he did all of these things to make my brith milah a wonder simcha for all to enjoy.

This is Henry Mazer to whom I extend my heartfelt thanks. Alec Seth Krimsky

Brit Milah poem dedicated to Henry Mazer, Esther and
Myra for preparing the meal after Brit Milah.

Alec and Naomi sitting on entrance to second floor new bathroom on October 1972 in 108 Westbourne Terrace.

Zadie & Bubbie Skolnick with Alec Krimsky. He told me that he would not be able to attend Alec's bar mitzvah. I encouraged him but he died after Naomi was born.

FROM BROOKLYN NY TO BROOKLINE MA

Over the sidewalk cross Corey Road
to Mazer's house we go;
the kids know the way
on Thanksgiving day
through the rain and melted snow.

Over the sidewalk cross Corey Road
walk fast the time draws near
to pass the plates
and sit with mates
and enjoy each other's good cheer.

Over the sidewalk cross Corey Road
wash our hands without delay
after eating later
to thank our creator
for this is Thanksgiving Day.

Over the sidewalk cross Corey Road
On Yom Hahodaot
mindful of yore
when our spirits did soar
we shall soon light the Chanukiot

Over the sidewalk cross Corey Road
to Mazer's house we go
for all to eat
is Mazer's treat
for which we thank him so.

Sung to the tune of "over the River and
Through the Woods to grandma's house we go."

"Over the River and Through the Woods" to Mazer's
House we go to enjoy a thanksgiving dinner.

Chapter 46

RENT CONTROL IN BROOKLINE

The yuppies living at 329 Summit Avenue, above our first apartment as a married couple, were rowdy, so we moved to 403 Washington Street in Brookline after a year. We rented a spacious three-bedroom apartment on the third floor of a building owned by the realtor Maurice Gordon. His apartment manager, Herbert Breitstein, was very accommodating by repairing, painting, and retiling the bathtub. Dorothy enrolled in Northeastern University, transferred credits from Harvard University Summer School, and completed her MA in secondary school counseling before delivering our first son in May 1968. Our first son was a miniature mechanical toy with inputs and outputs and occasionally switch-off time to recharge his batteries. After my working day, Dorothy would hand him to me and I would bathe him and stimulate him to where he did not want to sleep. He has not changed. It was autumn of 1968. Heat in the apartment was intermittent, and we had a baby. On some days, the temperature dropped below sixty degrees Fahrenheit, and I became concerned. Dorothy expected me to do something. I explored the basement and the boiler, talked with the custodian, and learned about the condition of the heating system. It needed attention. The custodian told me that parts were on order. I waited patiently, and still there was insufficient heat. More time elapsed. I heard more excuses. Remembering how I grew up in Coney Island in a cold apartment, I decided to go downtown to Federal Street to the real estate office of Maurice Gordon, my landlord, and plead with him or his representative to fix the heating system. His secretary was polite and promised to present Mr. Gordon with my message. Everyone was out of the office, and no one was available to handle complaints. The secretary assured me that Mr. Gordon would do everything to restore full heat in the building. I believed her and went home, thinking that I actually accomplished something. I was wrong. I accomplished nothing, but I did not know this at the time.

I continued my trips into the basement and spoke with Frankie, the custodian. Since I majored in thermodynamics and structures for my MSME that I received in 1965 from Northeastern University, I believed that I could understand heating systems. I learned about the hardware and the behavior of the hardware from the custodian. I grasped the problems but not the solutions. We still were without heat and moving into the coldest part of the winter.

I wrote a letter to the landlord, stating that I was putting my rent into escrow until the heat was working. Attorney Al Kramer was on the staff of Governor Frank Sergeant. He lived in an attached building in which we shared the same heating system. He met with me and agreed to put his rent into escrow. Governor Sergeant later appointed Al Kramer a judge in the District Court of Quincy a few years later. Al Kramer became famous after promulgating a novel idea to keep repeat drunken drivers off the roads by imposing hard punishment and alcohol treatment. The state of Massachusetts adopted a watered-down version of Kramer's model by permitting repeat offenders to avoid jail sentences by agreeing to receive help with their alcoholism. He retired from the Quincy District Court in 1993 after serving the bench with distinction. He continued to speak out for tough sentencing for repeat drunken driver offenders. In 2005, the Massachusetts State Legislature passed a bill named after Melanie Powell who was killed by a repeat drunken driver. Melanie's Law would severely punish repeat drunken drivers. The federal government already took action by denying transportation funds to states that do not have laws or programs to deter repeat drunken drivers. The legislative wheel in Massachusetts grinds slowly. The proposed bill has been watered down by the state legislature.

I received notices from the landlord to pay the rent. I notified him about the absence of heat and the escrow fund. The last notice from the landlord was a threat to evict me. Not wanting to expose my wife and child to an eviction, I yielded by paying all the back rent and felt helpless. The laws at that time did not protect tenants from unresponsive landlords. Al Kramer received similar notices and legally maneuvered to delay implementation of the eviction. Months later, he finally moved from the premises without paying his back rent.

During this time, the *Brookline Chronicle Citizen* and the *Boston Globe* uncovered a growing trend among large landlords in Boston and Brookline to chop up apartments and rent to students, most of whom attended Boston University (BU), thereby increasing rental income for the owners. BU admitted students in excess of the available space in the dormitories. Families were leaving Brookline. As a consequence, the size of the Hebrew school at Kehillath Israel substantially decreased. Senior citizens were also driven out of their apartments.

Brookline has a town meeting representative form of government. The town of Brookline is administered by a five member board of selectmen (BOS) and an executive secretary who carries out the wishes of the BOS. The BOS usually meet once a week on Monday after 5:00 p.m. to discuss town issues for permits, licenses, grievances, etc. The town meeting serves as the town legislature and currently consists of 240 elected citizens of Brookline spread among fifteen precincts. The Town meeting members vote on budget issues, zoning issues, school issues, capital funding, salaries of town employees, new construction, etc. The town meeting usually occurs once a year around March and more often if necessary. Selectmen are usually long-term residents who have served Brookline for many years on one of the many volunteer committees and who are voted into office.

The Brookline Board of Selectmen, in response to a troubled social climate at the time, issued a request for volunteers to serve on a new Rent Control and Grievance Board (RCGB) to mediate disagreements between landlords and tenants. The RCGB had no formal authority but could recommend compromises. The discussions usually resulted in nonbinding recommendations. I volunteered to serve on the RRGB and was interviewed by the board of selectmen. I explained my views to them about building code violations, escrow funds, and unresponsive landlords. Louise Castle was the chairman. Attorney Sumner Kaplan was one of the five selectmen. I was not picked but was cornered after the interview by Sumner Kaplan, who liked my passion and suggested that I contact Attorney Herbert Goodwin, who was also not picked. Craig Bolon, a physicist at Harvard, volunteered to serve and was also not picked. Tutored by Sumner Kaplan, we three rejects met and formed the Brookline Tenants Council. I was determined to do something, but I had no experience or knowledge about town government or politics. This was all very new to me. I was in over my head. I wanted to do something.

Herb Goodwin, who was later appointed a judge for the Brookline Municipal Court by Governor Dukakis, was our leader. Herb was the brother of Richard Goodwin, former speechwriter to President John Kennedy. Richard was married to Doris Kearns Goodwin, noted historian and biographer of President Lyndon Johnson. Herb had the requisite legal knowledge and experience. He was also a tenant. He knew the town. His wife Rhoda, a clinical psychologist, was absolutely engaging and charming with an infectious sense of humor. Herb and Craig knew people from the Democratic Party. The Brookline Tenants Council expanded quickly to about twenty people. Herb, in my eye, was an admirable leader with integrity. He was absolutely trustworthy and knew the law and understood the strains on the tenants. He was a tenant in an apartment on Thatcher Street owned by Ida Gottleib, who, as many other large landlords at that time, failed to address building code violations. The Brookline Tenants Council urged the Building and Health Departments to enforce the building and sanitary codes. Code violations were apparent in Brookline, but the town had a history of nonenforcement.

Potential rent control supporters were invited to meet at Sixty-First Griggs Terrace, home of Mrs. Anne Jackson, a long-term town meeting member. This was my first introduction to local politics. She was a very gracious, classy lady who lived in an exquisite single-family house furnished with memorabilia from faraway travels. Professionally, she screened schoolchildren for eye problems. She advocated progressive causes and participated in the 1963 march on Washington DC for civil rights. She was an artist, and the walls in her house were adorned with her works. We entered a warm house; and she prepared the usual tea with cookies and other refreshments, introduced ourselves, and started to talk about the new degradation of civility, denial of civil rights, and unfair treatment of tenants by avaricious landlords. Between the discussions in her house and in the home of Attorney Herb Goodwin, the Brookline Tenants Council was born. Ms. Jackson was a supporter of fairness toward tenants and eventual rent control. She really saw beyond her own needs. She lived to ninety-five and died on 13 August 2005. She was buried on 15 August. I was on my way to Seattle, Washington, on 15 August. Otherwise, I would have attended her funeral. I am sure that many local politicians remembered her contributions to civility and progressive ideas.

The Brookline Tenants Council had many meetings in Herb's house and a large rally at the Devotion School. We invited many speakers with different viewpoints. We pushed for strong laws to protect tenants from evictions, large rent increases, and code violations. Pro-landlord supporters warned the attendees of the dangers of "rent control legislation" and charged that the run-down South Bronx neighborhood in New York City was caused by rent control. "No one will invest in new housing in Brookline," "We need more investment, not less," "Rent control will discourage investment and only more investment will increase the housing stock." But people needed protection now. There is a long path from increased investment to having sufficient heat for my infant son. I viewed the arguments as unreal. Time had run out. Tenants needed protection from greedy and unscrupulous landlords. Yes, it sounded like Communism.

By consensus, the Brookline Tenants Council (BTC) developed an action plan to be implemented immediately. Our plan was to query all the candidates for the annual town meeting about their support for strong rent control by-laws and ask for their support for strengthening the enforcement of the building and sanitary codes. We would then publish this information in the newspapers. The *Brookline Citizen* newspaper printed the weekly statements of Herb Goodwin; the Brookline Tenants Council was in the news. The Brookline Tenants Council had acquired name recognition and credibility thanks to the efforts of our spokesman, Herb Goodwin.

We queried the candidates for every townwide office from selectman to town meeting member. We collected and shared the data with one another. We recorded the names of candidates we supported for election on slips of paper. The slips were sorted geographically. Each of us was assigned a specific geographic area to inform tenants by inserting slips into mailboxes. Each of us carried hundreds of slips, and over three to four weeks before the town meeting, we inserted the slips into the mailboxes of all the fifty-five thousand residents of Brookline. I covered Fairbanks Street, Washington Street, and some apartments on Beacon Street. The winter was ending, but there was still a chill in the air. I walked on Sundays and often at night. I preferred the late night hours because no one would stop and question me or challenge me. I smiled at people who saw me insert the slips into mailboxes, and I avoided any conversation.

One resident asked if I was being paid to distribute the slips. I replied, "No, this is a total volunteer effort." This was a numbers game, and there was little time to engage in conversation late at night. My wife knew where I was going, but I don't think she was too happy with me running around the neighborhood late at night. I returned often at 1:00 a.m. from these midnight forays, walking all around my neighborhood, satisfied that I was doing all I could to effect protection for tenants. I went to work the next day exhilarated with hope that Maurice Gordon would be ultimately humbled by passage of new by-laws that would provide more protection for renters. Almost all the candidates supported by the Brookline Tenants Council were elected to the town meeting, but it was not enough to pass real protective by-laws for tenants. Since one third of the town meeting members run for office each year, we needed to repeat this effort the following year.

The Rent Review and Grievance Board chaired by Chairman Attorney Carl Sapers heard hardship cases and tried to mediate, but the RRGB had no enforcement authority. Stronger by-laws were needed. Rent control was needed. People accused Herb Goodwin of pandering to the public for eventual political gain. There are always people who mistrust the motives of people with integrity because the attackers have no strong moral conscience. Herb Goodwin did not run for higher political office. I do not recall that Carl Sapers was ever accused of pandering, yet he was eventually elected as moderator of the town meeting, an office he held for nine years with distinction. Attorney Carl Sapers was never appointed as a judge even though he was a partner at the same law firm (Hill and Barlow) as Mike Dukakis who eventually became governor of Massachusetts. Mr. Sapers became an expert on design and construction law. I wonder if his experiences on the RRGB listening to alleged building code violations from tenants influenced his decision to study and gain expertise in architectural design and construction law.

My next-door neighbors were Isadore and Sara Alpert, an engaging senior couple who explained to us that rent control in Brookline, an old Yankee town, would never be established. We were fruitlessly spending our time. He worked for the Action for Boston Community Development (ABCC), a human services agency assisting over one hundred thousand low-income families and individuals to fight poverty and promote self-sufficiency through education, job training, and family support initiatives. Mr. Alpert had been peripherally around local politicians and claimed to have understood their mind-set. Who was I, a newcomer to Brookline, to overturn the status quo? There is nothing more powerful as an idea whose time has come. The time had arrived. He would be proven wrong—really wrong. The tenants supported rent control candidates, and the majority of Brookline residents were tenants. The BTC tapped into a rich political vein.

Next year we again polled the candidates for town meeting. We stuffed all the tenants' mailboxes with slips containing the names of candidates supported by the BTC. This time, however, I received a notice from the Brookline Post Office telling me that mailboxes are federal property and it is illegal to use mailboxes for purposes other than delivery of US mail. I never found out who caught on and reported us. I ignored the directive, and anyway, we had completed the task. Almost all candidates supported by the Brookline Tenants Council were elected. We did it! The town meeting now had more pro-rent control and more members who supported tenant protection by-laws than two years ago. The town meeting members recognized that the RRGB was not working and replaced it with by a Rent Control Board with increased powers to limit rent increases. The state legislature cooperated by passing enabling legislation. This strong rent control by-law was challenged, and the challenge was defeated in the courts. Brookline had rent control. Boston and Cambridge soon followed. Tenants who felt threatened had new tools. All housing except owner-occupied two-family housing was placed under rent control. Unrestrained greed by landlords was curtailed. Commonwealth Avenue is lined with BU dorms. Boston University was told to build more dorms to ease the housing pressure, and it did.

During the years of the great rent control debate, the *Brookline Chronicle Citizen* published letters for and against rent control legislation. One of the more interesting and energetic opponents was Attorney Gerald Fogelman who described himself as a small landlord. He remodeled multifamily houses and expected to be rewarded for his initiative and investment. He owned several old buildings occupied by multiple students. He received citations from the building department about the condition of his buildings. He argued that rent control was a denial of due process and was inherently unfair. In a letter to the *Brookline Chronicle* on 2 November 1972, he proposed converting rental units to owner-occupied condominiums. However, not all tenants could afford the costs of purchasing rental units as condominiums. If landlords insisted on condominium conversion, should tenants be forced to leave or be forced to purchase their rental unit? Should the rent control board decide these issues? Mr. Fogelman, an admitted libertarian, opposed all forms of government restraints. We had a series of newspaper debates in which I challenged his views that property rights were more important than the rights of people to whom property is rented. He saw landlordism as absolute, and I saw landlordism as an opportunity to earn a fair return within certain restraints. The demand for housing exceeded the supply, and this unbalance skewed the housing market. This skewed market was advantageous to landlords who chopped up large apartments to invite unrelated tenants to increase their rental income. It seemed to me that this was inherently unfair. Government was needed to restrain greed and end the unresponsiveness of the most egregious landlords at least temporarily. The free market for housing in Brookline needed correction before rent controls could be abolished. Attorney Fogelman took advantage of a skewed market he did not create.

A few years later, Mr. Fogelman sold his property, divorced his wife, moved to Jerusalem, and purchased a donkey that he used to carry goods including fliers for religious classes that he distributed to tourists. I met him outside the walls of the old city of Jerusalem distributing such leaflets but without his donkey.

Many landlords converted their apartments to condominiums after enabling legislation was passed in Governor Dukakis' administration. Condominium owners cared for their property. Initially, condominium costs were low; but as demand increased, so did their cost. Rent control in Brookline became an administrative nightmare during the ten years after passage. However, tenants had protection until the housing stock increased and students had more dorms.

The newly formed Rent Control Board would have teeth. On 20 September 1970, I wrote a letter to the board of selectmen asking that Attorney Carl Sapers, chairman of the Rent Review and Grievance Board, not be appointed to the newly formed Rent Control Board, which was to replace the RRGB. I received a written communication from the executive secretary, Mr. Richard Leary, that he received my letter and placed it on file. Sapers was involved with the Brookline Foundation for Housing whose mission was to provide affordable housing using government subsidies when appropriate. Mr. Sapers had verbally threatened me because of a letter I wrote to the *Brookline Chronicle Citizen* in which I complained that he raised the rent of Prof. Joseph Gartner after the Brookline Foundation for Housing took possession of a two-family house. The Gartners received an eviction notice. The rationale offered by Sapers was that the Gartners would not want to stay in the same building with tenants who had subsidized rents. The Gartners offered to pay the increased rent. The element of sensitivity was missing and possible conflict of interest was present, which is what prompted me to write to the selectmen. I recommended that he not be appointed to any future rent board. He was not appointed. Mrs. Marion Dubbs, who and her late husband founded the Concerts for Brookline Youth, was appointed as head of the Brookline Rent Control Board.

During the vigorous debate over many months, the heat in my building improved. We lived at 403 Washington Street for four years. Since owner-occupied two-family houses were exempt from rent control, in 1972 we purchased and occupied a two-family house. We used the rental income to improve the building. I learned lessons about the value of home ownership and laws of supply and demand of housing from hearing all the arguments during those frenetic days. The rent control by-law encouraged the emergence of other prorent control liberal organizations who pandered to the tenant votes. The Brookline Tenants Council had vanished after a few years and was replaced by the Brookline Tenants Union (BTU). The BTU supported tenants' rights and other liberal measures. About ten to fifteen years after the rent control by-law was enacted, it had run its course. The rent control bureaucracy and by-laws were terminated but not without resistance from a coalition of liberal groups such as the BTU and PAX, the newly formed propeace organization that had emerged in response to the Vietnam War. During the rent-control years, code enforcement had improved, condominium conversions started, rent increases were restrained, landlords recognized their obligations, housing construction increased, BU built dorms for their students, and the bitter rancor had gradually subsided to where market forces influenced rental costs. Eventually the 403 Washington Street building was sold as condominiums.

In the long run, rent control is undesirable because the bureaucracy for implementation is untenable (an administrative nightmare) and the return on investment is constrained by nonmarket forces. Bureaucracies would have to make economic decisions for landlords about profit, fair rent, return on investment, need for repairs, etc.

However, rent control should be used as a last desperate measure to protect tenants when all else fails. I am proud to have worked with some really fine people who saw their civic duty and acted instead of just pontificating. Rent control provided protection for elderly, for families, and for aggrieved tenants against the unrestrained greed of certain landlords who ignored their responsibilities to maintain their property in good order.

As a final source of personal satisfaction, Boston University declined to accept the offer of $1 million from Maurice Gordon to name the new school of nursing building after him. Nurses paraded around the new building with uncomplimentary placards, denouncing the offer with accusations that Mr. Gordon was a slumlord. I never characterized him as a slumlord. In my opinion, he was an unresponsive wealthy landlord. Maurice Gordon was humbled, and I felt a certain satisfaction. He sold his property in Brookline. He died a few years later in Florida. He reminded me of Tsar Nicholas II who was unresponsive to the hardships of his subjects. He enjoyed a privileged life until all was taken from him by the Leninist Bolsheviks who eventually executed him and his family in a basement in Swerdlovsk, an ignominious end to the Romanoff Family who once ruled over eleven time zones.

We moved from 403 Washington Street to 108 Westbourne Terrace in Brookline in 1972. Years later, we received a rent control exemption certificate from the Rent Control Board since Dorothy and I owned and occupied a two-family house. Our struggle for tenants' rights became a distant memory but one that I will forever remember with fondness. Craig Bolon resumed his career in physics, and Herb Goodwin was appointed as judge to the Brookline Municipal Court where he presided with distinction until his retirement. He was honored by the town of Brookline on November 1, 2001, for his years of dedicated public service. My wife, Dorothy, was elected to the Brookline town meeting and served for twelve years until she was defeated by the efforts of the Brookline Tenants Union and PAX who supported more liberal candidates. The BTU dissolved when rent control was finally abolished. The *Brookline Chronicle Citizen* newspaper disappeared, and with it went the core history of all the events surrounding a tumultuous decade in Brookline politics.

I am proud of my service to the Brookline Tenant's Council to bring rent control to Brookline, screw Maurice Gordon, and protect tenants from landlord greed. Where else could a newcomer be accepted so quickly into the body politic to effect change? This could never happen in New York. Herbert N. Goodwin was our maximum leader for rent control. He was a municipal judge for 12 years and a former attorney for the Justice department. He died on 26 June 2015.

Chapter 47

LINCOLN LABS AND THE LIGHT GAS GUN TO STUDY MISSILE REENTRY PHENOMENA

From 1964 to 1966 I accepted employment at Lincoln Labs in Lexington, MA as the supervisor of a light gas gun facility. The gas gun was an 18foot long steel barrel through which various projectiles were propelled by acontrolled rapidly expanding exploding gas. Projectiles emerged from the barrel at 2-3 times the speed of sound. The projectiles (cones and spheres) entered a vacuum chamber with low argon or nitrogen gas pressure. The projectile left a wake of ionized gasthat could be photographed using Schlieren photography. Lasers were pointed into the chamber through quartz windows and the absorption of the laser beam by the ionized wake could be measured. Hence the electrical properties of the wake could be studied. Scientists studied the wake with the eventual purpose of constructing sensors based on the ionization wake left by hypersonic missiles entering theEarth's atmosphere. My job was to manage the facility and fire one shot per day, have all the equipment calibrated and ready to work. After each shot, the barrel had to be cleaned, new projectiles had to be machined, residual gases were pumped from the tanks and new gases injected. The projectiles were stopped by a series of aluminum plates in the second chamber. I took one such 2 foot X 2 foot plate home for use as a cooking blech on top of our gas stove. It fit perfectly. I even made two lamps from the spent plastic cylinders used to drive the projectiles down the barrel of the light gas gun.

I published several technical papers during my employment at Lincoln Labs when I was the supervisor of a light gas gun facility. The purpose of the facility was to fire small projectiles (cone shaped) into several vacuum chambers. The scientists used lasers and microwaves to study the wake left by the projectiles. An understanding of the properties of the wake was an essential part of National Defense.

The most interesting paper I presented to the 13thmeeting of the Aeroballistic Range Association, 29 August 1967, in Quebec, Canada. It was entitled "Optimization of the Center of Gravity of Composite Axisymetric Solids." The center of gravity of a solid cone is ¾ of the distance to the bottom which is beyond the center of pressure which is why we needed a composite cone made of two different materials; the more dense material being the tip and the less dense material being the frustrum. The light gas gun fired small cones that had to be made in two parts in order for the center of gravity to be closer to the tip than the center of pressure. The tip had to be heavier than the frustum for aerodynamic stability. The conical tip was brazed to the frustrum of the cone. Anyone who shoots arrows at a target understands this principle. At Lincoln Labs the tip of tungsten was brazed to the titanium frustrum. The composite center of gravity of the cone cannot exceed 2/3 of the height of the cone because that is the aerodynamic center of pressure. The CG is moved toward the tip as the ratio of the density of the two materials increases.

The geometric model I used and the equations for a cone made in two parts, a tip and a frustrum brazed at the joint, are shown in the following pages. The Greek letter rho is used to denote density.

The math demonstrates that for a density ratio of 4:1, the center of gravity is forward of the center of pressure allowing for a stable flight. It turned out that the brazed joint for a density ratio of 4:1 was forward of the center of pressure for aerodynamic stability. The center of gravity of a solid cone = ¾ hand falls behind the center of pressure which makes the cone inherently unstable in flight and that is why the cone is made in two parts. The drawings of the geometric model and the equations are shown on the following pages.

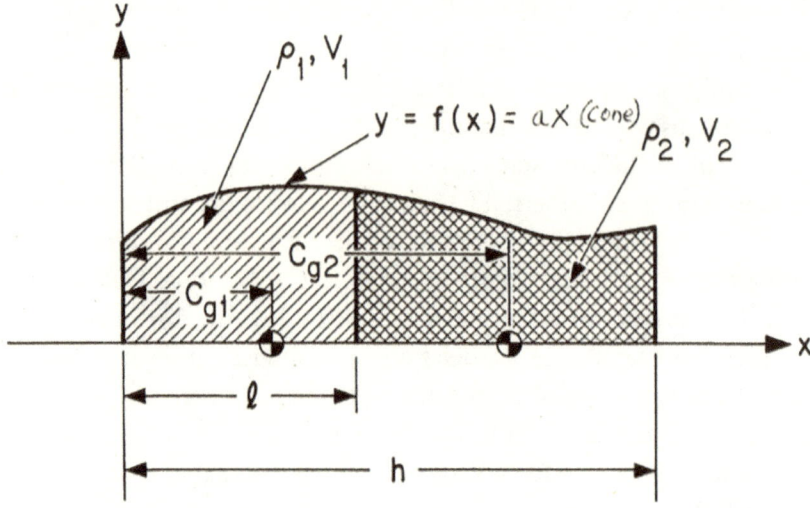

Fig 1 Geometric model of a composite axisymmetri solid.

What value of l/h is needed to make Cg/h a minimum value? A minimum value of Cg/h is needed for a maximum correcting moment of the cone traveling at hypersonic speeds.

Return to the basic equation for Cg/h.

$(Cg/h)[2Z/3(l/h)^3 +1] = 0.25 + Z/4(l/h)^4$; Let Z= 3 as before.

Take the derivative of d(cg/h)/d(l/h) and set it equal to zero. Then solve for l/h.

The final equation is: $2(l/h)^6 + (l/h)^3 = 0.5 (l/h) + 1.5 (l/h)^5$

For which the solution is l/h = 0.72, and Cg/h = 0.253.

The design of the hypersonic tungsten-titanium cone has thus been optimized.

The math describes the design of the hypersonic tungsten-titanium cone.

Making a substitution for the ratio of densities:

$P(1)/P(2) - 1 = Z$ $P(1)$ = density of the tip, $P(2)$ = density of the frustum

The solution becomes:

$(Cg/h)[2Z/3(l/h)^3 + 1] = 0.25 + Z/4(l/h)^4$

The density of titanium = 4.85 grams/cc. The density of tungsten = 19.3 grams/cc

The ration of densities = 3.97. Therefore $Z = 3$.

Assume that $Cg/h = 0.25$ as a guesstimate

$0.5(l/h)3 + 0.25 = 0.25 + 0.75(l/h)4$

$l/h = 0.666$

Why did we select $Cg/h = 0.25$? Selection was not arbitrary.

In Fig. 1 we see a composite axisymmetric solid whose tip is of volume V_1, density ρ_1 and whose frustrum is of volume V_2, density ρ_2. The total height (or altitude) is h and tip length is ℓ. The function which generates the axisymmetric solid is of the form $y = f(x)$. Taking moments about the origin, the over-all center of gravity can be expressed as

$$Cg = \frac{\rho_1 V_1 Cg_1 + \rho_2 V_2 Cg_2}{\rho_1 V_1 + \rho_2 V_2} \qquad (1.)$$

where

$$Cg_1 = \frac{\int_0^\ell \pi x y^2 \, dx}{\int_0^\ell \pi y^2 \, dx} \qquad (2.)$$

and

$$Cg_2 = \frac{\int_\ell^h \pi x y^2 \, dx}{\int_\ell^h \pi y^2 \, dx} \qquad (3.)$$

Hence

$$Cg = \frac{\rho_1 \int_0^\ell xy^2 \, dx + \rho_2 \int_\ell^h xy^2 \, dx}{\rho_1 \int_0^\ell y^2 \, dx + \rho_2 \int_\ell^h y^2 \, dx} \qquad (4.)$$

Rewriting equation (4)

$$\frac{\rho_1}{\rho_2} \int_0^\ell y^2 (Cg-x) \, dx + \int_\ell^h y^2 (Cg-x) \, dx = 0 \qquad (5.)$$

Making a substitution for the ratio of densities:

P(1)/P(2) -1 = Z   P(1) = density of the tip, P(2) = density of the frustrum

Making a substitution for the ratio of densities:

$P(1)/P(2) - 1 = Z$ $P(1)$ = density of the tip, $P(2)$ = density of the frustrum

The solution becomes:

$(Cg/h)[2Z/3(l/h)^3 + 1] = 0.25 + Z/4(l/h)^4$

The density of titanium = 4.85 grams/cc. The density of tungsten = 19.3 grams/cc

The ration of densities = 3.97.   Therefore $Z = 3$.

Assume that $Cg/h = 0.25$ as a guesstimate

$0.5(l/h)^3 + 0.25 = 0.25 + 0.75(l/h)^4$

$l/h = 0.666$

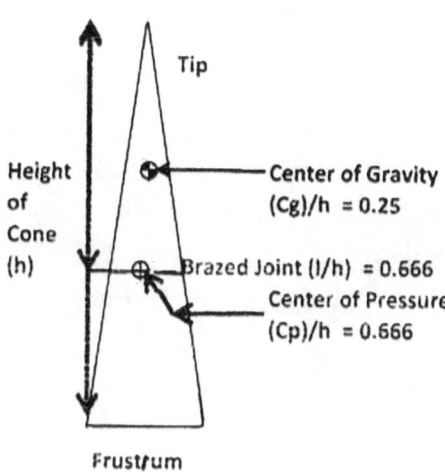

Height of Cone (h)

Tip

Center of Gravity (Cg)/h = 0.25

Brazed Joint (l/h) = 0.666
Center of Pressure (Cp)/h = 0.666

Frustrum

Making a substitution for the ratio of densities:

$P(1)/P(2) - 1 = Z$ $P(1)$ = density of the tip, $P(2)$ = density of the frustrum

The solution becomes:

$(Cg/h)[2Z/3(l/h)^3 + 1] = 0.25 + Z/4(l/h)^4$

The density of titanium = 4.85 grams/cc. The density of tungsten = 19.3 grams/cc

The ration of densities = 3.97.   Therefore $Z = 3$.

Assume that $Cg/h = 0.25$ as a guesstimate

$0.5(l/h)^3 + 0.25 = 0.25 + 0.75(l/h)^4$

$l/h = 0.666$

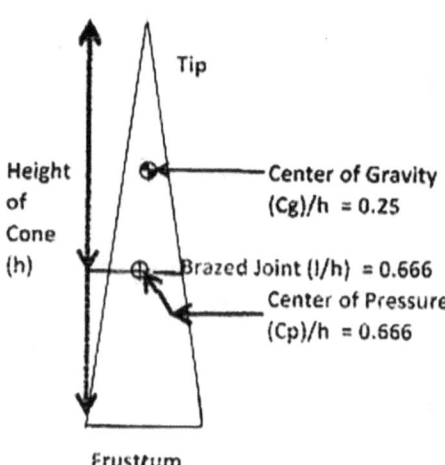

Why did we select Cg/h = 0.25? Selection was not arbitrary.

What value of l/h is needed to make Cg/h a minimum value? A minimum value of Cg/h is needed for a maximum correcting moment of the cone, traveling at hypersonic speeds.

Return to the basic equation for Cg/h.

(Cg/h) [2Z/3(l/h)^3 +1] = 0.25 + Z/4(l/h) $^{4;}$ Let Z= 3 as before.

Solve the equation for (Cg/h). (Cg/h) = function of (l/h); (l/h) becomes the independent variable.

Take the derivative of (Cg/h) with respect to (l/h) and set the derivative equal to zero. Solve for l/h.

The final equation is: 2(l/h)^6 + (l/h)^3 = 0.5 (l/h) + 1.5 (l/h)^5

For which the solution is l/h = 0.72 and Cg/h = 0.253.

The design of the hypersonic tungsten-titanium cone has thus been optimized because the center of gravity is as close to the tip as possible for maximum aerodynamic correcting moment.

The math describes the design of the hypersonic tungsten-titanium cone and provides the framework for trade-offs of material density and location of the brazing joint.

This example of using mathematics to define the design of the cone is elegant and demonstrates the power and beauty of mathematics to define a stable projectile travelling hypersonically in a partial vacuum of 40-80 torr in order to study the wake as means of identifying missiles flying above the atmosphere directed toward the United States. The ultimate goal of The ARPA program was to study options for national defense. I was proud to have participated in this program.

I presented this paper at the Frontenac Hotel in Quebec where we stayed. The hotel overlooked the St. Lawrence River. The view was magnificent, and we explored old Quebec City.

I learned during the 1967 Arab-Israeli War that my supervisor was disappointed at Israel's remarkable victory. He knew that I was Jewish. I left early Friday evenings and did not go to various luncheons, and after the stunning victory, he would say "They don't belong there" that I took to mean that the Jews do not belong in that part of the world. He believed that the United States must have helped them out. I was in no position to argue with him. But he and most Americans were shocked at the result of the six-day war. The job lasted two years, and then I was released because the ARPA contract expired. My supervisor made no attempt to place me elsewhere. The light gas gun facility was closed and the building used for office space.

Chapter 47.1

MY INTERACTION WITH UNCLE MUNYA

In 1926 Munya was eighteen years old and decided not to immigrate to the USA on a visa arranged by his father who lived in Philadelphia. My father went in his place. Two years later, at the train station when his two sisters and mother left Russia for America, my grandmother knew she would never see him again. Munya married and worked as a printer. He was drafted and emerged as a major in the artillery corps. His division pushed the Germans east toward Konigsberg in East Prussia near the Baltic Sea. The Germans were killed, captured, or escaped by sea. The Germans never returned Konigsberg, and the Russians renamed the city Kaliningrad. It was incorporated into Russia. His wife, Frieda, and son, Salim, were relocated to safety in Siberia. My father rarely spoke of him, and I never even knew that he existed. The family lost contact with Munya before, during, and after WWII.

Approximately in 1960, Aunt Pauline, sister of Munya, learned that he was still alive living in Kiev. She arranged to contact him. My cousin Elaine traveled to Europe and managed to visit him in Kiev by driving a car through Germany and Poland, quite a brave feat at that time. Pauline still remembered to speak Russian and arranged to visit him in Russia. She told us that the government provided him with a refrigerator so he and the Communist government would not be embarrassed. She arranged for Munya to visit the USA. His wife was not allowed to accompany him. Russian Jews were not allowed to leave the USSR at that time. The Communist government feared contamination by the West. Our family connection is described in chapter 1.

Munya wrote a series of letters to me, wishing us well and hoping that he could attend Alec's bar mitzvah whom he met when he stayed with us for about a week in the fall of 1969. Alec was about one and a half years old at the time. Alec ran around the house and sat on Munya's lap. Munya wrote later that it is a bit too late for him to attend Alec's bar mitzvah because he was about sixty-three years old in January 1969. His handwriting was clear. I paid a Yiddish scholar to translate the letters for me in 2012. Bar mitzvah meant something to him, but he opposed religion. Go figure!

He exchanged photos when he visited us and by mail. He used an English dictionary and I used a Russian dictionary to communicate difficult words. Now there are computerized translation programs. I wish we had one in 1969. He tried to learn English even at his age, and I tried to learn Russian. He went for walks in Kiev and attended the cinema even seeing American films. He wrote that he heard Mario Lanza sing in the movie. He attended concerts and heard Stravinsky and Gershwin. He heard the orchestra playing a symphony written by his son, Salim. Salim in Russian may be Shalom in Hebrew or Salum in Arabic. He was probably named after Munya's father, Samuel, whom he did not see after Munya turned sixteen years old. He was proud of his only son, Salim, and Salim's son Igor who attended musical college. Salim's daughter, Anna, later studied at the Moscow Conservatory. She became a concert pianist, and Igor became a piano teacher. He referred to himself as Zaide Munya and his wife as Bubbe Frieda. In every letter, he wished us well and gave special mention of Alec. He never saw or knew Naomi or Jonathan.

Munya wrote that he and Frieda are atheists in a letter to me dated 14 April 1969 in Yiddish. He sent me many letters to me mostly about wishing us well, asking about our children, and his describing activities in Russia. He said that he did not believe in a God who sits in heaven, the Garden of Eden, or the messenger of death (malach hamaves). He said that he believes in humankind (mentchlichkeit), but we could not discuss philosophy because of language difficulties. He said that he did not want to discuss these matters because he did not want to disturb my religious sensibility. He said, "There will come a time when you will start to look at life around you with different eyes." These are profound statements and were never expressed to me by any of his siblings. I would have enjoyed arguing with him, but the language barrier separated us. I could not tell him of his misperceptions based on the lies and misinformation he has been fed about Jews in America and our core values of being Americans. He wrote that he studied Chumish and Gemorrah and sang very well. However, the level of his knowledge was based on fairy tales, and he was never exposed to sophisticated Jewish thinking. He was influenced by the Communist government to abandon all religious and independent thinking. He had to survive by surrendering all religious identity; however, the culture remained, and he was able to read and write Yiddish, and he read from the Yiddish newspapers in Russia.

Munya wrote that he believed in "humankind." Unfortunately, I did not have the Yiddish or Russian language skills to question his thinking or provide arguments by Rav Soloveitchik, Rambam, words of the prophets that have come true, or the anthropic principle or evolution by design and not be accident. I was unable to talk about the wisdom in the Torah that could not have been written by any mortal.

He lived long enough to see Elly on a visit when Elly taught Torah in Talinn. Elly flew to Moscow with a translator. But Elly could not argue Torah with an eighty-seven-year-old Russian Communist who did not speak English or Hebrew. The Union of Soviet Socialist Republics (USSR) formally ceased to exist on 26 December 1991. After seventy-five years, the great experiment in Communism failed in Russia. I do not recall if Munya lived to witness that momentous event. Salim and his two children seemed to be less dogmatic than Munya. Near death, Munya admitted that he made a mistake in not coming to America in 1924 when his name was on the visa.

Our cousins living in Russia, Cherkessk, August 1994. Left to right: Igor, Salim, Svetlana, Polina, Anna, Daniel and Galya Krimsky. They all live in Russia because Uncle Munya refused to come to the USA when he had a chance.

Grandma Rose, Uncle Munya, Dorothy & Alec Krimsky during visit by Uncle Munya (DYADA Munya)

Chapter 48

POLAROID

In October 1969 I received a phone call from Gregory Lindin who interviewed me for a process/design engineering position at the Polaroid Corporation in Cambridge, Massachusetts. He was to become my supervisor for the next fifteen years. I was fortunate in being assigned a variety of engineering tasks across many disciplines in measurement, process control, design, materials, environmental engineering, and safety. Finally, I left the unstable military industrial complex to join private industry. My quantitative skills that I used for the past eleven years were not required. I would design and test hardware to develop "instant movies." I designed and tested prototype machinery and components to manufacture film for instant cameras and later for instant movies. We were called the sesame division, and all of us were subject to the same security rules that I later learned by working for the federal government. The ultimate objective of our program was to design an affordable instant movie system consisting of camera, processor, and film cassette. I was a witness to the remarkable technical development of instant movies and instant slides on a small scale and then witnessed the scale up to complete a huge plant at Norwood, Massachusetts. I worked on many engineering problems and climbed the corporate ladder with two promotions in nineteen years.

I was accepted for the executive development program until management found out, after testing me, that my left brain performance of analytical skills was off the chart and my right brain skills were average. I did not quite fit into their defined mental cubbyholes as a Polaroid manager. I also took physical stress tests, and the technicians had my heart pumping at 180 beats per minute on a treadmill. I was declared a noninsurance risk with a dominant left brain, conforming to an internal set of ethical rules, which makes me nonconforming as a top-level manager but with a high-energy and high-performance personality. I did not know any of this until the psychologists explained it to me. They told me who I was. I concluded that I was a nerd. Now I began to understand why I could not become a corporate manager. I worked there for twenty years, ending as chief design engineer for photovoltaic development. I was scheduled for another promotion. My boss reported to the vice president for R&D. I had a great career.

In 1985 Dr. Lawrence Kaufman asked me to work for him at Polaroid. He developed and managed a joint venture with Spire Corporation in Bedford, Massachusetts. The overall task was to develop the hardware for light sensors using amorphous silicon to be used in Polaroid cameras. Use of amorphous silicon for this application was promised to be a technical breakthrough. If the efficiency of converting sunlight into DC current was high enough, Polaroid could develop and market solar panels for producing electricity.

In May 1987, Spire Corporation reported in *Solid State Technology* magazine (p. 56) that the Solar Energy Research Institute (SERI) confirmed the efficiency of a spire-produced gallium arsenide solar cell at 23.7 percent. This was confirmed by Sandia National Lab and NASA as the highest efficiency solar cell ever produced. An amorphous silicon cell produced at Spire and tested by SERI was 10.5 percent. NASA is using 20 percent efficiency solar cells to provide power for the space station. Spire was far technically ahead of anyone else at that time to manufacture prototype solar cell panels.

In 2014, I contracted to rent my roof facing south to NRG Solar for placement of nineteen solar panels. After solar energy is absorbed by the atmosphere and reflected by the panel glass, each panel converts about 11 percent of the sun's energy into DC current when the sun is shining. Some energy is lost from DC to AC conversion. The solar constant above the earth is 127 watts/foot^2. Approximately 7.7

watt/foot^2 is lost through the atmosphere. The panels deliver about 13 – 14 watts/foot^2. Their efficiency is about 11 percent. I learned the technology by working on the joint venture between Polaroid and Spire Corporation from 1987 to 1989. I attended technical conferences about photovoltaics and the future applications.

My primary assignment was to design and supervise construction of a vacuum chamber large enough to conduct experiments by using flammable gases such as silane, hydrogen, and methane; toxic gases such as diborane, phosphine, and arsine; and corrosive gases such as silicon tetra fluoride and boron trifluoride. The gases broke down in an RF field. Boron and phosphorus bombarded the amorphous silicon-heated substrate, thus "doping" the amorphous silicon chip that turned it into a semiconductor that released electrons when struck by photons coming from the sun. Arsine and phosphine were highly toxic, and the threshold limit value (TLV) was parts per billion. We also used argon and helium to purge the copper tubes carrying the gases into the vacuum chamber. Even minute amounts of oxygen would contaminate the amorphous silicon chips that were growing and reduce the efficiency of converting sunlight into electricity.

As the chief design Engineer, I was responsible for safety of the photovoltaic site in Waltham. On 5 May 1988 I delivered a paper entitled "Hazardous Gas Management at a High-Tech Facility" about safety handling of toxic gases at the First Annual Polaroid Health, Safety, and Environmental Technology Symposium at Bentley College in Waltham, Massachusetts. I still have the DVD. I purchased Telos toxic gas detectors and interacted with the emergency medical staff at Waltham Hospital just in case one of our employees accidentally sniffed toxic gas. That was the first and last of such a symposium.

How to safely lift the vacuum chamber was a major problem. A major discussion topic among the scientists and technicians was how to safely and reliably lift the chamber without contaminating the inside of the chamber, within a reasonable cost. Also, the chamber had to be put back in the same place on the table constructed for that purpose. The traditional method was to use an overhead crane with a chain and pulley. I ruled that out as too expensive and repositioning the chamber would be a continuing problem. I purchased a hydraulic lift to raise automobiles and modified it to lift the 791-pound chamber vertically. The system was built as I designed it on paper, and the day of testing arrived. The chamber was cantilevered to the hydraulic lift. Some technicians worried that the torque on the hydraulic lift was too great and the chamber would topple. But the center of gravity was close to the center of the table so the table legs were far enough apart to prevent such a catastrophe. I recall Professor Dillon from Brooklyn College who taught us statics and told us that we were there to learn how to think for ourselves. If my design failed, I was finished. Judgment day arrived, and we tested the hydraulic system to lift the vacuum chamber. I started the hydraulic pump, and the chamber moved upward without shaking. Everything worked perfectly as I believed it would. My judgment was never again challenged by the PhD researchers for whom I built the vacuum chamber reactor. It was a moment I will forever relish.

The gases were introduced into a vacuum chamber in small precise amounts, and a radio frequency signal was initiated that broke down the gas molecules and some deposited onto the amorphous substrate. Any contamination in the vacuum chamber by air molecules would render the test results unsuitable. The vacuum chamber had to be absolutely clean with no traces of air.

The gas lines entering the chamber had to be oxygen free, and to do this required purging the gas lines with pure argon using an assigned vacuum pump. The chamber had to be opened occasionally to test and replace the amorphous silicon substrate. The chamber was made of stainless steel with quartz ports, valves for the vacuum pumps, ports for ionization, and thermocouple gauges to measure pressure. The chamber weighed 791 pounds. From 1987 to 1988 I wrote purchase orders for $500,000 for all the components needed to build the chamber, control panels, and housing for the deadly gases. That was the best assignment I ever had, and my boss recommended me for another promotion. This effort was to end abruptly, and the joint venture collapsed. Spire asked Polaroid for seed money, and Polaroid refused and was soon facing a leveraged buyout.

FROM BROOKLYN NY TO BROOKLINE MA

In spring of 1988, Roy Eisner of the Disney conglomerate announced that he purchased 5 percent of the outstanding Polaroid stock as the start of a leveraged buyout. Polaroid had an overfunded pension program and owned buildings in Cambridge near Kendall Square with low returns on the investment (ROI) and too much liquid assets. Polaroid failed to market the instant movies. The company had invested about $500 million over twenty years in the instant-movie program and was not able to recover this investment because VCR tapes were introduced at the same time. Polaroid was ripe for a takeover. My job was in jeopardy since Eisner would probably divest the nonprofit research divisions in which I worked. Six months earlier, Polaroid created an employee stock option plan (ESOP) in which I enrolled. Polaroid matched employee contributions that were used to purchase Polaroid stock at lower-than-market prices to encourage employee ownership in order to incentivize employees. I did not need further incentives.

Eisner challenged the ESOP in the courts by saying that the ESOP was designed to frustrate a takeover. This attempted takeover was called a leveraged buyout because the proceeds from the sale of parts of the company would pay for the costs of buying the company. Every day during the spring and summer was filled with rumors and uncertainties about our future. Polaroid defended itself by lowering its expenses by initiating a "reduction in force" and borrowed about $500 million to buy back much of the available stock at a price higher than the market price. The stock rose from $28 to $50 per share. Eisner sold his shares at the higher price and walked away with millions of dollars. Polaroid was left with enormous debt.

My job disappeared. My whole division was cut. We had a photovoltaic lab in on the top of Bear Hill Road in Waltham overlooking Route 128. On a clear day, we could see the top of Mount Wachusett on which I spent hours skiing in the winter with my children. A grand Westin Hotel is located on the bottom of Bear Hill Road clearly seen from Route 128. I was directed to stop all research and dispose of all the high-priced lab equipment in our photovoltaic lab. All this pained me, but I was still being paid to follow orders.

The equipment in our lab consisted of vacuum chambers and plumbing, vacuum gauges, RF generators, power supplies, vacuum pumps, diffusion pumps, cross-purge assemblies, and turbo-molecular pumps made by Leybold-Heraeus in Germany. I issued request for proposals from universities for Polaroid to provide this equipment for free. They had to submit proposals for how they would use the equipment. Boston College submitted the best proposal for graduate research in vacuum depositions. They sent over a truck, and we packed and deposited all the useful equipment into the vehicle. It hurt me to see how much good research equipment we gave away, equipment for which I wrote specs and personally purchased. A few months later, I contacted Boston College and was invited to see how graduate students were using the equipment. I learned that one of the lab professors of physics was Prof. Rein Uritam, associate professor of physics, husband of Justine Uritam. Now the following paragraph is an amazing story, almost unbelievable.

In the 1980s asbestos was sprayed onto the steel beams during the construction of Newton North High School. This was an acceptable method to protect the steel beams from melting during hot fires. Asbestos was used as a flame retardant and noise absorber. However, in the 1970s asbestos was also identified as a carcinogen responsible for asbestoses and mesothelioma, a rare form of lung cancer. During the construction of Newton North High school, Justine Kent-Uritam, a social studies teacher, lodged a complaint with the Newton School Committee about the asbestos used in the construction and was ignored. She was not even a science teacher. She was perceived as a hysterical teacher out of her area of expertise. The newspapers exposed the story. From my experience with asbestos at the Maimonides School, I knew I could I could help her. I called her up, asked to see her, and requested samples to determine if the material was asbestos and to identify if the material was chrysotolite, the most dangerous kind of asbestos. I visited her in her classroom. She handed me an envelope, and I provided the samples to Marilyn Barry, a microscopist at Polaroid. She used a 5800 power microscope with phase-contrast capability and compared her photos with the photos in the McCrone catalog to identify the asbestos as the most dangerous kind. This asbestos consisted of thin long fibers that lodged in the lung and were difficult to remove. I brought the Polaroid photos back to Justine-Kent Uritam, and she was thrilled that my analysis supported her complaints. Eventually, the Newton School Committee admitted their error and voted to implement an asbestos abatement program costing millions of dollars. The social studies teacher beat the architects and construction engineers with a little science and eventual backing of the Massachusetts EPA. It was her husband who was involved in receiving the Polaroid laboratory equipment I released to Boston College. I met him and explained the story to a surprised husband. His wife obviated administrative arrogance and conventional wisdom to expose a threat to children's health and safety by risking her own credibility. She deserved a medal. Justine is a banking consultant and environmental activist with the town of Dover, Massachusetts. In my mind, she is a heroine because stood up against the so-called experts despite ridicule. My career at Polaroid came to an end on 30 November 1988.

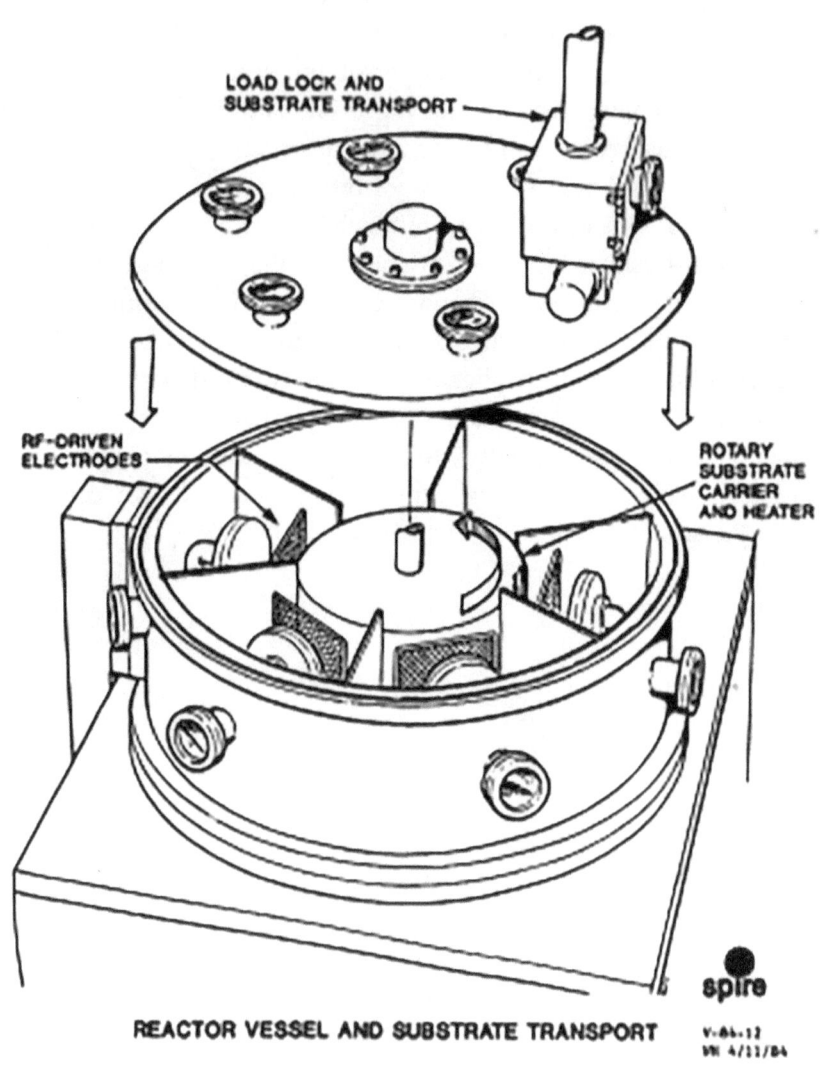

Formal drawing of the reactor assembly.

FROM BROOKLYN NY TO BROOKLINE MA

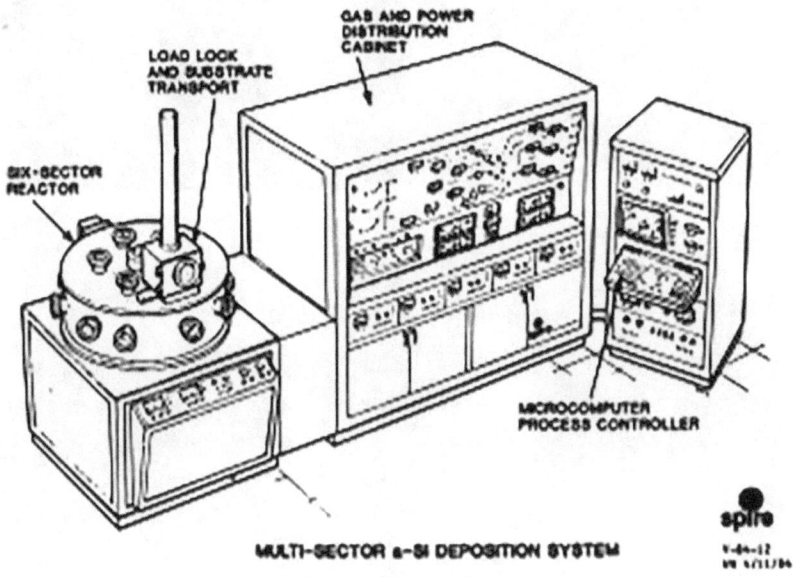

MULTI-SECTOR a-Si DEPOSITION SYSTEM

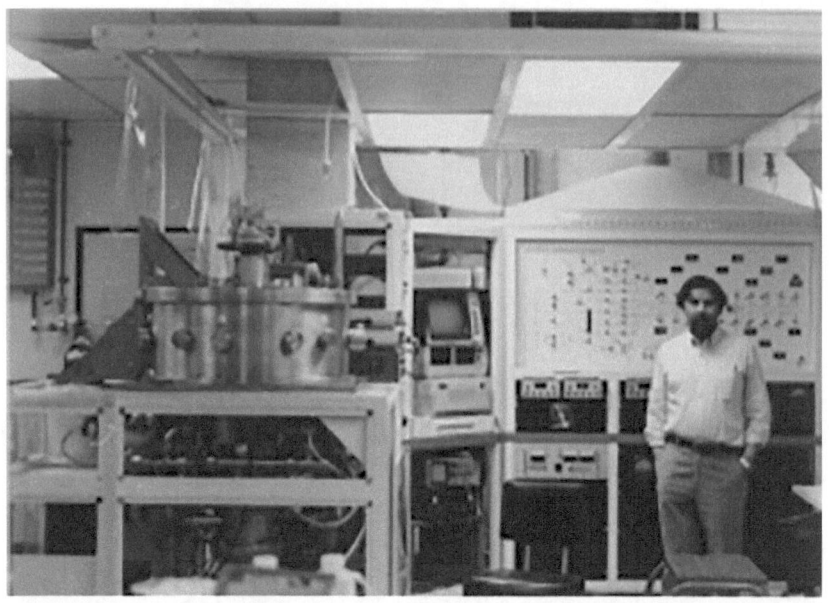

Dr. Vikrom dalal, Chief Scientist for the Amorphous Silicon
Program standing alone near the control panel.
Sid Krimsky was the Chief Engineer for the design,
construction, and testing of the reactor

FROM BROOKLYN NY TO BROOKLINE MA

Sid Krimsky standing near the Reactor Chamber (780 lbs) support stand and hydraulic hoist. Design drawings lie on top of the reactor plate.

MEMORANDUM # 84517

TO: Distribution
FROM: S. Krimsky
DATE: 11 September 1984
SUBJECT: Summary of a-Si Meeting of 11 September 1984.

Sid — you are doing a great job. Roy 9/15

A meeting was called by S. Krimsky to continue to clarify strategies for Reactor II shakedown. We reviewed the punch list of items scheduled for completion by 11 September 1984. Additional tasks were added which should permit us to demonstrate an argon plasma by Friday, 11 September 1984. K. Fields has responsibility for following items except where noted.

Item	Expected Date of Completion	Status
Inner cylinder attach skirt	9/11	Complete
Install inner cylinder 0.1 from top	9/11	Complete
Bracket transfer alignment check	9/11	Complete
Check clearance between skirt and top flange	9/11	Complete
Denote TC/ION gauge power supplies (C. Clahasey to advise)	9/11	Complete
Apply 12 VDC to test Brooks Valve	9/14	Wait for load lock
Feed-thru (Huntington to ship)	8/31	Not here yet
Adapter plate installed	8/31	Complete
Load lock	8/31	Being electropolished
Water lines to turbo pump	9/11	To be done by 9/12
Turn on turbo backing pump & check rotation	9/11	Complete
Turn on Fomblin oil filtering system	9/11	Complete
Look for gross leaks	9/17	Work continues
Install inner components: separators, it/f VAC, ground screen — disassemble, clean and install	9/11	To be done by 9/12
Install heater to inner cylinder with wires	9/11	Deferred to 9/25

The Amorphous Silicon Reactor lifted above its base. Report showing status of development and comment by Roger Little, President of Spire Corp., with whom Polaroid had a joint venture. Technician holding hammer is a prank.

Chapter 49

RABBI MOSES COHN

Elly Krimsky was enrolled in the first grade of Maimonides Hebrew Day School in September 1974. Naomi Krimsky was enrolled in the kindergarten in September of 1975. Jonathan was enrolled in kindergarten in 1981. Maimonides integrated a rigorous secular education with the best Jewish day school education northeast of New York City. Dorothy was copresident of the PTA for two years with Roberta Warren, Naomi Lopkin, and Linda Galper. I served on the board of directors and chairman of the house committee and energy committee. We had a vested interest in the school and wanted the best education for our children.

In the autumn of 1977, the Maimonides School Committee sent a letter to all parents announcing that Rabbi Moses Cohn, principal of the Maimonides School, agreed to retire in June 1978 and wished him well. Rabbi Cohn's signature appeared on the bottom of the letter. Rebbitzen Dr. Atara Twersky, chairman of the Maimonides School Committee, was the force behind the letter. Atara Twersky was married to Rabbi Dr. Yitzhak Twersky, who held the Nathan Littauer Jewish Studies chair at Harvard. He was a scholar of great renown. Parents were surprised to learn about this forced retirement. Federal legislation prohibiting forced retirement based on age had not yet been passed. There was one major problem. When we asked Rabbi Cohn about the retirement letter, he told us that he never agreed to retire in June 1978 and he never signed the letter.

In general, parents mistrusted the school committee because of their noncommunication and not sharing the rationale for policy decisions. Younger parents—highly educated, paying dearly for tuition—expected to be informed and participate in major educational decisions and have their concerns addressed. These younger parents, with expectations arising from living in an open society, were a generation removed from those who first enrolled their children in Maimonides School where no one questioned school policy.

The control of educational policy by the school committee and the contributions of Rabbi Cohn in modeling Maimonides School after his own educational experiences in Germany, at the Realschule where he was imbued with "Torah im Derech Eretz," are described in Seth Farber's book *An American Orthodox Dreamer, Rabbi Joseph B. Soloveitchik and Boston's Maimonides School*. Rabbi Cohn implemented the Rav's vision "to develop an academically excellent curriculum with the best teachers from local public and private schools" (p. 122). He introduced innovations in secular and Judaic studies that enhanced the academic level immeasurably (p. 123). I always felt that there was uniqueness to him despite his gruff exterior, but I never studied under him; I only knew him as an adult with children in the school.

Many parents were irritated by this treatment of a Rosh Yeshiva of being discharged for age. Rabbi Cohn came to Maimonides in 1941 after having escaped from the Mirer Yeshivah in Poland. He traveled across the Trans-Siberian railroad to Shanghai and arrived in the United States before the declaration of war against the axis powers. He had served as a teacher and principal at Maimonides School for almost three decades. The Maimonides School's Parents and Teachers Association (PTA) discussed an appropriate response at a series of meetings. The PTA listened to Mrs. Devorah Cohn who was a teacher and wife of Rabbi Cohn, parents, and teachers, all of whom supported his retention. The PTA voted to have a committee of three people (trio) to gather the facts and meet with the school committee to negotiate a settlement that might include an extension of one or two years beyond age sixty-five to give the community enough time to adequately prepare a banquet, time for Rabbi Cohn to prepare for a change, and time for the school committee to find a replacement. The three committee members were Dr. Jonas Galper, Mrs. Judith Hellman, and Sidney Krimsky. I was proud to work with people of such strong moral conviction. From autumn 1977 until June 1978, Rabbi Cohn's forced retirement was the major talk of the Maimonides community. The members of the school committee were Dr. Atara Twersky, Mrs. Joyce Kosowsky, Dr. Avraham Hoelzel, and Dr. Meyer Weiner. The school committee spokesperson was always Rebbitzen Dr. Atara Twersky, daughter of Rabbi Dr. Joseph Soloveitchik.

The parents' committee decided to conduct a survey by polling all the parents about retaining Rabbi Cohn for one or two more years to allow for a smooth transition. The results indicated that two-thirds of the parents supported the retention of Rabbi Cohn. We met with the school committee to present our findings and asked the School committee to modify their decree. Dr. Galper was our primary spokesman and pleaded on behalf of Rabbi Cohn. However, they said they were bound by rules of confidentially and would not discuss the rationale for their decision. They did admit that they have been receiving a number of complaints about him over the years and only hinted about some improprieties. We pointed out that many of the complaining parents supported his retention, which came as a surprise to Dr. Meyer Weiner. "We have already made a determination," said Mrs. Joyce Kosowsky. A reversal of their decision to retire Rabbi Cohn would project weakness to the community.

However, after much discussion, the school committee agreed to submit this issue before a bais din (Jewish Court of Law) to get a psak. We were asked to stop all discussion until the bais din made a ruling. All discussion ceased for three months. The psak never came. The bais din agreed to not hear this case because of the association of the school with the father of Rebbitzen Dr. Atara Twersky, Rabbi. Dr. Joseph Soloveitchik. In March or April, we were told of this development. Fairness and integrity were not in her vocabulary. She would not consider delaying implementation of the decision to retire Rabbi Cohn.

The chairman of the Maimonides board of directors (BOD) was Mr. Maurice Saval. The whole issue of forced retirement and respect for the Rosh Yeshiva was discussed at several meetings. The

BOD proposed to hold a large banquet as a fund-raiser to honor Rabbi Cohn with an appointed BOD member as chairman. The BOD made no public effort to convince Dr. Atara Twersky to retain Rabbi Cohn for another year or two. Certain members of the BOD accused Dr. Galper, Mrs. Hellman, and me for stirring trouble to push the school into providing a larger pension for Rabbi Cohn. We were accused of being his tools. The nameless person who said that could not conceive that people acted morally out of conviction. Rabbi Cohn refused to participate in any banquet arranged by the BOD whose purpose was to raise money from his forced retirement.

Rabbi Moses Cohn told members of the committee that Rabbi Soloveitchik told Rabbi Cohn years earlier that Rabbi Cohn could stay at Maimonides as long as he wanted. There would always be a job for him. However, since the Rov's wife died and the Rov's health diminished, he became more dependent upon his daughter to provide care. He was in no position to contradict his daughter's ruling. The committee members never approached the Rov about discharging Rabbi Cohn.

When we learned the *bais din* refused to consider this case, we knew we had lost. We used our remaining time from March 1978 to June 1978 to plan a banquet to honor Rabbi Cohn for his accomplishments at the Maimonides School for almost three decades of uninterrupted service. Mrs. Barbara Leibowitz was asked to chair the banquet at the Sidney Hill Country Club. Aside from the speeches, we presented a slide presentation of Rabbi Cohn's life from growing up in Altoona, Hamburg, to his escape across the Trans-Siberian Railroad from the Mir Yeshiva. He was instrumental in acquiring transit visas through the Soviet Union. I prepared transparency slides from photos given to me, took my own pictures, and traced his long journey on the Trans-Siberian Railroad on a map. Dr. Galper and Mrs. Judith Hellman wrote the script. I suggested that we engage Esther Edelman, a supporter of Rabbi Cohn, to read the script because of her able theatrics, elocution, and enunciation. She added to the occasion. Mrs. Devorah Cohn, who also had quite a story to tell about her own escape from Slonim before the Nazis invaded her town, was forever grateful to us about how we treated her husband

and how we did not allow this injustice to happen without opposition. Our efforts gave them dignity.

The following poem that describes the unfolding of events was prepared from notes and recollections of real events as they were evolving. It was meant to be read as a ballad and was understood at the time it was written. The superscript numbers reference explanations that were written a year later and were needed to understand the meaning behind the words in the ballad. The explanations follow the ballad.

The Departure of Rav Cohn

Here is a tale of parents deluded [1]
and of discussions from which they were excluded. [2]
Only through persistence, courage, and tenacity
were they able to attract a crowd of such capacity. [3]

In the thirtieth year of his administration
the School Committee decided upon Rav Cohn's excitation. [4]
They made a determination, his employment would cease
the complaints would end, in the school would be peace.

"Ten years of complaints are too much to bear,
in 19 months we'll discharge him from there."
"We can still preserve his dignity
by implementing our school retirement policy." [5]
"We shall send him a letter and clearly state
mandatory retirement will seal his fate." [6]
"Our private discussions have always met without opposition
and to challenge them now would be religious sedition." [7]

The chairlady had her say, her views did prevail, [8]
To Rav Cohn a letter was sent in the mail. [9]
He chose not to answer to preserve their reputation.
Their letter if made public, would give them aggravation. [10]

FROM BROOKLYN NY TO BROOKLINE MA

They sent a shaliach to discuss his leaving, [11]
hoping he would agree without any grieving.
Rav Cohn refused to be treated so
and told the shaliach to pick up and go.

In Oct 77 the chairlady without peer [12]
told him he must leave by the end of the year. [13]
All was kept secret until it became known [14]
that the School Committee was determined to oust Rav Cohn.

In Jan 78 a letter was sent [15]
to all parents about Cohn's retirement.
The parents learned that he did not agree
to leave his job so gracefully.

The faculty disapproved of the committee's action [16]
and by their vote showed their dissatisfaction.
A meeting was held by the PTA and Mrs. Cohn did say
"My husband never vacationed, rarely called in sick,
he built the school brick by brick." [17]

Those parents who felt his ouster was a sin
were relieved when the case went to bais din. [18]
All the parties were told to cease all debate. [19]
The rabbonim would decide Rav Cohn's fate.

A decision would be rendered competently
but two months passed uneventfully.
The parents learned to bais din's disgrace
that no rabbi would handle this unusual case. [20]

So the parents together by letter and phone
organized a petition to retain Rav Cohn.
Three parents were selected to present a petition [21]
and to articulate the parents' opposition. [22]

The date was set, the meeting occurred
in the school at night which was preferred. [23]
Their arguments were brief, their rebuttal was fixed, [24]
their conclusions were reached in 76.

The trio asked the reasons for their decision.
The committee answered with no precision.
The reasons are many so they did say
and Rav Cohn's confidentiality we can not betray. [25]

But 2/3 of the parents signed the petition and exclaimed [26]
that Rav Cohn in his position should be retained. [27]
But the members spoke with singular mind [28]
and not one dissenter did the trio find. [29]

The trio recognized the difficulty of their task
and persisted in further questions to ask.
"For whom is the school run?" they asked the committee. [30]
The committee had reasons to which only they were privy.
"We allowed him to retire with grace, honor, and dignity
but your petition has breached every confidentiality." [31]
Rabbi Cohn can not remain in this building any longer. [32]
Our position we cannot state any stronger.

"Our obligations we must discharge
in the best interests of the school at large." [33]
Since further arguments proved bereft [34]
the committee was thanked and the trio left.

The trio was promised that other qualified candidates the committee
would seek [35]
but the trio learned the selection was concluded the previous week. [36]
Some parents still believed the replacement selection was impartial
but the trio concluded the process was farcical.

FROM BROOKLYN NY TO BROOKLINE MA

The trio returned to the parents and reported.
Their requests having been denied, they consorted
To express their feelings by undertaking further obligations
by preparing a banquet with open invitations. (37)

The trustees learned of these activities
and at a Board Meeting expressed their proclivities.
They appointed a manager to chair the event (38)
and to raise money from Cohn's retirement. (39)

Since the Board was presented with the parents petition
and not one voice was raised in opposition, (40)
for them to use forced retirement to raise money
was viewed by parents as not so funny.

So the parents were incensed at the turn of events
and revised their plans and exercised good sense
by working harder not less
to make the banquet a huge success. (41)

The banquet preparations proceeded
and the planned attendance was exceeded
to honor and pay tribute through acclamation
by recognizing Rav Cohn's work and dedication. (42)

Here is a tale of parents deluded (43)
and of discussions from which they were excluded.
Only through persistence, courage, and tenacity
were they able to attract a crowd of such capacity.

June 1978

Explanations of the Poem: Work Completed June 1979

1. A number of untruths perpetuated by the school committee.
   a. Rabbi Cohn agreed to retire June 1978.
   b. A bais din that would resolve the issue about his forced retirement (specific bais din) was never identified.
   c. Majority of parents wanted him out.

2. School committee considered in June 1976 to retire Rabbi Moses Cohn based solely upon complaints they had received over the years and without really understanding the preferences of the Maimonides's parents. A parent who says to a child "I am going to kill you" rarely actualizes his or her frustration. Complainants signed the petition to retain Rabbi Cohn for a year or two. Members of the school committee were surprised to see the long list of parents who signed the petition.

3. Over 550 persons attended the banquet to honor Rabbi Cohn. Banquet was arranged outside of official school channels, and that irritated the leadership. Barbara Leibowitz was the banquet chairperson. She demonstrated impeccable taste with the colors, arrangements, and programming. Esther Edelman read the script for the life history of Rabbi Cohen with emphasis about his escape from the MIR Yeshivah to Shanghai, his arrival into the United States, and his contributions to the Maimonides School. Her clarity of voice, enunciation, and articulation stunned the audience. The script was crafted by Dr. Jonas Galper and Mrs. Judith Helman who agonized over each word. Sid Krimsky prepared the slides for the slideshow and operated the projector. Mrs. Linda Galper, past PTA president, hosted the meetings with help from Dorothy Krimsky who also served as a past PTA president of the Maimonides School. Both contributed ideas to the process and script. Dr. Jonas Galper was the master of ceremonies.

4. Decision was made about November 1976 at a school committee meeting. Hypothesis: Rabbi Shapiro urged the decision and threatened to leave unless Rabbi Cohn retired. School committee urged him to wait until Rabbi Cohn reached sixty-five.

Rabbi Shapiro claimed his hands were tied and he could not initiate or implement his perceived beneficial policies. School committee wanted him for the job because he studied under Rabbi Dr. Isadore Twersky at Harvard and he was a known and controllable entity. He would also take direction from Rabbi Dr. and Rebbitzen Dr. Atara Twersky.

5. By retiring Rabbi Cohn at sixty-five, no questions would be asked regarding the real motives for his forced retirement. The retirement policy was a surprise to the parents. There was a story at the time that Rabbi Soloveitchik told Rabbi Cohn ten years earlier that he could remain at Maimonides for as long as he was able. Rabbi Soloveitchik never made such a public statement about Rabbi Cohn in 1978.

6. Rebbitzen Dr. Atara Twersky's explanation: "Mandatory retirement at sixty-five is a school policy. Extended service is the exception. It only appears as a new school policy. Other personnel have remained beyond sixty-five by exception." Policy was rarely if ever enforced. Forced retirement at sixty-five is an American legal issue. Forced retirement of a Rosh Yeshivah is a halachic issue. US courts have held after 1978 that age alone is not a reason for forced retirement.

7. School committee decisions were always private and confidential except when leaked by spouses and children, and this did occur. (As one example, the decision not to rehire Chaim Parchi was leaked by the son of a school committee member to his class before this was discussed with Mr. Parchi.) Their decisions were never challenged. Dr. Jonas Galper perceived an injustice and gave voice to the majority of parents who opposed the decision to discharge Rabbi Cohn under these circumstances. Highly intelligent and very articulate, Dr. Galper constructed the arguments favored by the parents.

8. Rebbitzen Dr. Atara Twersky

9. Letter to Rabbi Cohn from the school committee

10. Words used by Rabbi Cohn! The contents of the letter might have embarrassed the school committee.

11. To discuss terms of his departure and retirement

12. There was none like unto her in Boston; she was the lifetime chairperson of the Maimonides School Committee.
13. June 1978
14. The information could not be contained any longer.
15. Parents were sent a letter announcing the retirement of Rabbi Cohn to which he never agreed.
16. A faculty meeting showed loyalty to Rabbi Cohn by voting for his retention.
17. The PTA leadership was behind the petition. These are the exact words used by Mrs. Devorah Cohn.
18. School committee's idea. The deck was stacked against the petitioners.
19. Pressure from the PTA ceased.
20. There was a united front.
21. Parents selected—Dr. Jonas Galper, Judy Helman, and Sid Krimsky—to represent the PTA.
22. The response of the parents was the results of several factors:
    a. Perceived unfairness to which Rabbi Cohn was treated
    b. Dislike of the autocratic methods used by the school committee
    c. Dislike of the excessive secrecy and perceived elitism under which school committee policies were discussed

Operational methods of the school committee are more suitable to nondemocratic countries with a less-educated populace. Clearly every issue is not so sensitive to require executive sessions.

23. Mutually agreeable since all parties had daytime employment. It was the only item upon which everyone agreed.
24. School committee was intransigent. They made a commitment to Rabbi Shapiro.
25. Trial by implication: The TRIO was supposed to trust the school committee as acting in the best interests of the school and community. Reasons were only hinted as something they were duty bound not to circulate.
26. He would remain as principal for one to two years or in another capacity commensurate with his age, experience, and skills.

27. He would serve for one or two years beyond June 1978. What harm would it have done? Rabbi Cohn would have agreed to two more years. This extension would have healed the community, allowed enough time to plan a memorial banquet, and would have enabled the planners to use the banquet as a fundraiser through the selling of ads. An extension would have dispelled any innuendoes surrounding breach of confidentiality.
28. Members of the Maimonides School Committee: Rebbitzen Dr. Atara Twersky, Dr. Myer Weiner, Mrs. Joyce Kosowsky, and Prof. Avraham Hoelzel. They were all well educated. Dr. Atara Twersky held a PhD in history and taught history at Brown and Nichols School, Dr. Myer Weiner was a dentist, Mrs. Kosowsky taught mathematics at one time, and Professor Hoelzel taught German language and culture at the University of Massachusetts, Columbia Point, Boston.
29. There was a united front.
30. Issue is still not satisfactorily resolved because recipients of services should have opportunity for input, which still does not happen. The school committee neither seriously solicits nor listens to the parents, although they argued that their actions regarding Rabbi Cohn's dismissal showed that they were responsive to the wishes of the parents.
31. Paraphrasing their actual words, the school committee really wanted everything handled quietly. They shunned publicity, and there was no opportunity to question them about their policies.
32. Exact words used.
33. School committee is the custodian of school values and virtues. Parents and students harbor school vices.
34. IBID 4
35. School committee promised the trio that there would be a fair selection process for a new principal. However, they made a commitment one week prior to our meeting to hire Rabbi Shapiro.
36. Rabbi Shapiro had been selected one week earlier.
37. Everyone was invited. Not everyone attended. Rabbi Soloveichik had a class at YU and did not attend. Some came and left early

before the slide show such as Rebbitzen Dr. Atara Twersky. Rabbi Shapiro personally thanked the banquet committee members for making such a memorable event for Rabbi Cohn. He stayed to the end and said he was moved by the occasion. It was believed that Rabbi Shapiro's father was discharged from a yeshiva based on age. Rabbi Shapiro must have been sensitive to the issue of forced retirement.

38. The board of directors wanted to usurp the leadership of the parents' committee and appoint a BOD trusted member to chair the banquet.
39. The revenues from the banquet and ad book would exceed banquet expenses. Those who favored Rabbi Cohn's removal would praise him. Rabbi Cohn refused the offer of a banquet arranged by the board of directors. We don't know what kind of financial pressures were put on Rabbi Cohn by the school leadership to get him to disassociate himself from the parents' effort. Since he had the most at stake, his resistance to the board's wishes and continued acceptance of the parents' effort required courage.
40. The Maimonides board of directors accepted the decision of the school committee. There was no debate among board members at the meeting although some members expressed private concern. Some parents who signed the petition were accused of being used by Rabbi Cohn for him to achieve a higher settlement. Members of the parents' committee were accused of being tools of Rabbi Cohen and acting against the best interests of Maimonides School. Rabbi Cohn decided not to obtain an attorney since he believed this would exacerbate an already-volatile situation. Most board members did not see the issues as having moral components.
41. Live music, good food, photographic displays around a pool, good speakers, and an audio visual presentation were the elements of the testimonial banquet.
42. First paragraph is repeated because only now at the poem's end are the events surrounding the delusions comprehensible to the reader.

FROM BROOKLYN NY TO BROOKLINE MA

EPILOGUE (written in 1979–1981) a la *Macbeth*

Fair is foul
and foul is fair
these inverted words
hover through the air.

Truth is false
false is true.
Whom to believe?
What to do?

To act or not to act,
that is the question.
Whether 'tis better to suffer silently
the outrageous claims of those who rule
and be rewarded for silence or to give expression to the gnawing of
    conscience
with a predictable vindictive reaction without a time boundary. **
    See Below!

POSTHISTORY

** The children of the parents who dared challenge the school committee were identified and rewarded by the administration of Maimonides School for the deeds of their parents during their attendance at the school.

Several of the major players died during the past fifteen years.

Rabbi Dr. Isadore Twersky, Nathan Littauer professor of Jewish Studies at Harvard and husband of Rebbitzen Dr. Atara Twersky, died from cancer in 1997.

Mrs. Judith Helman, English principal of Lubavitch School in Brookline, died from cancer.

Rabbi Prof. Joseph Soloveitchik, "The Rav," died from Alzheimer's disease.

Prof. Avraham Hoelzel, a confessed adulterer, moved from Brookline to Quincy and died from cancer. He married his paramour. His wife remarried and lives in Israel.

Rabbi Moses Cohen died. Mrs. Devorah Cohn continued to teach at Maimonides. She retired by choice and moved to Monsey, New York.

Mrs. Esther Edelman, voice of the banquet, died from cancer.

Rabbi Cohn was lucky to escape the horrors of Europe to travel through Russia to Japan and then to the United States. I doubt if he was aware of the FUGU plan to place fifty thousand Jews from Eastern Europe in Manchuria (named Manchuko after a Japanese invasion) to develop the resources of Manchuria, build towns, and live in peace with the Japanese rulers. Rabbi Marvin Tokayer uncovered this plan in researching the attitude of the Japanese toward the Jews living in Shanghai during WWII. It is all in a book entitled *The Fugu Plan*.

FROM BROOKLYN NY TO BROOKLINE MA

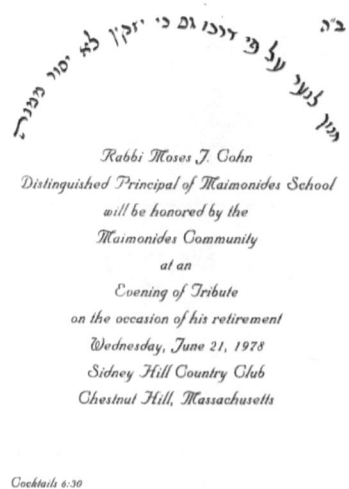

This is the invitation sent to the Maimonides Community to pay tribute to the retiring principal, Rabbi Moses Cohn. The Hebrew translation from the Book of Proverbs is "Train a child in the way he should go, and even when he is old, he will not depart from it."

This is a photo of Rabbi Moses Cohn and his wife Devorah standing outside of the Maimonides School after graduation ceremonies circa 1970.

Chapter 49.1

CLIMBING MOUNT SINAI

In August 1985 I traveled alone to Israel to attend the wedding of Joshua and Chagit Breuer. I signed up for a two-day trip into the Negev through a local tourist agency. I had to be at a hotel in Eilat in the morning where a minibus would meet me. There were thirteen tourists from different countries in the minibus plus the Israeli guide. His name was Motti. Motti was a dark-skinned Israeli, probably Yeminite, who spoke English, Hebrew, and Arabic. He was wearing IDF clothing, so I assumed that he completed his military obligation. The minibus stopped at the Taba Crossing. We showed our passports to the Egyptian customs agents. We were transferred to a new minibus with Arabic license plates (I assumed it was Egyptian) with an Egyptian driver. Motti loaded the minibus with food consisting of eggs, pita, chumus, cucumbers, tomatoes, coffee, and lots of water.

We traveled into the Negev along the coast of the Red Sea until we stopped at Nuweiba, a Bedouin encampment, to rest and buy some food. I remember that the Beduins were hospitable and offered us coffee, dates, etc., at reasonable prices. Camels were tethered to the desert sand, and we were advised not to get too close.

We left the encampment and drove to somewhere between Saint Catherin's Monastery and Mount Sinai, which the Arabs called Jebel Musa, Mountain of Moses. We encamped for the night in a large tent with mattresses on the desert sand without any sheets. Some women objected to the mixed sleeping, but Motti did not budge. We all slept in our clothing. Conditions were sparse. Motti asked me to collect all the passports that would be returned the next morning. I felt uncomfortable asking tourists for their passports. Motti explained that this was Egyptian law and we had to comply. I presumed that the Egyptians did not want anyone sneaking off in the middle of the night. Motti prepared supper.

We lay down on the mattresses about 8:00 p.m. because we had to be up at 4:30 a.m. for breakfast and be prepared to leave at 5:30 a.m. The passports were returned to us. The sun was rising as we approached Mount Sinai. The minibus went as far as it could. We exited the bus and started to walk to the top of the mountain. The sun was rising, the air was dry, Motti reminded us to drink. We had canteens. We climbed past markers on the trail, Coptic churches, Christian symbols on rocks, and discarded trash in Arabic writing all the way to the top. After a few hours, we encountered steps that led us to the top.

Going in the other direction were young people from an American church who slept at night on the mountaintop, collecting the trash by the roadside and placing it into large Mylar garbage bags. What a mitzvah! Motti told us to leave nothing on the mountain. In about four hours, we arrived at the top, and I put on my tallit and tefillin. I did not want to miss an opportunity to daven shachris on the top of Mount Sinai. I saw a Coptic church on the top and even went inside, but it was bare except for the Coptic markings on the walls. The temperature was in the eighties, but the air was dry. The view from the top was fantastic. There were no clouds in the completely blue sky. I could see for a hundred miles in four directions. North was Israel, south was Saudi Arabia, west was Egypt, and east was Jordan. I looked around, and there were other mountains higher than Mount Sinai, and I recalled in the Torah reading that Mount Sinai was not chosen for its height. There was little vegetation on the top to obstruct the view. The shape of the mountain was more rugged on the side facing Egypt. We climbed on the side facing Jordan. That was a manageable climb. Climbing on the other side seemed really difficult.

I looked below and saw an entire almost-flat field and imagined that hundreds of thousands of people filled that field while Moses spoke with God on the mountaintop. Slightly below the Coptic church was a large rock with the inscription "P. A. Philbrick." Who was P. A. Philbrick who carved his name on the rock? I wondered if he was related to the former Philbrick Estate and Philbrick Road on which Maimonides School was built.

We descended the mountain in half the time to ascend, entered the minibus, and drove to Saint Catherine's Monastery. Motti pointed out the "burning bush" near the monastery. It was never consumed by fire. In the monastery, we walked around and saw the famous skull room with the skeleton heads of former priests separated from their bodies stacked haphazardly in a room. Motti pointed out ancient writings on large stones that were believed to have been written by the Israelites when they were in the desert. We returned to my hotel in Eilat.

After I returned to America, I contacted the Brookline Historical Society. My hunch was correct. P. A. Philbrick was a wealthy man who owned an estate on Philbrick Road. He traveled to Alexandria via ship, hired guides and camels, made a safari to Mount Sinai, and carved his name on the stone. The long arm of Maimonides School stretched all the way from Brookline to the top of Mount Sinai.

View of the plain from the top of Mt. Sinai looking East toward Jordan. Hundreds of thousands of people camped on the plain waiting for Moses to return from the mountain top. How was Moses able to communicate to over 2 million people waiting on the plain and base of Mt. Sinai remains, to my mind, an unanswered question.

Chapter 50

MICROSCIENCE, ANTI-SEMITISM, AND THIEVERY

Even before I left Polaroid in November 1988, I found employment with a small private engineering company Microscience in Norwell, Massachusetts, on the South Shore. I physically departed Polaroid in October but collected two salaries for one month. About 1,500 people left Polaroid with me including my boss, Larry Kaufman, and his boss George Fernald, vice president of R&D. I would report to the owner of Microscience, Tony Drybanski, who spoke with a British accent but whose origins were clearly in Poland. Microscience Corporation built vacuum deposition systems for other companies and laboratories. Vacuum deposition was a newly developed high-tech method to coat silicon substrates for light-sensing, photovoltaic, and manufacturing of electronic circuit chips. This is exactly what I did at Polaroid. It was a perfect match for me. The photovoltaic technology for generating electric power was in its infancy, and I would grow with it. I designed support structures, vacuum chambers, and accessories as well as purchased standard parts such as instruments, stainless flanges, stainless steel piping, valves, etc., for processing hazardous gases.

I worked with another engineer, August Westner, whose origins were German but we had a similar mind-set with respect to a work ethic except that he came in on Saturday and worked late Friday evenings. I worked long hours during the week but left early Friday and did not work on Saturday. Drybanski did not like this and made some remarks about remaining competitive and company loyalty. Passover was coming, and I needed time off. I did not have much accumulated leave since I had only been there for six months.

But there was another issue. My purchase orders for parts had to be reviewed by the marketing manager. He obtained the contracts to build systems for universities and other companies. He always claimed to obtain better prices from his vendors than did I. He negotiated volume sales, squeezed the suppliers for better prices, and obtained price advantages so he claimed. I never saw his purchase orders.

Before Passover 1989, Microscience was not doing well financially, and I was perceived as not being as useful as when I was hired. Besides, the marketing manager was buying all the parts and getting better prices. Tony knew I would take leave on Passover and all the Yom Tovs were in the middle of the week. I was the only Jewish employee. So he brought me into the office and apologized for having to fire me. I did not live up to his expectations. He did not know that the marketing manager was privately negotiating with outside vendors for a job and buying excess parts. He promised contracts that never materialized. The marketing manager left shortly after I was discharged. I could not charge Tony with discrimination, but I smelled it. He was careful how he spoke with me. He predicted that my next job would last long and wished me luck. I left with two weeks' salary.

After I was discharged, I learned that the marketing manager obtained kickbacks from his own vendor list and wound up buying more parts than we actually needed in anticipation of acquiring big contracts. He was a real operator and turned out to be a thief. Microscience went bankrupt and closed within a few years.

Vacuum processing chamber and base I designed for Microscience Corp. in Norwell Massachusetts.

Chapter 50.1

CONSULTING AT CIBA CORNING CORP.

After my employment at Microscience Corporation ended, I was offered a temporary consulting job at Ciba Corning Corporation in Medfield, Massachusetts. Ciba Corning manufactured circuit boards for a blood analysis tester. The program manager reported to me that every spring the reject rate of circuit boards increased to unacceptable levels and the company engineers could not determine the cause. The voltages on components were less than called for on the specifications. I observed and carefully documented the manufacturing process from purchasing components to assembling, the circuit boards, soldering, degreasing, cleaning, and drying the circuit boards. I used my experience as a Polaroid process engineer to determine that a film remained on the circuit board after degreasing with water in an ultrasonic vapor degreaser. I pressed Scotch magic tape on the circuit board before and after welding and washing and observed a thin film on the tape. I also used de-ionized water on the circuit board before and after washing and observed the contact angle. The data indicated that there was a residue on the circuit board after washing.

I convinced Ciba Corning to pay for a secondary ion mass spectrometry (SIMS) test to analyze the contaminants on the circuit board. The main contaminant was sodium. There were other contaminants, but sodium predominated. That was it. I solved the problem because sodium is electrically conductive and would drain away electric current from the components on the circuit board, thereby reducing voltages of the components. But what was the source of the sodium? I had to use my knowledge of water treatment I learned at Polaroid. The water department in Medfield dumped copious amounts of sodium hydroxide into the public water supply to neutralize the acid rain coming from the Ohio Valley every springtime.

The program manager did not want me to talk with the water department engineers to ask them to reduce the sodium hydroxide additive because Ciba Corning was dumping some contaminants into the sewer. Therefore, I recommended a reverse osmosis water treatment hardware to remove the metallic components from the water supply used to remove the solder flux from the circuit boards. I wrote the specs for an RFQ (request for quotation), and Ciba Corning selected a contractor to install a reverse osmosis system. I told them to call me if the problem reoccurred after installation of the reverse osmosis system and I would not bill them. They never called.

Chapter 51

DEPARTMENT OF DEFENSE AND MY THIRD CAREER START

I left Polaroid in November 1988 after an attempted leveraged buyout by Roy Eisner of the Disney conglomerate that was eventually withdrawn. I accepted an immediate offer from the Microscience Corporation in Norwell, Massachusetts, south of Quincy, to design vacuum processing equipment for thin film depositions. The owner, Tony Drybanski, developed a dislike for me when I asked to leave early Friday nights and take vacation days during Passover 1989. I worked long hours to make up the time, but the owner was unimpressed. The other employees worked on Saturday. After seven months, I was dismissed. I sensed anti-Semitism. The small firm had developed financial problems and within two years went bankrupt. I realized later why I preferred large companies to small companies. I could lose myself and preserve my independence in a large company. Employees can cover for one another. Employees are more closely micromanaged in a small company. I applied for unemployment insurance for the first time in my life.

    I identified an opportunity to market home water filtration systems made by the National Safety Associates Corporation (NSA). The national marketing manager got me started, and I learned a lot about water filtration and marketing. Dorothy helped me, but we were not really successful enough to stop collecting unemployment insurance.

Hanscom Air Force Base in Bedford, Massachusetts

In the summer of 1989, after meeting my employment advisor at the state unemployment board in the JFK building in downtown Boston, I decided to visit the Thomas O'Neil Federal Building a few blocks away and view the new art exhibition in the atrium. There was a hiring fair for just that day for federal jobs at Hanscom AFB. I submitted my résumé that I always carried with me to a personnel lady who told me that the US government was not hiring engineers, but she would accept and circulate my résumé. I was called for an interview within six weeks and hired after an extensive interview.

I was among the last handful of engineers hired at Hanscom AFB in November 1989 because the Berlin Wall was dismantled in November 1989 and the base commander, Lt. Gen. Gordon Fornell, envisioned a reduced need for engineers to develop and acquire communication systems to thwart the Soviet threat. Very few electronics engineers have been hired to work directly for the US government at Hanscom AFB since 1989. Work has been outsourced to private contracting firms.

I recall my first awakening about working as a DoD federal employee. Our secretary was upset because she received a phone call (just after I received a government phone and a working number) from an upset woman who was trying to locate her daughter working at Hanscom AFB. She made lots of phone calls, spoke with an operator, and could not locate the person with whom she wanted to speak. She was obviously frustrated and insulted our secretary who asked me, the newest employee, to handle this irate woman. The phone call was transferred to me, a higher-level employee, than the secretary. I calmly asked the woman about her problem. She was exasperated and finally said, "I want to speak with someone from the government." I responded with confidence "Lady, I am the government. Hold on while I locate the person with whom you want to speak." I found the new employee and let her use my phone. I was overcome. I realized then, even after I recited and accepted the oath of my position to defend the Constitution of the United States, that

I represented the government of the United States. My actions could reflect positively or poorly upon the US government.

For twenty years I worked on developing communications and imagery systems for collection, processing, transmission, display, and exploitation of civilian and military intelligence collected against the enemies of the United States. I was exposed to high-level security briefings and had access to many secure federal buildings, contracting firms, and a dozen military bases including Ramstein, AFB, Germany, for conferences where these matters were discussed. While in Germany, I attended conferences in buildings used to train the Panzer Corps before and during the Second World War. I read the German plaques on the walls extolling their bravery and sense of duty to the fatherland especially in North Africa. The barracks were later occupied by the French and the Russians before the fall of the Berlin Wall. I saw the plaques for bravery in three languages. I visited Sachsenhausen and Dachau concentration camps during that trip. I presented a slide showing in shul during Showa week.

None of the documents upon which I wrote comments or the documents I authored or the PowerPoint Presentations I made or the tens of thousands of e-mails are releasable to the general public.

APATS

I experienced several amusing incidents. I was assigned to be program manager for the Antenna Pedestal Assembly Test Station (APATS). APATS enables a depot operator to automatically detect and fault-isolate defects within MILSTAR Antenna Pedestal Assemblies. MILSTAR is an assemblage of satellites that enables ground based operators to communicate beyond the line of sight (BLOS). The Antenna Pedestal Assembly has to continuously and accurately point to the MIL-STAR satellite, which makes EHF/UHF communication possible between ground, air, and transportable MILSTAR terminals. The government oversight team consisted of MITRE and contractor support. Raytheon was the prime contractor. The cost to develop and test the test station was $16 million. Work was completed by December 1996.

Several months prior to completion, Raytheon in Waltham informed us that the space in the assembly area would be needed for other programs and we had to find a home for the test station that occupied about two hundred square feet; otherwise, Raytheon would bill the DoD for storage costs. I had to find a home for the APATS and make sure that operators were trained to use the equipment. An obvious choice was Robins AFB near Atlanta, Georgia, because it was one of the largest USAF depots on the East Coast. I set up a meeting with the military officer responsible for all USAF equipment used at Robins. I explained the capabilities, requirements for electric power, cooling and heating, and maintenance training for the operators with a series of PowerPoint slides. APATS may be shipped to cold and hot climates to test the ground-based antennas. After the presentation, the senior officer asked me how many times did I expect APATS be annually used. "Perhaps once or twice annually," I replied because the ground-based antennas also built by Raytheon were not breaking down. Under new congressional guidelines, Robins had to show a profit from their maintenance activities by means of interagency transference of funds. Operational funds would be transferred from the agencies using the MILSTAR antennas that needed repairs. Accepting the APATS would lower his profit margin and he could not add this equipment to his inventory. He would have to pay for training of operators who might use the APATS only once or twice a year and keep the APATS in a state of readiness. This surprised me, and I reported to my boss. He suggested McClellan AFB near Sacramento, California, one of the largest USAF depots on the West Coast.

I traveled to McClellan AFB and repeated my dog-and-pony show using the same PowerPoint slides. The officer in charge said that he would accept the APATS hardware but there was one problem. McClellan was on the BRAC (base realignment and closure) list and may close within one year. Did I want to risk sending the APATS to McClellan for a year and then have it sent elsewhere and retrain soldiers in how to use the equipment? It made little sense.

My boss had no further suggestions, so I called the air staff. The air staff (captains and majors) report to the chief of staff of the USAF.

Finally one officer suggested that I contact the army staff. Perhaps an army depot would accept the equipment. Time was running out, and Raytheon kept reminding me of inventory charges. A US army officer suggested that I contact Tobyhanna Army Depot in Pennsylvania. I made the phone call and traveled to Tobyhanna. The Tobyhanna Depot is huge and contains all equipment needed by the army. Robots travel back and forth on the floor, locating items requested by soldiers to conduct operations around the world. The items are sent to the loading platform, packaged, and sent to an air base the next day for shipment around the world. Requests come in via the Internet and transmitted to the same robots that locate the items and bring them to the loading platform. I asked the senior officer, "What about profit incentives and base closure?" "Son, this is the army. We will accept anything that benefits our soldiers, never mind profits, and this base will never close. We made a big mistake by allowing the air force to become a separate service." In 1948 President Truman signed an executive order creating the USAF as a separate service after being convinced by the USAAF (United States Army Air Force) brass that a separate service was needed because the air force had a strategic mission. I shipped the equipment to Tobyhanna and was invited to observe the set-up.

Selling Software for AWACS Aircraft Communications Equipment

Another amusing incident was not so amusing at the time. The DCGS (distributed common ground system) uses a digital radio and display system that received intelligence about the location of friendlies and enemies in the battlespace. Each participant (ground, air, and sea) used radar to locate all the participants, friendly and unfriendly, in the battlespace that may have extended hundreds of miles from a central location. The radio had a video monitor that displayed the locations using icons. This was developed by MITRE Corporation and took about twenty years. The basic specs were released for commercial development and became available in cars, trains, and planes as a visual display and global positioning system (GPS). Each participant had a narrow digital time slot to report data using TDMA (time division multiple access). I was responsible for authoring the security classification guide for the entire JTIDS Program developed and paid by the USAF.

The data collected on airplanes and seen by pilots and navigators was classified and could be downloaded to military bases around the world. The air staff's direction to me was the names of the air bases around the world capable of receiving such data were to be treated as unclassified. So therefore the names of an air base in Germany and South Korea that were capable of receiving such data were to be treated as unclassified. The names of US bases that could receive such data were also treated as unclassified. I wrote the security classification guide (SCG) in that way. The entire document I had prepared had to be approved by HAFB (Hanscom Air Force Base) Security, and security sent it to the NSA (National Security Agency) for approval. I sought approval from many DoD agencies. NSA returned with comments disapproving the document because the air base in Germany and Korea argued that their site for receiving DCGS data was to be classified. I was trapped. NSA disagreed with the air staff. I worked for the air staff, not NSA. However, the ESC (electronics system command) commander at HAFB would not approve any document disapproved by the NSA. I needed NSA approval.

I presented technical arguments to the NSA opposing their opinion. I received e-mails, highly classified, from the director of the NSA, General Michael Hayden (called DIRNSA), warning me that the two overseas bases wanted the fact classified that they were able to receive JTIDS data. Was this petulant or irrational by the NSA? General Michael Hayden signed the documents. Finally I was informed that the Status of Forces Agreements with these two countries was the basis of the caveats by the NSA, and the NSA was working to revise the Status of Forces Agreement. The NSA managed to revise the agreement with Germany but not with South Korea. The air staff was furious, but I had to make a decision, and the last e-mail from Gen. Michael Hayden, DIRNSA, convinced me to follow his direction. I followed his direction and wrote the document as he instructed. The air staff was not happy. A few weeks later, NSA sent a delegation to the Security Department at HAFB to ensure that I followed their direction. The air staff backed down.

A few weeks later, I received a phone call from an American colonel stationed in South Korea, asking me what to do with a large sign posted above JTIDS HQ announcing the name of the organization. I told him to remove the sign and burn it. A few years later, I learned from my government replacement that the Status of Forces Agreement with South Korea had been revised and public recognition was unclassified. I was proud and pleased of my participation to maintain the Status of Forces Agreement with the Republic of South Korea.

Purchase of Communications Software by a Foreign Country

I received another assignment to review a request from another country to purchase AWACS (airborne warning and control) aircraft including the electronics for communication, command, and control including all the software for the JTIDS (joint tactical information distribution system) that provides for battlefield awareness to US forces. The JTIDS radio receives radar data for location of friendly and enemy forces and displays the information as icons on a video screen. Requests for military sales are presented to the US embassy who forwards the request to the Foreign Military Sales (FMS) Office in the Pentagon. If the FMS office cannot handle the technology, then the request is forwarded to the program office where an engineer is assigned the task of determining if the sale of advanced technology will compromise national security. I was assigned the task. The country said that they would not purchase AWACS aircraft without the computer codes for JTIDS software. The AWACS Program Office wanted to sell AWACS aircraft, which had been approved by the White House, but this approval did not mention software codes. I studied the problem and visited the FMS Office at the Pentagon and reviewed the specific technology the air staff did not want to share with foreign countries and also reviewed CIA reports on the trustworthiness of countries to protect US classified and sensitive technology. I returned to Boston and wrote a classified report that we could sell all the hardware but not the JTIDS codes for software and provided all the rationale. The AWACS Program Office personnel met with me and requested that I reverse my conclusion based on the national political consequences of not selling the software codes to a friendly nation. This could result in a protest to the White House by the country who wanted to buy the software codes. The meeting was unfriendly. My rationale was based on the defense needs of the United States and not on the needs of another country. Political implications did not weigh in my report. The AWACS Program Office did protest, and my report was reviewed by a full colonel who agreed with me. The last I heard was that the country purchased all the hardware and software but without the codes for the software.

Y2K Compliance

From 1998 to 2002, the USAF set up a Y2K compliance section at the Pentagon. I was tasked to certify sixteen weapons systems for Y2K compliance and to coordinate my efforts with the Pentagon Compliance Section. I had to report status to my boss who was Colonel Charles Jones, a scuba diver, comedian, and astronaut. We released contracts to software vendors to have them identify old programs using century logic that required only two numbers to define dates. It seemed that every computer programmer was employed a few years prior to Y2K. All the software for navigation, precision-guided missiles, battlefield awareness, and communications had to be changed to incorporate the twenty-first-century dates using four numbers to define the year and also work correctly during leap years. Simulation programs for each of the sixteen systems had to be developed and tested. The simulation programs had to be tested as if we already were in the twenty-first century.

If the dates and times were wrong after midnight on 2000, I would receive a telephone call from the assistant to the director, asking me to report the next day to assess the damage and outline how we were going to fix the problem. The next day was New Year's and a holiday, but if called, I would have to appear. I received no phone calls. Tuesday morning I was informed by the director that all the sixteen weapons systems were tested during on New Year's Day and all registered the correct times and dates. The next hurdle was to see if the dates and times were correct during 29 February 2000, a leap year. All systems recorded the correct dates and times. My assignment ended a few months after Y2K.

Unfortunately, on 9/11 my former boss, retired Colonel Charles Jones, was a passenger on the United Airlines airplane that crashed into the World Trade Center. There is a plaque to his memory at the gazebo on Hanscom Air Force Base. I visit his plaque every opportunity I have when I return to the air base. His name is carved on the stone wall surrounding the World Trade Center Memorial.

Able Danger

As part of my training to be a middle manager, I was accepted in a program to better understand the roles and responsibilities of Congressional Intelligence Committees. We attended lectures by PhDs who studied Congress and briefed by several congressmen and staff members. I attended some congressional hearings. The most fascinating of my training was attending the hearing about "Able Danger." Able Danger was a classified military planning effort led by the US Special Operations Command (SOCOM) and the Defense Intelligence Agency (DIA). It was created as a result of a directive from the Joint Chiefs of Staff in early October 1999 by chairman of the Joint Chiefs of Staff Hugh Shelton to develop an information operations campaign plan against transnational terrorism and to identify terrorists prior to 9/11.

According to statements by Lt. Col. Anthony Shaffer and those of four others at the congressional hearing that I attended, able danger had identified two of three al-Qaeda cells active in the 9/11 attacks. The 'Brooklyn cell' was linked to the "Blind Sheik" Omar Abdel-Rahman and the September 11 attack leader Mohamed Atta, and three of the 9/11 plot's other 19 hijackers. Shaffer warned us that the Chinese have already started to hack into SCADA systems (supervisory control and data acquisition systems) for the flow of oil, nuclear power systems, finance and banking systems, telecommunications, water delivers, truck transportations, etc.

The Pentagon "ordered five key witnesses not to testify," according to Senate Judiciary Committee Chairman Arlen Specter. "That looks to me as if it may be obstruction of the committee's activities," Arlen Specter, R-Pennsylvania, said at the start of his committee's hearing into the unit. Analysts had created charts that included pictures of then-known al-Qaeda operatives and connections with US residents. Charts were displayed at the hearing.

Able Danger was the name given by General Hugh Shelton, chairman of the Joint Chiefs of Staff, to have the military track legal entrants into the USA who were suspected terrorists or suspected accomplices of terrorists. The suspicious reports were provided by the Central Intelligence Agency (CIA). The military officers monitored phone calls, e-mails, behavior, etc., of the suspected terrorists. The Able Danger officers compiled a terabyte (thousands of pages of data) that they offered to the FBI, but the FBI refused to read or accept such data that was acquired illegally. These suspected terrorists were legally here in the USA. Congress Curt Weldon from Pennsylvania heard about this gross infringement on individual freedoms and exposed the whole thing. Weldon demanded that Congress hold a hearing on this subject.

I attended the hearing. The hearing room was packed with reporters and video cameras. I arrived early and was lucky to obtain a seat. Able Danger was an illegal program, which is why the FBI wanted no part of this. The military officers, on advice from the military lawyers, pleaded the Fifth Amendment. Arlen Specter was in charge of the hearing and was livid that the officers refused to testify. The hearing lasted about one and a half hours and ended at lunchtime. Spector promised to reconvene sometime in February. There were other committee meetings that I did not attend. Later the officers admitted that terabytes of data was shredded. All the tracking data was shredded. The attitude of the military was that "if the executive branch [Justice Department and FBI] does not want the data, then we do not want to incriminate ourselves." So nothing came of this except to spend federal funds. Readers can Google Able Danger.

FROM BROOKLYN NY TO BROOKLINE MA

E Corridor in the Puzzle Palace (Pentagon)

During one of my trips to the Pentagon, I walked into the outer office of the secretary of defense. A secretary sat in the outer office. She saw that I had a DoD badge. I asked her if I could just look inside. The office was empty. She said yes; so I walked inside and saw the seal of the United States, the desk, files, flags, computer, and the table where he stood to review documents (shtender) used by Donald Rumsfield, SECDEF. I could not imagine that a kid from Brooklyn would ever visit the office of the SECDEF. A few years earlier, Colin Powell, a kid from the Bronx, was the SECDEF.

I ended my service to the US government 30 June 2010 after twenty years. I spent the last two weeks of my career with the DoD shredding documents and being deprogrammed. I was presented with the Civilian Achievement Award upon my retirement. I was awarded two USAF Achievement Medals, one for certifying sixteen weapons systems for the Y2K transition and the other for authoring the first Program Protection Plan for JTIDS.

Espionage

I spent two weeks at the National Security Agency (NSA) at Fort George Meade in Maryland undergoing training. I was exposed to classes in cryptography and espionage by members of the Central Intelligence Agency (CIA), Defense Intelligence Agency (DIA), and NSA that was called "No Such Agency" because of the secret nature of its work to defend and protect the United States from domestic and foreign enemies.

I was briefed on espionage committed against the United States from revolutionary times to recent events. Espionage is prosecuted under Title 18 of the US Code. Espionage is defined as the providing of classified material to a representative of a foreign interest. Who commits espionage, what is the motivation, who suffers, and who pays were the subjects of our briefings. Of special interest were the cases of Aldrich Ames, Robert Hanson, Walker Family, and William Pelton. During WWII Richard Sorge, a spy for Russia, convinced

Joseph Stalin to move the Siberian Army, poised to defend Russia from an expected invasion from Japan, to the eastern front to push the German armies from Moscow and St. Petersburg. We learned how the United States and England intercepted encrypted messages that convinced President Wilson to enter WWI. We learned about the work of Alan Turing during WWII to build an Enigma machine to intercept military-encrypted messages from Nazi headquarters to far-flung military units including U-boats. We learned about damage assessment reports and who is assigned. We learned about the US vulnerability to espionage, cyberhacking, cyberdefense, and cyberoffensive operations.

We learned about moles, double agents, and converted spies. We learned that one hundred persons from 1975 until 2010 were charged with espionage or attempted espionage. Of the one hundred persons, twelve were sentenced to life in prison. No person sentenced to life in prison has ever been pardoned at least from 1975 to 2010. The remaining eighty-eight were given lesser sentences, deported, swapped for Americans accused of spying, eluded the FBI, or died in prison. Three convinced the court that they were double agents and were sentenced to zero time. We learned about the Rosenberg case. I acquired so much information that I briefed several divisions of federal employees and once briefed 250 employees at Lockheed Martin for ninety minutes on espionage. I managed to acquire a declassified diagram from the National Archives made by David Greenglass of an explosive lens used in the "Fat Man" atomic bomb that was dropped on Nagasaki to end WWII. Greenglass was the brother of Ethel Rosenberg and cooperated with the FBI to convict the Rosenbergs. Security personnel at Hanscom AFB trusted me to not release material above the secret level. My briefings were first reviewed by high-level security personnel before presenting my PowerPoint slides. I felt that I was really trusted by higher-level DoD personnel. I even had to prepare damage assessment reports several times when classified material could not be accounted. I was the security manager for eight years as an additional duty. I enjoyed the work and was trusted and respected.

Education

Working as a direct federal employee for the DoD opened many doors of education. I applied to attend the Air Command and Staff College, which is designed for captains and majors, to qualify for higher ranks. The program takes about a year to complete with reading assignments, exams, and a thesis. My subject of my thesis was the military strategies of Gen. Douglas MacArthur during WWII.

After, I applied to attend the Air War College and was selected. My classmates were mostly lieutenant colonels who were eligible for promotion to full colonels in the USAF. We read material about worldwide military strategies by other countries and studied important battles and why they were lost and won. The subject of my thesis was the air war of the 1967 Arab-Israeli conflict. I examined many essays from both sides of the conflict. I had to rewrite my thesis twice before it was accepted.

I attended the National Defense University at Fort Myers, Virginia, for four days, studying national defense strategy including cyberwarfare, defensive, and offensive operations. On display was the final uniform worn by General Colin Powell, chairman of the Joint Chiefs of Staff whom I first met at CCNY in the ROTC. Student participation was expected, and the class was well attended by civilians and military personnel. Civilian employees were required to show so many hours of education per year to stay current with national defense, new technologies, new oversight requirements established by Congress, and any new rules of ethics. Ethics training by JAG (judge advocate general) attorneys were conducted semi-annually, and attendance was mandatory. The rules are based on avoidance of impropriety and avoidance of embarrassing the US government (except in breaking laws). Some of the guidance could have been taken from Pirkei Avos. The lawyers presented real cases of ethics violations and the resulting consequences such as loss of clearance, reduction of grade, and negative performance reports. The government had me on a leash, but it mattered not because of the benefits and employment security. I achieved level III (highest) in two fields: program management and system planning, research, development, and engineering.

Closing Ceremony of the APATS Program (Antenna Pedestal and Test Station) at the Raytheon site in Marlboro, MA. Sid Krimsky was US Gov't Program Manager and Ron Garon was the Raytheon Program Manager

FROM BROOKLYN NY TO BROOKLINE MA

Colonel Jeffrey Katz, USAF, awarding me a 10 year service pin on 6 Nov 1999.

Author sitting next to a mockup of "Fat Man" atomic bomb dropped on Nagasaki on 9 August 1945 to end the war against Japan that was initiated on 7 Dec 1941 by their dastardly attack on Pearl harbor. Fat Man was an implosive bomb with a plutonium core. Mockup sits outside the U.S. naval Museum at China Lake in California. About 120 Fat Men were produced between 1947-1949 and were all retired in 1950. I was sent to China Lake to observe software performance during war games.

Collection of citations, medals and awards at my retirement ceremony 29 June 2010 at the Hanscom Air Force Base Chapel

Retirement ceremony for my boss, Colonel James Shaw and his wife at the Concord Brodge.

FROM BROOKLYN NY TO BROOKLINE MA

DEPARTMENT OF THE AIR FORCE
HEADQUARTERS ELECTRONIC SYSTEMS CENTER (AFMC)
HANSCOM AIR FORCE BASE MASSACHUSETTS

Mr. Sidney Krimsky,

On the occasion of your retirement after twenty years of dedicated service as a Civil Servant in the United States Air Force, the ESC engineering leadership expresses its heartfelt thanks and deep appreciation for your patriotism, diligence, and adroit application of advanced engineering skills to Air Force acquisition processes.

Having entered government service after twenty years' successful experience as a practicing engineer in industry, you became a key player in many sensitive, mission-critical programs at ESC, including the Distributed Common Ground System (DCGS) where you successfully revised and guided the DCGS Security Classification Guide (SCG) to multi-agency approval within six months after being assigned the task. In the same period, your scheduling team facilitated the successful delivery of three advanced sensor systems to the warfighter.

Your patient, mentoring, collaborative style and selfless pursuit of workable solutions in complex situations are in the highest traditions of the Air Force Civil Service. For your hard work and unimpeachable example, the ESC engineering leadership expresses its eternal gratitude and wishes you and your family the best of all possible futures.

TIM RUDOLPH
SL Ph. D.
Chief Technology Officer

Chapter 51.1

ACT FOR AMERICA

During my employment with the Department of Defense, we were briefed semi-annually on terror threats to the United States by the Air Force Office of Special Investigations (AFOSI) stationed at Hansom Air Force Base. Sometimes briefers came from Washington to provide classified PowerPoint slides. During the 1990s we learned about terrorist cells in the USA from Middle Eastern countries and the goals of the cells. The cell members were here to raise funds for overseas charities and to learn about our infrastructure. These briefings were classified, and we could not talk about this outside the briefing room. What happened on 9/11 was a result of careful planning by terrorists using information obtained by others.

After 9/11, Act for America was started by Brigitte Gabriel, a Lebanese Christian who with her family was mistreated by the radical Muslim terrorists starting in 1972. She and her family escaped to Israel and worked as a translator and radio host in Israel before immigrating to the USA. She graduated college and worked as a marketing consultant until 9/11. She escaped from Lebanon in order to avoid future terrorist attacks by radical Muslims, and she saw what happened here as a wakeup call. I learned about MEMRI (Middle East Media Research Institute) and Act for America while trolling the Internet. MEMRI employs scholars who translate speeches from Arab leaders and scholars into English. Brigitte Gabriel speaks Arabic and English fluently and started to lecture small groups that grew in numbers about the threats faced by Americans from radical Islamists.

The numbers grew to thousands and tens of thousands. She prepared brochures and DVDs and presented lectures about the threats to Western societies. The lectures were emotional as she described her own disrupted life as a teenager in Lebanon.

I contacted the national organization, found material on the Internet, and called up the Boston chapter president who was a Coptic Christian and whose family had to leave Egypt. He is a civil engineer, so we had a good exchange at Kupel's, sitting outside, eating bagels. I joined Act for America and attended numerous meetings at veteran's hall, synagogues, and once at a Christian monastery.

Act for America has grown to 190 chapters and about 180,000 members and a full-time lobbyist in Congress. Act for America has connections to patriotic groups around the USA. The purpose of Act for America is to disseminate information about radical Islam, influence the States and Congress to pass the ALAC program (American Laws for American Courts), identify persons with radical Islamic leanings, and disseminate information about the Koran and its contents inimical to Western values. The national coordinator assisted us to form a local chapter in Long Island. I was instrumental in starting an Act for America chapter in Long Island. Dorothy and I attended the National Convention in Washington, DC in September 2015. We were moved by the enthusiasm of the attendees, mostly veterans, patriots, and people disappointed with the policies of the United States Government making concessions to Muslims that diminish our fundamental freedoms enshrined in the Bill of Rights.

Chapter 51.2

TRIPS TO BERLIN, GERMANY

During September 2000, Dan Towers and I traveled to Germany on government business to attend meetings about the efficacy and performance of our hardware and software designed to acquire battlefield intelligence and also to attend a SAR/SLAR (side airborne radar/side-looking airborne radar) Conference in Berlin, Germany, attended by representatives from NATO countries. The classified meetings were held in a former Panzer training facility in North Berlin not too far from the Sachsenhausen concentration camp. The US military officers advised us to extend our business trip to visit Sachsenhausen and also Dachau. It was an education for me. On the barrack walls of the Panzer facility, I saw plaques awarding unit citations to the Panzer divisions for performance in North Africa during WWII. I read the German plaques, and it sent shivers up my spine. The facility was later occupied by the French, and I saw citation plaques in French. I toured Checkpoint Charlie and the Potzdammer Plaza that used to be no-man's land between East and West Germany. The Berlin Wall fell during 1999, and we saw remnants of the broken wall. I visited Sachsenhausen and Dachau concentration camps and showed my slides at various Holocaust memorial meetings.

In 2012, Dorothy and I visited Berlin; and we saw all the tourist sites, multiple memorials to the Holocaust, and Jewish museums. We toured inside the Oranienburger Synagogue made famous by the photos of flames coming through the windows during Kristallnacht in November 1938. I was transfixed by the rebuilt synagogue, walked to the very top, and saw all the exhibitions. We visited Sachsenhausen concentration camp. All the concentration camps have been sanitized. The stench is gone. The corpses were buried. The barbed wires are no longer electrified. The barracks are gone except for a few at Auschwitz. The Russians who liberated Auschwitz used the wood from the barracks as fuel. We saw Auschwitz and Theresienstadt during a trip to Prague during 2001. There are museums at all the camps we saw. The horrors that emerged from anti-Semitism can be seen in all the museums we saw, but the presence of the museums has not erased anti-Semitism.

Berlin is the nexus of dictatorship under Kaiser Wilhelm II; democracy under the Weimar republic; Fascism under Hitler; barbarism under Hitler, Himmler, and Heydrich; Communism under Stalin and Ulbricht; and finally democracy and free enterprise under Konrad Adenauer (nicknamed Der Alter, meaning the *old one*, because he was ninety years old) and Ludwig Erhard (nicknamed Die Dicke, meaning the *fat one*). Berlin is where WWII started and that is where it all ended, and the Soviet War Memorial in the center of Berlin opposite the Tiergarten describes it all. We went to Berlin to better understand what happened and what has been accomplished.

Kadimah Pub in Berlin near the Oranienburger Synagogue-
Reminds me of Cong. Kadimah-Toras Moshe

Sign posted on the wall of the Oranienburger Synagogue: lNacht
5 Sept 1866 – 5 Sept 1966
This synagogue is 100 years old and was set on fire on
Kristallnacht by the NAZIS on 9 Nov 1938.
During the Second World War 1939-1945 it was destroyed by
bombing in 1943. The front of this House of God should be for
all times a place of monument and memory. Forget it not.
Jewish Community of Greater Berlin
Board of Directors
*September 1966

FROM BROOKLYN NY TO BROOKLINE MA

Dorothy Krimsky between two soldiers at Checkpoint Charlie between East and West Berlin

Chapter 52

SYNAGOGUE PRESIDENT

In the spring 1977, I was approached by Dr. Hillel Besdin and asked to accept a nomination as shul president. I was to replace Robert Cohen who served as president for fourteen years. These elections were noncompetitive to avoid bad feelings and possible fracturing of the congregation. I served as president for ten years and two more years as copresident with Dr. Jeffrey Houben. We divided the work. He handled ritual and programming matters. I did finance, house, and administration matters. I made many administrative changes. I modified the by-laws to simplify them and the administration. I designed the first mechitzah under the rabbi's direction and guidance. Eliezer Halbfinger and I constructed the first mechitzah in one day (it happened to be Labor Day) by using pine lattice available from Home Depot that I purchased for $20. When congregants returned for Maariv, it was completed and installed. Naturally, I received a few complaints, and some people left the synagogue. They objected to a mechitzah. Rabbi Halbfinger personally spoke with everyone who objected. I used lattice because it had the largest openings and the width of the panel was at the minimum height allowed by Rabbi Moshe Feinstein. We also replaced the two secretaries Gertrude Markson and Ann Derby with a computer-savvy person, Gregory Yurkovsky, who set up the Yahrzeit and other mailings on computer. Gregory came from Russia, learned computers and accounting, and had a day job at Northeastern University. At shul, he worked at night.

I replaced the Adler machzorim used for the high holidays, with its archaic English translations, with the red Birnbaum machzorim.

From Henry Mazer, Marvin Levenson, Jack Sugarman, and Rabbi Halbfinger, I learned what it means to be part of a community. I tried to transmit this concept to my children. I could never have done this without the support of my wife, Dorothy. She managed the household affairs during all the times I attended meetings and met with individuals about assignments, personnel conflicts, and personal issues. She was always there for the children.

In June 1999, I ended my ten years as president. During the next two years, Jeffrey Houben and I shared the duties of president. Shul members insisted on honoring me for my twelve years of service with a banquet to raise money for the shul. I insisted that Dean Solomon and Charlotte Rosen also be honored. This would be our fifteen minutes of fame. It was a wonderful occasion with all my children, grandchildren, and mother present. At that time, she was able to walk up some steps. Rabbi Elly Krimsky represented our family, and these are the words he spoke.

PRESENTATION TO SIDNEY KRIMSKY delivered by Rabbi Elly Krimsky

> Bir'shus Miori v'rabbi, Rabbi Halbfinger, my Grandma, Rose Krimsky, Ava Mori, Ima morasi

> *On behalf of my siblings, Naomi, Yitzy, & Jonathan, I would like to sincerely thank the congregation for bestowing this well-deserved honor on my father. We join the shul in honoring and congratulating Dr. Dean Solomon and family and Charlotte Rosen and family in the tribute they share with our father. Our thanks to the hard working committee who organized this dinner and the honor—Susan Miller and Frannie Linda. Since we are obligated to honor and respect our parents 24 hours a day seven days a week for the duration of our lives, a dinner such as this makes our loving task a bit easier, and provides us with a unique*

opportunity to share our unique mitzvah with the public. My words are those of my siblings.

Over a century-and-a-half ago, Rabbi Samson Raphael Hirsch, confronted the tides of assimilation and the enlightenment in Germany. Without apology and with his brilliant wisdom and sensitivity, he wrote, debated and ultimately saved Orthodox Jewry in Western Europe. In a move for which I am daily grateful, Hakadosh Baruch Hu placed Rav Hirsch's great grandson in the life of my father. They took a Yiddish class together at City College, both individuals knowing it would be easy (and satisfy language requirements for graduation). Reb Shlomo Breuer's life was tragically cut short in the spring of 1992 but I know that my family and I are lucky to have known him and encountered such a great man.

I quote from remarks my father delivered at the bar mitzvah of Shlomo's eldest Breuer grandson, his son Joshua's son b'chor, this past summer in Israel. "He was the first rational Orthodox Jew I encountered in the modern world. He thought and acted halachically, not from emotion but from reason. I could relate to that. I was attracted to his clarity of thinking, love of people, unpretentiousness and Sophie's hospitality. Shlomo's wife, also a great grandchild of Rav Hirsch. If such people could observe shabbos, believe in kashruth, put on t'fillin and yet be rational and friendly, then I must further explore this very model of living. I would learn, not so much what Shlomo said but what he and Sophie did; especially their midos." My parents were honored that Shlomo put off a return trip to Israel to serve as one of the two witnesses at their wedding. The other witness, Reverend Moshe Holcer, signed my sister's k'subah and to this day maintains a close relationship with us, as do his children and grandchildren.

My father's absolute intellectual honesty brought him to where he is today. In Pirkei Avos we read "Akavia ben Mhalalel says: Consider three things and you will not come into the grip of sin: Know whence you came, whither you go and before whom you will give judgement and reckoning." This mishna so accurately depicts my father's outlook.

Know From whence you came.

My father always reminds us that we are all descended from Ukranian peasants. We joke about it and I recall the black bread I brought back on one of my trips to the Soviet Union which my father kept in the freezer until Pesach. To him that loaf was more valuable than a vintage bottle of single malt scotch, for it represented our lineage, our simple progenitors. When I was young and was flirting with a life as a journalist, my father told me, "Why don't you make the news, not just report it." My father's devotion to our humble family tree was genetically passed to him from his father, for whom I was named and for my grandma Rose's father, Zeide. It should be noted that Zeide Isadore Skolnick, in his later years also hosted my father for Shabbos, and sowed the seeds that moved my father to return to the Mesorah. My father will always speak of his time with Zeide with fond memories and my brother was named after him, his middler name being Yitzhak. My father's positive experiences with "Zeide" can be described in the fact that my father walked from his home in Coney Island to his grandfather's shul in Brownsville, East New York on Yom Kippur, to spend Ne'ilah with his grandfather.

Know where you are going and before whom you give judgment and reckoning.

My father's path is the path of truth, and he assiduously and joyously lives his life in pursuit of the ultimate emes. Jonathan reminded me of a conversation to which he was privy. My father was talking with some younger members of the shul. They were discussing health issues, ways in which one can extend their days. My father declared in total seriousness that "If palm oil were good for you, I would drink it." Seeing that he had a crowd, he continued, "If hot dogs were good for you, I would eat them. Finally to make his point clear, as if we didn't understand it at first, he proclaimed that if AIDS were good for you, I'd go out and get it."

My father's pursuit of truth, however, never comes in conflict with sensitivity or genuine concern. My father is the Cal Ripkin of the work force—taking only less than a handful of sick days in his 35+ year working career. He feels, as does Chazal, that if someone pays you a salary to work, you need to earn your keep and perform your duties to the best of your abilities. He has no tolerance for underperformance. When I would come home with C's in science, he didn't show his disappointment in my struggles to master the science he so loves; he merely asked me if I was trying my hardest and believed me when I told him that I was.

We are especially proud of the donation of books to the Synagogue library by our chilkdren.

Portable aron (cupboard) made from original woodwork of aron taken from Cong. Toras-Moshe in Roxbury, MA.
Translation: It is a Tree of Life to those who grasp it, referring to the Torah.

Rabbi Abraham Halbfinger spiritual guide for our family from 1966 until his death on 22 September 2012. We did not fully appreciate what we had until we lost it.

Chapter 52.1

KADDISH FOR KADIMAH

On Sunday evening, 29 April 2012, the congregation members voted 54–24 to accept the recommendation of the board of directors to replace Rabbi Azriel Blumberg with a rabbi from Yeshivat Chovevai Torah (YCT), an "open Orthodox" rabbinical training school, against the wishes of Rabbi Emeritus Abraham Halbfinger. He urged the selection committee not to bring in a graduate from YCT. YCT graduates are not accepted in the RCA. Their time spent on learning from traditional Jewish sources is less than the graduates of RIETS (Rabbi Isaac Elchanan Theological Seminary). YCT (Rabbi Avi Weiss) ordained a female rabbi contrary to thousands of years of Jewish tradition. YCT adopts a more lenient position to Halacha somewhere between Conservative Judaism and Orthodoxy. Yeshiva University (YU) graduates are employed at YCT, but YCT graduates are not employed at YU.

Dorothy and I were disappointed. Rabbi Halbfinger came to Kadimah-Toras Moshe in September 1966, one month after Dorothy and I attended services. I was appointed to the board of directors (BoD) in June 1967 by Henry Mazer and served on the BoD continuously. I served in every capacity at KTM: president from 1977 to 1989, *Gabbai* for eight years, chairman of the energy committee, *Baal Tokaia* for thirty years, chairman of the school committee for two years (when KTM had a school for the first and second grades), associate treasurer, and chairman of the house committee. I was co-president with Dr. Jeffrey Houben from, 1989 to 1991.

I also designed and built with Alec's help three sections of the mechitzah, designed and oversaw the construction of the outdoor succah, cleaned up the coatroom with the help of Cheryl Sisel, designed and supervised construction of the remodeled coatroom and repaired it after the collapse of the shelf because the lag screws were supported by drywall and not cement blocks, designed and installed the outdoor mailbox, installed a peephole for security in the side door, supervised the repair of the outside stone wall, replaced a defective outdoor defective wall electric light fixture in the succah, provided comments that helped to reject the proposal to relocate KTM and build a large apartment building on the parcel, purchased computer and peripherals to automate the office, and designed and constructed a portable *aron* for the Torah to dwell overnight in a house of *shiva*.

As president, I introduced many changes into our governing process such as reducing the number of BoD members from twenty-eight to fourteen because the shul had fewer members after the merger in 1962–1964, eliminating the position of associate treasurer because the occupant had no assignment, opening the kitchen to anyone under rabbinic supervision who wanted to prepare a Kiddush or luncheon, introducing computers into the KTM office with the help of Larry Smith, promoting transparency by opening BoD meetings to the members (except for executive sessions), and introducing the finance committee/executive committee as an ad hoc committee to advise the president about finances and sensitive matters. KTM was the first Boston shul to provide a room for the Student Struggle for Soviet Jewry (SSSJ). We opposed the closing of the JCC on Sutherland Road and Barry Shrage, probably out of guilt feelings, and established and funded the Brookline Brighton Development Fund that awarded grants for synagogue projects. KTM benefited from being awarded a few grants. The fund was based on the interest earned from the net income from the sale of the JCC to Heritage House. Barry Shrage deserved our appreciation.

The BoD voted eleven to hire the YCT rabbi, two abstentions, and two to hire the one of the two other candidates. The membership then had an opportunity to express their opinion and to vote. The final vote was 54–24. The opponents needed one-third of the voters to reverse the BoD decision, or twenty-six members. Four more votes were needed to oppose Rabbi Berman, and some people simply did not vote in person or by proxy.

After the decision of the membership to hire a YCT rabbi, against the wishes of Rabbi Halbfinger, I decided to sever all connections with KTM in May 2012 and continue my religious life with the *Ashkenazic Minyan* in the Sephardic shul on Corey Road. The parents of young children were adamant to bring in a dynamic rabbi who could respond to their needs. In my opinion, they chose theatrics over substance.

More than that is the fact that I was marginalized since June 2011. The last time I *davened Shabbos Shachris* was in June 2011. I was asked by Herb Klaver approximately twice a month to daven Shabbos shachris. When Herb stopped coming, for medical reasons, the other two gabboim did not call me but instead called nonmembers and one new member. I was not called to do the *HafTorah* on the Yahrzeit of my father. I did it about ten times during my forty-six years but was not asked during the past five years. Only a few times did I read my own HafTorah, Parshat Parah. The gabbai's excuse was that he thought I did not want to daven Shabbos shachris. He called me up to apologize after Rabbi Halbfinger spoke with him. I spoke with Rabbi Halbfinger who asked me not to leave KTM after forty-six years. I meant a lot to the shul, and the shul meant a lot to me. In view of the fact that the president misspoke when he said several times that we would not bring in a Chovevai rabbi and that Rabbi Halbfinger would review all *smichot* before bringing in anyone, and since none of this happened, it was time to leave and open a new page in my religious experience.

FROM BROOKLYN NY TO BROOKLINE MA

Our family outside 108 Westbourne Terrace in Brookline, MA where we lived from 1972 -2013.

Chapter 53

LIFE'S GOALS: SECURING PROFESSIONAL EMPLOYMENT, GETTING MARRIED, AND RAISING A FAMILY

My father drummed into my head not to become a house painter. He must have been frustrated belonging to the Painter and Decorator's Union and having to pay dues and hope there was work for him when he reported to the union hall. He did not enjoy working for bosses but yet did not have the requisite skills to work for himself. His choices were limited. My choices were broader and deeper. My playmates in elementary school and junior high school appeared to have more of an outgoing personality as they were able to talk about sports and the trivia of life with a fluency that exceeded my own. As they grew older and out of adolescence, we separated. They dated as a group and then paired off with girls, engaging in rituals that were a mystery to me. I was unable to make small talk especially about movie stars, celebrity personalities, and sports. I knew about school work, and that was all. I took solace in taking things apart, building things, and saving things such as coins and stamps. The word *nerd* had not yet been invented.

In junior high school and high school, I learned that I had a liking for languages, mechanical drawing, and mathematics. Mr. Benjamin Braverman, in the tenth grade, asked me what I wanted to do after graduation. I never thought of asking anyone. There were no real career counselors at high school. I was unprepared to answer him, but I said that I wanted to become a draftsman. He suggested that I study engineering. I worked hard in his class (called fusion math because it combined algebra and trigonometry). I volunteered to present the homework assignments on the blackboard almost every day. I never heard of engineering as a career except as a train driver. I looked it up in the dictionary. He was the only teacher that ever asked me about my future. From the tenth grade, my heart was set on engineering—nothing else. High school math especially analytic geometry and trigonometry and the use of a slide rule became my passion. I loved the order, symmetry, and absoluteness of the axioms, propositions, proofs, and conclusions of plane geometry taught by Ralph Ellis. I regret very much that I never contacted them while in college or after college to personally thank them for their attention to me and being such fine teachers.

My singular goal was to graduate Lincoln High School, enter CCNY, and graduate with a degree in engineering. Nothing would deter me. Later after graduation, my goals evolved to include finding a partner, getting married, and raising a family. My parents were unequipped to talk with me about this, so I had to reason things out by myself just as my engineering professors had taught me. "The most important thing you will have to take out of my class is the ability to think for yourself," said Professor Dillon who taught us the laws of Newtonian mechanics, statics, and dynamics.

My first professional job was in Sacramento, California. Finally, I had a challenging job, decent wages, and disposable income to buy clothes and an automobile. I had no social structure or workable plan to meet someone, get married, and model a life. In California, I observed the hedonism, absence of families, and social disconnections. After a year, I decided to leave and found a job in Boston after two years in the Sacramento existential desert. I tried to implement my plan in Boston by making contact with MIT Hillel, Harvard Hillel, and even attended Radcliff mixers. There were almost no unmarried Jewish girls at work, and my request for dates was refused. Connections at Hillel did result in a few social connections. But I was on my own.

Dorothy moved to Cambridge, Massachusetts, in 1965 to attend Harvard Summer School in the education department. We met at a party arranged by her brother and his friends who were attending grad school at MIT. I saw Dorothy a few months later in front of the Harvard Coop and suggested we go out. She had friends who had no cars, so I suggested we all go in my Peugeot to Cape Cod and have a picnic. We did have a picnic and within a few weeks paired off. I visited Israel in August 1965, and upon my return, we resumed our friendship. We became engaged in March 1966, drove to New York City, and I met her family for the first time. Her mother had different expectations. After all, I was balding, thirty years old, five feet five inches tall, with small parents and relatives of modest means, and was born of Ukranian Jewish peasants—not exactly what her parents, both born in America, expected. However, I was strong, Jewish, healthy, and had a fine education and a good job. Had I met them before we were engaged, the outcome might have been different. The rest is history.

My parents had almost given up on me, so they were pleased that I announced my engagement. Dorothy was an object of immense curiosity for my parents and relatives. But she endeared herself to all of them.

Dorothy and Jonathan Krimsky with Theodore Bikel somewhere near the Boston Public Garden.

Simma Hollander holding a fallen branch that became the Krimsky Family Tree with all the grandchildren's names engraved on the wood.

Bikel was a wonderful performer. I saw him last in the play in Washington, D.C. The Disputation of Barcelona (July 20-24 1263) that was held at the royal palace of King James I of Aragon in the presence of his court. It was a debate between the Ramban (Nachmanides) and the Christian Clergy.

The first time I heard Theodore Bikel perform was a recording of the Town Hall Concert around 1959. He was absolutely hilarious with his deep resonant voice explaining how future archeologists would treat the artifacts found in Washington, DC and how American Russian Émigrés' react coming to the Kretchma, a Russian Night Club. He appeared frequently at rallies to free Russian Jews trapped in the Soviet Union called "refuseniks" because they were refused exit visas. We saw him in the Boston Common where he sang and spoke about the plight of the refusniks. His recordings marched with technology from 78 RPM records to open reel tapes to VHS tapes to cassette tapes to DVDs. I own many of his recordings. He was born in 1924 and died 21 July 2015.

Our three wonderful children at the wedding of Alec Krimsky.

Mezinka dance at Alec's wedding. Visible: Marilyn and Alan Peltzman, Yossi Hollander, Jonathan Krimsky holding baby, Yitzy Hollander, Chaya Krimsky, and Yocheved Krimsky as bride.

Naomi Krimsky watching Master Chef Henry Mazer preparing food in our Synagogue for her bas-mitzvah.

Chapter 54

ASSISTING DEBORAH ONIE TO RECOVER HER REPUTATION

During the spring of 2009, we learned that Mrs. Deborah Onie's contract with the Maimonides School was not renewed. She was Jonathan's teacher in the sixth grade. Our relations with her were only professional, not social. Her husband took up her cause, and we started to believe him from information provided by her husband, Larry, that she was unfairly treated. He asked for my assistance because my three children had graduated from Maimonides School with a good education for which I was grateful. I paid complete tuition. I was not beholden to Maimonides or involved in business dealings with the school or any member of the BoD. I was involved in preserving the dignity of Rabbi Moses Cohen. Parents who were involved with preserving the dignity of Rabbi Moses Cohen in 1978 had grandchildren in the school and were available only for moral assistance. The parents feared retribution to their children and/or their grandchildren. Judy Hellman had died. My record was clean, and I was not subject to any business or financial influences with anyone associated with the Maimonides School. My ultimate boss was the secretary of defense.

This is what happened: Mrs. Onie was teaching sixth-grade general studies for twenty-one years. Her supervisor was Nancy Posner, general studies principal. Rabbi Beeker taught sixth-grade Hebrew studies. His supervisor was Rabbi Stewart Klammer, Hebrew studies principal. Five boys in her class and in Rabbi Beeker's class were judged to be behavioral-problem students. The principal of Maimonides School wanted these students to leave. The students scored low grades in the *Lemudei Kodesh* (Hebrew) studies. They scored satisfactory or high grades in general studies. Rabbi Stewart Klammer asked Mrs. Onie to lower their grades. She refused, stating that their test scores did not merit such treatment and their behavior was acceptable in her classes. Her refusal was deemed to be "insubordinate" by Rabbi Klammer and wrote negative performance reports. Next semester he exchanged her classroom for a smaller classroom and wrote negative performance reports in preparation for not renewing her contract. She claimed harassment and protested to the Maimonides School Committee. Meanwhile, Dr. Atara Twersky, chairlady of the school committee, resigned; and she was replaced by David Schiff, a Maimonides alumnus and member of the board of directors and a pillar of the community. Harassment continued with negative reports. Finally, at the end of the spring semester, she was told that her contract would not be renewed. She appealed to the school committee for reasons and was not provided with any. She asked for her performance reviews and was told they were not available.

She demanded to see her performance reviews and any letters of approval from parents. Parents who learned that she was being discharged after twenty-one years were unhappy, and many wrote letters of appreciation to her and to the school. Some of the files about her were released including a "defamatory report." A defamatory letter authorized by Rabbi Stewart Klammer, Hebrew principal, and written by Nancy Posner, general studies principal, was circulated to the members of the school committee. Mrs. Onie challenged the content of the defamatory letter.

Mrs. Onie requested a bais din three times and was refused by the school each time. The bais din refused to issue a subpoena to members of the school committee. She was irate because she claimed the information in her files was invented and untrue. The members of the school committee did not exercise due diligence by challenging the content of the defamatory report. If any of the charges in the report were true, she should have been fired immediately. Some of the positive letters and commendations she received over the years had disappeared from the school files. She and her husband appealed to the community for some kind of justice. Her reputation was tarnished. She appealed to the Boston bais din for a hearing several times and was turned down each time.

Having nowhere to go, she appealed to the Massachusetts Commission against Discrimination (MCAD). The MCAD subpoenaed the files, and she read all the reports and sought legal assistance.

The report was prepared during her employment. The chairlady of the school committee was Dr. Atara Twersky, and she took no action after reading the report. David Schiff was selected as the replacement for Dr. Twersky after she resigned. David Schiff and Rabbi Klammer were good friends. It was Schiff who did not renew her contract. She had been teaching for twenty-one years at Maimonides School.

The MCAD found probable cause for a jury trial. The content of the letter was refuted in a jury trial, and both defendants, Posner and Klammer, were found guilty of defamation. Mrs. Onie was awarded a settlement.

Meanwhile, her attorney, Paul Manoff, was contacted by someone from Maimonides, and a conversation ensued about potential future work. He was compromised and did not report this to the court. He was disciplined by the board of bar overseers by means of a temporary disbarment.

Mrs. Onie reapplied for her prior position after her replacement left after two years. She was not accepted. The interviewer wrote a negative report about the interview, which Mrs. Onie challenged by appealing to the Massachusetts Commission against Discrimination (MCAD). She again appealed to the Boston and RCA (Rabbinical Council of America) bais din but was refused each time. The case was scheduled to go to a hearing before the commissioner in Nov 2010. Maimonides kept offering her a settlement, which she resisted. Finally, just before the hearing and learning that the community of rabbis was indifferent to her fate and her hurt, she accepted a settlement, and the complaints officially ended.

I had a hand in consoling her, collecting documents, newspaper articles, and e-mails in which I asked for the school by-laws, name of the president, and name of the corporate clerk. I never received a response. Even Barry Shrage, president of the CJP, was unable to obtain a copy of the current by-laws of the school. The CJP donates money to an organization without naming a live president and providing active by-laws. The Maimonides school administration again refused her request for a bais din and refused to apologize for circulating evil and incorrect reports about her performance. The school finally settled out of court.

The entire history was documented in a fifty-eight-page report and sent to all the alumni who provided e-mail addresses to the school. The report was also sent to significant rabbis in New York and Boston who did not respond to a teacher whose reputation was besmirched and found that she was defamed by her principals in a Hebrew day school in a jury trial. The indifference of the community was more disappointing than the scurrilous charges levied against her. This speaks volumes about the rabbis in Boston and New York (bais din of America) to whom Larry Onie appealed to hear this case. They allowed an evil document to go unanswered and a Jewish teacher to be besmirched. She received no help from the Jewish institutions designed to help her and therefore had to appeal to the secular courts. RCA rabbis refused to assist a Jewish teacher obtain justice.

I'm proud of what I did to alleviate her helpless situation about her besmirched reputation. I was disappointed in the response of the community who appreciated Mrs. Onie but would not lift a finger to help her. Their loyalties to the school, to their friends, and to the principals exceeded their loyalty to honesty, integrity, and truth meaning Torah. This whole business and the experience of trying to delay the forced departure of Rabbi Moses Cohn soured my respect for the Boston and RCA (bais din of America) batai din. The batai din refused to assist a Jewish teacher in a Hebrew day school—how sad and disappointing.

Mr. Onie and I tried to find the by-laws and see if their charter allowed the school to make such arbitrary decisions. The principal of the school would or could not release the by-laws. We appealed to the attorney general of Massachusetts since Maimonides is incorporated and is supposed to be supervised by the Brookline Superintendent of

Schools. The AG and superintendent could not help us. We appealed to the Combined Jewish Philanthropy head Barry Shrage because Maimonides is the recipient of CJP funds. You would think that the CJP would want to understand the administrative structure of recipient organizations. Barry Shrage requested a copy of the by-laws and his request was denied. It seems that Rabbi Klammer was a loose cannon. We learned that Maimonides Hebrew Day School is not accredited by the state-accrediting agency. We learned that parents either did not know or did not care. The reputation of Maimonides for academic excellence is well-known, and that is all that concerns parents besides tuition costs.

Lessons Learned from the Onie Experience

- Absence of accreditation does not deter parents from enrolling their children in a Jewish day school even if they know that the school lacks accreditation. Maimonides as of 2012 was not accredited.
- Church-based schools do not have to conform to their own by-laws.
- Church-based schools are not required to provide by-laws to donors, parents, or officers.
- The attorney general of Massachusetts can provide no assistance in obtaining by-laws.
- Church-based schools are exempt from filing 990s with the IRS.
- All schools in Massachusetts are supposed to be supervised by the local superintendent of schools, but AGs avoid meddling and supervising Jewish day schools unless there are physically unsafe conditions.
- Church-based schools are not required to provide notes of board meetings to anyone.
- Church-based schools that provide false information about teachers can be sued for libel in local courts.
- Church-based schools need not inform donors or parents about governance issues.

- Church-based schools need not account for major investment losses to donors or parents.
- It is not unethical for members of boards of directors of church-based schools to recommend their own law firm to provide legal counseling and charge for billable hours.
- Firing teachers who refuse to lower grades has legal consequences if teachers are willing to spend the time to seek redress through the MCAD and courts. Maimonides School will not repeat this faux pas.
- Firing teachers on the basis of age alone is illegal. If teachers are willing to seek redress through the MCAD and the courts, they may win and receive a settlement.
- Providing libelous and/or incorrect information about teachers to the MCAD and courts has legal consequences if malice can be proven. It is unlikely that Maimonides will repeat this faux pas.
- Any settlements received by the teachers are accompanied by a gag order.
- There are serious ethical consequences to the plaintiff's lawyer if defendant's lawyers offer or suggest potential work to plaintiff's lawyers during discovery or trial. This is like a sting operation, and any lawyer who cooperates may be disbarred as was Paul Manoff who was compromised by the lawyer representing Maimonides School when they discussed future cases.
- Although all the local rabbis, who are community leaders, agree that aggrieved Jewish teachers who teach in a Jewish day school should seek Jewish courts (baitim din) to resolve any differences, the same leaders may refuse to call a bais din and issue subpoenas to relevant rabbis involved in a dispute—an astounding degree of hypocrisy. The American legal system offers the best remedies for aggrieved plaintiffs; the bais din falls short. This includes the bais din of America.
- Teachers who were unjustly treated (as determined by a trial or being offered a settlement) can expect no support

from the Jewish community. The overall Jewish community has become desensitized to mistreatment of teachers. A sense of collective ethics is missing.
- The personal ethics or the behavior of the school board or management board members is cognitively dissonant from the teachings of Torah. The insensitive response to teacher dismissals for spurious reasons, without explanations, by school board or management personnel at Maimonides School was astounding. This is contrary to the values taught in a Jewish day school that espouses Torah values.

These experiences plus our experience to preserve the dignity of Rabbi Moses Cohn educated me to the realities of "Jewish justice." Only the American legal system offers the best chance of an aggrieved Jewish person to obtain justice.

I spent about two years listening to the narrative of Deborah Onie mostly by her husband who fought intensively to preserve her reputation and redress, what we both believed was an obvious injustice. The following essay was printed in the Jewish Advocate on April 18, 2008 page 13 entitled "Maimonides School Matters."

In his essay on Parshat Mishpotim (Feb 1,2008) Rabbi Korff wrote that "it is forbidden to go to the secular courts when conflicts between Jews can be settled within the framework of Judaism and the authority of the "Rabbinic Courts." In the Feb 8 edition, he also wrote, "for dealings between mankind, atonement is only possible when persons face each other as did the Cherubs with the arc and the tablets between them."

These principles were well implemented in the landlord-tenant dispute between the landlord Simcha Mindick and the tenants in the building he owned. Both parties agreed to use the Rabbinic Court, faced each other, and accepted binding arbitration. The dispute was resolved without going to the secular courts thereby saving all parties legal expenses. The process and the resolution received favorable publicity in the Jewish Advocate and other Boston newspapers after the compromise was announced.

The leadership of the Maimonides School in Brookline did not follow those principles when Rabbi Moses Cohn was not rehired because he attained age 65, despite a majority of parents that urged the school committee to retain him for one or two more years to prepare for a transition and a proper departure banquet that would have raised funds for the school. The school committee met with parents and both sides agreed to have a Rabbinic Court resolve this issue.

The school committee then asked the parents to cease all discussion during Rabbinic Court deliberations. About two months later the school committee admitted that there was not going to be a Rabbinic Court. Parents suspected that no Rabbinic Court would hear this case because Maimonides was the Rav's school. Supporters and opponents of Rabbi Cohn were not allowed to face each other in a Rabbinic Court. The school deprived itself of an opportunity to raise significant funds.

Several years ago, when Mrs. Deborah Onie was not rehired by Maimonides School, two defamation reports submitted by the two principals, were placed in her personnel file that purported to justify the rationale for her discharge. After the end of the school year, she obtained her personnel file, and for the first time became aware of and read the defamatory reports. She claimed that the reports were a fabrication. She requested three times to have a Rabbinic Court review her case to restore her reputation. She wanted a face-to-face meeting with the authors of the reports.

Three times Maimonides School refused her request for a Rabbinic Court and was forced to seek justice in the secular courts. Several years of depositions have ended and her case awaits a trial date decision. The legal cost to the school may have been several hundreds of thousands of dollars. Insurance or private funding may be covering the cost, which explains why the expenses appeared nowhere in the financial report.

The same school policy of not using a Rabbinic Court was implemented when Mrs. Evelyn Berman and Mrs. Phyllis Schwartz were not rehired. The teachers claimed discrimination, decided to fight and sought justice by filing a complaint with the Massachusetts Commission Against Discrimination (MCAD). The MCAD found for the teachers and Maimonides settled out of court by paying a large monetary sum. The plaintiffs agreed to not talk about their settlements. The legal costs may have been covered by insurance or private funds.

Based on the Mindick case, plus many other cases that come before the Boston Rabbinic Court that we never hear about, I am sure that the Rabbinic Court would handle this and other matters fairly, confidentially, and competently. However, the Maimonides School leadership rejected use of the Rabbinic Court.

The secular courts can only deal with facts and matters of law. The Rabbinic Courts deal with facts and halacha. Halacha includes issues of ethics and morality. Secular courts do not deal with ethics and morality unless the issues fall within the law. It is to the advantage of Maimonides School leadership not to have their actions examined through an ethical lens. Therefore the Maimonides leadership will seek the secular courts and pay the legal fees.

With respect to these decisions, transparency is opaque. The donating public does not know who is responsible for avoiding Rabbinic Courts. Is it the board of directors, the 8 or 9 shareholders, chairman of the board, school committee or the executive director?

Maimonides School is an outstanding academic institution in New England that imparts Torah and secular knowledge to its students. My three children graduated Maimonides with an education that enable two to earn smicha and my daughter to teach lemudi kodesh. Their teachers imbued them with Torah values.

One of the core Torah values of Maimonides School (from the web site) is that "the school must provide an all-encompassing religious atmosphere in which the observance of halacha in the totality of its ethical and ritual components is central." Is constantly choosing the secular courts over the Rabbinic Courts consistent with the core values? I think not.

Chapter 55

PERSONAL VALUES AND PHILOSOPHY

My values were formed by my associations and life experiences before I was married. My view of justice, ethics, and morality were innate; and some were learned from my father who never broke promises. He was reliable. It is not something you learn in school. I learned about not breaking commitments from my father. My studies of the Torah about what is right and wrong only reinforced my prior beliefs.

Free Will

Why did the Almighty also hide his face during the Holocaust is a question that confounded many Jewish scholars including Rav Joseph Soloveitchik. The best answer I heard is from Rabbi Gedalia Fleer, a worldwide traveler, lecturer, and Torah scholar.

The Almighty agreed to allow "free will" at the time of creation in a covenant with Satan. Free will allows the opportunity to do good and/or evil and allows for "tschuvah." A covenant, unlike an agreement, or promise is supposed to last forever. Breaking that covenant means that the Almighty cannot be trusted to keep his promise. However, God made another covenant with Abraham, Isaac, and Jacob. That covenant is to not allow the Jewish people to disappear. God made other covenant with Moses, and that is to never allow the Torah to disappear. Whenever there is an existential threat to the Jewish people or the Torah, God will intervene in the historical process. God also made a covenant with Noah never to again flood the earth.

God made an agreement, not a covenant, for the children of Israel to acquire the land of Israel and to keep it, providing they obeyed the words in the Torah. The prophets of the Almighty spoke his message about returning to Israel and repentance. Unfortunately, the people did not listen, and the result was destruction of both temples and exile. Acquiring the land of Israel was not a covenant; it was made as a promise with conditions.

As evil as it was, the Holocaust was not sufficient for the Almighty to break his covenant about free will. The Holocaust did not rise to the level of an existential threat. The proof is the resurgence of Jewish practice in Israel and around the world, the growth of Israel, and the increase of Torah study worldwide. At the end of WWII, this growth was unforeseen. There are many stories of strange, unexplained, unnatural occurrences in the various wars since 1948 that favored Israel. Hopefully, the Jewish people learned their lesson and will keep their part of the covenant. God will still allow free will but will still keep his part of the covenants he made with Satan, Abraham, Isaac, Jacob, and Moses.

Raising Children

Children have different innate abilities. Better not to push them but to allow them to nurture their own interests in their own way. Parents provide the basic raw materials including analysis of alternatives. Schools provide the knowledge, and shuls provide the inspiration. That is how it is supposed to work. Children just have to try as hard as they can, and they will emerge successful. The path is more important than the end result.

Compliments and Criticisms

Beyond a certain age, compliments and criticisms convey little meaning and may be largely ignored by accomplished rational people who are beyond all pain and suffering.

Offending People

There are always people who are easily offended when their views are challenged. They need to visit a "dermatologist psychologist" to acquire thicker skin.

Punishment

I developed a "no-fault punishment" system when children fought. Rather than spending unproductive time assessing blame and dispensing punishment to the guilty, I punished them both equally by sending them to their rooms or depriving them of something or threatening to deprive them unless they stopped fighting or arguing over trivia. They would be angry at me and have to learn to cooperate with each other and not cause trouble. Better to be angry with me than with each other. Any punishment must be "immediate, precise, and overwhelming" but infrequently applied so that the recipient really understood what went wrong. Hitting a sibling initiated the harshest of responses. Arguing is acceptable and even encouraged, but hitting is not allowed. I believed in few rules at home, but those rules we had were rigorously enforced.

Disciplining Grandchildren

Our philosophy is to support the parents, allow parents to discipline their children, and only to bring gifts and spoil them. I did not appreciate when Dorothy's parents tried to impose their values on our children, and I am sure that my children would not appreciate if we impose our values even though our values are already congruent to the values of our in-laws and our children and spouses. We are fortunate that all our children and spouses have solid Torah values, and all Dorothy and I can do is be role models for our grandchildren and help whenever we can.

Complaints

When faced with nagging complaints, I would repeat that I am not raising a generation of kvetches, contentious whiners, and complainers. Let us find a solution. Complaining just feeds on itself and solves nothing. Complaints are unproductive unless they lead to action. As I grow older I observe that many complaints are based on 'emotional speculation' which are complaints devoid of facts.

DER

When faced with an irrational outburst to a trivial event or deprivation, I would tell them that you are having a disproportionate emotional response (DER) even to a four-year-old. Repeat it often enough, and it will get their attention. My mature grandchildren still remember when I told them that they are having a DER. Now they can laugh at the wording.

Reason for an Education

After having volunteered for three years to assist teachers teaching STEM subjects, as part of the RE-SEED Program and dealing with a few resistant students, I arrived at the following discourse. I would ask the students why they are in school. Their answers would be as expected: My parents force me, it is the law, my friends go to school, etc. My answer to them is that the reason they are in school are none of these. The reason they are in school is because the students want to be listened to when they grow up. It is the fundamental reason they are in school. It follows that to be listened to requires a knowledge base. No one wants to listen to a dummy. The brain starts out like an empty DVD with no information written to it. In time, information is written to the DVD subject to recall. Kids understand the meaning of an empty hard drive or DVD. Wanting to be listened to appeals to any student. No one wants to be ignored. In other words, it is in their own self-interest to go to school and try to learn. That is how I appealed to them.

I also told them that it is in my own interest for students to graduate, find good jobs, and pay taxes to fund my ongoing social security and medicare benefits.

Responsibilities and Commitments

We have to help one another out as best we can and just take responsibility. When adults accept responsibility, children will learn to accept responsibility. Don't make promises and commitments unless you are sincere about implementation. Children learn to distrust people when parents break even simple promises because children learn that it is acceptable to break promises. Better not to promise than to make and break a commitment. Even showing up on time is a promise because it shows how you respect the other person's time. Being late is breaking a promise.

Marriage

A criterion for a continuing marriage is the three *C*s: communication, compromise, and consideration. Breaking any of these may *C*s may result in a divorce, which also is characterized by three *C*s: condemnation, cost, and convalescence. Ralph Kramden and Alice Kramden had a perfect marriage. She was a perfect straight lady and listened to Ralph and his zany ideas but did as she wished and allowed Ralph to think that he was "king of the household." Jackie Gleason and Audry Meadows were perfectly matched for their roles.

FIRPS, WIMPS, and Heroes

We have become a nation of FIRPS (feckless incapable of responding to problems), and certain individuals have become straight-jacketed to where they are unable to take action. Men have become feminized. We see this on modern TV where men are no longer portrayed as macho. The manly heroes of another era such as John Wayne, Alan Ladd, Gary Cooper, Bert Lancaster, Broderick Crawford, George Raft, John Garfield, Gregory Peck, Kirk Douglas, etc., all of whom accepted responsibility and acted to do justice, no longer exist. Now we have the comic book characters of the past who seek justice. Parents are supposed to demonstrate strength, fair play, ethical behavior, and healthy habits. Deviations or compromises from the ideals of the past century cause cynicism, skepticism, and hypocrisy.

We also have become a nation of WIMPs. WIMP means weak individual managing people. Bosses who fear telling the truth and mislead their employees are prime examples.

We live in a nation of FIRPS managed by WIMPs.

WIMPS and FIRPS share common features:

Cognitive distortion exists when false beliefs are genuinely held.

Entropy dissonance exists when human energy produces little useful work.

Cognitive dissonance exists when there is a difference between reality and cognition.

In the study of cosmological models, WIMP means weekly interacting massive particle. Physicists studying the cosmos have proposed a model in which WIMPs may be responsible for dark matter that suffuses the entire universe. Gravity should have attracted all the galaxies toward a central point within the universe instead of galaxies receding from one another. WIMPs may constitute much of missing antigravity matter that pushes the galaxies away from each other. WIMPs rarely interact with ordinary matter and are hard to detect and find. Sociological WIMPs are plentiful and easy to find.

"Lashon Hora" (Evil Speech)

"Lashon hara" is used (1) as an excuse to avoid critical discussion, (2) to avoid a serious discussion that would make someone feel uncomfortable and (3) and as a cover-up to silence someone from speaking the truth. So we live with our delusions, avoid confrontation, and allow unethical behavior to continue. FIRPs and WIMPs hide behind lashon hara.

"Institutional arrogance" requires institutional *tschuvah*. We find such arrogance in private companies that ignore customers at their peril. We also find such arrogance in nonresponsive, nontransparent government agencies whose employees cannot be corrected. We also find it in Hebrew day schools that refuse to share governance documents. Sometimes the only tool available to encourage transparency is lashon hara followed by exposure.

Soup

Soup, especially on cold Boston nights, has to be served steaming hot. Cold soup is worse than no soup. Fruit soup in the hot summer is an exception.

Truth versus Shalom Bias

If a choice has to be made between truth and shalom bias, then I always choose truth because shalom bias not based on truth cannot be sustained. This can be challenging at times. Jeremiah said in verse 17:9, "The heart is most deceitful of all and it is fragile; who can know it?"

Loyalty

Loyalty to friends or an institution is risky because it may compromise honesty, integrity, or truth if a conflict arises. This is what happened in the Catholic church when pedophiliac priests were moved around. Cardinal Bernard Law was more loyal to his fellow priests and the institution he served than to the values of honesty, integrity, and truth. Integrity by Boston rabbis was compromised when Rabbi Moses Cohn and Mrs. Deborah Onie challenged decisions made by the Maimonides School Committee to dismiss them and asked for assistance from the bais din and no assistance was forthcoming.

Justice

People bullied by institutions capture my attention. I usually side with the victim. Tenants bullied by landlords and the treatment of Rabbi Cohn are examples of institutional bullying. A Jew is forbidden to stand idly by while a fellow Jew is being bloodied (figuratively). My inspiration is from Isaiah 1:17–18: "Learn to do good, seek justice, strengthen the victim, do justice for the orphan, and take up the cause of the widow. Go forth, now let us reason together." Reasoning has to be based on objective truth. A favorite saying of mine is "Emes, Emes, Tirdof" in Hebrew, which is a take-off on "Tsedek, Tsedek, Tirdof" from the Torah. Truth, truth shall you pursue, even though the pursuit of truth may result in trouble for the pursuer. No good deed goes unrewarded.

Stubbornness

Stubbornness means disagreement with my mother, a genetic trait I inherited from my maternal grandfather.

Noise

I have always been bothered by loud noises especially at weddings. The hosts and the rabbis seem to have no influence to have the band lower the volume of the music. Yet I know from my experience at Polaroid Corporation that exposure to noise has a deleterious effect on hearing. Constant exposure to noise (noise is undesired sound) can produce hearing loss. I either wear earplugs at weddings or stuff wet tissue paper into my ears to reduce the sound levels penetrating my eardrums. At Polaroid, I purchased ultrasonic vapor degreasers to clean oil-covered plastic parts prior to assembly into Polaroid cameras. This was an effective way to remove all mold oil and chads (small plastic slivers) on the plastic parts. Unfortunately, the machines that I purchased produced ninety decibels of continuous sound. The OSHA limit for an eight-hour day is eighty-five decibels. I had to do something to avoid a potential lawsuit from people who became sick. So the corporate doctor and I interviewed employees, and we concluded that some employees really developed symptoms from the noise levels. We moved some employees away, provided ear muffs for some, tried the baffle the sound, and rotated employees. Some employees never complained. The noise did not bother them. That is how I learned about the physiological effect noise has on health, not just hearing loss. I advise everyone to wear ear protection at weddings.

Proudest Nonemployment-Related achievements

Getting married, raising a family with three wonderful children, fighting for rent control, participating in Rabbi Cohn's banquet, improving our old house we purchased in 1972, being elected as a synagogue president, and helping Mrs. Onie restore her reputation were some of our social and political achievements. The nerd struck back!

Growing Old

Growing old and staying healthy requires attention to avoidance, diet, exercise, genetics and luck. I avoided smoking and drugs. My Diet eventually focused on vegetables, fruits, grains, minimal red meat, and no hard cheese.

I prepared for growing old at age 25 when I joined the Cambridge YMCA. I watched Harry lePore, in his late 50s or early 60s teach calesthenics to dozens of Y Members. I used the Naulilus machines to stretch my muscles and ligaments. I jogged around the track for a mile every week. I jogged from 1200 Massachusetts Avenue along Memorial Drive to the Eliot Bridge and back along the Charles River. I skied and climbed mountains in New Hampshire before I was married. I taught my children how to ski and we climbed mountains in New Hampshire. I learned to sail on the Charles River and Boston Harbor breathing in the fresh air. I walked all over Cambridge and sometimes into Brookline to eat at Rubin's. I lived and matured in Massachusetts for 53 years.

Chapter 56

THE DIVORCE

The divorce between Sheldon Krimsky and me had its roots in our adolescent experiences. I used to pick on him without reason. Once I refused to let him in the house because he forgot his keys. I wanted to teach him a lesson. Sheldon attended Hebrew school until bar mitzvah age. He read his haftorah in a small synagogue. There was a small collation followed by a small party in our home in Coney Island to which my zadie and our paternal relatives were invited. My parents did not have the resources to make a large bar mitzvah party in a hall as was done for me. My mother bought a large bakery cake and cooked some food. A few relatives showed up: Zadie, Aunt Rae, Aunt Annette, and Cousin Elaine. I never asked my brother if he felt deprived because he did not have a large recognition of his bar mitzvah. He seemed indifferent. His exposure to yiddishkeit was Hebrew school lessons, bar mitzvah, and trips to my zadie during Passover. He was indifferent and disinterested in anything my zadie had to say about shul life. I was more interested, but there was a limit to my interest. Zadie's children did not attend his seders. He said that he made seders for me. His children Ida, Natie, and Heshy had no interest in learning about the European culture Zadie left behind or of the serious Jewish scholarship transmitted over thousands of years from Israel to Russia. After WWII ended, his children wanted economic opportunities, homes, and families. Any spiritual interest was absent.

Over the years at Brooklyn College and later Purdue University, I strongly suspect that my brother was affected by the antiwar riots during the sixties by left-wing ideologies of peace, love, and freedom from social restraints. His eulogy for our father, who died in December 1966, reflected his dislike for organized religion consciously or unconsciously. From disinterest to indifference, to atheism, to hostility was the path my brother followed. He deplored the mindless Judaic rituals with incomprehensible ancient language. I avoided these topics with him because I was not in a position to argue with him using any form of reason. Sheldon studied all the philosophers for his PhD and understood all their arguments for denying religion and God. He developed a liking for Marxism. When I mentioned to him that under Marxism people suffered, he responded, "Well, they are not doing it right." When I asked him about incentive in Russia, he said that there are state-created incentives. However, millions of people were dissatisfied and wanted to leave Russia. Individual initiative was suppressed by the Communist regime.

My father belonged to a union and complained about the bosses. He visited the union halls to get work. My brother may have been influenced by the capitalistic bosses who inflicted hurt to the working men. Sheldon developed a dislike for big business and the influence they exert on the working class and, in general, the evils of the capitalistic system. Any sensitive person familiar with the travails of the working class would agree with him.

After Dorothy and I were married, Sheldon visited us and especially developed a relationship with Alec. He would visit us after work, eat supper with us, and talk with Alec.

Sheldon, Carolyn, and our parents were invited to meet Mrs. Boriss, Carolyn's mother, at her home in Long Island. My mother recalls that Mrs. Boriss served bacon and ham and my mother was appalled. I do not think she complained because to complain is to start a bad relationship with potential in-laws. But Mrs. Boriss and Sheldon knew that my mother kept a kosher home and did not buy bacon or ham. Sheldon was indifferent.

Dorothy and I were invited to his wedding with Carolyn. We met her for the first time at the wedding. We asked Mrs. Boriss in advance that the food be kosher. Mrs. Boriss refused to spend the additional cost for kosher food. No one else really cared, and the

FROM BROOKLYN NY TO BROOKLINE MA

bride and groom did not care. I asked for kosher meals for Dorothy and me, Max and Sonya Katz, and my zadie. Kosher meals were provided but only after much discussion. The kosher food was double wrapped in foil.

Sheldon asked me to make a toast at his wedding. Just before toast time, he asked me if I would mind if Patrick made the toast. Patrick was married to Carolyn's sister. What could I say? I did not want to mar the affair, so of course, I agreed. Patrick made the toast. He divorced later. So much for Patrick!

After he married Carolyn Boriss, we learned from my mother that she disliked her father, Max Boriss, who paid for her trip to Paris to study art. Max Boriss was a businessman. Sheldon would visit us every month or so with his two children, Alyssa and Elliot. Our children played together, but Sheldon would frequently oversee what my children were talking about to his children to ensure his children were not contaminated by Jewish teaching. All my children were enrolled at the Maimonides School, and this had an effect in their outlook. Carolyn rarely came with him; she had little to say to me or Dorothy. Dorothy and I even attended an art exhibition of her work at a gallery in Cambridge or Boston. I did not understand her work, but so what? She was my sister-in-law, and we tried to be civil.

Carolyn disliked me and could not justify me to her liberal friends after learning that

- a. I worked for the DoD and supported the USAF's mission to destroy things and people;
- b. I used "Roundup" to kill dandelion weeds instead of pulling them out of the ground;
- c. we owned a two-family house and collected rent (I was a kulak, wealthy landowner);
- d. we practiced Orthodox Jewry and were members of a fundamentalist religious sect;
- e. we had three children, were therefore selfish, and should have stopped after number two;
- f. I used chemicals in my house for cleaning, polishing, stain and paint removal, etc.;

g. I was not an academician and had no business proffering advice on major issues; and
h. she viewed herself as creative and me as a noncreative lackey of corporate America. We lived in different realities.

For item *e* above, when Carolyn learned that Dorothy was expecting a third child, she asked if Dorothy would abort. Dorothy responded, "If I did, I would not tell you." Our view was that a deliberate abortion of a potentially healthy baby is an embarrassment and murder of life, not to be done and certainly not to be broadcast. We did not ask and do not know if Carolyn had abortions.

It became obvious that I did not fit in with her Cambridge illuminati. She was embarrassed that I wore a *kippah* to Alyssa's graduation from Cambridge High and Latin School and attended the collation afterward at their home in Cambridge wearing a kippah. She developed "chemical sensitivities," and I was perceived as unsympathetic to her allergies. After all, I was only an engineer; and what did I know about chemical sensitivities, corporate abuses of employees, and social injustice? Sheldon was even surprised that Polaroid allowed and encouraged me to purchase all the safety equipment I needed as safety manager for the many projects for which I had responsibilities as chief design engineer. I went beyond federal OSHA guidelines. I worked for corporate America. How could this be? I could tell that my treatment by Polaroid management did not fit his business model of corruption and profit above all else.

In 1993 Naomi was married in Beth El Synagogue in Newton, Massachusetts. Sheldon and his family were invited. I informed them that the walls of the synagogue hall had been painted about two weeks prior to the actual event. Carolyn did not attend, citing her chemical sensitivities. Only Sheldon and Alyssa attended. They were not invited to Jonathan and Chaya's wedding in 2004. Elly invited them to his wedding in 2006, and they did not attend. I told Elly that it was a wasted invitation. We were not invited to Alyssa's wedding. Since she intermarried, I would not attend if asked.

I did not understand any of this at the time, but over years, I sensed the pattern. I integrated her behavior and conduct, and that gave me insight into her personality. In 1995, after the fateful telephone call, the quiescent latent venom emerged.

We attended Eliot's bar mitzvah at Tufts, and then we walked to the Charles Motel in Cambridge for a kosher meal for which the food was double wrapped. There was really no spiritual content, and I was not invited to give a drosha, so I prepared nothing. But we offered two books as gifts in addition to cash. One book was *Pirkei Avos, Ethics of the Fathers* and the other was entitled *Permission to Believe*, which is a philosophical treatise appropriate for a thirteen-year-old, presenting arguments about God's existence. Carolyn threw the books back to me and said, "What about *Ethics of the Mothers?*" I was dumbfounded and took the books back. This was a bar mitzvah gift, and her response was boorish indicative of poor breeding.

At that encounter, she called me a fundamentalist. A fundamentalist is an unsophisticated, not fully developed individual. The fact that I was the inheritor of thousands of years of Jewish tradition and thought plus having three college degrees meant nothing to her.

So what was the triggering event?

In 1995 Salim Krimsky, accompanied by his two children Anna and Igor, was invited by the Tufts University Music Department to give a series of concerts of Russian Jewish music composed by Salim Krimsky and with Anna as a piano accompanist. Sheldon was a professor of urban economics at Tufts and arranged the concert through the music department. Dorothy and I attended the concert. Salim was interested in making the arrangement permanent and having Tufts sponsor his trips to America. Sheldon and I hosted Salim and his children for the time he was in America. I met him at JFK Airport and drove him to my house, and Sheldon came later. Sheldon drove him almost each day to Tufts to prepare for the concert. Salim wanted to make a good impression on his American hosts and on the music department at Tufts. Salim and his children dined with us and even spent one Shabbat at our home, respecting our tradition.

On a Sunday morning, Sheldon was scheduled to drive from Cambridge to our house to bring Salim to Tufts University to discuss with the head of the music department and musicians about his pending concert and how he wanted it presented. Salim wanted a permanent relationship with Tufts and to have Tufts University pay for trips to the USA. This meeting was important to him. Sheldon was expected around 10:30 a.m. At ten fifteen or so, Sheldon was not here, so Salim urged me several times to call to see if he was on his way. At first I demurred and said that Sheldon is reliable and will be here on time. He nagged, and finally I called. Carolyn answered the phone. I told her why I called, and she questioned why I made the phone call. "Don't you know that Sheldon is reliable? He is not meticulous about time." She started to question me about the purpose of the phone call. I tried to be civil and explain that Salim needed reassurances because he was nervous, did not want to be late, and this meeting was very important to him. She continued to challenge the need for a phone call, and I finally said something like "Carolyn, this conversation is going nowhere. Good-bye," and hung up.

That night in the parking lot, Sheldon confronted me and said that I was rude in hanging up on her. I tried to tell him what happened. It was hopeless. I told him that I did not intend to offend her, but I made no apologies. He told me that all conversations with her have to go through him. I found this demeaning and disrespectful of women. Carolyn was an educated woman with an MA in art studies and history. In other words, I was forbidden from speaking directly with her. I found her emotional, very sensitive to every word and nuance, especially coming from me whom she perceived as a fundamentalist antediluvian troglodyte. At an earlier meeting in her house, she actually said that I was a fundamentalist, meaning "religious fundamentalist," and I was forcing this down the throats of my children, thereby condemning them to a life of limited options and religious captivity. Instead of confronting issues, she used epithets. This is typical of the left. She needed to see a dermatologist to acquire thicker skin.

We exchanged a series of letters. Sheldon insisted that I apologize. Apologize for what? I told him that I would have a thoughtful response to all the letters upon my return from Israel. I dissected his and her letters analytically and told them why I disagreed with his statements and conclusions. My letter must have appeared as a shock to them because I challenged almost every assumption. As a college professor, Sheldon is used to receiving papers from obsequious students who want good grades, not from family members who question every unproven statement.

My mother was always bothered by this major rift between Sheldon and me. In her eyes, he is a good boy and could do no wrong. I am stubborn and should apologize. Dorothy should become involved. My mother marveled that Dorothy talks with her brother and sister-in-law whose daughter Eva married a non-Jew, Peter Bacevich. Her brother's son Jesse also married a non-Jew and was divorced. Uncle Albert is tolerant, respectful and understanding of our religious preferences. I am proud to have him as a brother-in-law. Sheldon is hostile to religion, and that makes the difference. In addition, Uncle Al's wife, Anita, is a rational, loving person who attended Alec's Brit Milah and was always positive about our ongoing family relationship. She never expressed dissatisfaction with our personal choices just as we never criticized their choices. God created men and women with free will.

Columnist Dennis Prager wrote "From Karl Marx to today, the Left has always hated people on the Right, not merely differed or been angry with them. The question is: why? Here are three possible answers. First, the left thinks the right is evil… Second, when you don't confront real evil, you hate those who do… Third, the left's utopian vision is prevented only by the right… Hatred of conservatives is so much part of the left that the day the left stops hating conservatives will mark the beginning of the end of the left as we know it."

Chapter 57

GRANDCHILDREN

As of August 2013, Dorothy and I have been blessed with twelve grandchildren. My mother had five grandchildren and would have had fourteen great-grandchildren, twelve great-grandchildren from my side, and two from Sheldon's side had she lived to August 2013:

NAME	BIRTHDAY	DAYS	gematria		SUM
Ephraim Boruch Hollander	23 May	174	331	232	563
Yossi Kalman Hollander	15 Aug	227	156	220	376
Simma Meira Hollander	16 Sept	259	115	256	371
Tamar Yaffa Hollander	28 Sept	271	640	95	735
Aryeh Leib Krimsky	28 Nov	332	216	42	258
Tziporah Krimsky	28 May	148	331		331
Yeshaya Simcha Krimsky	20 Feb	51	395	352	747
Malka Krimsky	12 Oct	285	95		95
Yaakov Yedidiah Krimsky	9 Aug	221	182	29	211

Rachel Krimsky	9 May	129	238	27	265
Yakira Sarah Raizel Krimsky	9 April	99	325 505	257	1087
Akiva Pesach Krimsky	31 July	212	118	148	266
Shoshana Raizel Krimsky	18 July	199	661	257	918
Shaina Hollander grt- grand daughter	14 April	105	259		259
Reuven Krimsky	5 May	126	259		259

Other Important Dates:	
Mar 17 Abba's birthday	
Mar 24 Naomi's birthday	
May 26 Elly's birthday	
May 26 Uncle Al's birthday	
June 18 Ima's birthday	
June 25 Grandma Rose's birthday	1935
June 27 Elly's and Yocheved's anniversary	2007
June 28 Chaya's birthday	
Aug 14 Ima's and Abba's anniversary	1966
Aug 17 Naomi's and Yitzy's anniversary	1992
Aug 28 Jonathan's and Chaya's anniversary	2006
Sept 7 Yitzy's birthday	
September 8 Albert's and Anita's anniversary	1976
September 20 Jonathan's birthday	
November 13 Yocheved's birthday	

We are confident that our thirteen grandchildren will carry Torah into the next century. From a grandparent's perspective, all are different but all will carry the seeds of Torah in the decades to come.

At Simma's bas mitzvah on 6 November 2011, I was asked to say a few words and they are at the end of this manuscript. My zadie would be proud that his great-grandchildren became rabbis and his great great-grandchildren will learn Torah and transmit its values into the twenty-first century. His line of Torah knowledge he brought from Russia took seed in me through a series of remarkable coincidences. His other grandchildren and possibly great-grandchildren are forever lost in the Torah world as they became integrated into the American culture, unknowing of the richness and core values of the Jewish tradition. They never had a chance to investigate and make a choice. For me, was it luck or destiny?

Our first grandchild, Ephraim Boruch Hollander.

FROM BROOKLYN NY TO BROOKLINE MA

Birthday Gift for me. Note that the number of members of each family are mapped to the words Happy Birthday Zaidy!

Aryeh and Chaya Krimsky at Rubin's restaurant in Brookline

Yedidiah, Malka, Friend, Tziporah, Yakira, Rachel, Shai, & Aryeh Leib Krimsky on front steps of Jonathan and Chaya Krimsky's house in Clifton, NJ. during the summer of 2015.

Bas Mitzvah of Simma Hollander, oldest grandaughter.
Top Yitzy, Simma, Naomi, Ephraim
Bottom: Yossi, Sid, Dorothy, Tamar

FROM BROOKLYN NY TO BROOKLINE MA

Tziporah Krimsky grating potatoes to make chanukah latkes in our Brookline home

Making Latkes with Aryeh, Tziporah, Yeshaya and Malka Krimsky

Car wash by Yedidiah, Rachieli and Yakira Krimsky. Summer 2015

Aryeh leib and Grandma Rose in the garden of
Golda Meir House in Newton, MA

Eight of our thirteen grandchildren. On top: Yedidiah and Tziporah. Teenagers Yossi and Ephraim holding Aryeh Leib, Tamar Hollander, Simma Hollander, and Shai Krimsky. Thanksgiving 2000.

Hollander children with Grandma Rose at the Golda Meir House in Newton, Massachusetts

Chapter 58

NORTHEASTERN UNIVERSITY AND THE RE-SEED PROGRAM

I accepted an offer to work for AVCO Corporation in Wilmington, Massachusetts, in September 1960 and promptly moved to 1200 Massachusetts Avenue in Cambridge, Massachusetts. How exciting it was to live near Harvard Square with all its quaint shops, restaurants, and beautiful green scenery striding the Charles River. How I loved to jog up and down Memorial Drive west to the Eliot Bridge and east toward MIT. How different from the heat and hedonism of California. AVCO sponsored a tuition-paid learning program at MIT. I had my transcripts from CCNY and Sacramento State College sent to MIT and was accepted as a special graduate student in the department of aeronautics and astronautics. I studied compressible fluid flow, numerical analysis, and radiation heat transfer. Some of the professors wrote the engineering textbooks I used at CCNY. After two years, I left AVCO and MIT. I could not afford to pay the tuition on my own. Besides, my father became ill and reduced his working hours and finally had a heart attack. I helped to financially support my parents for two years until my mother found work and was able to pay the rent. My brother was in graduate school, was self-supporting, but had limited funds.

I transferred all my credits from CCNY, Sacramento State College and M.I.T. to Northeastern University and enrolled as a graduate student in ME by taking classes at night with some tuition assistance from my employers over several years. I completed my MSME in June 1965 followed by a Massachusetts state certification and license as a professional engineer. I still hold a PE license. I returned to graduate school at NEU earned an MBA in 1987 with tuition assistance from Polaroid Corporation. I was inducted into Beta Gamma Sigma, the honorary MBA Association, immediately upon graduation because of a high GPA.

I retired from the Department of Defense in June 2010 and attended a science fair at Northeastern University (NEU) looking for volunteer opportunities to maintain my technical sharpness and give back to the schools that made my career possible. I met Prof. Michael Selivitch who told me about the RE-SEED program at NEU (**R**etired **E**ngineers and **S**cientists **E**nhancing **E**ducation through **D**emonstrations). I was interviewed by Paul Conroy, RE-SEED administrator, who enrolled me for the first training session in September 2011. I was asked in October 2010 to oversee a robotics club at the Revere Elementary School. I accepted the offer and had fun with sixth graders as they built Lego robots from kits. Next year I taught physics to ninth graders and their teacher. The third year I was asked by the principal of the Revere Elementary School to teach general science and physics to the students. I designed and built simple machines that demonstrated force, motion, distance torque, magnetic force, and energy. I used basic math only for students in the higher grades. The kids loved the hands-on demonstrations for which they conducted the measurements. The teachers arranged their schedules so I could cover all the students in one day. I was even asked to train new volunteers in the "hands-on methods" or "activity-based learning" I used in the classrooms.

After we moved from Brookline, I met with the CCNY provost, associate provost, vice president of the CCNY alumni association, and the coordinator of student services (Dr. Bruce Billig) in order to transfer part of the RE-SEED business model to CCNY. I spoke with Dr. Lisa Coico, president of CCNY, who promised to look into all this. The dean of the College of education, Dr. Mary Driscoll, nixed the whole idea. She stated in a letter to me that she did not have sufficient resources to implement a RE-SEED type program. I. Efforts at Hofstra also proved fruitless... The principals of the South Shore and Shulamith Day Schools appeared interested but their teachers do not seem interested. We shall see what happens.

I arranged to meet with the Director of Science Education at the World Trade Center Building number 7. I had a three-way discussion with the director and the Executive Director of the RE-SEED Program, Prof. (physics) Christos Zahopoulos of Northeastern University. The view from the 20th floor was phenomenal. He seemed interested but never returned my follow-up phone calls. I had a 3-way teleconference with the Assistant Director of Education of the State of New York in Albany. He also seemed interested but did not follow-up on my phone calls.

Massachusetts public school students in the 8th grade score the highest grades for science and math throughout the whole country. Yet the bureaucrats and administrators are unable to develop a program to allow retirees in the classrooms to assist teachers to enrich the state curricula and provide mentoring service as volunteers. What is more is that New York State spends the most money to educate public school students than any of the other 49 states. The only help for struggling students is to hire tutors. Retired teachers are available as tutors and they are recommended by active teachers. The idea of tutoring without charge is unheard of except for children with indigent parents. This was never my experience in Boston. The RE-SEED volunteers inn Boston wanted to give something back to society for having had a successful STEM career. New York is a different culture.

PEIR

Unable to volunteer as a STEM (Science Technology Engineering and Math) retiree in the New York public or private schools, I had to do something to keep busy and my mind occupied. Attending to grandchildren and house repairs were not enough to occupy my time. Many of the homilies I listened to in Young Israel of West Hempstead, I heard before from the Rabbis in Boston. A synagogue member told me about PEIR (Personal Enrichment in Retirement) group at Hofstra University. The PEIR Program provides opportunities for intellectual stimulation, cultural enrichment and personal growth for retirees age 55+. Classes, discussions, and social meetings are planned and facilitated by PEIR members and guest speakers. Subjects in literature, history, religion, philosophy, science, political and social science, performing arts, medicine, economics finance and technology are presented by the members to an audience of members. Presentations are held about 4 days per week in the mornings and afternoons.

A diverse body of men and women attend the presentations. I never heard of such a group in Boston. I presented lectures in areas with which I was very familiar such as espionage, cryptography, Nobel prize winners in physics about neutrinos, physics of the catapult with a demonstration model, number theory, Second Temple Jewish History, and the life of William Randolph Hearst based on a 600 page biography. This is a wonderful opportunity for seniors to remain alert and interact with like-minded retirees.

I had two 3-way telecoms with the Assistant Director of Education of New York State and the Director of Science Education of New York State. The other party was Prof. (physics) Christos Zahopoulos, Executive Director of the RE-SEED Program at Northeastern University. Both Directors seemed interested but my follow-up calls were not answered so I have to assume that they were not interested.

I applied to an ad seeking tutors at the Huntington Learning Center in Lynbrook, NY. I was interviewed and passed two exams testing me in math and general science. The questions were similar to Regents exams I took 60 years ago in High School. I had to submit three references. I will become a math and science tutor for high school students and paid an hourly salary; something I did as a volunteer in Boston. The New York State culture is different.

I had a three way conversation with the Assistant Director of Education of the State of New York with Prof. Christos Zahopoulos, Executive Director of the RE-SEED Program. Prof. Zahopoulos is a full-time professor of physics at Northeastern University. I also had a three way conversation with the Director of Science teaching of the State of New York. Both seem interested in the concept of using

STEM retirees as volunteers in the New York public school system to assist teachers to implement the STEM curricula. However, nothing came of this.

I explained that the 8th grade students in Massachusetts scored the highest grades in math and science in the whole country via NAEP exams; it did not influence them to make further inquiries and start a pilot program. My hopes for being a volunteer were dashed. In Massachusetts, the teachers, principals, parents, & students welcomed retired STEM volunteers to provide enrichment, conduct of experiments, and mentoring students. Tutors earn about +$100/hour in New York schools. Students needing tutors whose parents cannot afford the fee may be on their own. Teachers recommend retired teachers as tutors. In Massachusetts, volunteers wanted to give something back to society for having had a successful STEM career. That does not seem to be possible in New York. What is more is that the cost per pupil in the public schools in New York is the highest in the country.

Chapter 59

EPILOGUE

In July 2011, my last uncle, Perry Fishbein, died. His wife Ida, Zadie's daughter was a dutiful wife who took care of him at home as best as she was able. I never had a relationship with him or my uncle Natie who died a few years earlier in Albequerkie, New Mexico. My uncle Heshy died in Northbridge, Los Angeles, after an earthquake. I regret never having a relationship with the families and cousins on my mother's side. The divorce between me and my brother is her reward for constantly criticizing the half brothers and sisters on her side because of her hatred for her stepmother. Would you want a relationship with someone who constantly criticizes your mother?

The following paragraph sums up my feelings about moving out of Massachusetts. I said these few words on Saturday 31 August 2013 during a special Kiddush we sponsored to celebrate the births of Yakira Sarah Reizel and Akiva Pesach.

> *Even though we arrived from another shul on the other side of the tracks, I want to thank Rabbi Hamaoui, Rabbi Benmergui and the Sephardic Shul members for making Dorothy and I feel welcome. There is a wonderful warm and spiritual environment here that we will carry with us when we move to West Hempstead, Long Island.*

FROM BROOKLYN NY TO BROOKLINE MA

In this week's parsha, Moshe comes to realize that his assignment is over. He lectures Bnai Israel who are still children in his mind because he watched them mature, as a father, and he knows that they will stray from the advice he gives them. Moshe came to be our teacher and our leader by a series of unexpected occurrences. His assignment ended and he departs from the scene. His assignment lasted 40 years from the Burning Bush to Jericho. My assignment lasted longer.

I graduated from CCNY in New York in 1958 and moved to California with employment in the "Rocket Racket" working on the Polaris IRBM in Sacramento.

In 1960, by a series of unexpected occurrences, I was offered a high tech job in Massachusetts. I moved to Cambridge and re-connected with Prof. Shlomo Breuer, Z", TS", L" Talmudic Scholar whom I befriended at CCNY, and a great-grandson of Rabbi Shimshon Raphael Hirsch. He moved to Providence, Rhode Island to earn a PhD and later to Boston. I also met Rabbi Moses Holcer, of Beth Shalom in Cambridge. His family became a model to emulate for living a Jewish life. I changed jobs many times but chose to remain in Massachusetts despite attractive opportunities in other states. In 1965 I travelled alone to Israel to explore the land and people. I met my wife Dorothy during that year. She moved from Queens, New York, obtained a teaching job at Winthrop High School and attended Harvard Summer School. I returned from Israel and presented photographic slides to several groups about Israel and especially how Jerusalem appeared before the 67' war.

SIDNEY KRIMSKY

What a privilege it has been for me and my family to work and grow in Massachusetts for 53 years, living so close to Jewish educational institutions, the sites of the Revolutionary American history, great universities, hospitals, and shuls. Although our three children were born in Boston, graduated Maimonides School, (at a cost of $103,000) and 350 checks over 20 years) studied in Israel, and graduated from YU and Stern College, they never forgot their Boston roots. Dorothy was co-chairman of the Maimonides PTA and I served on the Board of Directors and was chairman of the Energy Committee. I was president of Cong. Kadimah-Toras Moshe for 12 years. The financial investment at Maimonides School was well worth it when I compare the results of midos and character my children exhibit when compared with children who attended public school. Public schools today are unlike the public schools of the 1950s.

After my mother died in December 2012, we decided to move closer to our children and grandchildren who live in Connecticut, Long Island, and New Jersey. Our two new grandchildren were born after my mother died. Yakira Sarah Reizel, daughter of Rabbi and Yocheved Krimsky was named after my mother Reizel and my grandmother Sarah (Sonya) whom my mother adored. Akiva Pesach, daughter of Rabbi Jonathan and Chaya Krimsky was named after Dorothy's uncle Paul, who was an active participant in Jewish life in Queens.

After living in Brookline for 46 years, I feel that my existential assignments here have ended. For us, it is time to move on. On 4 November 2013, we are moving to West Hempstead, Long Island, where I shall await my next assignment.

Chapter 60

PERORATION: BYE-BYE, BROOKLINE

2 February 2014

Marvin A. Kleckner
Town Administrator
Town of Brookline
11 Pierce Street
Brookline, MA 02445

Dear Mr. Kleckner,

My wife and I moved to Brookline in 1967, purchased a house in 1971, and recently moved on November 2013 to West Hempstead, NY. We moved to be closer to our children who live in the tri-state area, NY, CT, and NJ. My wife Dorothy was a Town Meeting Member for 12 years and I served for three years on the Brookline CATV Committee. I was also a member of the Brookline Tenants Council during 1967-1969 when we fought for rent control. Attorney Herb Goodwin was our leader. We succeeded when the Town Meeting passed the "Rent Control and Grievance Board" by-law that limited rent increases in multi-family units and insisted that code violations be remedied.

    We lived in Brookline for 46 years. So naturally we were pleased to have been randomly selected to participate in a survey about the

Brookline Community. The survey never arrived. Our mail is being forwarded by the US Post Office to our new home address. So perhaps we are off the list but I do have some remarks about Brookline that I would like to share with you because I reflect the attitude of many residents.

Brookline offers many services to the elderly, children, and teenagers. Public transportation is readily available. The building dept was very helpful for me to acquire the variances I needed to improve my house. The Town Meeting works and reflects the positions of most residents. The schools have a high rating and that is why parents want their children educated in Brookline rather than Boston. The police and fire Departments respond quickly to every call. The libraries are well provided. Streets are cleaned and plowed although Westbourne Terrace, where we lived, was never plowed to the standards of other streets. Single stream Collection of recyclables' was a great idea and seems to work really well. Green space and parks are well maintained.

There is a dark side. There has been an unfriendly attitude toward motorists. The use of credit cards with parking meters did not work out very well. Instead of doing a pilot program, to learn if the meters would work during really cold or snowy weather, the Town just installed lots of new meters. Many had to be removed after consumer complaints. This was not thought-out.

In West Hempstead, where we moved, there are no parking meters. Driving to the US PO or Stop and Shop is so much more pleasant. There are no parking meters in front of banks, grocery stores, barber shops, or the public libraries. There are parking meters in the nearby Five Towns and near the public buildings in Hempstead. Parking is permitted over night on public streets in West Hempstead. It seems that Police do a good job keeping us safe without an overnight parking ban. Brookline should sell more overnight parking stalls to raise revenue.

The Transportation Dept of Brookline eliminated one lane of incoming and outgoing traffic at Coolidge Corner. There is always a bunch-up of cars during rush hour on Beacon Street at the Coolidge Corner intersection. The Dept of Transportation created bicycle paths and the cars have to slow down spewing their fumes as they sit and idle. The cyclists are breathing the fumes from the idling cars as they cycle up and down Beacon Street. The traffic lights are not well coordinated. More time should be allowed for East-West traffic than for traffic entering from side streets.

The Transportation Dept. eliminated the U-Turn at Williston Road, making it really inconvenient for motorists who have to drive almost to Cleveland Circle to make a U turn to go to Shaw's Supermarket.

Now the Town wants to increase the cost of waiting time at the meters near the T stops. The Town wants to increase revenue using any means. Brookline is becoming like Cambridge in using parking meters to raise revenue. This only discourages customers from parking and shopping at local merchants. Driving to the Post Offices on Beacon Street or Brookline Village is a hassle.

After we moved into Brookline, the Selectmen believed that high density buildings, such as La Fountain on Beacon Street, would increase tax revenue from rents and this would more than compensate for the cost of needed additional services. So here we are 30 years later with more people living in Brookline. Have the taxes collected from the increased density of people kept up with the cost of additional services? Property taxes for my property in Brookline increased about $188/year or about 3.85%/year compounded annually.

Enclosure # 1

PROPERTY TAXES OVER THE YEARS
108 Westbourne Terrace, Brookline MA 02446

Year X	Real Estate Tax Y
2013	$ 10,263.38
2012	$ 10,263.52
2011	$ 9,534.40
2010	$ 9,234.84
2009	$ 8,854.40
2008	$ 8,907.88
2007	$ 8,412.00
2006	$ 8,377.76
2005	$ 8,086.18
2004	$ 7,902.72
2003	$ 7,540.44
2002	$ 7,510.20
2001	$ 6,744.50
2000	$ 6,379.36
1999	$ 6,112.68
1998	$ 5,772.12
1997	$ 5,568.40
1996	$ 5,617.40
1995	$ 5,442.34
1994	$ 4,849.12
1993	$ 5,002.50
1992	$ 4,822.66
1991	$ 4,751.83
1990	$ 4,554.22
1989	$ 4,552.94
1988	$ 4,654.98
1987	$ 3,557.16
1986	$ 3,557.16
1985	$ 3,597.44
1984	$ 3,031.20
1983	$ 2,231.33
1982	$ 2,920.60
1981	$ 2,940.00
1980	$ 2,714.00
1979	$ 2,970.00
1978	$ 2,873.00
1977	$ 2,708.00
1976	$ 2,596.00
1975	$ 2,396.00
1974	$ 2,173.00
1973	$ 2,074.00
1972	$ 2,030.00

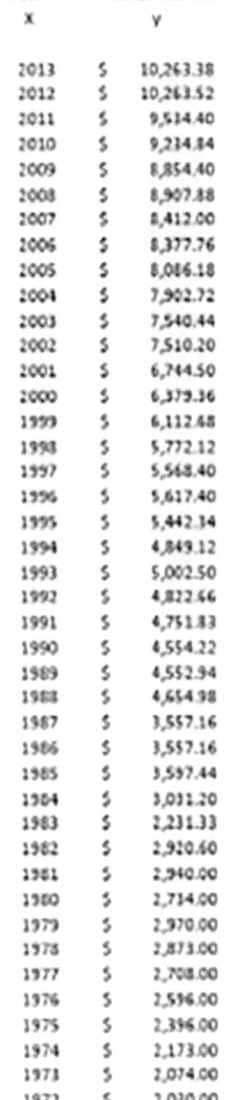

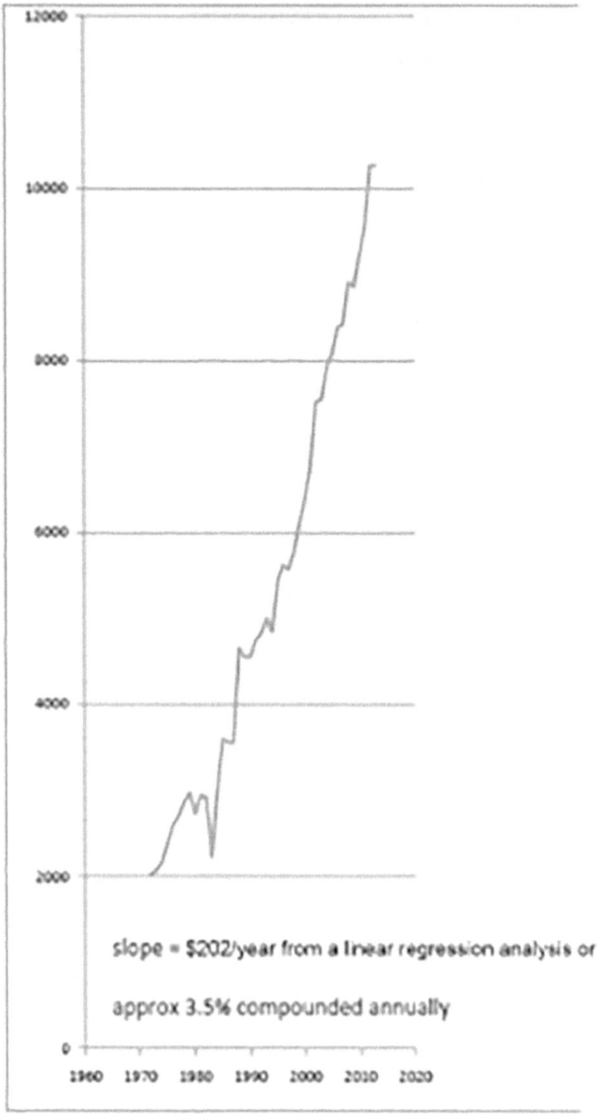

slope = $202/year from a linear regression analysis or approx 3.5% compounded annually

The increase in property taxes has been slightly less than the average cost of living from 1971 to 2013 ($4.22%). This reflects careful financial management of the Town to the credit of the Advisory Committee and the Selectmen. During the same time, the value of my house in Brookline increased 8.0% compounded annually from 1971-2013 which shows that Brookline is a desirable place to live. The value of the house I purchased in West Hempstead has also increased. The value of the house we purchased in West Hempstead increased 2.9% compounded annually from 2001 to 2013, more slowly than the average consumer price index from 1971-2014. So in my opinion, property taxes in Brookline increased slower than expected because of increased revenue from high density buildings and control of expenses.

Period	Avg CPI	Tax increase	Property Increase Brookline	Property Increase West Hempstead
1971-2014	4.22%/year	3.85%/year	8.0%/year	2.9%/year

Brookline Town Meeting members keep talking about affordable housing. When taxes keep rising, rents increase thereby discouraging tenants from moving to Brookline unless they receive a rent subsidy.

The military and the law enforcement agencies have come to rely on more technology to provide for security of the residents. Cameras on streets are an example of this reliance. Brookline is a safe community because of the efforts of the Police Dept and use of cameras on public property is a small price to pay. The electronic age has made absolute privacy obsolete. Has anyone polled the merchants on Beacon Street about their attitude concerning cameras? Do the objectors to cameras own Easy Pass cards, shop on the Internet, bank or pay by credit card?

If they object then, their privacy has been compromised. The technology exists to warn motorists about an impending accident and will soon be added to cars. You can imagine how this information can be stored and/or transmitted to the insurance company who may use this information to identify more risky to less risky drivers and use this to adjust insurance premiums. This is a further example of loss of privacy coming within, I would say, about 10 ten years.

The recent by-law about restricting leaf blowers to 67 db of noise has been vigorously pushed by a progressive town meeting member. In my opinion, this is a silly law that requires that leaf blowers be certified by the Town and limited to 67 db. This is an example of over-regulation and micro-management by persons with an extreme liberal agenda who complain about the government controlling our lives. The maximum allowable exposure under OSHA for noise in the workplace is 85 db on the A scale for an 8 hour day. I measured the noise level at weddings and it can reach 102 db five feet from the loudspeakers. Excessive noise exposure can cause hearing loss. There are no regulations restricting noise levels at indoor events in Brookline or anywhere else. With leaf blowing, people are engaged in honest work, performing a service, by blowing and collecting leaves. The power of their gas-operated machines enables them to work fast on lawns. If homeowners are bothered by the noise, they can close the door and windows. The noise level drops quickly with the inverse square of the distance from the blower to the listener. The people blowing leaves should be wearing ear protectors. Restricting leaf blowing between 15 Sept and 15 May just seems excessive micro-management and yet the same "progressives" oppose intrusive use of cameras on Beacon Street.

Brookline is becoming a Town with increasing density because of being next to Boston and BU. On Brainerd Road, for example, three new huge developments with condos have been constructed within the past few years. The density of Boston will spill over into North Brookline. Increased people density means more cars on the streets.

Eliminating the need for plastic bags seems like a good idea. But the Town should provide canvas bags for about $1.00 each for about six months to customers at the large grocery stores. Grocery stores can continue to use paper bags but should eventually charge for paper bags. Eventually all stores should be asked to conform. Brookline might also eliminate the sale of bottled water and Styrofoam cups because the plastic bottles and cups are not biodegradable. Drinking filtered tap water is the way to go.

Why is South Brookline untouched by the addition of 500 more students in the school population? There is plenty available unused land. Take a piece of the golf course and build a new KG-12 school for 500 students. Why add to the density and burden of the Lincoln, Pierce, Runkle, and Driscoll schools? I realize that this is not a simple problem because of where the children live. Parents want the children to attend a nearby school but this may not be possible without burdening existing schools, traffic, and school bus transportation.

In summary, the quality and nearness of schools and town services make Brookline a great place to live. Real Estate taxes, under control, track the cost of living. Attitude toward motorists is less than desirable.

Sidney Krimsky, P.E. Massachusetts
(Past Resident of Brookline for 43 years.)
357 Walton Street
West Hempstead, NY 11552
(516) 489-0508
bzkrimsky@verizon.net

Chapter 60.1

REMARKS ON THE BAT MITZVAH OF SIMMA MEIRA HOLLANDER ON 6 NOVEMBER 2011, 9 CHESHVAN 5772

Yitzy asked me yesterday to say a few words and he trusts me not to sound foolish. I may not be asked again.

In the Haftorah reading yesterday *Lech Lecha* we read the words of Yeshaya, Isaiah, *Mi Pa-al V-Asaw* which means, according to the Stone Chumish, "Who wrought it and accomplished it?" Accomplished what? The Prophets speak to us in multiple time zones, past, present, and future. In the prophet's present, he tells us that G-d will make dust of the idol worshipping nations. Of the past the prophet reminds us who created the earth, stars, and sky. What about the future? The Torah also speaks to us in the future and Moses would be pleased to know that Samuel B. Morse used a quote from the Torah to speak to us in the future. Samuel B. Morse, inventor of the telegraph, transmitted the first telegraph message on 24 May 1844 from Washington, DC, to Baltimore over an electrical wire that read "What hath G-d wrought?" He used a quotation from Numbers 23:23, *Ma Pa-al Kali*, very similar to the words of Isaiah. He invented the Morse code, a series of long and short key strokes on a telegraph machine similar to BITS 0 & 1 pounded on a computer keyboard. So what has this to do with Simma Meira? The statement "What hath G-d wrought" has metallurgical and theological meaning. Wrought Iron is made by pounding and fashioning iron when hot into unique designs such as a wrought iron fence. The metal is tough and yet soft, a desirable a metaphor for any young lady entering adulthood.

Theologically, wrought means carefully formed and fashioned with care. The gematria of Meira is 256 and the gematria of *Ma Pa-al Kali* is also 256. The number 256 is a special number in mathematics. It is 2^8 power represented by 8 BITS in the binary number system, which is needed to characterize all the keystrokes on a computer keyboard plus use of special characters. *Pa-al means* to do that which is G-dly, that which is right, to fashion laughter, joy, simcha, to be helpful, reliable, and responsible, all attributes of Simma Meira. So "What hath G-d wrought?" Naomi & Yitzy with G-d's help wrought Simma Meira. After all it was the Almighty who created the laws of biology that makes life, growth, and consciousness possible and we are proud to have her as our eldest granddaughter and we are confident that she will set an example for Tsiporah, Rachel, and Malka and all the girl cousins on the Hollander side. Dorothy and I wish her mazal tov and hatzlocha on this day of her awakening into a beautiful bas Israel.

Chapter 60.2

BAS-MITZVAH OF TAMAR YAFFA HOLLANDER ON 6 NOVEMBER 2016, 5 CHESHVAN 5777

Any message for a bas-mitzvah should be informational, relational, and inspirational.

The first is informational.

The name Tamar has three letters, Tuf, Mem, and Resh. The Gematria = 640 and I found it difficult to make a meaningful connection. I had to explore something else. So I asked myself how many Hebrew words can these three letters form if they are permuted using the three letters, two letters of the three, and one letter of the three. I learned that the three letters Tuf, Mem, andResh can account for fifteen different Hebrew words. Three letters permuted can form 6 words. The three letters taken two at a time also form 6 words. Each letter alone can forma meaningful word. The three letters Tuf, Mem, Resh permute to six words as follows: Tamar meaning dates, Ramat meaning a hill or elevation, Mar meaning Mr, meaning to contribute or donate, rotaim meaning to hitch up, bind up or bundle like to bind a Torah, and mutar meaning permitted. These are all positive nouns or verbs.

The permuted two-letter words are as follows: Mar meaning Mr., Tam meaning innocent or simple, Ram meaning high or lofty, Mait meaning deceased, R'Tam meaning Rabbeinu Tam, and T'R meaning the Rabbis taught. Except for deceased, these are positive adjectives or verbs.

So you can see that Hebrew is a very efficient language. All the combinations in the name Tamar are used to produce the maximum number of words. However the letters in Tamar in order taken one at a time also produce: Torat Moshe Rabbeinu.

The second is relational.

I learned a long time ago that on the bar or bat mitzvah day, there is always something appropriate sandwiched between the two earshot and possibly the haftarah relative to the bar or bas-mitzvah. So this is relational. Tamar's bat mitzvah today is sandwiched between parsha Noach and parsha Lech-Lecha. When Tamar was about three or four year sold I told her that I saw Noach build the tevah, the ark. Noach lived or traveled to the town of Heet in Iraq located near the Euphrates River. All the wood for the ark came from the cedars of Lebanon transported down the Euphrates River. Cedar grows in swamps and does not rot from exposure to water. Noach caulked the spaces between the logs with pitch or tar from the tar pits in the Town of Heet. The tar pits still exist as I heard from returning soldiers from Iraq. Heet is near Ramadi and Ramadi was liberated from ISIS in February 2016. I told her that we moved to Israel North of Iraq before the ark was finished and we did not drown by the flood because Israel was not flooded. I told her that the length to width ratio of the ark which is 6:1 and the 30 amot depth of the ark was designed to survive 30 foot waves in a storm. The ark was covered with horizontal black pitch stripes from the caulking between the logs to prevent water leakage into the ark. The ark drifted North East toMt. Ararat in Turkey. The Almighty told Noach "take yourself of every food that is eaten and gather it for yourself so it shall be as food." The lesson here is to prepare food for an impending disaster. Noach must have known how to cook and prepare food for people and animals. Cooking is a valuable skill. We know that Tamar likes to cook and bake andis good at it. Her chocolate cookies are addictive. I told her that I could describe the ark because I saw Noach build it but I left before it was finished. There is no evidence that Noach made chocolate chip cookies.

In parsha Chays Sarah Sarah was asked to lie about being the wife of Avraham. She was asked to pretend to be his sister, not his wife. Ramban said it was a sin to put her in danger but Sarah was a good actress and convinced the Egyptians that she was Avraham's sister. After all, she had no children at that time. Sarah was a great actress without having participated in "Drama for Life." The Torah does not record that Sarah had acting lessons. Tamar participated in many plays and learned to be an actress. She played Dorothy in the Wizard of Oz. Avraham also listened to Sarah about asking Hagar to leave. He must have respected her advice. She had a strong personality to allow Avraham to have a concubine and have a son. This exploded in her face when she insisted to Avraham that Hagar leave. Avraham told Hagar to leave. Avraham listened to Sarah so I think that she was really in charge of running the family. The lesson here is that women have more influence then they may think they may have. I believe that Tamar has a strong personality that has not yet emerged but will emerge in the future as she grows in her studies of Torat Moshe Rabbeinu.

Now we can be inspirational.

We start with a remarkable sentence from the prophet Yeshayahu from the HafTorah after KI Savo; 60-5.

The Stone translation of that paragraph is unclear. The Soncino translation is more precise. That is what I used however the words of the prophet carry multiple meanings for the past and the future. The future meaning was not fully explained to Yishayahu or even understood by the Rabbis who translated the Stone Chumash. Soncino says "you will see and be radiant and your heart will pulsate and be larger because the abundance of the sea shall be turned to you and the wealth of nations will come to you." I am confident that Yeshayahu did not know what I am about to tell you because he was not told. What does this have to do with Tamar? Be patient!

Fifty miles west of Haifa, in Israeli territorial waters, Joseph Langotsky, an oil geologist, in 2001 discovered a massive natural gas field 1-3 miles below the sea bed that is estimated to contain 10.8 Trillion cubic feet of natural gas, methane. The find is believed to be one of the largest such sources of natural gas in the world. Gas from Tamar is being produced.

This find will enable Israel to become energy independent and able to sell natural gas to other nations who will come to Israel to buy natural gas. The supporters of climate change promote burning natural gas to replace oil and coal as sources of electricity. The monetary strength or the wealth of nations will be used to buy natural gas. They will come to Israel just as Yeshayahu said 2,800 years ago to buy gas and that Israel's wealth will come from the sea. Joseph Langotsky has two daughters, Tamar and Dalit. He named the oil field Tamar. He named a smaller oil field Dalit. Addition areas of natural gas have been discovered nearby and are part of the Tamar gas-field. Tamar field has lots of gas. The sale of world-wide gas has increased and the cost of oil has decreased. The power of nations derived from selling middle-east oil will diminish with the sale of Israeli natural gas that burns clean with fewer pollutants thanks to Tamar. Tamar wealth is under the sea bed and Tamar spelled backwards is Ramat or elevation or hill. Spelling Tamar forwards or backwards, Tamar is meaningful.

In Deuteronomy Chapter 15:5 Moses is talking to the Children of Israel and translated in the Stone Bible he says "For Hashem your God has blessed you as he has told you; you will lend to many nations, but you will not borrow, and you will dominate many nations, but they will not dominate you."

While Israel's total external debt is US $95 billion, or approximately 41.6% of GDP, since 2001 Israel has become a net lender nation in terms of net external debt (the value of assets vs liabilities in debt instruments owed abroad), which as of June 2012 stood at a significant surplus of US$60 billion.

The three letters in the name of Tamar, taken one at a time, Torat Moshe Rabbeinu or backwards Rabbeinu Moshe's Torah should inspire her to continue on her journey to adulthood on the path taken by her siblings and parents, cousins and grandparents with the strength of Sarah and the skills of Noach.

www.ingramcontent.com/pod-product-compliance
Lightning Source LLC
Chambersburg PA
CBHW030314100526
44592CB00010B/431